The author

Ann Hoffmann has spent the greater part of her professional life working with or for writers. After a first job in publishing, she travelled widely in Europe and, on returning to England, spent four years as secretary/researcher to the well-known writer, the late Robert Henriques. In 1966 she established a research service for authors, which she ran until 1987. She now devotes the bulk of her time to freelance researching and writing her own books, which include *Research for Writers*, *They Were Not All Rogues*, *Bocking Deane* and *Lives of the Tudor Age* and *Majorca*.

In this expanded and revised edition of *Research for Writers*, Miss Hoffmann writes knowledgeably from personal experience on a variety of sources of information, on research methods, on some of the pitfalls to be avoided by the 'novice' researcher, on the particular problems facing writers of fiction and non-fiction and on the impact of the new technology on research.

Research
for Writers

Books in the 'Writing Handbooks' series

Developing Characters for Script Writing • Rib Davis
Freelance Copywriting • Diana Wimbs
Freelance Writing for Newspapers • Jill Dick
Marketing your Book: An Author's Guide • Alison Baverstock
Writing for Children • Margaret Clark
Writing Comedy • John Byrne
Writing Crime Fiction • H.R.F. Keating
Writing Dialogue for Scripts • Rib Davis
Writing Erotic Fiction • Derek Parker
Writing Fantasy and Science Fiction • Lisa Tuttle
Writing Horror Fiction • Guy N. Smith
Writing for a Living • Michael Legat
Writing for Magazines • Jill Dick
Writing a Play • Steve Gooch
Writing Poetry • John Whitworth
Writing Popular Fiction • Rona Randall
Writing for Radio • Rosemary Horstmann
Writing Romantic Fiction • Daphne Clair and Robyn Donald
Writing for Soaps • Chris Curry
Writing Successful Textbooks • Anthony Haynes
Writing for Television • Gerald Kelsey
Writing a Thriller • André Jute
Writing about Travel • Morag Campbell

Other books for writers

Creative Web Writing • Jane Dorner
The Internet: A Writer's Guide • Jane Dorner
Novel Writing • Evan Marshall
The Reader's Encyclopedia • William Rose Benét
Rewriting: a creative approach to writing
fiction • David Michael Kaplan
Word Power: a guide to creative writing • Julian Birkett
Writers' and Artists' Yearbook

SEVENTH EDITION

Research
for Writers

Ann Hoffmann

A & C Black • London

Seventh edition 2003

A & C Black Publishers Limited
37 Soho Square, London W1D 3QZ

ISBN 0–7136–6576–9

Under the title *Research for Writers* the third, fourth, fifth and sixth editions
were published in 1986, 1992, 1996 and 1999 by A & C Black Publishers Limited.

Previously published under the title *Research: a handbook for writers and journalists*
First edition 1975 Midas Books
Second edition 1979 A & C Black (Publishers) Limited

© 2003, 1975, 1979, 1986, 1992, 1996, 1999 Ann Hoffmann

A & C Black uses paper produced with elemental chlorine-free pulp, harvested from
managed sustainable forests.

Printed in Great Britain by Creative Print Design (Wales),
Ebbw Vale

Contents

Principal Abbreviations used in this Book

AGRA	Association of Genealogists and Researchers in Archives
APGI	Association of Professional Genealogists in Ireland
ARCHON	Archival gateway for Internet resources maintained by the National Register of Archives
ASGRA	Association of Scottish Genealogists and Record Agents
Aslib	Association for Information Management (formerly called the Association of Special Libraries and Information Bureaux), now part of the Taylor & Francis Group
BAC	Business Archives Council
BALH	British Association for Local History
BBA	*British Biographical Archive*
BBC	British Broadcasting Corporation
BFI	British Film Institute
BHI	British Humanities Index
BIS	[British Library] Business Information Service
BL	British Library
BLDSC	British Library Document Supply Centre
BLPC	British Library Public Catalogue
BNF	Bibliothèque Nationale de France
BNB	*British National Bibliography*
BNI	*British Newspaper Index*
BRA	British Records Association
BT	British Telecom
CARN	County Archive Research Network
CD-ROM	Compact Disk-Read Only Memory
CD-RW	Compact Disk-Rewritable
CILIP	Chartered Institute of Library and Information Professionals
DNB	*Dictionary of National Biography*
FAQ	Frequently Asked Questions

FFHS	Federation of Family History Societies
FRC	Family Records Centre
GRO	General Register Office
HMC	[Royal] Commission on Historical Manuscripts
HMSO*	Her Majesty's Stationery Office
ICA	International Council on Archives
IGI	*International Genealogical Index*
IHR	Institute of Historical Research
ISP	Internet service provider
IT	Information technology
ITC	Independent Television Commission
ITI	Institute of Translation and Interpreting
KIST	*Keyword Index to Serial Titles*
LA	Library Association
MDR	Manorial Documents Register
NA	The National Archives (Public Record Office and the Royal Commission on Historical Manuscripts)
n.d.	no date
NPO	[British Library] National Preservation Office
NRA	National Register of Archives
N.S.	New Style (dates)
NSA	[British Library] National Sound Archive
OED	*Oxford English Dictionary*
ONS	Office for National Statistics
O.S.	Old Style (dates)
PCC	Prerogative Court of Canterbury (wills)
PCY	Prerogative Court of York (wills)
PRA	Picture Research Association (formerly SPREd)
PRO	Public Record Office, now National Archives
SfEP	Society for Editors and Proofreaders
TSO*	The Stationery Office Ltd.
URL	Uniform Resource Locator
WAYB	*Writers' & Artists' Yearbook*
WWW	World Wide Web

* Prior to 1 October 1996 the acronym HMSO was used for the government executive agency which undertook various trading activities, including publishing. Since that date HMSO has been used for Her Majesty's Stationery Office, an administrative unit within the Cabinet Office. The Stationery Office Ltd. (TSO) is a private sector publishing company which on 1 October 1966 acquired the publishing operation of the government agency HMSO.

Note: For the sake of brevity and to avoid the clumsy repetition of 'he' and 'she' throughout the book, writers/researchers are referred to by the one pronoun, 'he'. No offence is intended to the female person.

Author's Note

WHEN I EMBARKED on this project in 1975 it was with the idea of setting down, for freelance writers faced with the daunting task of researching for publication for the first time, some fairly concise practical notes on methods and sources that would start them off along the right lines and at the same time help them to avoid some of the pitfalls. Although the book has grown considerably in the process, and this seventh edition enables me to revise the text yet again, it was never intended to be – nor, in view of the vast sources available to the modern writer, can it ever be – more than a guide. No one researcher can do more than scratch the surface, let alone compile a comprehensive research manual. Even had I now a team to assist me and the space of a CD-ROM to fill, it would be a daunting task, given the need to keep it up-to-date with the thousands of new reference works, in electronic and microform as well as in print, that are published each year. Not only would such a manual have to be priced beyond the means of the very people my little book is intended to reach, but it would defeat my prime purpose, which has always been merely to point the way and to encourage the researcher to *research*. The danger of making too much information available too easily and too speedily is that the recipient may be tempted to sit back, accept what is offered as gospel and not bother to delve further. This is not what I had in mind.

Researching, like writing, is an individual, creative process. It cannot be 'taught'. In his quest for original material – and who does not dream of stumbling upon a cache of hitherto unknown, unpublished papers or the answer to a problem that has baffled scholars for several generations? – the writer never ceases to learn. All the time he is probing, absorbing, selecting, adding to his store of knowledge of sources of information largely by trial and error. Either he has a 'nose' for it or he has not. If not, unless he has time on his hands, he would be well advised to use the services of a professional. An elementary grasp of sources can of course be gleaned from a textbook and a few days' intensive study in a good reference library, or online; this has immense value as a springboard. After that he is on his own. Invariably he will find himself, at different stages of his research, thrust into the unaccustomed roles of student, librarian, interviewer, detective and private investigator, and much else besides.

Throughout the compilation of this and previous editions, therefore, I have kept in mind the many time-consuming problems likely to be encountered by a novice writer/researcher, whether he is concerned with fiction or with non-fiction. I have dared to suggest, from my own experience, ways in which these problems may be tackled. Like all craftsmen, I have my favourite tools – principally those tried and trusted reference works that served me well during my years as a professional researcher. Over the last decade I have taken on board many of the newer, electronic aids. Laying these out alongside one another on the work bench, as it were, for fellow craftsmen to pick up, handle and use as they see fit, has been a joy and a challenge. They may not constitute the particular assortment that a colleague would select – indeed, they are a somewhat mixed bag, being drawn in the main from my own research activities and thus inclined more to the factual, historical and biographical than to the scientific or technical. But I can vouch for them absolutely as loyal and steadfast helpmates, and I am confident that they will go on for some time yet to help others solve some of those alarming and often seemingly insoluble conundrums that have the nasty habit of cropping up at the worst possible moment in a writer's working day. If, in the long term, there may result books and features and theses that are not only better researched, but researched with less strain and less burning of the midnight oil on the part of their authors than was once the norm, then the putting together of this book, the seventh time round, will have achieved its purpose.

Most professional writers and journalists now make full use of the new information technology (IT). Terms such as 'database', 'online', 'CD-ROM', 'World Wide Web' and 'email' no longer need explanation. Many of those 'technophobes' who not long ago were stubbornly maintaining their 'anti-computer' stance have since succumbed, have successfully mastered the new skills and now 'browse', 'surf' or 'trawl' the Web regularly along with the rest. There can be very few people today who do not know that in 21st-century speak a 'browser' is no longer someone who browses among books but a powerful program for accessing the World Wide Web.

The younger generation of writer-researcher, computer-literate from an early age, takes for granted not only speedy access to information worldwide,but the facility, when armed with little more than a mouse, a modem and a keyboard, to communicate and exchange ideas internationally at relatively low cost. Never before has so much source material been so instantly (and surprisingly inexpensively) accessible. Unfortunately, the problem today is not one of the quantity of information available at the press of a key, but the *quality* of that information – or, to phrase it differently, the *quantity of misinformation* lying in wait for the unwary.

Increasingly the computer encroaches on our professional and domestic lives, so that soon there will be very little that can be accomplished without it. Nevertheless, as individual writers and researchers, I still believe that we should treat the Internet with some caution. More importantly, I believe that as individuals we should remain free to make use only of those elements of IT that work for us personally. No more. We should never feel we *have* to 'go online' simply to 'keep up' with friends and colleagues, or because the media tells us how wonderful it is. And *never* if we become so worried about the skills involved that the problems of which key to press, and in what sequence, start to interfere with the creative process.

Already the Internet impinges on pretty well every aspect of our daily routine, be it in banking, shopping, travelling, writing, or any other activity, and regardless of whether or not we are 'online'. As book buyers or researchers, every time we enter a bookshop or library or archive centre we have the benefit of a computerised catalogue. For those who are not yet themselves online there are opportunities to access the Internet and the World Wide Web at the local library or cybercafé.

The new technology has transformed the working lives of writers and researchers, and we are indebted to it. The manufacture of the Xerox photocopying machine several decades ago liberated us from the tedious task of copying long texts by hand; today we are able, thanks to the personal computer and the information scientists, to benefit almost instantaneously from recent research anywhere in the world. The present generation cannot conceive how, less than a quarter of a century ago, any of us got by without photocopy and microfilm, let alone without CD-ROM and email. I do however question whether some of these seemingly miraculous techniques, in banishing the tedium, may not also have shed a little of the 'magic' along the way? Is it possible that bringing up a text on screen can genuinely match the thrill of holding in one's own hands a medieval charter complete with original seal, or the handwritten letter of, say, Queen Victoria or Winston Churchill? Perhaps accessing a database the other side of the globe generates its own particular brand of magic. If so, I have yet to experience it. Speaking for myself, I shall always be thankful that I was able to do the bulk of my professional researching at a time when nearly always you were entrusted with the original newspaper, the original document. These days, understandably, in the interest of conservation, 80 per cent of the time the closest you get is a microfilm.

When I prepared the last edition of this book in 1999 I was rather in the dark as to the proportion of my readers who were online and those who, for financial or other reasons, were not. This time round, on the assumption that most of you have, or are at least considering, access to the Net, I have written a separate chapter on online research. As before, websites and email addresses are given, where relevant, throughout the book – and there are more of them. At the same time, I feel I must reassure the 'technophobes' who hold fast to pen, paper and typewriter. The theme of my book has always been, and remains, library and archive research. I believe strongly that, for many years to come, researchers and writers will go on using the traditional methods and sources outlined here. A computer may give you speedier access to up-to-date information, and may lighten your task in other ways, but it cannot and will not do all your work for you. Remember the protagonist in A.S. Byatt's *The Biographer's Tale* – the biographer who, having been told of the uses of the Internet for research, 'took to it with pleasure, but it did not beat the library, not yet, with its catalogue, and its books full of bibliographies full of books full of bibliographies.' * Similarly, you too are bound to continue to do the bulk of your research

---

* Quoted by kind permission of Dame Antonia Byatt. *The Biographer's Tale*, Chatto & Windus, London, 2000.

in the library and the archive centre. Books and journals will continue to be published in printed as well as in microform. And for many readers of my generation who were brought up to research on the printed or written page, and for whom the page is friendlier than the screen, taking a volume from the bookshelf and leafing through the pages may still seem quicker than loading a CD-ROM and scrolling up and down on the monitor. The old techniques of note-taking and face-to-face interviewing will still be practised. Those of you who have tried to use a computer and decided it is not for you – yet – take heart. You will not be outlawed overnight. Nor will any sane editor reject a well-researched, well-written work purely because it is submitted on A4 paper (now called 'hard copy') rather than on disk – though it is true that most editors today expect both. 'Books do not seem likely to be replaced by personal computers,' wrote Lord Rees-Mogg in *The Times*, reassuringly, on 18 May 1998, 'reading from a screen is work, but reading from a page is pleasure.' * However much my younger readers may protest – and they have a right to do so, for theirs has been a totally different education – that is a sentiment I heartily applaud.

Mark Twain, the first writer known to have delivered a book to his publisher in typescript, purchased one of the early Remington typewriters in 1874. Five generations on, in 2003, some bestselling authors still choose to write in longhand and to pay a professional typist. The message is clear: the age of electronic authorship – and, it follows, electronic research – may have arrived, but you are still free to suit yourself.

One of the difficulties I always have in compiling a new edition is to judge which of the older titles to drop in order to make room for more recent works. Inevitably, with so much new material to hand, some titles have to go. I am of course only too well aware that in the present economic climate, libraries are having to cut down on the renewal and purchase of their reference stocks, which means that researchers without easy access to a copyright or university library may be at a disadvantage. To this end I have taken the middle road, discarding what I personally consider to be 'dead wood' (titles that have been superseded by more up-to-date, improved works), while retaining as many as space permits of the well-established or one-off reference books that still rank among the best on their subject. If this time round I have inadvertently axed one or two of my readers' favourites, I ask their forgiveness. May I suggest that before they chuck out the earlier edition, they make use of the blank pages provided at the back of this one to keep a note of such titles?

Since 1999 there has been a noticeable shift away from the printed book and CD-ROM towards the electronic product, insofar as bibliographic and major reference works are concerned, with an ever-growing number of texts and databases now accessible on the Web. It is a trend which I have tried to reflect in my revision.

As before, books and other publications mentioned in the text are listed alphabetically by title at the end of the relevant chapter rather than in one long bibliography at the end. (Listing by title rather than by author runs contrary to recognised

---

* Quoted by kind permission of Lord Rees-Mogg.

bibliographic practice. Its continuance in this edition is, I hope, justified for reasons of quick reference: the works themselves are referred to first by title in the text and users of earlier editions will have become familiar with this method.) Database files mentioned in the text are now listed in the bibliographies. Electronic, microform, CD-ROM and DVD editions have been included where most relevant. Publication on film, fiche, CD and DVD being such a fast-growing industry, to have attempted more would have been at best incomplete; it would also have added considerably to the bulk (and thus the cost) of this book. A researcher who is 'on the ball' will ask at the library enquiry desk; even if he does not, the competent librarian or archivist will usually bring such editions to his attention. Regrettably, it is not possible always to indicate those titles which are out of print, as the situation changes constantly and reprints or new editions may become available during the lifetime of this book. Most of the out-of-print titles mentioned will be found in the larger public libraries or may be borrowed through the public library lending service; but researchers needing to use such books over a long period are recommended to 'shop around' for them in secondhand and antiquarian bookshops (and even jumble or car boot sales), or to visit one of the bookfinding websites recommended on pages 58–9.

The need to deliver my revised text some six months before publication (the preparation and writing therefore up to ten months ahead) makes it impossible to be fully up-to-date, but readers who follow my guidelines for using library catalogues and bibliographies should have few problems in tracing recently published material or new editions of existing works. One major difficulty for me has been the number of changes in publishing in recent years, with many independent publishers being taken over by the larger groups, and so many excellent titles allowed to go out of print or discontinued. Addresses and telephone numbers are a constant irritation, changing as they do, with unpredictable and infuriating frequency, along with websites and email addresses. Depending on the month of publication, even annual guides are to some extent out-of-date by the time they appear. This aspect – or hazard, if you like – of modern living is one we simply have to learn to accept. In this edition, as well as fax numbers and email addresses for most libraries and other sources, I have included some of the major websites of use to the researcher. I strongly recommend readers to compile a personal websites/email address book.

I should like to take this opportunity to express my gratitude to the many librarians, archivists, curators, press and public relations officers, publishers and others who have so efficiently and courteously dealt with my enquiries on a multitude of subjects over the years, and most especially to the staffs of the British Library and the Public Record Office. I am also indebted to several fellow writers, research colleagues and librarians who made constructive comments on the first six editions, most of whose suggestions are now incorporated. My thanks also go to the team at A & C Black (Jessica Hodge and Katie Taylor) and, by no means least of all, to my copy editor, Hilary Lissenden, for her meticulous work on this new edition.

My mail-bag since first publication (1975) makes it clear that *Research for Writers* has been of some assistance not only to the novice researcher and writer for whom it was intended – and even on occasion to those who make a hobby of entering competitions – but also to those more experienced 'diggers' who, so they tell me, suffer occasionally from extraordinary lapses of memory or mental blocks that result in their wasting precious time searching for information which in fact may be close at hand in their own reference collection or in a local library. To all these people I dedicate this seventh edition. In return, the greatest compliment they can pay me will be to *treat the book as a working tool, to annotate it profusely, and to update it as their research requires.* My publishers have again been persuaded to include a few blank pages for personal notes. If, by the time these blank pages are filled, the book starts to come apart at the spine through constant usage, hopefully there may be another edition in the pipeline. By then, it is likely that new editorial blood will have been recruited, bringing with it fresh ideas and – who knows? – possibly an entirely new format to the text. Whatever its future may be – and I sincerely hope that the book *does* have a future – I shall always feel happy to have originated it and to have had the satisfaction of keeping it up-to-date for the best part of three decades. In the meantime I trust that this revised edition will please, and serve equally well, both the dedicated pen-pusher among my readers *and* the 'mouse potato' * – not forgetting those in between who hover nervously on the brink of 21st-century technology and venture into cyberspace and the digital age only now and then. As always, comments and suggestions for future editions will be most gratefully received.

A.H.
Tunbridge Wells, 2003

---

* A person who spends most (or too much) of his time sitting at the computer. Applicable to the majority of writers today?

Chapter One

The Writer as Researcher

EVERY WRITER, UNLESS he is creating a work of pure fantasy, has to do research. The nature and depth of that research will vary enormously, according to the subject of the work, the field of writing (feature, novel, biography, history, thesis, children's story, etc.) and whether it is aimed at the academic, popular or juvenile market. Whereas the scholar may have comparatively unlimited time (and, if he is lucky, also a research grant) which allows him to follow up pretty well every relevant line of enquiry in detail, the journalist's 'copy' must be on the sub-editor's desk at a given hour, and he is always pressed for time. Both texts must be correct, up-to-date and original – in other words, properly researched and well written.

In the end-product the academic work, with its notes and references, bibliography and index, may look to be the more meticulously researched, but this can be a deception: the thousand-word newspaper or magazine article, in order to present its data in a convincing, accurate and readable way and to show that its author is fully conversant with the latest events and/or published studies on the subject, may well involve as much, and sometimes more, research in proportion to its length. Whatever the field of authorship, the writer has to know a great deal more than he actually puts into words if what he writes is to ring true – and this applies as strictly to fiction writers as to journalists and historians and biographers. Ernest Hemingway, in an interview published in *Paris Review* (Spring 1958), put this very well. 'I always try to write on the principle of the iceberg,' he said. 'There is seven-eighths of it under water for every part that shows. Anything you know you can eliminate and it only strengthens your iceberg. It is the part that doesn't show. If the writer omits something because he does not know it, then there is a hole in the story.'*

In ideal circumstances an author would write only of what he knows. No one, however, possesses first-hand knowledge of every trade or profession in which he wishes to place his characters; few can afford to visit all those far-off lands that they

---

* The same author, in *Death in the Afternoon*, expounds on this theme at greater length in a memorable passage worthy of framing and hanging above every writer's desk. It will be found at the end of chapter 16 of the novel.

are tempted to use as 'local colour' in their work. In most short stories or novels or plays, therefore, there are bound to be some people, some situations and some settings that are beyond the personal experience of the writer, and for which he must rely to some extent at least on secondhand material – that is to say, on what others before him have observed and recorded, on printed statistics and factual data, and often on the recollections of third parties. The writer of history or historical fiction has no choice but to rely on documentary sources, either in print or in manuscript. In all these instances the research done must be thorough and, as far as possible, undertaken *in the round* (i.e. from more than one angle, avoiding reliance on any one source), or the result will be cardboard people, cardboard backgrounds and a loss of credibility in what may otherwise be an excellent piece of writing.

The prime importance of researching thoroughly before going into print cannot be over-stressed. Once his reader's confidence has been lost, the author will have an uphill battle to regain it. All too often a disillusioned reader or bright schoolchild will write and tell him where he has gone wrong, or – which is worse – may write and tell his editor or publisher, which in turn destroys their confidence and is likely to influence their attitude to the author's future work.

It is dangerous to rely on only one source for a given piece of information, however authoritative that source may seem to be. Mistakes occur all too frequently in even the most erudite book. They may not be the original author's fault at all, but the result of slipshod proof-reading in the editor's office or a printer's error that occurred at a later stage, such as when the typesetter re-sets a line to incorporate the author's or publisher's corrections. The sad thing is that once they are in print, mistakes are bound to be copied in good faith by someone else, and that person's work in turn will almost certainly be used as source material by another, and so on – so that even if a correction is made in subsequent editions of the original work, the misprint in that first edition may be perpetuated *ad infinitum*. By 'misprints' in this context is meant the mis-spelling of a proper name, a mis-quotation or a wrong numeral – the sort of error that would not necessarily be spotted by a general reader. The other kind of mistake, known as a 'literal' in publishing and printing, which may be a character set up in the wrong fount, or upside down, or two characters transposed, and the more obvious spelling mistake are more likely to be spotted at proof-reading stage.

Such are the hazards of authorship that the writer of non-fiction would do well to keep constantly in his mind's eye as he works the image of future trusting generations of students and researchers relying on his text as an authoritative source.

For most modern writers time is a precious commodity. Gone for ever are those halcyon days when Samuel Johnson could speak of a man turning over half a library to make one book; since his day millions more books have been written and published, and our libraries, archive collections and record repositories now house a bewildering and ever-increasing conglomeration of printed, manuscript, microfilmed, recorded and electronically produced material; there are also vast databases worldwide. More than ever before has it become essential for the writer/researcher to organise his working hours to the best advantage. He must know where and how to get at the information he requires in the quickest, as well as the most efficient and economical, way. As the great Dr Johnson also said: 'Knowledge is of two kinds. We know a subject ourselves, or we know where we can find information upon it.' While the specialist must know his pet subject inside out, there is no question but that for the general writer the knowledge of *where to go* to find what he needs is of the greater value. Quite apart from the fact that no one would want to become a walking encyclopedia, even if it were humanly possible to carry a mass of information on a variety of subjects in one's head all the time, most professional writers would agree that a sound knowledge of available sources (or, failing that, a reliable researcher on whose services they can call) allows them more time to concentrate on the creative activity. Nothing can be more distracting or more paralysing to the flow of ideas and their shaping into words than a nagging worry, 'Where on earth am I going to be able to find out about *that*?'

Seeking information implies curiosity, a characteristic inborn not only in the feline species but in the whole human race. We have all been researchers since we were in the cradle. Long before he can speak or read or write, a baby is obsessed by the desire to find out about the things around him. Attracted by the colour of an unknown object, he reaches out to touch it and, having seized it and found it pleasing to hold, usually puts it into his mouth. What does it feel like? Does it taste good? What is it made of? *What is* it? He has taken the first step along a path of discovery and enchantment that will last a lifetime. From that first childish desire to learn about objects, he progresses to curiosity about himself and his body, and then to other people and animals; from the happenings he observes in his immediate circle to those of history; through history to religion, and then to science and speculation about the future. He will never know it all, but if as he grows older he keeps alive his youthful sense of curiosity he will – especially if he becomes a writer – have endless resources on which to draw, and he will never be bored.

It is a well-known saying that a writer may be angry, disgusted, amused, uplifted or almost anything in between, and his work will be the better for it, but if he is bored it will be reflected in his writing. Robert Louis Stevenson held that life would be only a very dull and ill-directed theatre unless we had some interests in the piece. 'It is in virtue of his own desires and curiosities that any man continues to exist with even patience,' he wrote, 'that he is charmed by the look of things and people, and that he wakens every morning with a renewed appetite for work and pleasure. Desire and curiosity are the two eyes through which he sees the world in the most enchanted colours: it is they that make women beautiful or fossils interesting ...'* Because a writer's raw material is derived principally from a study of other human beings, their complex relationships, their strengths and weaknesses and idiosyncrasies, as well as their history, he can probably get away with being more openly curious than any other group of people – provided always that he does not offend by his looking or

---

* From the essay 'El Dorado' in *Virginibus Puerisque*.

probing. The arts of observation without seeming to observe and of probing without seeming to probe are skills that can – and should – be acquired.

While most writers are also researchers, not all researchers are talented as writers. The prime function of the researcher is to seek information; that of the writer is more complicated, for his duty is both to impart knowledge and to give pleasure – in other words, to entertain as well as to instruct his reader. And just as a factual book can give pleasure to the reader by the manner in which it is written, so the most absorbing and entertaining of stories can impart knowledge. The one thing a writer must never do, under any circumstances, however, is to distort the truth for the sake of a good story.

Everything that comes within the writer's own experience is grist to the mill and should be stored away, ideally in note form or on tape or computer, for future use. Ideas, an unusual turn of phrase, a gesture, a conversation overheard, brief descriptions of people or places, on-the-spot reports of events, even pain suffered (you think at the time you will always remember how it felt, but you rarely do): these will be of immense value, provided that they are kept in such a way that they can be turned up quickly when required. (Some practical suggestions for filing and storage are discussed on pages 20–22.) Naturally it is not possible to predict years in advance what you are going to need, so that how much or how little is noted and filed must be a decision for the individual writer, but it is a fact of life that once you throw something away, you need it. The Preface to Somerset Maugham's *A Writer's Notebook*, first published in 1949, makes interesting reading on this score, for the author admits that there were many years in which he made no notes at all, that he kept no record of his meetings with famous people. 'I never made a note of anything that I did not think would be useful to me at one time or another in my work,' he states, 'and though, especially in the early notebooks, I jotted down all kinds of thoughts and emotions of a personal nature, it was only with the intention of ascribing them sooner or later to the creatures of my invention. I meant my notebooks to be a storehouse of materials for future use and nothing else.' So spoke the short-story writer and novelist. It would be unthinkable for a diarist or biographer to fail to record his meetings with famous people.

In the course of his researching life, a writer will be faced with a variety of tasks. These may range from the simple checking of facts (dates, quotations, spellings, statistics) to the tracing of a contemporary account of some historical event, or the more complicated unravelling of someone's ancestry, or an authentic setting for a novel or play. The bestselling author Frederick Forsyth reckons to divide his research into four categories: *geographical* (which necessitates visits to places); *historical* (checkable in source material); *procedural* (which involves contacting and talking to 'inside' people); and *technical* (checkable facts). It will be obvious that there are wide differences, both of skill and approach, between the four, and that some of the categories overlap or merge.

In *factual research* (statistical, historical and technical), the enquirer knows precisely what he is looking for and what he expects to find, so that, provided he knows where to go for the information, he should encounter no great difficulty. Knowing where to go is the key here.

In pure *historical research* the scope is much wider, as regards both the material available and the use that is made of it. As no two writers, given the same plot and the same set of characters, will come up with an identical story, so no two researchers, confronted with the same documentary sources, will use those sources in an identical way. The basic facts – the skeleton – will be similar, of course, but whereas one researcher will explore a certain avenue in more detail than another and quote extensively from a document that in the eyes of his colleague merits no more than a passing reference, the second may be less selective on one aspect of the search but obsessive about detail on another, depending upon the angle from which their respective works are to be written and on the market for which they are intended.

Background research (which includes the geographical and procedural), usually required for a work of fiction, modern or historical, generally demands less discipline but, as a result, may lead the enquirer down some unforeseen channels and possibly end by radically changing the shape or character of his story.

Thus both historical and background research fall into the category of *creative*, as opposed to *factual*, research. In these fields the researcher, not knowing beforehand what he is going to find, must be alive to each and every clue he comes across, any one of which could lead to some vital discovery that could bring his work to life in an exciting and original way.

In general, an article or thesis will require either factual or historical research, or both; whereas most books will demand a mixture of all three types of research, in varying proportions according to their subject and what the writer already knows. In a biography, for example, some factual research will be necessary to substantiate a quotation from a letter or diary of a certain date; historical research to fill in the detail of an event in which the subject of the biography played a leading part; background research to permit the author to describe, say, the environment in which that person grew up. In an historical novel, dates and names and events must be factually correct, while background research will be important in order to bring it to life, to add accurate details of costume, food, manners, etc. of the relevant period. In a modern short story or play, the setting must be authentic and the characters must speak the right language (slang, dialect or technical idiom related to their occupations and age). Some of the problems and pitfalls, as well as the sources of information appropriate to each of these categories of research, are outlined in later sections of this book.

Whatever the subject or nature of the search, the procedure is roughly the same. You may begin with one solid fact or several – this may be a date, or an event, or a name, or sometimes merely an idea – and you build up your dossier rather like the Criminal Intelligence Service officer tracks down his suspect: with patience, persistence, and (hopefully) the occasional lucky break. You make full use of modern technological aids but do not eschew the conventional methods. It may take you months to ferret out one vital clue, or you may chance upon it straight away. Often it is just when you have returned despondently to square one from yet another in a series of blind alleys that you stumble on the missing link – and curse yourself for following up so many red herrings on the way. All professional researchers know the elation such an unexpected discovery produces. Nowhere is it more aptly described than by the university professor quoted in Dr A.L. Rowse's *A Cornish Childhood* as saying, '... I felt that curious thrill, the authentic sensation of the researcher ... It is as if you were to sit down and find you have sat on the cat. The thing comes alive in your hand ...' Peter Fleming, discussing the art of research with the late Joan St George Saunders of Writers' and Speakers' Research, the first professional research service in this country (there are several others now), likened it to fox hunting: 'The horns sound, one races for the first covert – then a halt while the hounds snuffle around in the undergrowth. Here the cunning hunter circles around the wood and knows instinctively which way the hounds will break. Off you go again and by the end of the day you are still there – perhaps to be blooded with success!'*

Writing is a solitary profession, more often than not practised in total privacy. Research, by sharp contrast, demands – indeed, flourishes on – a gregarious lifestyle, a talent for seeking out and mixing with the widest possible spectrum of the human race. The present generation calls this 'networking'.

Stories abound of writers reluctant to attend this or that function, fearing an evening of tedium and greatly begrudging the sacrifice of working time, only to find themselves seated next to some stranger who has fascinating information to impart which they would never otherwise have come across. The moral is clear. Raw material exists in abundance. It lurks in unexpected places. You have to find that material.

Most established writers manage the switch from the writing to the research mode very successfully. It is not difficult. The great thing to remember is that, when wearing your 'research' hat, you should 'network' intensively. And do keep up a private 'contacts' book, with names and addresses and telephone numbers, against that time in the future when you need to renew an acquaintance. Such a notebook could become your most precious research tool.

One of the researcher's thorniest problems lies in deciding when to call it a day. It is always possible – and tempting – to go on delving just a little further – provided, of course, that time and adequate funds are available. But you have to keep in mind the terms of reference of your work and discipline yourself accordingly. Only experience will enable you to acquire the 'feel' of the job, to know when you should follow your hunch and go off at a tangent, when to replace the reference books on the shelf and pick up your pen. The temptation will nearly always be there to continue researching 'for a little while longer'. All too easily you can slip into the comfortable routine of the perpetual student.

It is a bad thing to postpone indefinitely the real creative process. Indeed, to prolong researching unduly is regarded by some academics as an indication of a fear of

* Letter to the author from Mrs St George Saunders, 15 August 1975. Quoted by kind permission of Sir Alan Urwick.

the actual writing. Therefore once a certain stage in the research has been reached, it is best to press on with a first draft. A modest amount of further research will almost certainly be necessary, and possible, at a later stage, when you will know more precisely what you need or in order to update, to fill in any gaps or to explore aspects of your subject which you may have ignored at the outset but now wish to include. Very often an editor or agent, after a first reading of the author's typescript, will suggest modifications or additions; in the case of a book, it will be the copy-editor who will query with the author certain spellings or statements, some of which may involve extra research.

Modern society is constantly on the move, new studies appear every week, and since it now takes an average of between six or nine months from delivery of manuscript to the date of publication of a book, unless a writer is submitting an article of topical interest for almost instant publication in a newspaper or journal, it will be impossible for his work to be fully up-to-date. Modern typesetting procedures and the current practice of going straight into page proofs instead of first into galleys and then into page have made it prohibitively expensive for any but the most essential corrections and updatings to be incorporated at this stage – apart, of course, from printer's errors and 'literals'. You should not allow this to worry you unduly: it is the same for everyone, and a well-researched, well-written work will always achieve recognition as such.

In the fulfilment of his work, whether it be long or short, fiction or non-fiction, a writer usually experiences the deep sense of satisfaction that is the reward of a job of research well done. If it has not been altogether too traumatic an exercise, he may even go along with the view of the poet Robert Herrick:

> Attempt the end, and never stand to doubt;
> Nothing's so hard, but search will find it out.

Chapter Two

Organisation and Method

THE WRITER'S FIRST task, when embarking on a new project, is to survey and organise the material already in his possession. By the time you have done this, you will have a pretty good idea of how much additional research needs to be done. Then, and only then – and always bearing in mind the intended length and complexity of the end-product, as well as the time and funds available – are you ready to move on to tap other sources.

At this stage you should make a preliminary list of everything you need to find out, and where you think you will have to go to get it. The key here is to *plan ahead*. This does not apply to research you do on the Internet, to which you have instant access; but at libraries and other information centres, the books you want may be in use by other readers, so that you will have to wait a few weeks for them. The people you hope to interview may be busy or away. Information you send for may take longer than you anticipate to arrive. You will be surprised also at how much time and money you will save by taking the trouble to write down all those people and places you envisage having to visit: with the aid of a good map and gazetteer you can plan itineraries that take in several assignments on each trip.

Just as it is false economy to skip the amount of time necessary for a thorough study of basic material and sources, so it is foolish to neglect to give proper thought to setting up a system for the storage and easy retrieval of that material, remembering always to make suitable provision for material still to be acquired. Since both these operations cost money as well as time (time = money being a constant theme throughout this book), this is an appropriate place in which to outline some of the financial aspects of research.

COSTS OF RESEARCH

The first thing to remember is that it will always cost more than you expect. Leaving aside the question of working time, outgoings will include stationery and equipment, travelling and motor expenses, search fees (charged by some private libraries and by clergy for inspection of parish registers), the purchase of books, periodicals and newspapers, photocopying, photography, computer and fax supplies, telephone and postal expenses (these can be unexpectedly heavy), and, if you have one, the monthly subscription to your Internet service provider (ISP). Meals away from home when researching can be expensive, and you should not forget the lighting, heating and cleaning of a room used as office or study, since over the years this too can mount up – and if you are making an income from writing, most of such outgoings can be included as legitimate expenses to set against tax. The fees of a professional researcher, if employed, will be another major item, as will those of an indexer; and, at the end of the day, unless you are a good word processor/typist, you should allow for the cost of producing the final typescript in two or more copies. Computer-owners should remember to include the cost of the print-out from disk (the toner cartridges are not cheap).

It is an excellent idea to make a list of every conceivable expense you think you are going to incur – and then double it. Costs are rising all the time, and if a book takes four years to complete instead of the eighteen months you envisaged at the outset, this will play havoc with your budget. However, you will not have to fork out the total amount in one go, but as you proceed.

If you are fortunate enough to have a book or article commissioned, explain to the publisher or editor before you negotiate the contract or settle the fee just how much research expenditure is likely to be involved, and, in the case of a book, try to negotiate an adequate advance against royalties; this will probably be payable in instalments. Journalists may be able to arrange their assignments on an expenses-paid basis. In all cases, it is wise to keep a record of every item of expenditure, from a packet of paper clips to the hotel bill, and to ask for receipts for all major payments: you may not be a published writer when you start out, but if you end up as the author of a bestseller or even a writer with a modest regular income from his work, you will need to justify your expenses to the tax inspector.

It is always dangerous to state prices in print, especially in these days of inflation. As a guideline to the uninitiated, however, it should be borne in mind that at the time of going to press (spring 2003) freelance researchers and record agents are charging between £15 and £35 an hour, depending on the special skills involved. Typing costs vary: most agencies and home typists now offer a word-processing service, with inkjet or laser printing. (Consult advertisements on the back page of *The Author*, the quarterly journal of the Society of Authors, 84 Drayton Gardens, London SW10 9SB.) If you type your own work, remember that paper, ribbons, floppy/CD-RW disks, and ink or toner cartridges for the printer all cost money. (Members of the Society of Authors may order stationery through their fringe benefit scheme – provided they can collect the goods from the Society's office in South Kensington.) By shopping around locally you may find an outlet selling office and computer supplies at discount prices. Do not overlook the need for servicing your equipment from time to time: keeping even the faithful old manual typewriter up to scratch may cost in excess of £50 a year.

Photocopying varies from as little as 5p to 50p a sheet, according to size, to as much as £2 for A2 size copies from newspaper pages. The cheapest are those you make yourself on a coin-operated machine. 'Enhanced' photocopies and copies from microfiche or microfilm are more expensive. Bear in mind that applications by post not only cost more, but may also be subject to a minimum charge and handling fee. Some libraries offer an express service at additional cost. Genealogists and family historians constantly bemoan the fact that photocopies of birth, marriage and death certificates now cost £7 apiece if applied for in person or between £8.50 and £11.50 when ordered by post (see chapter 8, 'Family and Local History,' pages 142–64).

One major expense so often overlooked by a writer is the cost of quoting from copyright material: fees are liable to be charged for anything more than a few lines, although in practice some agents and publishers will be content, in the case of a short passage, with a suitable acknowledgment or possibly a free copy of the book. Quoting the words of songs is particularly costly. Reproduction fees for illustrative material, on the other hand, vary according to the size of the reproduction and the nature of the rights sought (i.e. British Commonwealth rights, world rights, etc.), but are normally not payable until the date of publication. Sometimes a publisher is willing to bear all or part of such expenses, and an author wishing to quote extensively from copyright material or to use pictures from private photographers, picture agencies or libraries would be well advised to ascertain the costs in advance and to discuss the financial division of responsibilities prior to the contract being drawn up for signature.

'Hidden' expenses include the number of free copies an author is expected to hand out. Normally he will receive six free copies of his book and may buy additional copies at a substantial discount. It is courteous to give signed copies to those who have helped to prepare the book for the press, such as the professional researcher, translator, indexer or proof-reader (where these are not taken care of by the publisher), and to the typist; copies should also be presented to anyone who has provided a substantial amount of material or granted the author access to private papers. The publisher is responsible for sending out review copies.

EQUIPMENT

No one would dream of taking up a sports or leisure activity without the proper equipment; nor should a writer or journalist embark on his researches lacking the few essential tools of the trade. It is true that pen and paper, the rudiments of shorthand or speed-writing, access to a good library, and an unlimited amount of time were once all that was needed, and although one might still 'get by' with these, today, when time is money (a recurrent theme of this book, for which I make no apology), it is both sensible and practical to make full use of all that modern technology provides to help us obtain the information we seek as speedily and as inexpensively as possible.

The basic equipment required can be divided into three groups: 1) the tools you take with you in briefcase or car when researching outside the home; 2) equipment for use in the writer's study; and 3) equipment that is 'desirable' (i.e. where funds permit) or for special assignments.

The suggested items are (excluding normal stationery):

To take out 'on the job'
Large briefcase and/or shoulder bag
Portable PC (laptop, palmtop or PDA) or alternatively a digital or micro/mini cassette recorder (sometimes called a pocket memo/electronic note-taker), with or without a detachable microphone if you are likely to do any interviewing (see pages 32–3), and with plenty of spare cassettes and batteries (take twice as many as you *think* you will need)
Portable 'digital' pen/computer pen (see below, page 16)
Camera (if the job requires it), either a compact or SLR, with generous supply of film, flashbulbs and batteries – or, better still (provided you have a PC with suitable software), a digital camera. *N.B.* An 'instant' or compact camera with auto-focus and auto-flash is perfectly adequate when pictures are required for research purposes only; otherwise a good SLR or digital camera is essential. The digital camera, although expensive, frees you for ever from the hassle of buying films and getting them developed and printed. Instead, images are loaded into an internal memory card which, once downloaded onto the computer, can be wiped clean for re-use; cards are available in a range of megabytes, the higher the MB the more images can be stored. (A 64 MB card stores up to 300 images.) Always buy the best camera you can afford, according to your needs, and if you are going for digital remember that the higher the number of pixels the better the image. (A minimum of 3 million pixels is recommended; 5 million gives superb results.)
Mobile phone/BTcharge card and/or other phonecard
Filofax/personal organiser, or failing that a pocket diary/telephone and address book
Clipboard (useful for writing on as you walk around or when interviewing)
Plenty of notepads
Pocket magnifier
Mini-stapler
Plenty of ballpoints and *pencils*, with sharpener and rubber. (Local record offices and most manuscript departments of libraries permit note-taking only in pencil.)
Ruler
Envelopes and stamps (Royal Mail ready-stamped envelopes are useful.)
Map of area to be visited
Local bus/rail timetables
Small cash book (for noting tax-deductible expenses on the spot: it is easy to forget unless you put them down at the time)
Spare pair of reading glasses (if used)
Torch
Loose cash (especially £1 coins), for cloakroom lockers and self-operated photo-copying machines (also useful for tea and coffee vending machines)

N.B. For security reasons most libraries and record offices require visitors to deposit briefcases or bulky packages before entering the search rooms. (Ladies are at an advantage here, if they have the kind of briefcase that doubles as a handbag – but there may be restrictions as to size, and at some places handbags must be deposited and essential items transferred to a transparent plastic carrier.) If you are asked to empty your bag, be sure that all your papers are securely fastened or in document folders so that you do not scatter them along the corridor on the way to the search room.

For the study
Word processor/personal computer (preferably with hard disk, CD-ROM drive and modem)
Printer (preferably inkjet or laser), with spare inkjet refill or laser toner cartridge
Fax machine
Good desk lamp (a long-life 'natural daylight' bulb is a good investment for close reading and proof-correction)
Filing cabinet or other storage system
Card index system
Large magnifying glass
Stapler/punch (better than paper clips for fastening notes)
Paper guillotine (for trimming half-used sheets of paper and enabling you to use off-cuts for notes and/or bookmarks)
Letter scales, leaflet with current postal rates and good stock of stamps in varying denominations (to save queueing at post office)
Highlighter felt pens in different colours
Soft pencils
Generous stock of yellow 'Post-it' notepads/multi-coloured index tabs
Lap tray (if you like writing by hand on your knee)

For the professional researcher and those on special assignments (in addition to the above list)
Sophisticated type of digital recorder, as used by most radio and TV reporters (essential if interviews or recordings are to be broadcast)
Camcorder, with supply of video cassettes
Telephone answering machine (now often combined with a fax machine)
Video recorder/DVD player
Paper shredder (essential if you handle confidential documents)
Photocopier capable of copying from bound volumes
Microform reader (if you use microfiche/microfilm at home). These are expensive, but secondhand or reconditioned machines are often advertised in the genealogical magazines (see chapter 8, 'Family and Local History', pages 159–64)
Modem for connecting to the Internet and other databases, plus all the necessary cables and software

N.B. It is wise to have a back-up computer in case your main one goes down (if this should happen, it will invariably be at the most critical moment). Keep your old one when you upgrade or buy a secondhand one cheap. Make sure it is compatible. Alternatively stow your old typewriter away in a cupboard or attic for emergencies.

Computers

Most professional writers and a high percentage of as yet unpublished writers now use personal computers (PCs). Journalists and researchers in all parts of the globe, no matter how remote, use their computers to access the Internet and the World Wide Web (WWW), which is the fastest growing information resource in the world, and to send and receive email and faxes. On the other hand, very many writers still buy computers purely for the word-processing facility.

It does not fall within the scope of this book to discuss the finer points of word processing or computing, let alone to recommend any particular brand of computer. It would be irresponsible of me to do so. The new technology advances at such a pace that anything I write today is more than likely to be out of date by the time this edition is published. However, a few basic guidelines may not be out of place:

Never rush into a purchase. There are many interesting packages and discounts on offer, both on desktop PCs and laptops, and it makes sense to shop around. Visit local dealers, browse through the latest computer magazines, talk to knowledgeable friends, preferably writers. At the end of the day the best advice you can get will undoubtedly come from a fellow author or journalist.

Buy the best system you can afford, preferably a multimedia computer, with a CD-ROM/DVD drive, and speakers. You may not need all the equipment now, but when later on you decide to go online and want to download chunks of data, or to run some of the more sophisticated programs on the market, or to go into self-publishing, you will be glad of it. The same goes for a printer, the inkjet or laser models giving the best results. Colour printers are fun, but not really necessary for the general writer, unless you intend to embark on desktop publishing.

The more powerful the processor, the faster it will work. The greater the capacity of hard disk and RAM, the more data that can be stored and the more programs run. Hard disk capacity today is measured in gigabytes (GBs) rather than in megabytes (MBs), which is some indication of the rate at which the technology continues to advance. Most systems can be upgraded later, to some extent, but do remember that the new software coming onto the market is increasingly greedy for disk and memory space. Think ahead.

Computers are sold online, by department stores, stationers and specialist dealers, and by mail order. I personally would always go for the specialist dealer or mail order company. Most dealers however seem to be notoriously indifferent to the special needs of writers: in their eyes spreadsheets, computer games and graphics all take precedence over word processing. Do your homework before you commit yourself.

Be sure to tell the dealer precisely what you intend to use the computer for. Insofar as word-processing software is concerned, most writers get along well with Microsoft Word or Wordperfect. It is worth emphasising here that it is definitely NOT a good idea to share your computer with the family, not least because games software is so much greedier, in terms of disk and memory space, than word-processing software.

If buying locally, insist on a one-to-one 'hands-on' demonstration. Draw up a list, however long, of everything you expect from your word-processing package (it may be line spacing, footnotes, page numbering, a search and replace facility, a word count, or just moving text from one page to another); ask to be shown how to carry out all these operations, and *make notes*. (The manuals supplied never seem to contain the very instructions you yourself need, and when you get home you will not remember.) Another thing to take into account is that you are going to be spending a good deal of time at work on the computer, so be sure to choose a keyboard and screen that you personally feel comfortable with. One of the advantages of buying from a local dealer is that he will set the whole system up for you and hopefully be around to deal with any teething problems that arise, as well as to upgrade it, if required, at a later date. If you purchase by mail order, the computer will be delivered with the software pre-loaded, but you will have to set it up yourself, with help from the manual or tutorial disk that accompanies the system; you will be given a technical support telephone number to ring whenever you need assistance.

Up to a few years ago when the book and magazine world was divided in its preference between IBM-compatible PCs and Macs (Apple Macintosh), writers were often influenced in their choice of computer by their editors or publishers. Macs run the Macintosh operating system and can read or convert PC disks; PCs run the DOS and Windows systems. Today, thanks to conversion software, most major word-processing packages usually work on both, so this is no longer a factor; nevertheless, it is wise to check both with your publisher and your dealer before you part with your money. For the purposes of desktop publishing Macintosh is the most favoured, on account of its graphics performance.

Many computer systems are now 'multimedia', and come with internal CD-ROM/DVD drives and stereo speakers. You must have a CD-ROM drive if you want to make use of the rapidly increasing number of reference works now being published in electronic form. A bonus for music lovers is that with this at your elbow you can listen to your favourite CDs as you work; for those who find computers stressful, soothing music may well avert potential bouts of 'computer rage'.

To go online you will need a 'modem', a device which enables your computer to communicate with other computers via the telephone. This may or may not come pre-loaded, or as a 'package' with the system, together with the necessary connecting cables and software. What you will almost certainly receive with a new computer is a large bundle of assorted software. Unfortunately, in order to get the sophisticated facilities that you do need, you may have to take on board all sorts of other options that, in your writing life, you will never use. It is a good idea to sort through these carefully at the outset and stow out of sight anything that does not relate to your work. In this way you will avoid the temptation of experimenting and thus wasting valuable creative time.

Portable computers – 'laptops', 'notebooks' and to some extent 'palmtops' and 'personal digital assistants' (PDAs) – are widely used by journalists and writers on the move. Points to watch when purchasing this type of equipment include compatibility with your desktop PC, battery life, and the size of screen and keyboard. A very small keyboard does not suit everyone, and you may prefer the type on which you write with a stylus on plastic. The more expensive portables are multimedia and have built-in modems enabling the user to send email and faxes, and to access the Internet. Handheld ('palmtop') models and 'computer pens' are useful for on-the-spot note-taking and have the advantage of fitting into a pocket or handbag. Also available are 'micro-computers' small enough to be slotted onto a belt. If you already have a PC at home, and need something just to make brief notes on as you work in the library or archive centre, or out on the job, a PDA or handheld computer may suit your needs. (Bear in mind, however, that the smaller the equipment, the more costly repairs are likely to be should it break down after the normal twelve-month guarantee has expired.)

There are other items of equipment and software of special use to writers and researchers:

Researchers who handle highly sensitive information should consult their dealers about digital shredders that safely erase all such material from the hard disk on their computer.

To protect your data from infection by the thousands of computer viruses now in circulation you should also invest in some virus-scanning software (this may come already loaded onto your new computer), and try to remember to update it regularly.

Writers and researchers who frequently need to store on computer large chunks of printed material from books or newspapers may find it worthwhile investing in some optical character recognition software (OCR). This is normally sold as a package together with a scanner. Ask your dealer about the best to suit your particular needs. Voice-activated software, which converts the spoken word into text on screen – a useful tool for the handicapped and those lacking in keyboard skills – is also now readily available, enabling the user to dictate to a PC at a speed of up to 160 words a minute. Not only are your spoken words transcribed instantly onto the screen, you can use your voice to command the PC to execute other functions such as formatting and editing text, surfing the Web, or simply to have your text read back to you (a useful timing device for speech writers). Although it has to be said that until recently, much sound-recognition software has been less than perfect, it *is* getting better. In fact, the day may not be far off when those of us lacking in keyboard skills (or simply too lazy to write in longhand) will routinely dictate our work onto word processors specifically designed for this purpose. Not only will these new machines take dictation, they will incorporate web browsers that learn and respond to voice commands. At the time of writing (early 2003) the Voice Xpress Professional software package, which includes a microphone and headset, sold by Dream Direct Ltd.,

Granville Way, Bicester OX26 4JT, is one of the most recommended. (More information from their customer enquiries, tel. 0870 7447 441.)

Handwriting recognition, or tablet-based computing, is one of the latest 'miracle' devices and will prove a godsend to researchers and writers. On the Microsoft Tablet PC, for example, you simply write on screen and have the ability to move, highlight, save, sort and search your handwritten notes. The 'digital' pens on the market will, when linked to appropriate software, store handwritten text or drawings and download them onto the computer screen – handy tools for those among us who begrudge the time spent typing up research notes. Some of these work with a small gadget clipped to the pad as you write or draw; others such as the Anoto incorporate a tiny camera as well as a processor and memory function (for more information and how to purchase online visit the website www.anoto.com). Watch out for other new inventions, which are coming thick and fast, and consult your dealer. (The pen which I forecast in the previous edition of this book, capable of 'learning' the user's handwriting and converting it to typed text on screen – invented by BT scientists and dubbed the 'SmartQuill' pen – has been licensed to another company and at the time of writing is not yet on the market.)

You should not confuse the 'digital' pen with the 'computer' pen, which is a tiny hand-held scanner for *printed* text, a godsend especially to researchers 'out on the job'. In this latter category there is the C-Pen, available in a range of portable and desktop models, some of which transmit text direct to the PC, while others are able to store between 1,500 and 2,000 pages of A4 text. As well as scanning, storing and downloading text, this wonderful gadget has a 'dictionary function', compatible with the Oxford, Merriam Webster and other major dictionaries, which will scan a word and display its meaning and/or translate it into several languages. It is also reasonably priced. (The C-Pen is available in the UK from Swains International PLC, Hunstanton, Norfolk PE3 6EW; tel. 01485 536200; email sales@swains.co.uk. For further details visit the following websites: www.cpen.com or www.swains.co.uk.)

Having extolled the virtues of these relatively new tools, I must add one word of warning. It would be unwise for any writer/researcher to succumb to the lure of too many widely advertised gadgets, without careful market research. Gimmicks such as pens that purport to write in an upside-down position, in water and on greasy surfaces, pens with a 'recording facility' (usually less than a minute), and the like are not for the serious researcher. One exception might be those pens with a built-in light, enabling you to jot down those brilliant ideas or phrases that inevitably occur to writers in the middle of the night, without disturbing your sleeping partner.

Other inventions will almost certainly hit the marketplace during the shelf-life of this book, and some of them will undoubtedly prove useful to the writer/researcher. I recall the days when I embarked on my career as a professional researcher, a time when we were all astounded by – and *very* appreciative of – the innovative 'Xerox' photocopying facilities (then available only in the major reference libraries) and the microfilm. Compared to today's prices, both were relatively expensive. We have come a long, long way since then. And will go further.

Photocopiers

Unless you do a great deal of photocopying, it is not really worthwhile purchasing a machine. Some of the cheaper desk-top models copy only from loose sheets, and not all those that take bound books give satisfactory results, especially if the volume to be copied is thick or tightly bound. Eager salesmen may promise copies at a fraction of the commercial cost, which can be tempting, but when you take into account the cost of materials, electricity, servicing charges, annual depreciation of the machine *and* operating – your valuable working time – there may not be a great saving. The value of having a photocopier at hand is the *convenience* of being able to run off copies instantly, without the need to make a special trip into town. Much depends, therefore, on how close you live to the nearest copy shop. Remember that you can use a fax machine to make a working copy of the odd sheet, but that this is not a permanent copy (it will fade after about six months). Many plain paper fax machines do however double as photocopiers.

ORGANISATION OF MATERIAL

There are few hard and fast rules in research, but it is wise to establish at the outset, and to adhere to, some systematic method of note-taking and data storage. There is little point in accumulating a mass of notes, press cuttings and other material unless you also devise a fairly foolproof system which will enable you either to bring up on screen or to manually locate what you want *when you want it*. Those who store manually should get into the habit of replacing any documents they have extracted immediately after use so that they can find them again later. (This will take only a minute or two at the time. It could take two hours, or more, if the document has been mislaid.)

Storage methods will differ according to individual circumstances and taste, and according to the type of material involved. Computer owners who set up personal databases will find them ideal for the storage of research notes and other information. The rest of us, soldiering on manually, divide into two camps: those who favour card indexes, and those who prefer notebooks, pads or loose sheets of paper, with a filing cabinet or cupboard large enough to house them.

Electronic storage

Building and maintaining a database on your PC is not difficult with the aid of your manual and the appropriate bibliographic software. Follow instructions, and try to keep it as simple as possible. Remember that the object of the exercise is to be able to access speedily everything you store. Remember too that in order to keep your database up-to-date you must regularly key in your research. This is not a problem if you use a portable PC or computer pen when out on the job: you simply load the data onto your desktop when you get home. But if you have to type up your notes onto the word processor and you do this when you are tired after a day's concentrated work, it is all too easy to make errors of transcription (we are all human). With a manual system you could have filed that same material, in note form, on paper, within minutes of getting home.

Always keep at least one back-up copy of your database on floppy disk or CD. It is a good idea to get into the habit of doing this each time you key in new data – it will take a few minutes at most and, in the unfortunate event of a crash, you will have lost nothing. You should of course always make a back-up copy of your current writing, after each session.

No one storage system is ever perfect. There is the added problem, if you are storing electronically, of what to do with the accumulation of photocopies, newspaper clippings, photographs, and correspondence. Or, for that matter, your original notes (which you must keep, in case you need to double-check something). The ideal solution is clearly a compromise: a database *and* a filing cabinet. (You will of course create a key index, suitably cross-referenced and regularly updated.)

Card indexes

The principal advantages of a card index are its flexibility and portability. It need not be expensive. All sorts of cartons, from shoe boxes to cereal packets, can if necessary be converted into filing receptacles; and for the one-off job a local printer may be persuaded into supplying slips of paper cut to size, which you can use instead of cards (but they must not be *too* flimsy). For permanent filing I recommend the commercially manufactured type of box in metal or plastic. You should buy only the kind of guide cards which have plastic or reinforced alphabetical tabs, as the cheaper variety will not stand up to hard wear. Record cards (ruled or plain) will withstand constant fingering better than slips. (For real economy, the researcher can always do what some professional indexers do, and once a particular job is finished, re-use the cards or slips by writing on the other side – preferably using a different coloured ballpoint so that there is no danger of confusion should the odd one be accidentally turned over.)

Cards or slips may be carried to and from the reference library or other place of research, as required, either in envelopes (clearly marked in subjects or whatever divisions best fit the job in hand) or in small packs secured by rubber bands. They can be sorted into alphabetical, subject or chronological order, either in one continuous series or per chapter and, if necessary, re-grouped as the work proceeds; coloured cards and coloured stickers (available in various shapes) may be used to denote different subjects or periods within each main division, and slips bearing brief cross references can be inserted as appropriate. The value of such a system is that its permutations are so great.

Loose sheets and notebooks

Many writers prefer to make their notes on larger sheets of paper. For them the shorthand reporter type of notebook is recommended, or there are various sizes of ruled pads, with or without punched holes, for fitting into loose-leaf ring binders or spring binders. Keeping notes in exercise books is not a good idea, unless a separate book is used for each section of the research, and even then it is advisable to number the pages and make a simple index in the front of the book, otherwise it may be difficult to locate the exact subject-matter when it is required.

For filing purposes it is best, when using sheets of paper rather than cards or slips, to note each item on a separate sheet or at least to leave a good gap between each item so that the notes can be cut up at home and each one slotted individually into its right folder or envelope. Although this may sound extravagant, writing on both sides of the sheet, unless it is on the same subject and clearly indicated by a bold 'PTO' or arrow at the bottom right-hand corner of the first side, is false economy – much valuable material has been 'lost' in this way. It is all too easy to gather up notes and file them without checking to see what is written on the back; nothing is more frustrating to the writer than to *know* that he has made a note of some vital fact or quotation or source – but *where*? It is also a good plan to get into the habit of putting material away as soon as possible after returning from the library, or after use. Otherwise the telephone may ring, there is nothing else handy on which to jot down a message, so the sheets lying on the desk are turned over, scribbled on – inevitably, sooner or later, something will go astray.

Working chronologies

Some writers engaged on an historical study or biography find it helpful to make themselves a working chronology to keep at their elbow while they work. This can be a straightforward listing of events or, in the case of a biography, may consist of a loose-leaf ring binder with the sheets arranged so that when the book is open, the left-hand page lists the happenings in the life of the biographee and his family, while the right-hand page lists outside events of approximately the same date. Ample space should be left between dates for subsequent insertions as research proceeds, to avoid the necessity of retyping pages. The time spent on the preparation of this simple working tool will be amply repaid by the ease with which the writer will be able to see his subject in perspective as he works.

Another useful system for the non-fiction writer is a small card index containing, on separate cards, a brief note of all the important points that must be covered, chapter by chapter. Before starting each chapter the writer can cast his eye over the cards and re-group them in the order in which he intends to deal with them. When that chapter is finished, anything that needs to be mentioned again later can be transferred on to the relevant section, so that he will not lose sight of it when the time comes.

Filing

If the documentation is not vast, the most convenient form of storage may be in large manila envelopes, clear plastic or multi-coloured document wallets, numbered or clearly marked as to subject or content; some researchers prefer the 'concertina' type of file or the folders secured with elastic that have up to nine divisions. For all but the simplest research collections, however, a steel filing cabinet will be a worthwhile investment. There are some small trolley-type cabinets on castors, which will suit the writer who likes to have his material at his elbow, at desk or armchair, wherever he works; otherwise the single- or multi-drawer cabinet, with or without suspension filing, is the best buy. As each book or writing project is completed, the material can be cleared out, parcelled up and stored elsewhere to make space for the next assignment.

So far as the storage of used material is concerned, the cardboard cartons obtainable free from wine shops and supermarkets are most useful; but photographs and manuscripts are best kept dust-free and flat in the kind of boxes still supplied with top-quality typing papers. For the perfectionist, or the writer who envisages the need to have quick access to his old material, there are excellent lightweight storage containers, ranging from collapsible box files to the more rigid corrugated-board storage cabinet complete with drawers. Valuable material should ideally be stored in acid-free containers in a cool and well-ventilated atmosphere, but for most purposes simple parcels loosely wrapped in brown paper and clearly labelled may be adequate. It is worth remembering that cardboard and brown paper allow documents to 'breathe', whereas metal does not; archive material such as original letters and diaries should not be kept for any length of time in a closed filing cabinet.

Whatever system you adopt, electronic or manual, there are two essentials that will prove their worth over and over again: 1) the establishment of a key for quick reference; and 2) a system of clear labelling. If you are not using your computer for this purpose, notebooks with alphabetical divisions or the most compact of desk-top card indexes are recommended, together with a supply of labels and felt marker pens in various colours. The card index, which may be kept in a box or in a rotary filing unit, should be as simple as possible, containing just sufficient information – either names and telephone numbers, or titles of books and periodicals, with page references and/or dates, or any suitable code of reference numbers – to send the user directly to the required source material.

A word of advice now to those who are setting up a new storage system – THINK BIG! As work progresses, you are bound to accumulate at least twice as much material as you planned for. Bear in mind, too, that a four-drawer filing cabinet takes up no more floor space than the single-drawer model. Few writers will be like the well-known historian and biographer who has admitted to having taken four years to decide to buy a proper filing cabinet and another four years to fill it – but those who do find themselves with empty drawers at the outset can always put them to good use. (Think of the peace of mind it will give you when you go away to research or on holiday to know that the one and only copy of your unfinished manuscript is securely stowed away, comparatively fireproof and out of the reach of vandals!)

The same goes for original material loaned to the writer. This is a big responsibility, and it is advisable always to make a point of photocopying or taking notes of what you need and returning the originals to their owners without delay. If this is absolutely not possible, at least keep the material in a safe place. Newspaper cuttings will go brown and photographs fade if kept in daylight for any length of time, and photographs can be easily damaged and rendered unsuitable for reproduction if left lying around on the desk. Some picture agencies require the borrower to pay substantial costs for the loss or damage of negatives or transparencies.

Books should always be treated with special care, whether they are loaned by private individuals or borrowed from the library. If they are to be handled a great deal, it is a good idea to cover them with plastic film or brown paper. *Never* write in the margins or turn down corners to mark a reference (unless of course the book belongs to you and you regard it as a working copy); and be very careful when photocopying that you do not bend it in such a way as to damage the binding. I now use 'Post-it' Index flags for quick reference; lightweight, in dispensers of fifty, and available in various colours, they can be written on, used over and over again, are easily removed and leave no mark on the page.

Take special care to write on the backs of photographs only with a very soft pencil; anything else can do irreparable damage. It is best to keep all illustrative material in a separate drawer, box file or filing tray, with each print inside a plastic folder or stiffened envelope. Elementary advice, maybe, but it is a fact that many photographs suffer through being left lying about unprotected; even if they are stacked underneath other papers they may sometimes inadvertently be scribbled on, and once that kind of damage is done it cannot be undone.

Those who handle a lot of original documents and photographic material may find it useful to look at the website of the British Library National Preservation Office (www.bl.uk/npo), which lists a number of very useful publications and also answers some FAQ; the free leaflets may be downloaded. While most NPO documentation is aimed at librarians and archivists, anyone who owns or handles original material will benefit from reading its 'Preservation Guidelines' document; also recommended are their booklets 'Good handling principles and practice for library and archive materials', 'Photocopying of library and archive materials' and 'Preservation of Photographic Material'. That excellent booklet, *Caring for Books and Documents* by A.D. Baynes-Cope, published by the British Library some years ago is, alas, now out of print but should be available at libraries. A free leaflet, 'The Care of Records: Notes for the Owner or Custodian' is on offer from the British Records Association, 40 Northampton Road, London EC1R 0HB (tel. 020 7833 0428; fax 020 7833 0416); you will be asked to send a stamped addressed envelope. (*N.B.* The BRA, founded in 1932 to promote the preservation, care, use and publication of records, is a registered charity, and donations are welcomed. For further information look at their website: www.hmc.gov.uk/bra.)

Three final tips:

1   Having set up the system that suits you and your project, do make an effort to keep the filing up-to-date, or the whole purpose will be defeated. If it is not possible to slot material away as it comes in, it is a good idea to keep some kind of 'pending' box or file, or a nest of filing baskets, into which you can put it until you have the time.

2   Remember that every good filing system has a 'Miscellaneous' file, and get into the habit of looking there for anything you cannot find instantly. As the 'Miscellaneous' file grows – and it is wise to allow plenty of space for it – new subject headings will suggest themselves and the appropriate material can be extracted and filed separately.

3   NEVER THROW AWAY ANY NOTES without keeping a record of the sources.

RESEARCH METHODS

Having established your storage system, electronic or manual, or ideally a combination of both, you are now ready to tackle the actual research.

If you are online, obviously you should make the Net your first port of call, visiting the websites relevant to your subject, browsing through library catalogues and posting questions to appropriate newsgroups. (See chapter 3, 'Online Research', pages 36–49.) Armed with the fruits of this initial foray, you will be ready to embark on more in-depth – or what I now privately call 'terrestial' as opposed to 'Net' – research. Your starting point here will almost certainly be a library or archive centre.

Using libraries

Finding your way round the library or libraries where you intend to do the bulk of your research is half the battle for the writer. The first thing to remember is that the librarian's job is to guide the researcher or reader to the right books; he is not paid to do original research for you. It is nevertheless astonishing how much a co-operative, interested librarian will do, and it is always politic to take him into your confidence about the scope of your research and what you are writing. Similarly, it is advisable to contact the librarian of a special library, either by telephone or letter, before making a first visit; provided he is given due notice of your interest, the librarian or one of his assistants will usually then prepare a preliminary selection of titles, and you can begin work without delay. If you do not do this, you may find that the librarians are tied up with other readers when you arrive, and you can easily waste half a day of valuable researching time.

In public libraries (lending and reference departments), and in the majority of special and private subscription libraries, you have access to the stacks and are free to browse among the books arranged on the shelves related to your subject. Most libraries today are computerised to some degree, and you are able either to use the computer terminal yourself, or the librarian at the enquiry desk may do this for you.

Where this is not the case, ask the library assistant how their particular catalogue or subject index is organised, and how to order.

At the major copyright and university libraries a certain number of reference works are on what is known as 'open access', that is to say on shelves where they may be consulted by the reader or from which they may be taken to the reader's desk (but not of course out of the reading room) and returned after use; all other titles must be applied for in the usual way. Where a library is not computerised you must look up the relevant shelf-marks in the general catalogue and fill out a requisition slip for each title. Ordering by computer has speeded things up dramatically: for example, at the new British Library the average waiting time is about thirty minutes (at the old premises in Bloomsbury you were lucky to get your books in two hours), and you see on screen straight away whether a book is in use by another reader or unavailable for some other reason. Nevertheless it is always wise to order what you need at the earliest moment (some libraries will allow you to reserve books a day or two in advance), and to fill in the short waiting period by using works that are on the open shelves or by consulting the catalogue for the next phase of your research. Because of lack of space, many libraries today are forced to 'out-house' selected classes of books; be prepared for these to take twenty-four hours or more to arrive.

Researchers wishing to use the British Library or other copyright libraries, those of the Imperial War Museum, National Maritime Museum, Royal Botanic Gardens and most university and museum libraries must obtain a reader's ticket, and it is advisable to do so in advance of your first visit – although temporary day tickets are normally issued on demand. Write to the Admissions Office of the relevant library for full details and application forms. You will probably be asked to supply two passport-size photographs, one of which will be incorporated into your pass, and in some cases for a letter of introduction.

On your first visit to a library or archive centre, devote a little time to familiarising yourself with the layout and with the cataloguing system. Where the catalogue is online, you will be guided every step of the way on screen. You do not need to know the full title of the item you seek, or even the author's name: one keyword, be it part title, part author's name or just the subject, should produce results.

A word of advice here for the uninitiated who find themselves confronted by an unfamiliar array of new technology equipment. DO NOT PANIC! There is nearly always an instruction manual, probably somewhat dog-eared as a result of frantic searching by other users in need of assistance, and usually pretty incomprehensible to the lay person! (To be fair, they *are* all nowadays much more 'user friendly'.) This manual will tell you which keys to press and in what order. Once you have pressed the first key, step-by-step instructions appear on screen to guide you through the next phase, and if you do something wrong a message will appear instantly on screen to that effect, with instructions on how to remedy the error. If all else fails, put yourself in the hands of a trained library assistant, who will do it all for you the first time. (In my experience, far from resenting such demands on their time, librarians are quite keen to show off their skills and to play with their 'new toys'; but this attitude will not last for ever. Watch very carefully: you will not be popular if you have to ask for help a second time.)

It is unlikely nowadays that you will find yourself in a library that is not online, but if this does happen, do not hesitate to ask a library assistant to explain any unusual features, and how to look up anonymous works, yearbooks and directories, or the proceedings of learned societies. Some libraries display a map showing the layout of the open reference shelves, or there may be a printed leaflet available. Most still have their old separate 'author' and 'subject' card indexes which you can search if all the computer terminals are in use (remembering that they will not be fully up-to-date), or you may come across a 'dictionary' type of catalogue which combines author, subject and title in one alphabetical listing. Occasionally you may have to use a catalogue on microfiche; if so, do be meticulous in replacing all microfiches in their correct numerical sequence after use, for the sake of subsequent researchers (and long-suffering librarians).

In smaller libraries the card index catalogue is usually cumulative, but in others there may be separate drawers or cabinets containing cards for acquisitions within a stated period. This 'Recent Acquisitions' section should not be overlooked. The trap here for the inexperienced lies in the word 'acquisitions', for although this section of the catalogue consists primarily of new titles, it will also include books that have been purchased or otherwise acquired recently – some of which may have been published some years ago. When you fail to find the book you are looking for in the general catalogue, therefore, always turn to this section.

The majority of libraries in the United Kingdom have adopted the Dewey Decimal Classification, which divides human knowledge into ten classes, each subdivided to accommodate subjects within each class. Try to memorise the main divisions, as follows:

000   General Works
100   Philosophy
200   Religion
300   Social Sciences
400   Languages
500   Science
600   Technology
700   The Arts and Recreations
800   Literature
900   Geography, Biography and History

The British National Bibliography (*BNB*) also uses the Dewey classification, and if you are seeking a published work on a certain subject, and do not know the author or precise title, you should go straight to the relevant class listing, as you would do in the library.

Note-taking

There are three 'golden rules' of researching:

1 Copy accurately
  Care must be taken to retain original spellings in quoted matter, using an editorial *sic* in square brackets if necessary. It is a good idea to get into the habit of double-checking all figures, proper names and page references immediately they are written or typed. For example, the date '1943' can so easily be copied as '1934' when one is tired (or more easily, because one's mind is on the year in which one is working, say, '1998' as '1989' or '2001' as '2010'!), and whereas it takes only a few seconds to verify the figure at the time, such a mistake can take hours to correct later – or may not be discovered until the work is in print. Writing unusual proper names and place names in block capitals in the researcher's notes also helps to avoid error and will save a lot of trouble if, several weeks later, the writer is unable to decipher his own hurried scribbles. There are surely very few people who, at some stage, have not mistaken a badly written 'cl' for 'd', or a 'uv' for 'w' – sometimes with dire consequences. It is especially important, when noting email addresses and websites, to make sure that you copy the dots and dashes, as well as the lower case and capital letters, correctly.

2 Check, double-check and, if in doubt, triple-check all facts
  Primarily where verbal recollections are given to the researcher by private individuals, but whenever and wherever possible in all other cases, especially if any doubts are entertained as to the accuracy of facts (even if printed facts), these should be verified in another source. Where confirmation of a fact or figure cannot be obtained and the writer remains in doubt, it is best either to avoid using it or, if you must, to state the source or sources relied on. The problem of 'conflicting authorities' is discussed in chapter 5 (pages 94–5).

3 Keep a note of all sources
  The importance of keeping full reference notes cannot be overstressed. Valuable time may be wasted if, for example, when your first draft is written, you wish to re-examine a particular source but cannot turn up instantly a note of the author, title, date and relevant page number, and preferably also the shelf-mark of the library where you originally saw it. Even more time will be wasted if you have omitted to follow the recommendation under (1) above to check page references on the spot and, failing to find what you are looking for at, say, page 241, you must thumb through a hefty tome, possibly without the help of an index, only to discover the right passage at page 421. (Whenever this happens, the shortcut is to try first all the permutations for the number originally written down.) Making brief cards or slips for each reference as you go along will halve the work when it comes to compiling a 'notes and references' section or the bibliography

(see chapter 11, 'Preparation for the Press', pages 189–99). Press cuttings and photocopies should be clearly marked with the book title, newspaper or periodical, plus volume number, date, publisher and page number where appropriate. Remember to do this before you hand in the volume or microfilm or replace it on the shelf.

What should you do when you come across an incorrect date or figure in a library book, perhaps a wrong page entry in an index? In the interest of future users, the temptation is to amend the text – in pencil, of course – but is it worth the risk of being expelled from the premises for life? The duty librarian is probably too busy to take much heed. My opinion is that if it is a modern title, provided you have the time and the inclination, you should write to the publisher asking him to make the correction in any reprint or new edition. If it is an old book, sadly there is nothing to be done.

Photocopying

All reference libraries and most other libraries and record offices operate a photocopy service, subject to the usual copyright restrictions and a ban on old or rare editions that might be damaged in the process. Microfilms and the type of photocopy suitable for reproduction can usually be obtained only from major libraries and record offices, and may take several weeks, but the electrostatic print or 'rapid copy' or 'xerox' as it is sometimes called, which is the most useful to the researcher, is often available while you wait or within twenty-four hours. Some libraries have installed coin-operated machines and expect you to make your own copies.

With material that is out of copyright there is no problem, but unless the copyright owner has given permission in writing, copying of all other printed matter is restricted to one article from any one issue of a newspaper or periodical, at any one time; or to a total of one-tenth of any one book in copyright. In all cases the applicant will be required to sign a statement that he has not before obtained a photocopy of the same extract, that he requires the copy purely for the purposes of research or private study and that he will not use it for any other purpose without the permission of the copyright holder. The cost is modest when one considers the amount of time it takes to copy a text by hand. Another factor to be borne in mind is that the photocopy is an *accurate* copy. When ordering photocopies from a library, it is essential to keep a note of the author, title, date of publication and edition of the source material, since these will not always appear on the photocopied sheets and the originals may not be returned to you; write these on the photocopies as soon as you receive them, and always before filing.

Commercial photocopying services abound in every city and major town these days, with self-operating machines at some railway stations, department stores and supermarkets. The quality of copies varies considerably, as does the cost; some places offer a substantial discount for a large number of copies made at any one time. These 'copy shops' are not usually over-worried about copyright and may well copy a complete book without demur, although in so doing both they and you, the purchaser, are breaking the law. Anyone planning to copy a large amount of text still in copyright should first apply for permission to the publisher.

Infringement of copyright by photocopying and scanning is a huge international problem.

Special arrangements exist for photocopying and scanning (digitisation) by UK universities and higher education establishments, government and public bodies, and industry. The Copyright Licensing Agency (CLA), founded in 1983 by the Authors' Licensing & Collecting Society (ALCS) and the Publishers Licensing Society (PLS) to collect photocopying income due to authors and publishers, has developed licences to meet the needs of these groups. For example, it recently agreed (but not without referral to the Copyright Tribunal) a scheme with Universities UK under which a blanket fee is paid per full-time student, with a copying limit of 5% of any one work. Back-dated to 1 August 2001, this scheme will operate for five years. Since September 1999 the CLA has administered a Digitisation Licensing Scheme, whereby scanning licences for individual works or parts of works are made available to universities, higher education establishments, pharmaceutical companies and churches. Looking to the future, it is envisaged that eventually digitisation will overtake photocopying altogether. For updated information contact The Secretary, The Copyright Licensing Agency Ltd., 90 Tottenham Court Road, London W1P 4LP (tel. 020 7631 5555; fax 020 7631 5500; email cla@cla.co.uk) or visit the website (www.cla.co.uk).

An updated edition of the British Copyright Council's very useful *Photocopying from Books and Journals: A Guide for All Users of Copyright Literary Works* is due soon.

Copyright

Copyright exists to protect the tangible form in which creative people such as writers, artists and musicians set out their original work. The key phrase here is 'tangible form', which this does not necessarily mean in print. There is however no protection for ideas or plots. Nor is there any copyright in titles, although the use of a title may be restricted where confusion is likely to arise between rival works, or between, say, a book and a film or play. There are special laws regarding composite productions (films, broadcasts, sound recordings, etc.), computer programs and, most recently, databases. The vast amount of in-copyright material now getting onto the Internet and onto pirated videos and CDs presents a major problem that even the new technology may find difficult to solve.

In the United Kingdom copyright exists as soon as the work in question has been set down in any medium. There are no formalities of registration, and it is not necessary for the work to be published. Book writers, scriptwriters, illustrators and translators also benefit from what are known as 'moral rights': these are 1) the right to be identified as the author whenever a work is published, performed or broadcast, called 'the right of paternity'; 2) the right to object to derogatory treatment, called 'the right of integrity'; and 3) the right not to have work falsely attributed to them.

While the right of integrity is automatic, the right of paternity must be asserted in writing: this is usually printed beneath the copyright line on the verso title page of a book. Moral rights do not apply to work published in newspapers, periodicals or collective works of reference.

In recent years the law on copyright has been harmonised within member states of the European Union, following the implementation of a series of Directives. The first of these, EU Directive 93/98, known as 'the Term Directive', came into force in the United Kingdom on 1 January 1996. The major amendment affecting writers has been to extend the term of copyright from the previous fifty to seventy years from the end of the calendar year of an author's death or, if the author or date of death is unknown, to seventy years from the date the work was first made available to the public. Thus the works of authors who died between fifty and seventy years ago, which had gone out of copyright under the fifty-year rule, are now protected under the new seventy-year rule, i.e. they are back in copyright for whatever period remains of seventy years from the date of their death: this is known as 'revived copyright'. Ownership of that copyright belongs to the person or company who owned it on 31 December 1995 or, if that person has died, or the company no longer exists, to the author's personal representatives. In the case of joint authors, the seventy-year rule is applicable to the last of them to die.

Another change under this Directive, and one of which all writers should be aware, is that the 'fair dealing' exception now applies only to work that has previously been published or made available to the public (see below, pages 29–30).

Special rules apply to pre-1989 material unpublished during the author's lifetime: such work remains in copyright for fifty years following its first posthumous publication, or until 2039, whichever is the shorter period – unless, that is, the 'life plus seventy years' rule is the longer, in which case, up to the end of the year 2039, that rule has priority. This is a complicated issue and one which all writers using private papers should bear in mind. Tim Padfield's *Copyright for Archivists* sets out very clearly the provisions of UK copyright law in this respect.

A further European Union Directive, concerning databases, has been effective since 1 January 1998. More recently there has been the EU Directive on Copyright and Related Rights in the Information Society, which became law in the UK on 31 December 2002; this new legislation provides protection for authors, performers and users in the digital environment within the European Union, as contained in the treaties of the World Intellectual Property Organisation (WIPO).

The current copyright statute of the United Kingdom is the Copyright, Designs and Patents Act 1988, which came into force on 1 August 1989, replacing all previous copyright statutes. International copyright is safeguarded by two separate conventions: the Berne Convention of 1886 and the Universal Copyright Convention of 1952, to which different countries adhere. Both conventions have been revised over the years, most recently in 1971.

In the United States the Copyright Act 1976, which came into force on 1 January 1978, replaced the old Act of 1909. It is important to remember that US copyright law differs from British copyright law in several respects.

For outlines of these various statutes, as well as the latest European Union Directives, see the articles on British and US copyright in the current *Writers' & Artists' Yearbook*. Fully updated information on copyright and electronic rights can be found on the website of the Authors' Licensing & Collecting Society (ALCS), www.alcs.co.uk. For those who are not online, there is a members' handbook, and a CD-ROM is available. (Apply to ALCS, Marlborough Court, 14–18 Holborn, London EC1N 2LE; tel. 020 7395 0600; fax 020 7395 0660.) A detailed guide to British copyright law, Denis de Freitas' *BCC Guide to the Law of Copyright and Rights in Performances*, is available through bookshops or from the British Copyright Council, Copyright House, 29–33 Berners Street, London W1P 4AA (tel. 01986 788122; fax 01986 788847; email copyright@bcc2.demon.co.uk). The Society of Authors publishes *Quick Guides* on the following: 'Copyright and Moral Rights', 'The Protection of Titles' and 'Copyright in Artistic Works, including Photographs', all of which are updated regularly. There is also 'What is mine is yours – at a price', an informative article by Kate Pool, Deputy Secretary-General of the Society of Authors, in the 2003 edition of *The Writer's Handbook*. A recommended title is Raymond A. Wall's *Copyright Made Easier*. Professional researchers should consult *Copyright for Library and Information Service Professionals* by Paul Pedley; watch out also for the forthcoming *Practical Copyright for Information Professionals* by Sandy Norman, due in autumn 2003, and very up-to-date.

British copyright law is immensely complicated. The 1988 Act, which replaced all previous statutes and sought to re-state the law of copyright in the United Kingdom, specifically forbids 'unfair dealing' in all works still in copyright. In practice this means that anyone wishing to quote substantially from a work in copyright must obtain permission from the owner of that copyright, normally the writer of the work in question, if he is still alive, or, after his death, his heirs and/or literary executor or person to whom the copyright may have been assigned. Biographers and historians should remember that although a letter *belongs* to the recipient, the copyright in it is vested in the writer of that letter and, after his death, for a period of seventy years or until the year 2039, to his estate; this applies also to letters published in the press. (See above, page 28, for special rules regarding copyright of unpublished personal papers.)

While the quotation of short passages for the purposes of criticism or review is deemed to be 'fair dealing', in all other cases involving more than a short phrase or a couple of lines of poetry it is advisable to obtain formal clearance. Generally speaking, the Society of Authors and the Publishers Association have agreed that the use of up to 400 words of prose (or a series of extracts of up to 300 words each, totalling no more than 800 words) from any one work, or up to a quarter of a poem, may be deemed 'fair dealing', *provided only that the words quoted are for criticism or review*. If you are quoting more than a short phrase from copyright material in any other context, permission should be sought, as the use of a 'substantial' part of a work without permission is an infringement of copyright. It goes without saying that acknowledgment should always be made to the author, title and publisher. The Society of

Authors' *Quick Guide* 'Permissions' sets out the position very clearly.

Writers should be aware of a major change on 'fair dealing' that came into force with the recent EU Directive on copyright in the information society (see above, page 28). Whereas hitherto the 'fair dealing' exception has related to *all* works in copyright, from now on it applies only where the work being quoted has previously been published or made available to the public.

It is important to allow plenty of time for the clearance of material you wish to quote. Write initially to the permissions department of the original publisher. If they do not control the rights, they should pass your request on to the author, his agent, literary executor, or, if relevant, to any subsequent publisher of the work. Foreign rights are frequently controlled by publishers or literary agents abroad, but the UK publisher should be able to provide a name and address to write to. A fee may be payable, the amount depending on the length of the passage or passages it is intended to quote and on the nature of the rights sought (i.e. British only, or British Commonwealth or world rights).

Advice on the reproduction of Crown copyright material should be sought from The Copyright Unit, Her Majesty's Stationery Office, St Clements House, 2–16 Colegate, Norwich NR3 1BQ (tel. 01603 621000; fax 01603 723000).

Clearing the copyrights on illustrative material is best left to a professional picture researcher or your publisher.

Difficulties sometimes arise in tracing copyright owners, especially in the case of unpublished material such as correspondence. A letter to the press may bring results, or try WATCH (*Writers and Their Copyright Holders*) on www.watch-file.com or http://tyler.hrc.utexas.edu. This ongoing Anglo-American project began in 1994 and is maintained jointly by the Harry Ransom Humanities Research Center at the University of Texas, Austin, USA and the University of Reading in the UK. Its regularly updated website contains the names and addresses of copyright holders or contacts for thousands of authors and artists, politicians and public figures, whose archives (in whole or in part) are housed in libraries or archives in North America and the UK. It can be searched free of charge.

Infringement of copyright can lead to heavy financial penalties. Researchers should be constantly on their guard against plagiarising another writer's text. Although there is no copyright in facts, it is essential to take care when making notes that you differentiate between actual quotations and your own précis. It is all too easy, months later, inadvertently to use the original author's words as your own, and then you may find yourself in trouble.

If you genuinely fail to locate a copyright holder, then you should include in your Author's Note at the beginning of your book a statement to this effect, saying that every effort has been made and that any inadvertent omission will be made good in subsequent editions. Your agent or publisher will advise on the precise wording of this statement.

A WATCH-recommended US publication is Richard Stim's *Getting Permission: How to License & Clear Copyrighted Materials Online & Off.*

Use of portable equipment in libraries

Most major libraries now set aside a section of their search rooms for those who wish to use laptops, computer notebooks or (more rarely nowadays) portable typewriters. Cassette recorders are permissible only by special arrangement with the librarian – this will depend on whether or not a private room, or part of a room, can be made available so that other readers are not disturbed. Dictating into a recorder undoubtedly saves time and fatigue, in the library, but can create problems of transcription back home unless proper names are spelled out and punctuation indicated; nothing at all will be saved if, at the end of the day, you have to go back to the original to check a quotation. Researchers will find a small pocket recorder of real value, however, where a good deal of interviewing or travelling has to be done: even if there are objections to using such a device during an interview, a quick dash to the car or hotel afterwards to record one's impressions while all is fresh in one's mind is very worthwhile, and so is a recorded on-the-spot description of buildings and scenes to be portrayed in a writer's work. For this purpose I have found the small battery-operated hand-held type of machine known as a 'pocket memo' or 'electronic note-taker' to be ideal. (You can speak into this faster than you can type onto a keyboard, and you can do it while walking around.) The Philips pocket memo 381 uses mini-cassettes of either 15 or 30 minutes per side, while the Olympus (slightly cheaper) takes micro-cassettes of one hour per side. There are small Olympus digital models that are only slightly more expensive and will record for up to 180 minutes. A 'state-of-the-art' digital recorder which uses a smart media card and has a downloading facility is essential for interviewing or sound recording, and here it is best to choose a model which will run both on batteries and on mains. Many digital recorders no longer require a microphone to be plugged in. If you intend to transcribe your mini- or micro-cassettes, you will need an appropriate transcriber, with foot pedal; most of the larger machines have a socket for plugging in a pedal (essential for tape transcription). Digital recordings can be downloaded into the computer.

The use of microform readers (for microfiche and microfilm) baffles some novice researchers. The machines do vary, and it is wise in the first instance to ask a library assistant to show you how to operate the particular model they have. It is very important never to touch the film with greasy fingers or to get it twisted, and always to rewind the film onto the original spool before returning it to the issue desk. (Nothing is more exasperating to the next user than to discover that the spool must be rewound!) Similarly, it is most important – for the sake of the next user – to replace all microfiches after use in the box or folder provided, *in the correct alphabetical/numerical order.*

In libraries where there are a number of microfilm readers installed, often close together, some people find they cannot do more than an hour or two's work at a time, partly because of the noise of other users constantly winding and rewinding and partly due to eyestrain. Some professional researchers tackle these difficulties by wearing earplugs and/or tinted spectacles.

Interviewing

Interviewing people, and getting the maximum information out of them, is a skill that is acquired with practice. There are no hard and fast rules, but here are a few tips from personal experience:

Always write or telephone in advance, stating clearly who you are, why you need the information, and precisely what it is you seek.

If time permits, take 'two bites at the cherry'. People are naturally on the defensive at a first interview, but when you go back a second time they already know you and will welcome you as a 'friend'.

Never ask a crucial or controversial question right at the start. If necessary, put the person being interviewed at ease, make some social small talk first. It can be quite productive sometimes to bring out your 'key' question almost at the end of the interview, as though it were an afterthought and not all that important – the interviewee will be relaxed by that time and much more expansive.

Don't assume that you can use a recorder. A lot of people are nervous of being recorded and will 'freeze' if you insist. A good plan is to have your machine tucked away in your briefcase and then, when the interview is well underway, you can say something like, 'This is tremendously good stuff, I can't get it all down accurately in my rusty shorthand...would you mind very much if I record it?' You can plug what is known as a 'conference microphone' into the little Philips recorder mentioned on page 31, stand it on the table and it will record up to 5 metres in each direction; the Olympus takes an ordinary microphone. Conference microphones can be plugged in to some digital recorders, but many recorders now on the market have an internal memory and do not require a microphone at all.

Offer to let interviewees see anything you intend to quote in print, and ask them how they wish to be acknowledged. And always write afterwards to thank them for sparing the time to talk to you.

The question of how far to trust information given to you from personal recollection is dealt with in chapter 7, 'Biography and Autobiography' (see pages 123–41).

Up to ten years ago Eve McLaughlin's *Interviewing Elderly Relatives*, written primarily for the guidance of genealogists and family historians, was virtually the only handbook for researchers (as opposed to personnel officers) on the subject in existence in the UK; now in an expanded edition, it contains many useful tips. Happily there have since been several titles, of which the following three are unfortunately out of print and unlikely to be reprinted, but should be available at libraries. *Interviewing Techniques for Writers and Researchers* by Susan Dunne offers a step-by-step approach, from the research and planning that are necessary beforehand to getting the best out of the interview and (increasingly important nowadays) avoiding libel. Sally-Jayne Wright's *How to Write and Sell Interviews* contains valuable advice on the interviewing technique: how to talk to anyone, from the man-in-the-street to the celebrity; how to ask the questions that get results; body language and telephone manner; even what to wear. *Interviewing for Journalists* by Joan Clayton is equally strong on practical advice. Both Jill Dick in *Freelance Writing for Newspapers* and *Writing for Magazines* and Gordon Wells in *The Craft of Writing Articles* deal briefly with the subject. A more recent handbook written primarily for journalists, published in Australia but available in the UK, is *Interviewing* by Gail Sedorkin and Judy McGregor. This reasonably priced paperback is crammed with invaluable tips for all interviewers, ranging from how to frame and use the 'icebreaker' question to naming (or not naming) sources, and the pitfalls to be avoided. Much emphasis is laid on the need for preparatory research if the interview is to be a success.

If you are nervous about interviewing or feel that you need to brush up your technique, enquire at the London College of Printing, Elephant & Castle, London, SE1 6SB (tel. 020 7514 6562; website www.lcptraining.co.uk) about the one-day courses that they run for journalists.

So much for search procedures and storage of material. Throughout the writing of this chapter I have tried to keep in mind the needs of the novice writer of fiction, the amateur family historian and the biographer. Hopefully I have included one or two tips that may be of use even to the more experienced. Students preparing theses and writers embarking for the first time on academic work are recommended to read Roy Preece's *Starting Research* and/or Nick Moore's *How to do Research*.

Another excellent title aimed at the academic writer is *Doing Your Own Research* by Eileen Kane, the revised edition of which contains a new chapter, 'The Library and the Internet'. *Lifting the Lid* by David Northmore is a guide to investigative research.

There are many ways of researching. Methods that work for others may not come naturally to you. Members of the younger generation of writers may scorn anything but the electronic. Many of the 'oldies' among us are scared stiff of the new technology, but may be tempted at some stage to give it a go. To them I would say this: yes, do consider storing your notes electronically, setting up your own personal database, surfing the Net. But give it time. Never let yourself be pressurised into taking on board in one go all that IT has to offer, simply to keep up with other writer friends – and *never* when you are already launched into or about to begin a major work. Always, always go for the methods of working and storage that you feel most comfortable with, those that intrude the least on your creative skills. That way, and only that way, you will save yourself a lot of unnecessary stress – and possibly also an unnecessary overdraft into the bargain.

The Author, quarterly journal of the Society of Authors, London; free to members, currently £8 per issue to non-members
BCC Guide to the Law of Copyright and Rights in Performances, by Denis de Freitas, British Copyright Council, London, 2nd edn, 1998

The Business of Writing, by Gordon Wells, Allison & Busby, London, 1998

'The Care of Records: Notes for the Owner or Custodian', British Records Association, *Guidelines 1*, 1997, available free (send a stamped addressed envelope) from the BRA, 40 Northampton Road, London EC1R 0HB

Caring for Books and Documents, by A.D. Baynes-Cope, British Library, London, 2nd edn, 1989

'Copyright and Moral Rights', *Quick Guide No. 1*, Society of Authors, 2002

Copyright for Archivists, by Tim Padfield, PRO, London, 2001

Copyright for Library and Information Service Professionals, by Paul Pedley, Aslib, London, 2nd edn, 2000

'Copyright in Artistic Works, including Photographs', *Quick Guide No. 11*, Society of Authors, London, 1997

Copyright Made Easier, by Raymond A. Wall, Sandy Norman, Paul Pedley and Frank Harris, Aslib, London, 3rd edn, 2000

The Craft of Writing Articles, by Gordon Wells, Allison & Busby, London, 2nd edn, 1996

Doing Your Own Research, by Eileen Kane, Marion Boyars, 2nd edn, 2001

Freelance Writing for Newspapers, by Jill Dick, A & C Black, London, 3rd edn, 2003

Getting Permission: How to License & Clear Copyrighted Materials Online & Off, by Richard Stim, Nolo Press, Berkeley, California, USA, 1999; also on CD-ROM

'Good handling principles and practice for library and archive materials', National Preservation Office, London, 2000 (booklet available free of charge from the NPO, The British Library, 96 Euston Road, London NW1 2DB)

How to do Research: The complete guide to designing and managing research projects, by Nick Moore, Library Association, London (now Facet Publishing), 3rd edn, 2000

How to Write and Sell Interviews, by Sally-Jayne Wright, Allison & Busby, London, 1995

Interviewing, by Gail Sedorkin and Judy McGregor, Allen & Unwin, Crows Nest, NSW, Australia, 2002

Interviewing Elderly Relatives, by Eve McLaughlin, 4th expanded edn, 1999 (available from *Family Tree Magazine*, 61 Great Whyte, Ramsey, Huntingdon, Cambs. PE17 1HL)

Interviewing for Journalists, by Joan Clayton, Piatkus Books, London, 1994

Interviewing Techniques for Writers and Researchers, by Susan Dunne, A & C Black, London, 1995

Lifting the Lid: A Guide to Investigative Research, by David Northmore, Cassell, London, 1996

'Permissions', *Quick Guide No. 10*, Society of Authors, London, 2002

Photocopying from Books and Journals: A Guide for All Users of Copyright Literary Works, by Charles Clark, British Copyright Council, London, 1993; new edn in preparation

'Photocopying of library and archive materials', National Preservation Office, London, 2000 (booklet available free of charge from the NPO, The British Library, 96 Euston Road, London NW1 2DB)

Practical Copyright for Information Professionals, by Sandy Norman, Facet Publishing, London, scheduled for September 2003

'Preservation Guidelines', document available free of charge from the National Preservation Office, as above

'Preservation of Photographic Material', National Preservation Office, London, 1999 (booklet available free of charge from the NPO, as above)

'The Protection of Titles', *Quick Guide No. 2*, Society of Authors, London, 1997

Starting Research: An Introduction to Academic Research and Dissertation Writing, by Roy Preece, Pinter Publishers (Mansell), now the Continuum Publishing Group, London, first published 1994; 2nd edn, 2000

Writers' & Artists' Yearbook, published annually by A & C Black, London; articles on British and US copyright

Writers and Their Copyright Holders (WATCH), joint project run by the University of Texas Harry Ransom Humanities Research Center and the University of Reading; online at www.watch-file.com or http://tyler.hrc.utexas.edu

The Writer's Handbook, ed. Barry Turner, published annually by Macmillan, London

Writing for Magazines, by Jill Dick, A & C Black, London, 2nd edn, 1996

Note: The *Quick Guides* published by the Society of Authors are free to members (with s.a.e.) and available to non-members at £2 each, post free, from the Publications Department, Society of Authors, 84 Drayton Gardens, London SW10 9SB (tel. 020 7373 6642; fax 020 7373 5768). Information concerning membership of the Society will be found on the website www.societyofauthors.org, or send an email to info@societyofauthors.org.

Chapter Three

Online Research

Within the past decade, information technology (IT) has transformed dramatically the way in which writers and researchers go about their work. The transformation has crept up on us with startling speed, and there is no going back to our old ways. Gone for ever are the hours spent poring over well-thumbed library catalogues and card indexes: all such preparatory work can now be carried out in advance, online, in the office or at home. No longer do we wait for weeks for information to reach us from the other side of the world: it appears on our screens within minutes. Our most senior librarians have reinvented themselves as 'information professionals', usually with a degree and/or strings of letters after their name. We too, faced with an array of keyboards and disks, 'plug-ins' and 'protocols', monitors and mice, have become IT practitioners – technicians in fact, in our own right. It is a new world.

Ten years ago a writer who claimed to do the bulk of his research on the Internet would probably have been regarded with some disbelief, almost as a nutcase. Today a writer who boasts he has no intention of even trying out email or attempting to browse the World Wide Web is looked upon as a bit of a fool. But he is a rare specimen.

The Internet and email have established themselves as permanent fixtures in our daily routine, and it is up to every one of us, writers and researchers especially, to make the fullest possible use of these new tools, both professionally and personally. Do not forget that present-day 'state-of-the-art' technology is 'multimedia', covering not only textual matter, but also graphics, sound and animation.

That said, admittedly 'the Net' is not without its imperfections; nor is it for absolutely everyone. If you are the kind of writer who has accumulated a sizeable reference collection over the years, and you like to spread out half-a-dozen books on the desk or study floor and flick through the pages, ferreting out information from this or that volume, comparing one text with another, you may be driven crazy by the slow manoeuvres you are forced into online and think it is not for you. If you are a 'technophobe' who comes out in a hot sweat at the mere sight of a computer, panicking over which button to press and when, to such an extent that the very process eats into your creative thought, then maybe you *should* think twice before you embark. But please do not, I beg you, dismiss it out of hand without a fair trial. Unless you give it a whirl, you will never fully comprehend what you might be missing out on.

The first important thing to remember is that the Internet is *not a substitute* for in-depth research into original sources; it is an *additional resource*. Think of it as a springboard. Respect it for what it has to offer. Handle it with care, as any skilled craftsman would handle his favourite tool, and it will surprise you with its flexibility and its worth.

There is plenty of help out there to get you started. Bookshops are awash with manuals (some, it has to be said, far better than others), crammed with advice on this or that technique, for shopping, banking, booking travel and theatre tickets, as well as for research purposes. In one short chapter it is impossible to detail every aspect of this new and exciting element in our lives. I shall merely outline the basic skills and resources, while at the same time spelling out some of the 'pros and cons' insofar as they concern the professional researcher. The finer points of word processing and using the Internet are in any case best gleaned from your tutor or a good handbook.

THE WORLD WIDE WEB

The Internet's most important component, the World Wide Web is the most powerful research tool and source of information yet known to man. In order to tap into this vast source you go 'online', and 'browse', 'surf' or 'trawl' its pages.

To judge from media publicity and sales talk, you might be forgiven for assuming that you have only to go online for all your research problems to be solved at the press of a few keys, and that from then on you will be able instantly to access everything you need from the comfort of your study armchair.

This is not so. Realisation of the information scientists' dream that one day – maybe – a vast online library will be created in cyberspace housing the full text of every book that has ever been published is a long, long way off, if it happens at all. (Which is good news for writers of works in copyright.) Meanwhile, more and more authenticated texts *are* coming online, more databases are created and more are regularly updated, thus making accessible a quantity of up-to-the-minute information that would have been undreamt of a decade ago. Unfortunately the quantity is not always matched by the quality.

Because in theory anyone can put anything they like on their own website, be it true or false, or simply unverified for factual correctness, the onus falls on you, the researcher, to check it out – and this is especially important if you intend to use that factual material in something you write and publish under your own name. Treat the Web therefore as the *first*, but *never the only*, library or information centre that you visit. Remember too that each website is only as reliable as the person who put the data onto it in the first place – while bearing in mind that human error applies also to printed books and all other documentation.

The Web consists of millions of linked pages of information on every subject imaginable. It is true that what you find there may be far more up-to-date than anything available in the terrestial library. But do not be fooled: sadly, as mentioned above, given the sheer volume of material in cyberspace, and its varied provenance, it is unwise to rely on it 100 per cent. Another trap for the unwary is that web pages are constantly being updated or amended, or may be removed altogether at whim, so that it can prove dangerous, in research terms, to rely on or quote sources other than those you know to be authenticated and more or less permanent. As with all other research you do, you should never skimp on the checking and double-checking. Be suspicious of anything that does not emanate from a known, authoritative source. With experience you will soon become quite clever at evaluating a website.

The great advantage for the researcher is that, unlike the library, the Internet remains open seven days a week, twenty-four hours a day, every day of the year. Whenever the mood takes you, or an idea strikes, you can access the catalogues of major libraries and universities all over the world. You can visit the websites of organisations and individuals at will and, once you find the information you want, print it out or download it onto your computer. Using the email facility, you can correspond globally with fellow professionals and contacts at minimal expense. You can post unlimited questions to newsgroups of your particular interests, join in their discussions, and receive regular newsletters on any subject you choose. You can also design your own web page or pages.

The downside is that you may find surfing the Web irritatingly slow, as you move from one link to another, or scroll endlessly through pages of advertising and irrelevant 'bumph' in order to find precisely what you seek. (But let's be fair, isn't it only too easy also to waste a lot of time in libraries?) Then there is the very real danger that unless you are exceptionally disciplined you may become altogether too addicted to the whole process – at the expense of both your writing time and your purse. You may also have to cope with receiving masses of time-consuming junk email (known in computer jargon as 'spam'). Worse still, you run the risk of exposing your computer to attack by virus.

All that said, the practicalities of going online are not complicated.

SUBSCRIBING TO AN INTERNET SERVICE PROVIDER

We will assume that a modem is installed in your computer. Now you must choose an Internet service provider (ISP). Should you pay a subscription or go for a 'free' provider? The answer is that basically, as with everything else in life, you get what you pay for: there is no such thing as a 'free lunch'. This is not to say that it isn't a good idea to take advantage of those unsolicited CD-ROMs that come through the post, offering you a free trial from this or that ISP. There is no better way of finding the one that suits you best – but be sure to cancel before the end of the trial period unless you wish to proceed, otherwise you will incur subscription charges.

Basically, the ISPs who charge are more reliable and offer additional services.

Check these out before you sign up. They are also a good deal less complicated to use. A choice of subscription is usually on offer, ranging from 'anytime', currently at around £12–15 a month, to 'off peak' (after 18.00 hours on weekdays and all day Saturday and Sunday), at between £5 and £9, or a fixed number of hours in the month (in which case you will be charged on your credit card for any excess). If you do not have a second telephone line you should consider taking out a 'broadband' subscription, which costs more (currently about double the 'anytime' monthly fee), but allows you to make and receive calls in the normal way while online.

If you opt for one of the 'free' services, be aware that you do have to pay, via your telephone bill, for every second you spend online. This is usually charged at local call rate, but the costs soon mount up, especially in the early days when you are finding your way around. There are disadvantages, too, in the shape of more advertising to wade through, and you may find that access is slow. (It is in the interest of the provider to keep you online as long as possible, since he earns commission from the telecom company for every call.)

Other factors to bear in mind before making a decision include the speed of connection and the time it takes for data to reach you. Check also that you are being offered a twenty-four-hour facility to call technical support at a local rate (some providers have been charging up to £1 a minute).

There are a number of ISPs to choose from, including those run by the major telecoms, such as BT and NTL, and the BBC. America Online (AOL, which now owns Compuserve) is one of the largest. Claranet, Freeserve, Demon, Pipex and Virgin are also popular. Shop around, ask other writers for recommendations, read the trade journals. Above all, suit your budget and your particular needs. Do not worry if you find later that you have made the wrong choice: it is easy to switch to a different provider.

There is an alternative way to go online, if you have no computer. For around £50 you can buy a TV Internet access box which plugs in to the Scart socket on your television set; this enables you to surf the Net and to send and receive emails without tying yourself to an ISP contract.

OTHER COSTS

There is a myth that cries out to be exploded about the costs of online research. Many people wrongly assume that once they have subscribed to an ISP everything else online comes free. This is far from the truth. A great many texts *are* out there, up for grabs as it were, and more *is* becoming available all the time. But if you are undertaking 'advanced' or scholarly research you must be prepared to find that many of the electronic publications/databases on offer are accessible only by subscription, and mostly at rates far beyond your pocket as an individual user. The only solution is to find the nearest library or institution which subscribes, or can be persuaded to subscribe, to the particular database or bases you need to use, and to weigh up the costs of travelling and travelling time against the subscription charge and the convenience of having that material online at home. In fact the choice may not be all that difficult: for example, a subscription to *Encyclopedia Britannica* doesn't cost the earth, will save you a lot of shelf space, and, furthermore, you will probably access it fairly often. Whereas unless, say, you are writing a book on women's rights, it is doubtful that you will ever recoup the cost of a subscription to the Chadwyck-Healey *Gerritsen Collection – Women's History Online 1543–1945.*

BROWSING THE WEB

Your ISP will supply the necessary software to connect your computer with theirs, through which you in turn connect to a vast network of computers worldwide. While computer software has in one sense become more complicated, and infinitely more greedy for disk space, there is no doubt that it is today much more 'user-friendly' than it used to be.

To connect to the Internet you first plug your modem into a telephone socket. In order to read pages on the Web you need what is known as a 'web browser' program, such as Microsoft Internet Explorer or Netscape Navigator; this is normally pre-installed on your computer. When you first connect, with this program running, the default or 'home' page will open. To access a different website all you have to do is to type in the appropriate address, known as the URL (Uniform Resource Locator). URLs normally start with 'http://www.', but in practice you can forget the 'http://' bit (it stands for Hyper Text Transfer Protocol) – the browser does this for you automatically – and begin with 'www.'. You then press 'Enter' on the keyboard. On the web page that opens on screen you will usually find a list of 'links' or 'hyperlinks' which direct you to additional information; click on these as appropriate, or scroll down to the next page on the site.

Web addresses are almost always written in lower case (no capital letters), and you must take care to type them with the dots and forward slashes in the correct places. After 'www.' comes the 'domain name' (the name of the person or company); this is followed by either '.ac', '.co', '.com', '.net' or '.org', indicating whether it is academic, a company, a commercial enterprise, an Internet gateway/administration host, or an organisation respectively; and then usually (but not always) by the global location, such as '.uk' for the United Kingdom, '.de' for Germany, '.au' for Australia. Where the address ends in '.com' or '.net' it is normally a US site.

USING SEARCH ENGINES

The most useful tools for the researcher on the Web are the various 'search engines' which, when you type in a keyword or topic, will look for and deliver on screen the relevant pages (often far too many!). Among the most popular at present are Altavista (www.altavista.com), Excite (www.excite.com), Google (www.google.com), HotBot (www.hotbot.lycos.com) and Yahoo! (www.yahoo.com), websites which you access by typing in their URL. The search engines differ slightly in their approach, but you will soon learn how to make the best use of them. Yahoo!, for example, is more of a subject-based directory than the others.

You should also take advantage of the growing number of 'metasearch engines', such as All-One-Search (www.allonesearch.com), AskJeeves (www.askjeeves.co.uk), Copernic (www.copernic.com), etc., which will search several (or up to several hundred) search engines globally to fulfil your request.

The golden rule for trawling the Web is to be as specific as possible in your request – in other words, narrow down as far as possible at the outset the precise information you seek, otherwise you will have to wade through a mass of material you do not want. This is known as 'refining' your search. I regard refining a search as not unlike trying to get through on the telephone to a top-notch City executive or VIP. You edge your way slowly towards the quarry, using the time-honoured researcher's attributes of persistence and cunning. You progress in stages from the switchboard through various secretaries and members of staff to the confidential PA, honing down your request as you go, never giving up – until, suddenly, with a bit of luck, there you are, at the fountainhead...

As in real life, the skill in this process lies in the choice of words and in the judicious use of 'operators' – which in computer-speak are not human beings but additions such as quotation marks or plus and minus signs ('+' and '-') to the keyword/topic; and more especially the 'Boolean' operators, named after the mathematician and logician George Boole, 'AND', 'OR', 'NOT', 'NEAR'. These are always written in upper case (capital letters). Such 'advanced search' techniques require practice, but you will soon become proficient. Before you log on to any search engine, it is best to prepare a list of keywords or phrases – and keep the list safe for next time.

It is worth remembering that all Internet searches take expertise and time, if they are to be successful. The telephone remains a researcher's steadfast tool and should not be overlooked. In my own experience of seeking information for this revised edition, I have frequently found a quick call to the right person faster, more informative, and cheaper, than an online search. This does of course depend on getting hold of the right person in the first place. Inevitably, it is the luck of the draw. The person you speak to may be charming, interested and willing to bend over double to help, or he may be totally uncooperative – in which case, as with the Web search, you try a different path.

KEEPING RECORDS

It is of the utmost importance to keep a record of the path to your information. A quick and automatic way of being sure to get back to those websites you visit regularly is to add them to 'Bookmark' or 'Favorites' on the browser ('Bookmark' on Netscape, 'Favorites' on Microsoft Internet Explorer) – simply click on the relevant icon and follow instructions. I also urge you to maintain a personal 'webography' or website directory, suitably indexed/cross-referenced under subject. It will pay good dividends in terms of convenience and working time.

There are scores of 'directories' of websites on the market, but somehow none of them ever contain all those that you need most. Even the lists of sites in the specialist handbooks for writers are lacking in this respect. The truth is that with so many sites out there, it is impossible to cater for every individual's needs. This is why it is essential to begin compiling your own list from the outset. By all means buy one or more of the latest printed guides, to start you off: I can recommend *The Good Web Site Guide 2003*, by Graham Edmonds, and also *The Rough Guide Website Directory*.

SAVING AND STORING WEB PAGES

When you need to save material found on the Web, you can either print out the relevant page(s), or you can 'download' it onto your computer for storage. The machine will hold the material in temporary memory for a given number of days. For more permanent storage you can copy it onto your hard disk.

Be sure to scan everything you want to download for possible viruses. Most new computers these days come with some form of anti-virus software pre-installed, and the on-screen instructions are easy to follow.

'Downloading' from a website to hard disk is not difficult. You simply click 'File' in the normal way, then select the 'Save as web page' icon and choose one of the options offered. When you do this for the first time, you should create a new folder where you want to store the material, then follow the on-screen instructions for saving it into that folder in one of a choice of formats. You can create as many sub-folders or files within the folder as you wish. As with all filing systems, it is essential to create a 'Miscellaneous' or 'Pending' file (call it, say, 'Download/Misc.' or 'Web/Pending') into which you can place downloaded material for later sorting. The whole process may take quite a while, depending on the length of the document(s) you are downloading, but you can check on how it is going by watching the blue bar in the bottom right-hand corner on your monitor. Remember that anything you download is subject to the normal rules of copyright (see chapter 2, 'Organisation and Method', pages 27–31).

Some documents on the Web (and on CD-ROM) are in Portable Document Format (PDF), i.e. 'locked', so as to preserve their original formatting. This means that whereas you can 'read' or print them, you cannot make any alterations to them. In order to read or print out PDF files you need to have the Adobe Acrobat Reader installed on your computer; this may be downloaded free on www.adobe.com/acrobat. Saving them to disk is more complicated: use the 'Help' icon the first time round and follow instructions.

If you want to print or save part of a web page, select the relevant text in the usual way, open the document to which you wish to transfer it, and use the 'Copy' and 'Paste' facilities to put it on the clipboard and paste it in the desired place.

YOUR OWN WEB PAGE

Going online offers the facility to create one or more Web pages of your own, at no extra cost. The content and design of such pages is however beyond the scope of this book. Take professional advice or, if you are tempted to have a go yourself, first read Jane Dorner's article 'Setting up a website' in the current *Writers' & Artists' Yearbook*.

EMAIL

Unquestionably one of the most important tools used by writers and researchers today is the electronic mail facility. 'Email' enables you to send messages to other Internet users worldwide and to receive messages from them (provided of course that they have an email address). To operate this facility you need an email program such as Outlook Express or Netscape, one of which may be pre-installed on your computer or will be provided by your ISP.

When you first sign up with an ISP you will be given a special 'mailbox' or electronic address (sometimes up to five addresses) through which you can send and receive mail; you will also be asked to choose a password, which under no circumstances should you divulge to any other person. The first part of the address you create yourself, usually incorporating your own name; this is followed by '@' and the address of the ISP. It will look something like annsmith@aol.com. Because each email address has to be unique, you will not be allowed your first choice if this happens to exist already (bad luck if you have a name like 'Ann Smith'), and you will have to add in another initial or middle name, or concoct something else (aresearcher@aol.com might work, for example). Be inventive.

Using your email address you can correspond with other Internet subscribers worldwide. For research purposes email is invaluable: it is easy to operate, cheaper and faster than the normal post (now dubbed 'snail mail'); messages normally reach their destination within minutes, and the reply often comes back just as quickly. You can send emails at any time of the day or night; incoming mail will be stored in your mailbox until you next log on. There are options to print, save, send to someone else or delete, at the click of an icon. And provided you keep up the Address Book on your program you will be saved the chore of having to type in the full address each time you email.

Journalists and writers frequently use email 'attachments' to submit copy to editors. By double-clicking on the appropriate icon (usually a paperclip) you can attach almost any length of word-processed document or digital image to your email; however, it would be unwise to transmit a whole book to your publisher without prior arrangement. In any case, emails are best kept as short as possible.

'Voice' emailing is a fairly recent facility, and at the time of writing by no means perfect. Watch out for new developments: it will not be long before 'video' and 'live video' emailing become the norm.

NEWSGROUPS AND DISCUSSION GROUPS

Among other sources of information on the Internet is a network of newsgroups and discussion groups called collectively the 'Usenet'. There are *thousands* of these groups, on virtually every subject you can think of, from the serious to the downright quirky; joining one or two that reflect your particular research interests sometimes elicits material unobtainable elsewhere. Many a precious nugget of information has been obtained by this means. Be selective, however – or you will find yourself wallowing in newsletters and messages, not to mention reams of junk mail.

As a member of a group you can 'post' to it messages (comments, queries or replies to other people's queries); these are known as 'articles' and are automatically received by everyone else in that group. You may be startled by the number of replies. It is not a bad idea to 'lurk' (i.e. read all the articles that are to-ing and fro-ing) at the outset, and you should also take the time initially to skim through the group's 'Frequently Asked Questions' (FAQ) as these may supply the information you seek, thus freeing you from the need to go further. Unfortunately the quality of what you receive cannot be guaranteed, and as in all research you should be cautious about using any unauthenticated material in print. (I have said this before, but it cannot be over-stressed.)

While there are no formal rules for participation in newsgroups, there is a universally accepted code of conduct known as 'Netiquette'. Breaching this code (i.e. sending a message in capital letters, which is known as 'shouting') could result in your being ostracised by that group.

Your ISP will provide you with a list of the newsgroups it carries (not all ISPs carry all newsgroups) and instructions as to how to access them, for which you need to run a 'newsreader' program such as Internet Explorer or Netscape. There is a list of groups on the Google websites (www.google.co.uk or www.google.com), with facilities to search or 'advance search' by topic. The Usenet home page at www.usenet.com has links to much useful information, including an index to newsgroups and an outline of Netiquette. You can also access Usenet through Google (select 'Groups'). The Google Group archive dates back to 1981 and now contains a staggering 700 million articles; it is updated several times a day.

CHAT ROOMS

Messenger services, or conferencing, is an alternative to email if you feel the need to 'chat' to people worldwide. Logged on to the Internet, and registered with one of several 'communications centres', you type what you have to say. This is transmitted instantly by the computer onto the other person's screen; he replies and his response appears in text on your screen; and so the conversation goes on... You can either 'chat' to an individual or join in a discussion between several people.

Unfortunately 'chat rooms' have acquired a somewhat dubious reputation of late, especially insofar as young people are concerned. It does not seem to me that they are of any great value to the serious researcher, unless he has a compelling need to talk 'live' to a colleague on the other side of the world. There is also the danger that 'chatting' can so easily become addictive and a waste of working time. The 'chat room' therefore will not concern us further in this book.

MAILING LISTS

If you are on email it may be worth your while subscribing to one or two mailing lists, also known as 'newsletters', on topics of special interest. ('Subscribe' is a misnomer: there is no charge.) Be extremely selective, however, or you will be pelted with trivial and often largely useless information.

There are details of thousands of mailing lists/newsletters on the www.topica.com website. Click on one or two subjects that interest you, and follow on-screen instructions on how to sign up. You might want to start with one called, intriguingly, 'Free Pint' (www.freepint.co.uk), whose newsletters contain a great deal of valuable advice on using the Internet for research. 'People Interested in Net Tips'(i.e. Pint) is compiled by a team of information professionals and has a membership of more than 56,000 worldwide. I was happy to see its reliability endorsed by Jane Dorner in her book, *The Internet: A Writer's Guide* (see page 47).

LEARNING NEW SKILLS

To the unitiated, what I have written so far in this chapter may seem nothing more than a bewildering, impenetrable maze, not least because of the Internet's strange jargon and the addresses that consist of long strings of lower case letters all joined together with sundry dots and forward slashes in between. If you are one of these bewildered souls, do not be unduly alarmed. Like all other worthwhile professional skills, that of using the Internet has to be learned, and to learn it you must be prepared to practise – and to make mistakes. The only way to acquire expertise is by trial and error, with or without tuition, and a good many hours spent with your nose in a manual. One of the best guides currently available is Hilary Coombes' paperback *Research using IT*, which assumes no previous knowledge, uses no unnecessary jargon, and offers a step-by-step guide to carrying out a reasearch project using online techniques.

As you would when visiting any library with which you are unfamiliar, allow yourself time to find your way around. Make full use of the 'Help' icon on screen and, if that fails, do not hesitate to ring the technical support team whose number is in your computer manual.

Take things calmly, one step at a time. Never, under any circumstances, kid yourself that you can master the skill with a deadline looming and your editor breathing down your neck.

If you lack patience or have little time between writing projects, go for some private tuition or enrol on a course at your adult education centre. It will be money well spent. Personally I found a few sessions of private tuition to be infinitely more productive than the long-drawn-out course: this way you can concentrate only on the essentials that you, as writer and researcher, need to know – and leave the rest, the graphics and the spreadsheets and so on, for another day.

Computer tutors frequently advertise their services in the local press, but it is advisable to get a recommendation from a friend or colleague. The public library should have details of the training opportunities in your area. For a 'hands on' trial without committing yourself, visit one of the numerous cybercafés that are opening up not only in London and the suburbs, but also now in towns all over the country. Find the one nearest you on the website www.netcafes.com.

A last personal recommendation, and I believe it is an important one: cultivate a few computer-literate friends locally to whom you can turn for advice when things go wrong. Inevitably, whenever you do encounter a problem – and you are bound to, sooner or later – it will be late at night or on a Sunday, when the technical support people are not on call. It is comforting to be able to talk to someone who is more than likely to have come up against the same difficulty – and who knows how to solve it. My experience is that computer buffs are a friendly crowd and will often bend over double to help a fellow user in distress.

And finally – to get you started on online research – here are three websites of general reference which are worth a try:

www.refdesk.com	a vast reference site on all subjects
www.ipl.org	the Internet public library
www.ask-a-librarian.org.uk	type in your question on screen and you will receive a reply by email within two working days (there is a limit of three questions per day!)

Numerous other sites are mentioned throughout this book wherever the relevant subject or source is discussed.

In the wake of the Internet and email 'explosion', the market has been deluged with literature on the subject. All handbooks go out of date rather quickly, but as I believe that many of the earlier books deal better with the elementary aspects of online searching – which subsequent manuals tend to assume that their readers already know – I continue to cite them here. There is, alas, space to mention only a few.

I cannot recommend too highly *Internet Research: Theory and Practice* by Ned L. Fielden and Maria Garrido, published in the United States. Its stated purpose is 'to make the Internet less forbidding and more comprehensive for researchers'. Practically everything the novice – or, for that matter, the experienced – researcher needs to know is covered, in a clear and reader-friendly style (which is a welcome change from that of some other manuals). The advantages and disadvantages of the Net are discussed; the techniques of online searching and the basic protocols explained; and much valuable advice given on specific Net skills and resources. There are separate chapters on the nature of research, Internet tools, information retrieval, and Internet subject resources; and appendices on writing the research paper and citation format. Most importantly, the book teaches good research methods. A paperback edition was published in 2001.

Until recently there were surprisingly few manuals on using the Internet that catered specifically for the needs of writers and researchers. There are two titles which I have found most useful, both written by Timothy K. Maloy and also published in the United States: *The Writer's Internet Handbook* and *The Internet Research Guide*. Although naturally slanted towards the needs of the American writer, these books contain much that will assist all writers and researchers insofar as search techniques and resources are concerned. (All the US titles above-mentioned should be available in the UK through normal bookselling channels or on the Amazon website www.amazon.com.)

Happily, within the last couple of years there has been a spate of Internet titles for writers published in the UK. Jane Dorner, who has built herself a fine reputation as the writers' Internet 'guru', has produced *The Internet: A Writer's Guide*, now in its second edition, as well as *Creative Web Writing* and *Writing for the Internet*. (The first of these titles is crammed with practical advice on making the best use of the Net, whereas the other two deal primarily with the creative side of writing for the new media, and so are not strictly speaking relevant to research.) I can also recommend *A Writer's Guide to the Internet* by Trevor Lockwood and Karen Scott, and *The Internet Writer's Handbook 2001/2* by Karen Scott. Two excellent publications by Internet Handbooks of Plymouth, *The Internet for Writers* by Nick Daws and *Books and Publishing on the Internet* by Roger Ferneyhough, have gone out of print, but are worthwhile shopping around for secondhand or borrowing from the library. (At the time of writing no information has been forthcoming from the publisher as to revised editions.)

What else is available to help the beginner? *The Rough Guide to the Internet* by Angus J. Kennedy and *The Internet Bible* by Brian Underdahl are both good value. There is a brand-new edition of Darrel Ince's *Dictionary of the Internet*. Newsagents and supermarkets sell a quantity of computer magazines, but these tend to be rather too technical in content and are not geared to the needs of the researcher. On the other hand, most issues of *The Author* and nearly all the popular 'writing' magazines (*Writing Magazine*, *Writers' News*, *Writers' Forum* and *Mslexia*, to name but a few) carry at least one informative feature on some aspect of the Internet which affects the writer. Gordon Wells' three titles, *The Book Writers' Handbook*, *The Magazine Writer's Handbook* and *The Business of Writing*, all contain sensible advice on word processing and the use of computers.

More advanced handbooks on Internet skills, written primarily for librarians and information professionals, include two titles by Phil Bradley: *Going Online, CD-ROM and the Internet* and *The Advanced Internet Searcher's Handbook*; *The Online Searcher's Companion* by William H. Forrester and Jane Rowlands; and two books by G.G. Chowdhury and Sudatta Chowdhury: *Information Sources and Searching on the*

World Wide Web and *Searching CD-ROM and Online Information Sources*. Although published several years ago, the *Keyguide to Information Sources in Online and CD-ROM Database Searching* by C.J. Armstrong and R.J. Hartley remains one of the best international guides for professional researchers. *Surfing on the Internet* by J.C. Herz, now out of print, is also worth borrowing from the library or acquiring secondhand.

If you are interested in an overview of the Internet and its impact on our society you may like to read either *Challenge and Change in the Information Society*, edited by Susan Hornby and Zoë Clarke, or *The Internet Galaxy* by Manuel Castells – or both.

The Advanced Internet Searcher's Handbook, by Phil Bradley, Library Association, London, 2nd edn, 2001

The Author, quarterly journal of the Society of Authors, London; currently free to members, £8 per issue to non-members

The Book Writers' Handbook, by Gordon Wells, Allison & Busby, London, 1995

Books and Publishing on the Internet, by Roger Ferneyhough, Internet Handbooks, Plymouth, 2000

The Business of Writing, by Gordon Wells, Allison & Busby, London, 1998

Challenge and Change in the Information Society, by Susan Hornby and Zoë Clarke, Facet Publishing, London, 2002

Creative Web Writing, by Jane Dorner, A & C Black, London, 2002

Dictionary of the Internet, ed. Darrel Ince, Oxford University Press, Oxford, 2nd edn, 2003

The Good Web Site Guide 2003, by Graham Edmonds, Orion, London, 2002

Going Online, CD-ROM and the Internet, by Phil Bradley, Aslib, London, 10th edn, 1997; paperback 1998

Information Sources and Searching on the World Wide Web, by G.G. Chowdhury and Sudatta Chowdhury, Library Association, London, 2001

The Internet: A Writer's Guide, by Jane Dorner, A & C Black, 2000; 2nd edn, 2002

The Internet Bible, by Brian Underdahl, John Wiley, New York, 1998; paperback, 2000

The Internet for Writers, by Nick Daws, Internet Handbooks, Plymouth, 1999

The Internet Galaxy, by Manuel Castells, Oxford University Press, Oxford, 2002

Internet Research: Theory and Practice, by Ned L. Fielden and Maria Garrido, McFarland, Jefferson, N. Carolina, USA, 1998; paperback, by N.L. Fielden, McFarland, 2001

The Internet Research Guide, by Timothy K. Maloy, Allworth Press, New York, 2nd edn, 1999

The Internet Writer's Handbook 2001/2, by Karen Scott, Allison & Busby, London, 2001

Keyguide to Information Sources in Online and CD-ROM Database Searching, by C.J. Armstrong and R.J. Hartley, Mansell, London, 2nd edn, 1997

The Magazine Writers' Handbook, by Gordon Wells, 9th edn, with Chris McCallum, Writers' Bookshop, Peterborough, 2003

Mslexia (For Women who Write), published quarterly by Mslexia Publications, Newcastle-on-Tyne

The Online Searcher's Companion, by William H. Forrester and Jane Rowlands, Library Association, London, 2000

Research using IT, by Hilary Coombes, Macmillan, London, 2001

The Rough Guide to the Internet, by Angus J. Kennedy, Penguin Group UK, London, 8th edn, 2002

The Rough Guide Website Directory, Penguin Group UK, London, 2nd edn, 2002

Searching CD-ROM and Online Information Sources, by G.G. Chowdhury and Sudatta Chowdhury, Library Association, London, 2001

'Setting up a website', by Jane Dorner, *Writers' & Artists' Yearbook 2003*, A & C Black, London, 2002; also in the 2004 *Yearbook*

Surfing on the Internet, by J.C. Herz, Little, Brown, London, 1995; paperback 1996, reprinted 1998

Writers' Forum, published monthly by Writers' International Ltd., Bournemouth

A Writer's Guide to the Internet, by Trevor Lockwood and Karen Scott, Allison & Busby, London, 2000

The Writer's Handbook, ed. Barry Turner, published annually by Macmillan, London

The Writer's Internet Handbook, by Timothy K. Maloy, Allworth Press, New York, 1997

Writers' News, published monthly by Yorkshire Post Newspapers, Leeds

Writing for the Internet, by Jane Dorner, Oxford University Press, Oxford, 2002

Writing Magazine, published bi-monthly by Yorkshire Post Newspapers, Leeds

Note: The Library Association (LA) and the Institute of Information Scientists recently merged to become the Chartered Institute of Library and Information Professionals (CILIP). In April 2002 Facet Publishing took over LA Publishing; titles published prior to that date are listed as LA publications.

Chapter Four

Basic Sources of Information and their Location

A WRITER'S RAW MATERIAL is derived normally from a combination of the following sources: personal knowledge, experience, and observation; printed, microfilmed or electronically stored material (i.e. books, newspapers, periodicals); unpublished documentary, recorded or filmed sources (manuscripts, family papers, theses, archive collections, tapes, photographs, videos, etc.); and other people's knowledge, experience and observation. Of these the most important must be the first-mentioned, since it is a writer's own viewpoint, drawn from his personal knowledge, experience and observation, which above all else puts a stamp of originality upon his work and distinguishes it from that of every other writer.

Except where the work in hand is one of pure reminiscence – and even then certain statements will probably need to be substantiated by fact – it is however not enough to rely solely upon your own knowledge. As soon as your original material has been studied and sorted according to the shape of the projected piece of writing, you must consider what are the other sources of information to be tapped.

PRINTED SOURCES

BOOKS

Printed books and information about books are obtainable primarily from bookshops, publishers and libraries. When you are engaged on a specific project, you will always find it worthwhile to acquire copies of the standard works on your subject, which you can keep at your elbow and either annotate in the margins or interleave with narrow strips of paper or markers on which you write some basic headings or other indications. It goes without saying that library books and books belonging to other people should *never* be marked in any way; but 'working copies' are a writer's essential reference tools and should be used to the best advantage.

New books may be purchased from booksellers or, in case of difficulty, direct from the publishers, and online. A good bookseller should be aware of what has been published recently on a particular subject and, through *The Bookseller* and other trade papers, as well as his contact with publishers' representatives, of forthcoming titles. He is usually able to find the required information more or less instantly, using one or more of a range of online trade bibliographies such as the Whitaker *BookBank*, *BookBank Global* or *BookBank OP*, or *Nielsen Bookdata*, all of which are updated very regularly. (*BookBank OP* covers UK and Europe and lists English-language books that have gone out of print since 1970.) If the title is not in stock, delivery may take a couple of weeks or more, depending on the publisher or distributor, and you may find it quicker to telephone one of the larger bookshops in London or one of the big provincial cities rather than wait for your local shop to obtain a copy. You can also order new books online at Amazon (www.amazon.co.uk), at Bertelsmann OnLine (BOL) (www.bol.com), at the Internet Book Shop (www.bookshop.co.uk), or through the major booksellers, all of whom are online.

An invaluable and inexpensive publication for the book-buyer is Lesley Reader's *Booklovers' London*. This slim paperback contains an amazing quantity of detailed information, not only on new, secondhand and antiquarian bookshops in London, but also on book-related charity shops and markets, libraries (public, specialist and academic), places of literary interest, festivals and much else. It has a most useful index, an area index and also a short list of useful websites.

If you want to keep fully up-to-date with the world of books it is a good idea to subscribe to *The Bookseller*, which is published weekly; there are two supplementary 'buyers' guides' in spring and autumn, to which you can subscribe separately and which are an excellent way of keeping abreast of forthcoming titles. It has to be said, however, that these guides are rather less comprehensive than they used to be.

You will probably be able to borrow most of the books you need for your research through your local public library or, if you are a member, a private subscription library or institution library. If you are a graduate you will be able to use a university library. When you want to obtain a new title reasonably quickly, be sure to put in an application as soon as you see it announced in the press. A modest reservation fee is payable at the public library, and normally you will not be allowed to retain a new book after its initial borrowing period if it has been requested by another reader. However, two weeks or so should give you ample time to make some notes and to decide whether or not you need to buy the book. At other libraries you may be able to keep the book until someone else asks for it.

So far as not-so-new books are concerned, if your public library does not stock what you require, you should be able to borrow them through the inter-library lending scheme operated by the British Library Document Supply Centre (BLDSC) at Boston Spa, Wetherby, West Yorkshire LS23 7BQ. The BLDSC loans books, journals, film, fiche and other types of documentation from its own collection; but requests for such material should be channelled via your local library or the British Library in London. Occasional users may order photocopies of documents through the 'Articles Direct' service (tel. 01937 546599; fax 01937 546210; email articles-direct@bl.uk).

Payment is by credit or debit card, and orders are normally processed within forty-eight hours. You can also register with BLDSC and order online. Material is loaned only to registered customers. For prices and other details of these and a wide range of services available, contact the BLDSC customer service (tel. 01937 546060; fax 01937 546333; email dsc-customer-services@bl.uk).

It happens sometimes that you cannot afford to wait even a few days for material – you need it for one chapter before you can proceed to the next – and then it may be worth the expense of travelling to your nearest copyright library or other major reference library. Remember, however, that you cannot count on seeing a very recent title there: acquisition and cataloguing processes take time. Sadly, due to cutbacks in spending, many libraries do not renew reference titles as regularly as in the past, and except in the larger libraries you may not always find the latest edition of the directory or yearbook you seek.

Copyright and reference libraries

Under the provisions of various Copyright Acts that have been passed since 1709, certain libraries are entitled to receive one free copy of every book published in the United Kingdom. These are: the British Library (London); the Bodleian Library (Oxford); the Cambridge University Library (Cambridge); the National Library of Wales (Aberystwyth); the National Library of Scotland (Edinburgh); and Trinity College Library (Dublin).

In all these libraries you can be confident of finding everything you need that has been published from the 18th century onwards, and also much earlier material (collections that have been bequeathed or titles purchased over the years in the saleroom). A small percentage of stock may have been destroyed during the last war or otherwise mislaid.

Graduates and other *bona fide* researchers and students are able to use the various well-stocked university libraries, of which the University of London Library, the John Rylands University Library of Manchester and the Sydney Jones Library of Liverpool University are excellent examples. There are also libraries at all the great London museums: the Imperial War Museum; the Caird Library at the National Maritime Museum (the largest maritime reference library in the world); the Natural History Museum; the Science Museum; and the Royal Botanic Gardens at Kew.

Among the major reference libraries open to the general public is the Westminster Reference Library just behind Trafalgar Square, London; some of the others are listed in Appendix I, pages 216–17. A visit to the nearest of these and to other reference libraries in the provinces may save you the expense of travelling further afield.

The headquarters of the British Library – the UK's national library, and the richest and most comprehensive in the world – moved a few years ago from Bloomsbury to purpose-built premises in the Euston Road, in north London, next door to St Pancras railway station. Since then the Library has operated from only three sites: St Pancras, where the main collections are now housed; Colindale, in north London, the home of the British Library Newspaper Library; and Boston Spa, near Wetherby, West Yorkshire, the base of the inter-library lending and document supply service.

At St Pancras there are eleven reading areas, on three levels: Humanities 1, Humanities 2 (which includes the Library and Information Sciences Service and the Recorded Sound Information Service), Rare Books and Music (where you can use the Listening and Viewing Service of the National Sound Archive), Manuscripts, the Oriental and India Office, Maps, and Science 1, 2 and 3 (spread over five reading rooms). Each has a staffed enquiry desk and a selection of informative leaflets describing its particular collections and services. At the core of the complex is a six-storey glass-walled tower housing the King's Library (the 65,000-volume collection of George III, presented to the nation by his son, George IV in 1823). As you would expect from a purpose-built new library, the facilities are excellent: easy disabled access, desks wired for personal computer use, computer terminals for online cata-logue searching linked to an automated book request system, and much else.

If you are visiting the British Library for the first time, you must allow yourself time to find your way around and to get to know the layout of open access works. There are two ring binders near the enquiry desk in the Humanities 1 reading room entitled 'Humanities 1 and 2 Title List', which will help. Or you might join one of the free 'Reader Induction Sessions': these take place at 11.00 and 14.00 hours, Monday to Friday, and last for about an hour. Book by telephone on 020 7412 7678 or by email reader-education@bl.uk.

Admission to the British Library, some other copyright libraries and most major libraries is free. A few, such as the Bodleian Library, Oxford, and Cambridge University Library charge a fee to non-graduates (according to status; details from their Admission offices). Some reading rooms are open to all without formality, others require a reader's pass. These are issued on personal application only and are for those who need to see material not readily available elsewhere or whose work necessitates the facilities of a large research library. You will be asked to state the subject of your research and to have your application signed by a university tutor or someone of authority who will vouch for you; a membership card of the Society of Authors or Writers' Guild may be sufficient. Take a couple of passport-size photographs with you (one will be incorporated into the pass).

Holders of public library tickets in their home town may use them to gain admis-sion to the special reference collections of all London public libraries and to borrow books from the lending branches. Tickets may also be used at other libraries by arrangement with the librarian.

Many libraries are open late on certain evenings in the week. At the British Library, the Humanities and Science reading rooms are open until 20.00 hours from Monday to Thursday; the Westminster Reference Library at 35 St Martin's Street, London WC2H 7HP, just off Leicester Square (tel. 020 7641 4636; fax 020 7641 4606; email westreflib@dial.pipex.com; website www.westminster.gov.uk/libraries/westref) is open until 20.00 hours from Monday to Friday. Some public libraries now open for a short time on Sundays. If you have to travel some distance, plan your schedule to make the maximum use of the longest possible working day. Books usually must be handed in well before the library closes, and photocopying orders are not accepted after a certain time, so that it is important to allow not only for ordering and paying for photocopies, but also for last-minute annotation.

For those who can afford it, a subscription to the London Library, 14 St James's Square, London SW1Y 4LG (tel. 020 7930 7705; fax 020 7766 4766) will prove very worthwhile. Members may take out ten books at a time (fifteen for country members, who may also borrow by post but have to pay the postage in both directions). Subscribers have access to the stacks and the use of a comfortable reading room, equipped with CD-ROM readers, and free access to the Internet. The computerised catalogue is accessible (members only) at www.webpac.londonlibrary.co.uk, and copies of the printed catalogue covering earlier holdings are available for purchase – a boon to those who live in remote areas or do not have Internet access, and wish to order by post, fax or email. The annual subscription, currently £150, may be set against a professional writer's tax; short-term subscriptions are available, without borrowing facilities (apply to the Membership Administrator for details).

Another London subscription library is the Highgate Literary and Scientific Institution Library, 11 South Grove, Highgate Village, London N6 6BS (tel. 020 8340 3343; fax 020 8340 55632; email admin@hsi.demon.co.uk); the subscription there is £50 for one person, £80 for a family. Among twenty-four other independent libraries in the provinces are those of Birmingham, Exeter, Leeds, Newcastle-upon-Tyne and Plymouth; for a full list visit the Association of Independent Libraries website www.independentlibraries.co.uk.

Special libraries

The use of libraries in general has been discussed in chapter 2. The questions that now arise concern location: how to find out about the special libraries that are likely to help you in your particular field, and how to locate in those libraries the particular books you need.

The first place to look is in the *Aslib Directory of Information Sources in the United Kingdom*. This gives a comprehensive listing of practically every library and source of information in this country; it contains a subject index, and details such as opening hours and the facilities available. The *Aslib Directory*, as it is known colloquially, is published biennially, and most libraries have the latest edition – ask for it at the enquiry desk. The Library Association's *Libraries in the United Kingdom and the Republic of Ireland* lists addresses, telephone numbers and names of librarians. Valerie McBurney's *Guide to Libraries in London*, which focuses on research collections, includes subject and organisation indexes and maps enabling the user to locate the relevant libraries. *The Museums and Galleries Yearbook* is a goldmine of information. The *Directory of Museum and Special Collections in the United Kingdom* is also excellent, containing details of the smaller as well as the best-known collections; and the *Guide to Libraries and Information Services* concentrates on the libraries of government departments and other organisations. There is a new publication from the British Library, *Guide to Libraries in Key UK Companies*. Another useful compilation is the CBD's *Centres, Bureaux and Research Institutes*.

The best up-to-date guides to libraries and research institutions internationally are *The World of Learning*, the *World Guide to Libraries* and the *World Guide to Special Libraries*. There is also *The Directory of University Libraries in Europe*.

Regrettably, space does not permit the mention here of more than a few individual libraries, named in the text under the various subjects of research discussed. A selective list of UK libraries is printed in Appendix I under subject headings, and of foreign libraries in London in chapter 10, 'Information from and about Foreign Countries'.

Catalogues and guides

The majority of libraries now catalogue their collections electronically, and it is rare nowadays to be confronted with a card index system. At the British Library, for example, where the old Open Access Catalogue (OPAC) has been replaced by a much enhanced version, the British Library Public Catalogue (BLPC), you have only to key in the name of the author, a title or merely a keyword, in order to find the material you seek. If you have Internet access at home, you can search this catalogue at www.bl.uk/catalogues; there are links to the catalogues of the largest university research libraries in the UK, as well as to many other catalogues worldwide. You can of course also use the old printed volumes. For example, the *British Library General Catalogue of Printed Books to 1975* is out of print but is still on many library shelves. *The British Library General Catalogue of Printed Books*, from 1976 onwards, ceased publication in 2000.

If, on your first visit, you are unsure how to proceed, don't waste precious researching time: ask for assistance at the reader's enquiry desk; it will be given readily. In most libraries free leaflets are available explaining how to search the catalogues. Be prepared to wait to do an online or CD-ROM search, as the terminals are in much demand.

Often you need information at the library on a subject about which you know next to nothing, let alone the name of any author or title. With online catalogue access, all you do is type in the subject or keyword; otherwise use the subject catalogue or a bibliography (see below). You should also consult the three-volume *Walford's Guide to Reference Material* (see page 86), which over the years has become known as the researcher's 'bible'; it has an excellent subject index. From 2004 this splendid research tool will be brought up-to-date to reflect the many changes in scholarship and science brought about by the digital age, under the title *The New Walford: Guide to Reference Resources*; a companion website is envisaged. The *Reference Sources Handbook* (formerly published as *Printed Reference Material and Related Information Sources*), written for librarians, is a first-class evaluation of reference books for research; although, sadly, it has not been revised since 1996, it still has much value. British Library readers will appreciate another older work, R.C. Alston's *Handlist of Unpublished Finding Aids to the London Collections of the British Library*. At the British Library the BLPC is linked to an automated book request system which enables the user to request or reserve any catalogued item; confirmation appears on screen either that the item requested has been ordered or if for any reason it is unavailable. You return to your desk, where a light flashes when the book or journal can be collected at the issue desk, usually within half an hour.

Bibliographies

If a bibliography has been published on the particular subject or person you are interested in, you should find a copy on the reference shelves together with other source books related to that subject. You can check whether a bibliography exists by looking at the *Bibliographic Index*, which is available in most major libraries in printed form and online. The *World Bibliography of Bibliographies*, compiled by a great 20th-century bibliographer, Theodore Besterman, is comprehensive only up to the mid-1970s. There is also the *International Bibliography of Bibliographies 1959–1988*. For more recent bibliographies you should check the subject index of the *British National Bibliography (BNB)*. The bibliographies of other countries are listed in volume 3 of *Walford's Guide to Reference Material* mentioned above, under 'National Bibliographies'.

The *British National Bibliography (BNB)*, published since 1950, is the most comprehensive listing of UK titles. Published weekly in print, monthly on CD-ROM, and now including digital and electronic publications, it also contains details of forthcoming books (up to sixteen weeks ahead of the *BNB* publication date). For further information contact the British Library National Bibliographic Service, tel. 01937 546585; fax 01937 546586; email nbs-info@bl.uk.

The Library Association (LA), 7 Ridgmount Street, London WC1E 7AE has published bibliographies on a variety of subjects over the years; these will be found in most reference libraries. Since April 2002 all LA publications have been published by Facet Publishing, which is owned by the Chartered Institute of Library and Information Professionals (CILIP). For more information, contact Facet Publishing (tel. 020 7255 0590; fax 020 7255 0591; email: info@facetpublishing.co.uk; website www.facetpublishing.co.uk). See note, page 49.

Readers unfamiliar with bibliographic practice should remember that the numbers given in a bibliography's index are entry numbers, *not* page numbers.

Electronic and other book information services

The use of the computer to access bibliographical data has transformed dramatically the researcher's routine. Most professional researchers are now skilled in online searching, at home as well as in the library, but if you are a beginner and are baffled, even frightened, by the computer terminals and the strange jargon, do not despair.

Help is readily available, both on screen and in the form of trained library assistants who will guide the uninitiated through the complexities. At some libraries the search can be done for you, with the cost based on staff time, time connected to the Internet and the cost of printing out the material. Ask at the enquiry desk if a computer search service is on offer.

On a totally different level, the Booktrust operates a Book Information Line (tel. 0906 516 1193) for members and non-members, weekdays 10.00–14.00 hours, calls charged at £1.50 per minute. It is always worth asking if they have a printed booklist on a particular subject. For further information contact Booktrust, Book House, 45 East Hill, Wandsworth, London SW18 2QZ (tel. 020 8516 2977; fax 020 8516 2978; email info@booktrust.org.uk; website www.booktrust.org.uk).

Tracing books

Often you want to trace a particular book whose exact title and author you do not remember. Provided you have a vague idea of these, or the approximate date of publication, it is no longer difficult. Whereas in the past this might have involved a lengthy search, nowadays you should be able to trace the item instantly by its keyword, via the British Library Public Catalogue (BLPC) at www.bl.uk/catalogues.

The earliest listing in this country is the *London Catalogue of Books*, covering the period 1700–1855. *The English Catalogue of Books*, volume 1 of which covers the period 1801–36 and later volumes (variously at three- and five-year intervals), continues until 1968. *Whitaker's Cumulative Book List* (from 1924) used to be published quarterly, with annual and five-year cumulations; in 1984 it was re-titled *Whitaker's Book List*, but has now been discontinued. The Whitaker bibliographic compilations, to which most booksellers and libraries subscribe, usually online, are also available on CD-ROM or microfiche; they are updated monthly and include forthcoming and recently out-of-print books. The microfiche edition of *Books in Print* should be available to readers for quick reference at all library enquiry desks. If you are searching at home, do not bother with the website www.booksinprint.com listed in many handbooks: when you log on you will find it is not the Whitaker but the US *Books in Print*, published by Bowker, and that you have to be a subscriber (at a cost way beyond the pocket of the individual) to search it. Get your local bookseller to do the search instead!

So far as American titles are concerned, the *National Union Catalog*, which replaced the old *Library of Congress Catalog* in 1948, and whose printed volumes are on the open shelves at the British Library and most major reference libraries, is especially useful as it gives authors' dates. Or you can access the current *Library of Congress Online Catalog* at www.bl.uk/catalogues/otherlibcats. For further reference look at the *American Book Publishing Record*, *Books in Print* (US), and the *Subject Guide to Books in Print*.

The best way of checking up on publishers and how to reach them is to consult one of several annual publications you should find in your local reference library.

These include the *Directory of Publishing*, the *UK and Irish Book Publishers Directory* and *Whitaker's Directory of Publishers* (*The Red Book*). Most contain a lot of other information (with addresses) relevant to the book trade. Pick out those firms who publish in your particular field or fields of interest and put yourself on their mailing lists. And keep an eagle eye open for reviews and advertisements in the national press. It goes without saying that you will be an avid browser in your local bookshop. ('Browser' in the old-fashioned meaning of the word!)

Obtaining out-of-print books

When you want to acquire titles that are out of print, either for your own reference collection or for work on a specific project, you have the choice of going to an antiquarian or secondhand bookdealer, using a professional booksearch service/independent bookfinder, or making an online search yourself.

If, for the sake of personal service, you go to your local antiquarian or secondhand bookseller, make a point of telling him of your special interest(s). He should then automatically let you know when suitable books come in and will advertise for specific titles on the Internet and in various trade journals. There should be no charge for this service and no obligation to buy when a quotation is forthcoming, subject to the book or books remaining unsold in the meantime; but the process sometimes takes several weeks. *Sheppard's Book Dealers in the British Isles* and *Sheppard's Book Dealers in Europe* are the handbooks most used by the trade; dealers may also buy and sell on the *Sheppard's Book Search* site. Private individuals will find the *Skoob Directory of Secondhand Bookshops in the British Isles* very useful. There is also a substantial listing of secondhand and antiquarian bookshops in *Booklovers' London*, mentioned earlier in this chapter.

Many leading UK booksellers, such as Blackwell's (Oxford), Hatchard's (Cambridge), and Heywood Hill and Maggs Bros. (London) offer customers a bookfinding service. Waterstone's booksearch service is based in Tunbridge Wells (tel. 01892 522700; fax 01892 521400). The thriving 'bookshop' town of Hay-on-Wye, which boasts almost forty specialist bookshops, has its own website offering a range of out-of-print titles (www.Haybooks.com).

There are a large number of individual bookfinding specialists spread throughout the UK, most of whom advertise regularly in the national and literary press or are listed in the 'yellow pages' directories. The International Booksearch Service at 8 Old James Street, London SE15 3TSA (tel. 020 7639 8900; email scfordham@talk21.com; website www.scfordham.com) offers a free service with no obligation to buy the book when found. Another highly recommended firm is Twiggers Ltd., 42 Charles Street, Barnes, London SW13 0NZ (tel. 020 8878 8644; fax 020 8878 7826; email booksearch@twiggers.com; website www.twiggers.com). It is a good idea to find a firm whom you can trust and keep them informed of your requirements. You may be asked for a modest search fee in advance. Twiggers, mentioned above, will search for four titles free of charge; if they have not been successful after a month, you may opt for an extended international search for up to three months on payment of £3 per title.

The Internet has proved to be a marvellous international market-place for buying (and selling) secondhand books. Amazon (www.amazon.com) and its UK counterpart (www.amazon.co.uk) now feature secondhand as well as new titles. Some of the other 'bookfinding' sites are definitely US orientated, i.e. www.alibris.com and www.bookfinder.com. One of the best sites in this country is UK BookWorld (www.UKBookWorld.com), on which you can search for titles, subscribe to an online bookshop or an email group, or register your interests (you will be notified when suitable books come in). At any one time this site claims to have a million out-of-print titles for sale. Another good UK site is www.justbooks.co.uk. Bibliofind (www.bibliofind.com) claims to be able to locate any title on offer, while the metasearch site www.addall.com scours the sites of thousands of bookdealers worldwide and lists the book or books sought by price (the cheapest first). You may also be tempted to try your luck on the e-Bay auction sites (www.e-Bay.com). If it is a rare or collectable title you seek, then go to Biblion at www.biblion.com.

The mail order firm Bibliophile Books (5 Thomas Road, London E14 7BN; tel. 020 7515 9222) sends out regular catalogues of book bargains free of charge, and you can shop with them online (www.bibliophilebooks.com) and make use of their advanced search page.

Obtaining out-of-print books from abroad has become much faster – and relatively cheaper – than it used to be, thanks to the Internet and payment by credit card. Be careful, however, about giving your credit card details to small or foreign companies online without checking that they are authentic and secure sites.

The *Books on Demand* programme of paper facsimile reproductions marketed by UMI (University Microfilms), now part of ProQuest Information and Learning Ltd., The Quorum, Barnwell Road, Cambridge CB5 8SW (tel. 01223 215512; fax 01223 215513; email marketing@proquest.co.uk) includes some 132,000 out-of-print titles ranging from the 15th century to the present day. For information on how to order, go to www.umi.com or to the ProQuest website www.proquest.co.uk (click on the UMI button), or telephone Customer Services at ProQuest, as above.

NEWSPAPERS AND PERIODICALS

The major holding in this country of national and foreign papers, popular magazines and periodicals is at the British Library: newspapers, fortnightlies, weeklies and some monthlies at the British Library Newspaper Library, Colindale Avenue, London NW9 5HE (tel. 020 7412 7353; fax 020 7412 7379; email newspaper@bl.uk), opposite Colindale Underground Station; all other periodicals at the main Library at St Pancras (96 Euston Road, London NW1 2DB). The major exceptions to this broad division are the pre-1801 London newspapers (the Burney and Thomason collections) and the Oriental and India Office collections, which are now at St Pancras, with some on microfilm at Colindale. British Library photographic reader's pass-holders are admitted to the Newspaper Library without formality; for others, short-term tickets will be issued on application in person to the Main Reading Room, subject to proof of identity bearing a signature. An annual pass will be issued to readers providing an address and proof of their need to use the Library on a regular basis. These passes are valid for Colindale only.

The Newspaper Library was opened in 1932 and has been growing fast ever since; its collections are available in hard copy, microform and on CD-ROM. An eight-volume printed *Catalogue of the Newspaper Library, Colindale* was published in 1975, but has now been superseded by the online *British Library Newspaper Catalogue* containing over 52,000 newspaper and periodical titles. This online catalgogue can be searched – by title, by place of publication, by date or by keyword – both in the Main Reading Room and in the New Reading Room (opened in 1996); there is a facility to print out searches. Go to www.bl.uk, click on 'Collections', then 'Newspapers', then 'Newspaper Library Web Catalogue'.

A copy of the 1975 printed catalogue is available in the Main Reading Room, where the open access reference shelves contain a large number of indexes to *The Times*, *The New York Times* and a range of other papers, long runs of *Willing's Press Guide*, *Benn's Media* and the *British Humanities Index* (and their predecessors), as well as many other bibliographical and historical reference works. In addition to the usual desks for readers, the Library has a limited number of places for microfiche readers, microfilm reader-printers and computer workstations with networked access to online and Internet resources. It is worth remembering that up to four items may be reserved forty-eight hours in advance of your visit (tel. 020 7412 7353 or email BookDelivery-Colindale@bl.uk). Because of the ongoing NEWSPLAN microfilming project (see below, pages 62–3), readers should be prepared for certain items to be unavailable for six months or longer; it is advisable to check by telephone with the Library in advance of your visit.

For some years now the Newspaper Library has been systematically microfilming its entire collection, so as to preserve the original newsprint from decay through constant handling. Most foreign newspapers are purchased on microfilm and since 1986 all UK newspapers are microfilmed on receipt. This is a great convenience both to the reader and to the library staff, as in many cases up to a year's run of a paper or journal can be housed on one spool, thus eliminating the handling of bulky volumes and conserving storage space. Microfilms of newspapers and journals are currently on sale (prices on application). Readers may make photocopies from microfilm, suitable for reference purposes only, on the microfilm reader-printers, using photocopy cards on sale at the Enquiry Desk in the Main Reading Room. Copies from microfiche and print-outs from CD-ROM and the Internet may also be made on a self-operated machine at the Library at a very reasonable 35p–70p per page, depending on size; photocopies from original newspapers, which are made only by staff, cost from 50p to £2 per page if ordered in the reading room, and from 75p to £2.60 if ordered by post (enhanced photocopies, printed on photographic paper, from £10.40 to £18.20 per page). Postal applications are subject to a minimum charge (currently £12).

These prices, which include VAT but not postage, valid from August 2002, are subject to change. An express service is available at extra cost (full details on application). All photocopying is subject to conservation restrictions and to the usual copyright regulations (only one article from any one issue of a paper or periodical at any one time, subject to a signed copyright declaration, for private study or research). Photographs (black and white or colour), colour transparencies and digital images on CD-ROM are also available (prices on request).

Tracing newspapers and periodicals

The researcher wishing to trace an early English-language newspaper will find all those published in Great Britain and Ireland before 1900 listed in the *British Library General Catalogue of Printed Books*. *Willing's Press Guide*, first published in 1871 as *Frederick May's London Press Directory*, and now issued annually, in two volumes, is one of the best quick reference guides to modern newspapers and periodicals both in the United Kingdom and internationally. (Until a few years ago it covered only the UK.) You should find an up-to-date copy in every reference library. It is online at www.willingspressguide.com, by subscription (there is a free forty-eight-hour trial period). A complete set of *Willing's*, together with several earlier newspaper press directories dating from 1846, is on the open shelves at Colindale; it includes an A–Z list, a list of publications under subjects, and (until recently) a list under English counties and towns. *The Newspaper Press in Britain: An Annotated Bibliography* edited by David Linton and Ray Boston, which contains a useful chronology of British newspaper history 1476–1986 and a location listing of papers and other archives, is highly recommended, together with its more recent companion volume, *The Twentieth-Century Newspaper Press in Britain*. Also very useful is the *Encyclopedia of the British Press 1422–1992*, edited by Dennis Griffiths, author of the very readable *300 Years of Fleet Street 1702–2002*. Forthcoming soon from the same source will be the *Encyclopedia of the World Press*, currently still in preparation. The British Library's own *Bibliography of British Newspapers* has been in progress since 1982, one or two counties per volume.

So far as foreign newspapers are concerned, *The Europa World Year Book* gives details of the press of each country; and volume 3 of *Walford's Guide to Reference Material* lists the various national source books under each country in both the 'Newspapers' and 'Periodicals' sections.

Benn's Media (formerly *Benn's Media Directory*) covers the whole world and is the oldest-established media guide: now in three volumes and published annually, it is directly descended from *Mitchell's Newspaper Press Directory*, which was first published in 1846. It covers newspapers, periodicals, house journals and much other related information on embassies and high commissions, news agencies, broadcasting and all aspects of the media including cable and satellite. A handy paperback reference and contacts guide to the media is the paperback *The Media Guide*.

In the British Library Public Catalogue (BLPC) you will find periodicals either under their title, place of publication, or – in the case of the transactions or proceedings of learned societies – under the name of the society. If you do not know the exact title or society name, you simply enter the keyword.

There are two invaluable finding aids for international periodicals: the *ISSN Register*, issued quarterly, listing periodicals from 180 countries, and *Ulrich's Periodicals Directory*, published in hardback and on CD-ROM, and also in an online version, *Ulrichsweb.com*, updated weekly. The *American Periodicals Series Online*, from ProQuest, is retrospective to 1740. Useful among the British Library catalogues online at www.bl.uk/catalogues is *Current Serials Received*. So far as British newspapers and periodicals are concerned, the quarterly *Serials in the British Library*, which has replaced the earlier *British Union-Catalogue*, is the standard guide.

Cynthia L. White's *Women's Magazines 1693–1968* is a classic in its field; a more recent study is *Women's Magazines: The First Three Hundred Years* by Brian Braithwaite, which has a useful 'births, marriages and deaths' section listing the successes, mergers and failures over the years. There is a brilliant collection from Primary Source Microfilm, *International Women's Periodicals*, spanning the 18th to early 20th century and some forty-five periodicals worldwide; also, from the same firm, *European Woman's Periodicals*, covering the period 1840–1940. David Reed's *The Popular Magazine in Britain and the United States of America 1880–1960* covers most aspects of magazine publishing in the period.

Finally, use should be made of the microfiche *Keyword Index to Serial Titles* (*KIST*), which lists all significant words in serial holdings of the British Library, the Science Museum Library and Cambridge University Library.

Now that *The Times* is on microfilm, you should have no difficulty in finding a library locally where you can access the complete run, starting with the first issue of 1 January 1785. Other papers may not be so easy to find in the provinces, but lists of newspapers (worldwide) that are available on microfilm, CD-ROM and online may be obtained from Primary Source Microfilm, The Gale Group, 110 St Martin's Lane, London WC2N 4BA (tel. 020 7257 2930; fax 020 7257 2940; email international@galegroup.com) and from Chadwyck-Healey, ProQuest Information and Learning Ltd., The Quorum, Barnwell Road, Cambridge CB5 8SW (tel. 01223 215512; fax 01223 215513; email marketing@proquest.co.uk). Primary Source Microfilm is in the process of microfilming the two major collections of *Early English Newspapers* (17th and 18th centuries) by Dr Charles Burney and his rival collector John Nichols, at the rate of 300 reels per year.

A huge preservation programme is underway to save some 3,500 fragile local and regional newspapers dating from 1800 to 1950. This *Local Newspapers in Peril* initiative, co-ordinated by the LINC NEWSPLAN panel of the Library and Information Co-operation Council, was made possible in 1999 by a £5 million Heritage Lottery Fund grant; the balance is to be raised from the newspaper industry, suppliers and the library sector. Eventually NEWSPLAN aims to preserve every local newspaper title in the UK; it will microfilm and digitise all those items most at risk and will install some 800 microfilm readers, with disability access, in libraries throughout the country. Microfilmed copies of newspapers will be provided in areas where they have been missing for years, and there will be online access to catalogues of newspaper collections. The first stage of this ambitious project, the Newsplan 2000 Project, running from 2001 to 2004, is well underway: 1,500 titles (300,000 reels of microfilm) to date. For more information visit one of the following websites: www.bl.uk (click on 'Collections', then 'Newspapers', then 'Newsplan'); www.newsplan2000.org/background or www.bl.uk/concord/linc/newsplan.

Indexes to newspapers

The most valuable of British newspaper indexes to the researcher is the *The Times Index*. The official index has been published since 1906, and an earlier, slightly less accurate version, known as *Palmer's Index to The Times*, from 1790 to June 1941. The *Index* is now published monthly, with annual cumulations; since 1973 it has included references to the *Sunday Times*, *Times Literary Supplement*, *Educational Supplement* and *Higher Education Supplement*. Other newspapers in the United Kingdom which publish or have at one time published indexes are the *Financial Times* (May 1912–20, and more recently from 1981), the *Glasgow Herald* (annually from 1906) and *The Guardian* (from 1986). All these indexes are on the open shelves at Colindale, together with indexes to several American papers such as the *New York Times*, *The Washington Post*, *Chicago Tribune* and *Los Angeles Times*, and indexes to a few Commonwealth and foreign newspapers. Microfilms of indexes to a number of British and continental newspapers are published by Primary Source Microfilm (The Gale Group – formerly Research Publications International) of Reading. Others are now online.

A major research tool starting in the 1990s is the *British Newspaper Index* (*BNI*) on CD-ROM. This covers fifteen newspaper titles: *The Times*, *The Sunday Times*, *Financial Times*, *The Guardian*, *The Observer*, *The Independent*, *Independent on Sunday*, *The Daily Telegraph*, *The Sunday Telegraph*, *Daily Mail*, *The Mail on Sunday*, *The Times Literary Supplement*, *The Times Higher Educational Supplement*, *The Times Educational Supplement* and *The Times Educational Supplement* (*Scotland*). UMI (University Microfilms, now part of ProQuest Information & Learning Ltd., The Quorum, Barnwell Road, Cambridge CB5 8SW; tel. 01223 215512; fax 01223 215513; email marketing@proquest.co.uk) offers a number of abstracting and indexing databases including *Newspapers*, which provides access to the *New York Times*, *The Washington Post*, *The Wall Street Journal* and other US newspapers. There is also the *Historical Index to The New York Times, 1851–1922*.

Indexes to periodicals

The earliest index to periodicals is *Poole's Index to Periodical Literature*, which covers the period 1802–1906; its comparatively recent author index is extremely useful. The *Reader's Guide to Periodical Literature* is an American publication that dates from

1900, now available in print and online; its English equivalent, the *Subject Index to Periodicals*, first published in 1915, changed its name to the *British Humanities Index* in 1962. Some of the more specialised indexes of interest to the researcher are the *Wellesley Index to Victorian Periodicals, 1824–1900*, the *Applied Social Sciences Index and Abstracts* (*ASSIA*), *Abstracts in New Technologies and Engineering* (*ANTE*), which has replaced the *Current Technology Index*, the *British Education Index*, and a series published by H.W. Wilson of New York, of which the *Art Index*, the *Biography Index*, the *Business Periodicals Index*, the *Humanities Index*, the *Index to Legal Periodicals and Books* and the *Social Sciences Index* (the last two formerly published as one index 1965–74, and before that date as the *International Index*) are the most likely to be of interest to the UK writer/researcher. (Your library may have these in electronic format, as the Wilson *OmniFile Full Text, Mega Edition* or *Select Edition*.) *Library and Information Science Abstracts* (*LISA*) is an important database which is international in coverage. The online *Periodicals Contents Index*, from Chadwyck-Healey, covers periodicals in the humanities and social sciences published since 1770, and *ProQuest 5000*™, from the same firm, provides full text access to 3,500 newspapers and periodicals, with indexes and abstracts of another 3,500, going back to 1971.

Among the indexes to particular magazines which are of immense value to researchers are those to the *Gentleman's Magazine*: the printed index volumes cover the period 1731–1819, with separate indexes to the biographical and obituary notices. *Notes & Queries* carries indexes to each volume and cumulated indexes for every twelve volumes. Both of these publications are excellent sources of information on a variety of subjects. Among recent indexing projects has been the index compiled by Geraldine Beare to the *Strand Magazine* 1891–1950, a valuable source.

The majority of modern periodicals carry volume indexes, which are a great help in tracing material quickly. Where there are no such printed indexes, you have to skim through the contents page of each issue to find a particular paper or feature; alternatively, apply to the editorial office of the publication concerned, if this is still in existence, where an index may be held on computer or in card index form.

Most public libraries keep long runs of local newspapers, county magazines and publications of their local historical and archaeological societies; these will also be found on the shelves of county record offices.

The British Library Science, Technology and Innovation Information Services (see Appendix I, page 233) houses a vast number of scientific and technical periodicals, including those formerly at the Patent Office Library.

The researcher wishing to trace a medical paper should do so in the US National Library of Medicine's *Index Medicus* (website www.nlm.nih.gov), which indexes some 3,800 journals worldwide and to which most medical libraries subscribe.

Press cuttings

Press cuttings have a value, as a starting point, in all research but (in my opinion) should be used with care and never as a substitute for original research. Any collection of cuttings is only as reliable and comprehensive as the person or persons selecting and assembling the cuttings were (or are) reliable and conscientious.The major exception to this has to be the admirable press cuttings library of the Royal Institute of International Affairs at Chatham House, 10 St James's Square, London SW1Y 4LE (tel. 020 7957 5723; email libenquiries@riaa.org), which contains much material of value to researchers on foreign and Commonwealth matters. The collection prior to 1940 is on microfilm, that of the period 1940–70 has been transferred to the British Library Newspaper Library at Colindale (indexes at Chatham House); the present library collection runs from 1971.

The Press Association News Library, now at the PA News Centre, Central Park, New Lane, Leeds, West Yorkshire LS11 5DZ (tel. 0870 830 6824; fax 0870 830 6825; email newslibrary@pa.press.net; website www.palibrary.pa.press.net), has a collection of some 14 million cuttings from 1928 onwards, as well as a photo bank of 5 million pictures. This archive is open to the general public seven days a week (Monday to Friday 08.00–20.00; Saturday and Sunday, 08.00–18.00). Alternatively, research is undertaken by in-house staff on a commercial basis (rates on application). A photo-copying service is available.

Another press cuttings library, very popular with journalists and researchers, is the privately owned Hans Tasiemka Archive at 80 Temple Fortune Lane, London NW11 7TU (tel. 020 8455 2485; fax 020 8455 0231). It contains a wealth of cuttings from the 1850s to the present day.

Many newspapers, libraries, trade associations and other professional bodies hold cuttings collections, and it is always worth asking what they have and having a look at them: you may well pick up leads for further research in this way.

OFFICIAL PUBLICATIONS

Most British official publications are available at the main reference libraries and public libraries. The former British Library Official Publications Library collection has been re-named the Social Policy Information Service and will be found at the new British Library in St Pancras in the Science 2 North reading room (tel. 020 7412 7536; fax 020 7412 7761; website www.bl.uk/services/stb/spis). It includes government publications of all countries, publications of the European Commission, the United Nations and other international and intergovernmental bodies. British Parliamentary papers, complete sets of *Hansard* and the *London Gazette*, current UK electoral registers and all the main statistical yearbooks are among a large number of reference books on the open shelves.

The current definitive source for UK material is the Chadwyck-Healey *UKOP*, available online and on CD-ROM. This combines the official catalogue of The

Stationery Office (TSO) and Chadwyck-Healey's *Official Publications Not Published by The Stationery Office*. For earlier publications, consult the microfiche *Great Britain: Stationery Office Catalogues of Government Publications, 1894–1970 and Consolidated Indexes to Government Publications 1936–1970*, also from Chadwyck-Healey. A vast amount of United Nations bibliographic information will be found on the CD-ROM *UNIBIS Plus*, which is retrospective to 1979 and now issued quarterly. You can also obtain information on the UN and its specialised agencies from the United Nations Information Centre, Millbank Tower (21st floor), 21/24 Millbank, London SW1P 4QH (tel. 020 7630 1981; fax 020 7976 6478; email info@uniclondon.org; website www.unitednations.org.uk).

On the European Union the best up-to-date sources are online (by subscription) from Chadwyck-Healey: *KnowEurope*, at www.knoweurope.net, and *European Access*, edited by Ian Thomson, also online as *European Access Plus*, at www.europeanaccess.co.uk. In print there is *The European Union Encyclopedia and Directory*, published annually by Europa Publications, London. New from Europa is a useful *Dictionary of the European Union*, alphabetically arranged and fully cross-referenced. An excellent introduction is John McCormick's *Understanding the European Union*, one of many titles in the Palgrave Macmillan *European Union* series. *EUROCAT*, on CD-ROM, is a complete catalogue of EU publications and documents. *Bona fide* researchers (but not students) may use the Library and Information Unit at the European Commission, Jean Monnet House, 8 Storey's Gate, London SW1P 3AT (tel. 020 7973 1992; fax 020 7973 1900/1910; website www.cec.org.uk/info). Westminster Reference Library, mentioned earlier in this chapter (see page 52) is one of the UK's three EU depository libraries.

MISCELLANEOUS PRINTED SOURCES

Articles, essays and quotations

The *Essay and General Literature Index*, covering work published since 1900, is the best place to look for miscellaneous articles and reviews. The *English Short Title Catalogue (ESTC)* is a unique source for books, lists, advertisements, song catalogues and much other printed matter; the material dates from 1473 to 1800, but is chiefly of the 18th century.

Quotations may be checked in numerous compilations available in every reference library and online (for recommendations, see Appendix II, pages 242–3). Full use should also be made of concordances to the Bible, and to Shakespeare, Tennyson and other major writers; one tends to forget just how time-saving these can be when one is reasonably sure of the author and when one has a major word or phrase to go on. *Granger's Index to Poetry*, with its title, first line, author and subject indexes, is indispensable. Another good tool is the *Cassell's Dictionary of Proverbs*, compiled by David Pickering.

Maps

The British Library's collection of maps (manuscript and printed) is one of the most important cartographic repositories in the world. The Maps Reading Room is on level 3 of the British Library, where there is a Map Reference Enquiry Desk to assist readers (tel. 020 7412 7702; fax 020 7412 7780; email maps@bl.uk; website www.bl.uk/collections/maps). The map catalogue is on CD-ROM and is separate from the British Library main online catalogue. There is a brand-new scholarly publication, *Maps in the Atlases of the British Library: A Descriptive Catalogue c.850–1800*, compiled by R.W. Shirley. Also highly recommended is another British Library publication, *English Maps: A History* by Catherine Delano-Smith and Roger J.P. Kain.

The Public Record Office, most local record offices and some libraries, such as the Bodleian Library in Oxford, the Royal Geographical Society Library and Birmingham Central Library, all hold special historical collections. Volume 3 of the *Catalogue of the National Maritime Museum Library* is another good source. A recent title from Phillimore, *Maps for Historians*, by Paul Hindle, is a practical guide and source of information. There is also the *International Bibliography of Maps and Atlases*, published by K.G. Saur on CD-ROM.

Stanford's, probably the world's finest map bookshop, at 12–14 Long Acre, London WC2E 2LP (tel. 020 7836 1321; fax 020 7836 0189; website www.stanfords.co.uk), sells antique and modern maps and atlases covering the world. (There are other branches in London and one in Bristol.) The first edition of the Ordnance Survey maps of Great Britain has been reprinted, and the historical series is still available. The modern editions, in an assortment of scales, may be purchased from Stanford's and all main Ordnance Survey agents, from the National Map Centre, 22–24 Caxton Street, London SW1H 0QU (tel. 020 7222 2466; fax 020 7222 2619; website www.mapstore.co.uk), or ordered through most booksellers. An interactive edition of the Ordnance Survey 2002 on CD-ROM is currently marketed by Dream Direct Ltd., Granville Way, Bicester, OX26 4JT (tel. 0870 7447 400; website www.eDream.co.uk). You may also like to visit the website www.multimap.co.uk.

Recommendations for atlases will be found in Appendix II, page 241.

Music and song

There is a wealth of material available to researchers. A good introduction is *Information Sources in Music*, published by K.G. Saur. Details of the British Library Music Collections and other music libraries in London will be found in Appendix I, on pages 229–30.

The New Grove Dictionary of Music & Musicians is the standard work, its second edition in hardback and paperback, also online (by subscription). On CD-ROM from K.G. Saur is the *International Bibliography of Printed Music, Music Manuscripts and Recordings*, covering the entire spectrum of music from the 15th century to the end of the 20th century. There is also *The Catalogue of Printed Music in the British*

Library to 1980. The *British Catalogue of Music 1957–1985* is published by K.G. Saur. Other bibliographies and catalogues of printed music are listed in volume 3 of *Walford's Guide to Reference Material,* under 'Music'.

The *Continuum Encyclopedia of Popular Music of the World* is a new comprehensive reference tool, with two volumes published to date (twelve volumes envisaged). Also from Continuum is Alyn Shipton's *A New History of Jazz.*

So far as periodicals are concerned, the *International Index to Music Periodicals* from Chadwyck-Healey is on CD-ROM and online; it has an ongoing 'Full Text' database online to which current and retrospective articles are constantly added. The *British Catalogue of Music* (three issues per year) and the *British and International Music Yearbook* are essential tools for any researcher in this field.

On opera, a standard work, reliable and very readable, is *Kobbé's Complete Opera Book.*

The *Song Index* and its supplement are useful sources for songs up to 1934, and there is also the *Song Catalogue* section of the *BBC Music Library Catalogue of Holdings;* the *Popular Song Index* and its supplements bring the catalogues up to the 20th century. *100 Years 100 Songs* covers the last century, in words and music.

Space does not permit me to go into the intricacies of research into hymns or nursery rhymes, but you should not have any difficulty if, as with any other kind of research, you consult either the BLPC, your reference library's subject index, or alternatively use one of the online search engines recomended in chapter 3, 'Online Research' (see pages 40–1) to find the standard works.

There is a classical music search engine on www.classicalsearch.com.

Sport

Although most clubs maintain their own collections of memorabilia, the most valuable historical archives remain in private hands; this material is unfortunately accessible only by personal introduction. That said, for published material there is a good Sports Library at Sheffield Public Library (tel. 0114 273 5929; email sports.library@dial.pipex.com), which houses a collection on all aspects of sport, including sports history. The Football Association has a library in London, at 25 Soho Square, London W1D 4FA (tel. 020 7762 4542; fax 020 7745 5515).

Among the sports museums are the British Golf Museum, St Andrews; the M.C.C. Museum at Lord's Cricket Ground; the River and Rowing Museum at Henley-on-Thames; and the Wimbledon Lawn Tennis Museum. On horseracing there are the Cheltenham Hall of Fame, the National Horseracing Museum at Newmarket and the York Racing Museum. There is a Rugby Museum at Twickenham. The best football museum is that of the Scottish Football Association at Hampden Park, Glasgow. (At the time of writing the Football Museum at Preston seems likely to close.) Details of all these museums will be found on the website www.umist.ac.uk/sport/mus.html.

Sporting statistics will be found in the yearbooks published for most sports (e.g. *Wisden's Cricketers' Almanack*), and in *Whitaker's Almanack* and *Pears Cyclopedia.*

The British Library publishes a useful sports bibliography series which includes *A Football Compendium*, *A Rugby Compendium* and *An Athletics Compendium*. The *International Journal of the History of Sport* is published quarterly, by Frank Cass; recent issues are online as well as in print.

Street and telephone directories

The Guildhall Library in London has a collection of street directories from the late 18th century, available on microfilm; many have been published by the Society of Genealogists, S & N Genealogy Supplies and Stepping Stones on microfiche or CD-ROM (see chapter 8, 'Family and Local History', page 164). There are two useful bibliographies: the *Guide to the National and Provincial Directories of England and Wales, excluding London, published before 1856*, by Jane E. Norton, and P.J. Atkins' *The Directories of London 1677–1977*. For present-day publications consult *Current British Directories* and *Current European Directories*. Most county record offices have sets of their local directories. These are extremely useful for checking addresses and names of neighbours, in biographical and family history research, as are the court guides (for the aristocracy) which also date from the late 18th century. The yellow pages of modern telephone directories may help you to find experts in a particular field.

Translations

The standard source is the *Index Translationum*, which has been published since 1932. Issued annually by UNESCO since 1949, it is now only online (at www.unesco.org/culture/trans), where it is fully searchable without subscription.

UNPUBLISHED SOURCES

Manuscripts and private papers

The major source of manuscripts in England is the British Library Department of Manuscripts at 96 Euston Road, London NW1 2DB (tel. 020 7412 7513; fax 020 7412 7745; email mss@bl.uk; website www.bl.uk). For access to the Manuscripts reading room you need a supplementary pass in addition to the normal reader's ticket; a letter of recommendation is required. There is a ten-volume *Index of Manuscripts in the British Library*, listing in one alphabetical sequence the holdings to 1950; more recent acquisitions will be found in the *Catalogue of Additions to the Manuscripts* series of volumes on open access. A good quick reference guide is *The British Library Guide to the Catalogues and Indexes of the Department of Manuscripts*. This useful booklet also lists the reference books on open access in the Manuscripts reading room and the catalogues available there of MSS holdings in other libraries. The Manuscripts catalogue itself may be searched online at www.bl.uk/catalogues.

If you wish to trace the location of other MSS or to ascertain whether any private papers exist, or to find out if such papers have been deposited or registered, you should first get in touch with the Royal Commission on Historical Manuscripts (HMC), currently still at Quality House, Quality Court, Chancery Lane, London WC2A 1HP (tel. 020 7242 1198; fax 020 7831 3550), but moving to the Public Record Office main building at Kew probably in the late autumn of 2003. In April 2003 HMC amalgamated with the PRO to form the National Archives (see below, pages 71–2).

The Historical Manuscripts Commission, established by Royal Warrant in 1869, maintains the National Register of Archives (NRA). The NRA consists of more than 43,000 unpublished lists and catalogues of manuscript collections (privately owned records and those held in repositories other than the Public Record Office, in the UK and abroad). Its indexes (150,000 references plus 300,000 connected records) may be accessed on the website www.hmc.gov.uk. Another register administered by HMC is the Manorial Documents Register (MDR), extremely useful to genealogists and local historians (see chapter 8, 'Family and Local History', page 158). *N.B.* Whereas at present these registers are open for consultation without formality, following HMC's installation at Kew researchers will need a National Archives reader's pass for access.

Also maintained by HMC is the NRA's electronic directory to repositories throughout the UK and in some institutions abroad, ARCHON, at www.hmc.gov.uk (click on 'ARCHON'); regularly updated, it aims by the year 2005 to provide an easily accessible gateway to all UK archives.

Publications of the Commission include a *Guide to Sources for British History* series and an ongoing set of *National Register of Archives Information Sheets* (for titles, see bibliography at end of this chapter). The HMC's *Surveys of Historical Manuscripts in the United Kingdom*, a select bibliography which lists completed surveys (published and unpublished) as well as those known to be in progress, is maintained online at www.hmc.gov.uk. The booklet *Record Repositories in Great Britain*, published jointly by the PRO and HMC, is revised every few years; for up-to-date information readers should consult ARCHON (see above).

Search facilities at the NRA include the use of computerised indexes: Personal, Business and Subject, as well as a Repositories File containing up-to-date details of record offices. A valuable research tool, published jointly by HMC and the Institute of Historical Research, is R.J. Olney's *Manuscript Sources for British History: their Nature, Location and Use*.

So far as literary manuscripts are concerned, you should look at the *Location Register of English Literary Manuscripts and Letters* and at the *Index of English Literary Manuscripts*, covering the period 1450–1900. Sadly, publication of the latter has been suspended beyond 1900 letter 'P' (see bibliography at the end of this chapter).

An excellent finding aid to unpublished material is the Chadwyck-Healey *National Inventory of Documentary Sources in the United Kingdom and Ireland* (*NIDS*), on microfiche and CD-ROM. Most major libraries subscribe, and there are useful leaflets explaining how to use the inventory. There is a similar series for documentary sources in the United States. *British Archives: A Guide to Archive*

Resources in the United Kingdom and Ireland, by Janet Foster and Julia Sheppard, is another indispensable reference tool, listing archive collections by town, by county and alphabetically; the introduction contains useful advice to the first-time user of archival material. David Iredale's award-winning *Enjoying Archives* is both practical and entertaining.

Researchers handling documentary source material for the first time should read Frank G. Burke's *Research and the Manuscript Tradition*; although written from the American perspective, it contains much practical advice of value to everyone working in this field. The British Records Association publishes a useful 'Archives and the User' series, regularly updated and reprinted (full details from the BRA, 40 Northampton Road, London EC1R 0HB; tel. 020 7833 0428; fax 020 7833 0416; website www.hmc.gov.uk/bra).

Public records

The National Archives: Public Record Office

The Public Record Office (PRO) at Kew, Richmond, Surrey TW9 4DU (tel. 020 8876 3444; fax 020 8878 8905; email enquiry@pro.gov.uk; website www.pro.gov.uk) holds official documents going back to the 11th century. Nowadays all government records are automatically deposited within thirty years and, with a few exceptions, are open to the public thirty years after their creation.

Formerly in Chancery Lane, central London, in recent years virtually all the records have been transferred to a purpose-built complex at Kew, where there are over 168 kilometres of shelving. (Census returns and non-parochial registers have been sent to the Family Records Centre; see chapter 8, 'Family and Local History', pages 147–8).

Admission to the PRO is free, but you must have a National Archives reader's pass (take with you some formal proof of identity bearing your signature, such as a driving licence or cheque card). Those who are not British citizens should present their passport or national identity card.

The PRO at Kew is a much friendlier place than it used to be in its old Chancery Lane premises. A number of 'Open Days' and other events, open to the public, are organised throughout the year. Academics and researchers have welcomed the extended opening hours, with two late evenings (Tuesday and Thursday) to 19.00 hours and Saturday opening (last document ordering 14.30 hours); see Appendix I, page 201 for full details. Provided you know the exact references, you may order up to three documents in advance of your visit (allow 1–2 days' notice) by telephone (020 8392 5200) or email (order@pro.gov.uk).

The reading rooms include a Research Enquiries Room, a Map and Large Document Room and a Microfilm Reading Room (where the microfilms are on self-service). In most rooms there are allocated areas where you may use your PC, typewriter or tape recorder. Document requests are made on computer terminals, and readers are issued with bleepers keyed to their seat number which let them know when they can collect from the issue desk. There are self-service printers for copying from microfilm and fiche, and an efficient reprographic service for ordering copies in a range of formats. If you are unable to visit personally, you can request copies to be sent by post or email.

To order documents – or photocopies – you must first ascertain to which class the files you want belong. All documents at the PRO are classified by department or ministry, rather than by subject. Once you have the class list, you look chronologically to find the piece number(s) you need to order. It is not as complicated as it sounds. There are several 'Introduction to Archive Materials' pamphlets available free of charge from the PRO bookshop and on the landing outside the reading rooms, and qualified staff are on hand to deal with enquiries and to help first-time users to operate the computer terminals. A research library containing some 150,000 titles on all aspects of British history adjoins the Microfilm Reading Room.

The PRO website www.pro.gov.uk offers a wealth of information on how to find information, as well as the complete catalogue, PROCAT (9 million file references).

Other records

Parliamentary records from 1497 are at the House of Lords Record Office, House of Lords, London SW1A 0PW (tel. 020 7219 3074; fax 020 7219 2570; email hlro@parliament.uk; website www.parliament.uk). Records of British rule in India to 1947 are in the Oriental and India Office Collections reading room at the British Library, 96 Euston Road, London NW1 2DB (tel. 020 7412 7873; fax 020 7412 7641; email oioc-enquiries@bl.uk; website www.bl.uk). The Imperial War Museum, Lambeth Road, London SE1 6HZ (tel. 020 7416 5000; website www.iwm.org.uk) houses documentary and illustrative material on the two World Wars, and the Churchill Archives Centre at Churchill College, Cambridge CB3 0DS (tel. 01223 336087; email archives@chu.cam.ac.uk; website www.chu.cam.uk/archives) is collecting papers of 20th-century politicians, scientists and both military and naval commanders; however not all of these collections are yet open to the public.

At the Guildhall Library, Aldermanbury, London EC2P 2EJ (tel. 020 7332 1868; website www.cityoflondon.gov.uk) you will find records relating to the City from medieval times, including those of many of the City livery companies (although some of these perished in the Great Fire of 1666). Consult the *Guide to Archives and Manuscripts at Guildhall Library.*

The National Library of Scotland, George IV Bridge, Edinburgh EH1 1EW (tel. 0131 226 4531; fax 0131 622 4803; email enquiries@nls.uk; website www.nls.uk) possesses a priceless collection of manuscripts, ranging from early monastic writings to modern political papers; there are printed and manuscript indexes. Also in Edinburgh are the National Archives of Scotland (formerly the Scottish Record Office) and the National Register of Archives (Scotland).

The National Library of Wales, Aberystwyth SY23 3BU (tel. 01970 632800; fax

01970 615709; website www.llgc.org.uk) houses over 4 million books and a vast collection of manuscripts, deeds, probate records, maps and other material (including an audio-visual collection) relating to Wales and the Celtic peoples.

The National Library of Ireland, the National Archives and Trinity College Library, all in Dublin, house many Irish records. You should also contact the Public Record Office of Northern Ireland in Belfast. (For these addresses and other details, see Appendix I, pages 201, 202, 226). When the old Public Record Office in Dublin was destroyed in 1922 most, but not all, of the records perished.

The addresses, telephone and fax numbers of all national and provincial record offices will be found in the HMC/PRO booklet, *Record Repositories in Great Britain* and online at www.hmc.gov.uk (click on 'ARCHON'). See also Appendix I of this book (pages 201, 203–13).

MISCELLANEOUS SOURCES

Broadcast and televised material

There have been many changes in the worlds of radio and television in the wake of the Broadcasting Act 1990. While these changes do not much affect the researcher into historical material, if you are seeking current information you should contact the relevant radio or television company direct. The most up-to-date handbook I have found is *Information Sources in the Press and Broadcast Media*, published by K.G. Saur in 1999. (Sadly, Barrie Macdonald's *Broadcasting in the United Kingdom: A Guide to Information Sources* has not been revised since 1994, but it is nevertheless still a useful reference tool.)

The Media Guide contains addresses and telephone/fax numbers of the various companies, as well as a list of independent producers (with telephone numbers). The Spotlight publication *Contacts* is also very useful in this respect.

Most sizeable reference libraries possess the Chadwyck-Healey microfiche editions of *BBC Radio: Author and Title Catalogues of Transmitted Drama, Poetry* and *Features, 1929–1975* and *BBC Television: Author and Title Catalogues of Transmitted Drama and Features, 1936–1975, with Chronological List of Transmitted Plays*. Also available on microfiche are the *Radio Times 1923–1994*, *The Listener 1929–1991*, and the *BBC Home Service: Nine O'Clock News, 1939–1945* (60,000 pages of newsreaders' typescripts).

The BBC Written Archives Centre, which is at Caversham Park, Reading RG4 8TZ (tel. 0118 948 6281; fax 0118 946 1145; email heritage@bbc.co.uk; website www.bbc.co.uk/thenandnow/wac) is open to *bona fide* researchers by appointment only. (Note that you can use the Centre's facilities only if you are working on an accredited academic or commercial project or have been commissioned to write a book or article.)

The BBC Sound Archives are not open to the public but may be accessed through the British Library National Sound Archive (NSA), which has now moved from

South Kensington to the British Library, 96 Euston Road, London NW1 2DB (tel. 020 7412 7440; fax 020 7412 7441; email nsa@bl.uk; website www.bl.uk/nsa).

One of the largest and most diverse sound archives in the world, the National Sound Archive, contains broadcasts and published recordings as well as a unique collection of unpublished recordings, dating from 1890 to the present day. Its online catalogue, CADENSA, which includes almost 2.5 million recordings (one of the largest of its kind in the world), may be searched online at www.cadensa.bl.uk, or at two special terminals in the British Library Humanities 2 reading room.

The Library and Information Service of the NSA is on open access, but if you wish to use the Listening and Viewing Service (located in the Rare Books and Music reading room at the British Library) you must make an appointment in advance. You will need a British Library reader's pass (see page 200). There is also a Northern Listening Service at the British Library's premises in Boston Spa, near Wetherby, West Yorkshire.

Under the terms of the new Broadcasting Act the National Film Archive is to maintain a national television archive. It is now the National Film and Television Archive (NAFTA), see below, pages 74–5.

Filmed and recorded material

The researcher interested in filmed material and the history of the cinema should contact the British Film Institute (BFI) at 21 Stephen Street, London W1P 1PL (tel. 020 7255 1444; fax 020 7436 0439). The BFI National Library at the same address and telephone number (fax 020 7436 0165; email library@bfi.org.uk; website www.bfi.org.uk/library/services) houses the world's largest collection of information on the cinema and television; it is open to non-members for reference (day membership available). The National Film and Television Archive, a division of the BFI, is administered from the same address, but the films themselves are stored at Berkhamsted. A viewing service is available for *bona fide* researchers.

If you need newsreel material, first contact the British Universities Film and Video Council (BUFVC) at 77 Wells Street, London W1P 3RE (tel. 020 7393 1500; fax 020 7393 1555; email ask@bufvc.ac.uk). On the Council's website www.bufvc.ac.uk you can search the British Universities Newsreel Project database containing some 160,000 records of all British cinema newsreels from 1910 to 1979; there is an explanatory 'Researcher's Guide Online'. You will not be able to see the actual footage there, but will be directed to the relevant source, probably British Pathé or British Movietone. Some newsreels are available on video. At Pathé recently the newsreels (1895–1970) have been transferred to digital tape, and an exciting new development is their website (www.britishpathé.com), launched in November 2002, giving researchers the facility not only to search their extensive database but also to download free clips.

The National Film and Television Archive (NAFTA) is housed chiefly at the J. Paul Getty Conservation Centre, Kingshill Way, Berkhamsted HP4 3TP (tel. 01442 876

301; fax 01442 289 112; email davidpierce@bfi.org.uk; website www.bfi.org.uk/collections/preservation/index.html). Some films are stored at other sites.

There are two indispensable guides for the researcher, although neither are absolutely up-to-date: *Film and Television Collections in Europe: The Map-TV Guide* ('Map' meaning the Mercury Archive Programme, Strasbourg), which contains detailed information on 1,900 film and television collections in 40 different countries, and *The Film Researcher's Handbook*, which is a guide to sources in Africa, Asia, Australasia, North America and South America.

Halliwell's Film and Video Guide and the *BFI Film & Television Handbook* are standard annual publications. Among a wealth of other titles I recommend *The Macmillan International Film Encyclopedia*, the Cassell/BFI *Companion to Cinema* series, the *International Dictionary of Film and Filmmakers*, *Halliwell's Who's Who in the Movies*, and the *Complete Index to British Sound Film since 1928*. For the early period of cinema, there is the mammoth *History of the Cinema 1895–1940*, a collection of 3,574 microfiches plus printed guide and index from Chadwyck-Healey. Keep an eye open, too, for mail order catalogues of special interest and historical videos and DVDs.

There is an International Movie Database online at www.imdb.com.

Oral history collections

Although the term 'oral history' is a fairly recent one, in fact this was the very first kind of history, as Paul Thompson has pointed out in *The Voice of the Past*. The growth of oral history study-groups today reflects an interest in and awareness of the value of this field of research, which demands quite different skills from those of the historian handling paper documentation.

Researchers interested in the subject should consider joining the Oral History Society; membership includes a subscription to the Society's journal, *Oral History*. Visit the website www.oralhistory.org.uk, or contact the Society direct at the Department of History, University of Essex, Colchester, Essex CO4 3SQ (tel. 01206 873333; fax 01206 873410), or through the National Sound Archive.

The best introduction to the subject, apart from the Thompson title above-mentioned, is *Oral History: Talking about the Past*, by Robert Perks; the same author has compiled *Oral History: An Annotated Bibliography 1945–1989*. Ruth Finnegan's *Oral Traditions and the Verbal Arts: A Guide to Research Practices* is a useful guide for the researcher, as is Ken Howarth's *Oral History*, in the Sutton *History Handbooks* series. In progress from Oxford University Press is the *International Yearbook of Oral History and Life Stories*.

The *National Life Story Collection*, an ongoing National Sound Archive project, is bringing together recordings of 20th-century people from all walks of life; this is bound to prove a valuable source for the next generation of researchers.

It is a sobering thought that already, at the beginning of the 21st century, less than 50 per cent of all records exist on paper, as opposed to those in filmed, recorded and electronic formats. This means that future researchers will be spending a far greater proportion of their working time looking and listening, rather than poring over the printed or handwritten page in the library and record office. Whether we like it or not, the revolution is underway, and we are going to have to get used to it, so the sensible thing to do is to prepare ourselves by acquiring the necessary new skills.

Theses

It is always worthwhile checking on dissertations, as these can be a most valuable source of information. Aslib has since 1950 published an *Index to Theses accepted for Higher Degrees in the Universities of Great Britain and Ireland*; it is now entitled *Index to Theses with Abstracts*. The universities of Oxford, Cambridge and London publish separate annual lists. There are *Abstracts of Dissertations* for Oxford and Cambridge going back to 1925, and lists for London in the University Calendar 1930–40, as well as *Subjects of Dissertations, Theses etc. for Higher Degrees* covering 1937–51. The Institute of Historical Research has published annual lists since 1901. Issued in May each year, *History Theses* consists of two parts: 'Theses completed' and 'Theses in progress'.

For North American doctoral dissertations and master theses consult the University Microfilms (UMI) *Dissertation Abstracts*, which contains a record of more than 1.5 million theses from the United States, Canada and the Pacific Rim since 1861. UMI is now part of ProQuest Information and Learning. You can search online by author, title, keyword or subject (www.proquest.co.uk, click on 'UMI') or telephone the customer services department at the UK office of ProQuest (The Quorum, Barnwell Road, Cambridge CB5 8SW; tel. 01223 215512; fax 01223 215513; website www.proquest.co.uk). A wide range of reproductions is available in print, microform and electronic formats.

Sadly, I feel the need to end this chapter on a cautionary note. However skilled one is at research – and we all get better at it all the time – finding authentic material is not easy. The much hailed 'Information Super-highway' is a minefield. Nothing is static: sources change; staff change; publishers re-group; long-established titles fall by the wayside. The Internet has proved to be less than 100% trustworthy. Nor, for that matter, are *all* books completely so. Libraries appear to spend so much of their budgets on videos that essential (essential, that is, to the researcher) yearbooks and other reference works on their shelves are long out of date. Frequently nowadays when we telephone, we reach only someone's voicemail. Worse still, people (yes, even library staff!) sometimes – if inadvertently – mislead you. There is a big difference between the qualified librarian and the relatively untrained library assistant. More than once in the course of revising this book I have been 'fobbed off' by an inexperienced library assistant with the wrong facts, either relying on old sources or hoping perhaps to rid himself of my persistent enquiries. I always now ask – politely, of course – for the date of all sources quoted. Be on *your* guard.

Abstracts in New Technologies and Engineering (ANTE), formerly the *Current Technology Index (CTI)*, now published by Cambridge Scientific Abstracts (CSA), Bethesda, Maryland, USA (UK office, East Grinstead), bi-monthly with annual cumulation; also as *ANTE Plus*, on CD-ROM, updated quarterly, and online (by subscription)

Abstracts of Dissertations approved for the PhD, MSc and MLitt Degrees 1925/6–1956/7, Cambridge University Press, 1927–59

Abstracts of Dissertations for the Degree of Doctor of Philosophy 1925–40, Oxford University Press, 12 vols, 1928–47 (BLitt and BSc theses are included in vols 10 and 12)

American Book Publishing Record, published weekly and monthly, with annual and 5-year cumulative volumes, by Bowker, New Providence, N.J., USA. There are sets of cumulative volumes from 1950 and one earlier volume for the years 1876–1949

American Periodicals Series Online, by subscription from ProQuest, Cambridge

Applied Social Sciences Index (ASSIA), published by Cambridge Scientific Abstracts (CSA), Bethesda, Maryland, USA (UK office, East Grinstead), monthly and online (by subscription)

'Archives and the User' series, the British Records Association, 40 Northampton Road, London EC1R 0HB

Art Index, published quarterly since 1929 by H.W. Wilson, New York; now monthly; online on WilsonWeb and WilsonDisc, updated monthly; also as *Art Index Retrospective 1929–1984* on WilsonWeb and WilsonDisc

Aslib Directory of Information Sources in the United Kingdom, published biennially, now by Europa Publications, London; 12th edn, ed. K.W. Reynard, 2 vols, 2002

An Athletics Compendium: A Guide to the UK Literature of Track and Field, compiled by Tom McNab, Peter Lovesey and Andrew Huxtable, British Library, London, 2001

BBC Home Service: Nine O'Clock News, 1939–1945, microfiche, Chadwyck-Healey, Cambridge

BBC Radio: Author and Title Catalogues of Transmitted Drama, Poetry and Features, 1929–1975, microfiche, Chadwyck-Healey, Cambridge

BBC Television: Author and Title Catalogues of Transmitted Drama and Features, 1936–1975, with Chronological List of Transmitted Plays, microfiche, Chadwyck-Healey, Cambridge

Benn's Media (formerly *Benn's Media Directory*), 3 vols, published annually by CMP Information Ltd., Tonbridge

BFI Film & Television Handbook, published annually by British Film Institute, London

Bibliographic Index, published since 1938 by H.W. Wilson, New York; now updated weekly on WilsonWeb, with retrospective coverage to 1984; *Bibliographic Index Plus* forthcoming

Bibliography of British Newspapers, British Library, London, in progress, 1982–

BookBank/Bookbank Global/Bookbank OP, see *Whitaker's* bibliographical services

Booklovers' London, by Lesley Reader, Metro Publications, London, 2nd edn, 2002

Books in Print (UK and European), see *Whitaker's Books in Print*

Books in Print (US), published annually by Bowker, New Providence, N.J., USA, 9 vols, with mid-year supplement, 3 vols; by subscription on CD-ROM, updated monthly, and online, updated weekly; also *Books Out-of-Print* online at booksoutofprint.com

The Bookseller, published weekly, formerly by Whitaker, now by VNU Entertainment Media UK Ltd., London; special 'Buyer's Guides', spring (January) and autumn (July)

British and International Music Yearbook, published annually by Rhinegold Publishing, London

British Archives: A Guide to Archive Resources in the United Kingdom and Ireland, by Janet Foster and Julia Sheppard, Macmillan, London, 4th edn, 2001

British Catalogue of Music, published by Cambridge Scientific Abstracts (CSA) UK, on behalf of the British Library; 3 issues per year

British Catalogue of Music 1957–1985, eds. Michael Chapman and Elizabeth Robinson, 10 vols, Saur, Munich, 1988–89

British Education Index, first issued 1958, now published by Leeds University Press, Leeds; 4 part-issues plus one annual cumulation

British Humanities Index, published since 1963 by the Library Association, London; now by Cambridge Scientific Abstracts UK, East Grinstead, quarterly, with annual cumulation volume; also as *BHI Plus*, on CD-ROM, updated quarterly and online (by subscription)

British Library General Catalogue of Printed Books: original edition to 1975 out of print; reprinted, with supplements, to 2000, by Saur, Munich, 1980–2001; CD-ROM by Saztec Europe, distributed in UK by Chadwyck-Healey, Cambridge; microfiche edition, British Library, London, 1986–2000; ceased publication 2000

The British Library Guide to the Catalogues and Indexes of the Department of Manuscripts, by M.A.E. Nickson, British Library, London, 3rd edn, revised by J. Conway, 1998

British Library Newspaper Catalogue, online at www.bl.uk/catalogues

British National Bibliography (*BNB*), weekly since 1950, with cumulative monthly, annual and some 5-yearly volumes; now published by British Library National Bibliographic Service, Boston Spa, Wetherby, West Yorkshire LS23 7BQ, weekly in print, monthly on CD-ROM

British Newspaper Index (*BNI*), from 1990, updated quarterly on CD-ROM, Primary Source Microfilm (The Gale Group/Thomson Learning), Reading

British Union-Catalogue of Periodicals, originally published in 4 vols by Butterworth, London, 1955–58; some supplementary vols; replaced in 1981 by *Serials in the British Library, q.v.*

Broadcasting in the United Kingdom: A Guide to Information Sources, by Barrie Macdonald, Mansell, London, 2nd rev. edn, 1993; paperback 1994

Business Periodicals Index, published since 1958 by H.W. Wilson, New York, monthly;

online on WilsonWeb and WilsonDisc, updated monthly; also as *Wilson Business Full Text*, updated four times a week on WilsonWeb, monthly on WilsonDisc

Cassell Directory of Publishing, see *Directory of Publishing*

Cassell's Dictionary of Proverbs, compiled by David Pickering, Cassell, London, 2001

Catalogue of Additions to the Manuscripts series, British Library, London

Catalogue of Official Publications Not Published by The Stationery Office, see *UKOP*

The Catalogue of Printed Music in the British Library to 1980, British Library, London, 62 vols; reprinted by Saur, Munich, 1980–87; ceased publication 2000

Catalogue of the National Maritime Museum Library, vol. 3, Atlases and Cartography, HMSO, London, 1971

Catalogue of the Newspaper Library, Colindale, compiled by P.E. Allen, 8 vols, British Library, London, 1975

Centres, Bureaux and Research Institutes, CBD Research, Beckenham, 4th edn, 2000

Companion to Cinema series, published by Cassell/BFI, London, various dates

Complete Index to British Sound Film since 1928, ed. Alan Goble, K.G. Saur, Munich, 1999

Contacts, published annually (October) by Spotlight, 7 Leicester Place, London WC2H 7BP (tel. 020 7437 7631; fax 020 7437 5881; email info@spotlightcd.com; website www.spotlightcd.com)

Continuum Encyclopedia of Popular Music of the World, Continuum, London, 12 vols, in progress, 2002–

Current British Directories, CBD Research, Beckenham, 14th edn, 2003

Current European Directories, CBD Research, Beckenham, 3rd edn, 1994

Dictionary of the European Union, by David Phinnemore and Lee McGowan, Europa Publications, London, 2002

The Directories of London 1677–1977, by P.J. Atkins, Cassell, London, 1990

Directory of Museums and Special Collections in the United Kingdom, ed. Keith Reynard, Europa Publications, London, 3rd edn, 2003

Directory of Publishing: UK, Commonwealth and Overseas (formerly *The Cassell Directory of Publishing*), now published annually by Continuum International Publishing Group Ltd., London

The Directory of University Libraries in Europe, Europa Publications, London, 2nd edn, 2003; also online

Dissertation Abstracts, from 1861, University Microfilms, Ann Arbor, Michigan, USA, online at www.proquest.co.uk

Early English Newspapers, Primary Source Microfilm, Reading, in progress (microfilm)

Encyclopedia of the British Press 1422–1992, ed. Dennis Griffiths, Macmillan, London, 1992

The English Catalogue of Books: first vol. 1801–36 and subsequent 3- and 5-year cumulations; discontinued (last vol. published 1969)

English Maps: A History, by Catherine Delano Smith and Roger J.P. Kain, British Library, London, 2000

English Short Title Catalogue 1473–1800, on CD-ROM, British Library, London, 1998

Enjoying Archives, by David Iredale, Phillimore, Chichester, 1985

Essay and General Literature Index, published since 1934 by H.W. Wilson, New York; now annually; also online updated quarterly on WilsonWeb and WilsonDisc; retrospective edition forthcoming

EUROCAT: The Complete Catalogue of EU Publications and Documents, quarterly on CD-ROM, Chadwyck-Healey, Cambridge

The Europa World Year Book, 2 vols, published annually by Europa Publications, London; online as *Europa World* from summer 2003 (by subscription)

European Access, ed. Ian Thomson, Chadwyck-Healey, Cambridge, in association with the UK offices of the European Commission, 6 issues per year; also as *European Access Plus*, online (by subscription)

European Union series, Palgrave Macmillan, Basingstoke

European Woman's Periodicals, Primary Source Microfilm, Reading; on microfilm (284 reels)

Film and Television Collections in Europe: The Map-TV Guide, Routledge, London, 1995

The Film Researcher's Handbook, compiled by Jenny Morgan, Routledge, London, 1996

Financial Times Index, from 1981, monthly with annual cumulations, also on microfilm from 1888, Primary Source Microfilm (The Gale Group), Reading

A Football Compendium: A Comprehensive Guide to the Literature of Association Football, compiled by Peter J. Seddon, British Library, London, 2nd edn, 2000

Gentleman's Magazine: General Index to the first 56 volumes (1731–86), 2 vols; *General Index... 1787–1819*, *Index to the Biographical and Obituary Notices, 1731–1780* and *1781–1819*, 2 vols: 1st vol, British Record Society, London, 2nd vol, Garland, New York and London

Glasgow Herald (now *The Herald*) *Index*, in printed form 1906–88; since 1989 by Scottish Media Newspapers, Glasgow, online only

Granger's Index to Poetry, first published 1904; now in its 14th edn, ed. Tessa Kale, Columbia University Press, New York, 2002

Great Britain: Stationery Office Catalogues of Government Publications, 1894–1970 and *Consolidated Indexes to Government Publications, 1936–1970* on microfiche, Chadwyck-Healey, Cambridge

The Guardian Index, from 1986, monthly with annual cumulations, University Microfilms (ProQuest), Cambridge; now included in the *British Newspaper Index*, q.v.

Guide to Archives and Manuscripts at Guildhall Library, Guildhall Library, London, 1989

Guide to Libraries and Information Services, eds. Peter Dale and Paul Wilson, British Library, London, 34th edn, 2003

Guide to Libraries in Key UK Companies, by Emma McKenzie, British Library, London, 2003

Guide to Libraries in London, compiled by Valerie McBurney and Paul Wilson, British Library, London, 2nd edn, 2002

Guide to the National and Provincial Directories of England and Wales, excluding London, published before 1856, by Jane E. Norton, Royal Historical Society, London, 1950; reprinted with corrections, 1984

Guide to Reference Material, ed. A.J. Walford; see below under *Walford's Guide to Reference Material*

Guide to Sources for British History: 1, *Papers of British cabinet ministers 1782–1900*; 2, *The manuscript papers of British scientists 1600–1940*; 3, *Guide to the location of collections described in the Reports and Calendars series 1870–1980*; 4, *Private papers of British diplomats 1782–1900*; 5, *Private papers of British colonial governors 1782–1900*; 6, *Papers of British churchmen 1780–1940*; 7, *Papers of British politicians 1782–1900*; 8, *Records of British business and industry 1760–1914: textiles and leather*; 9, *Records of British business and industry 1760–1914: metal processing and engineering*; 10, *Principal family and estate collections: family names A–K*; 11, *Principal family and estate collections: family names L–Y*; 12, *Papers of British antiquaries and historians;* Royal Commission on Historical Manuscripts, London, 1982–2003

Halliwell's Film and Video Guide, published annually by HarperCollins, London

Halliwell's Who's Who in the Movies, ed. John Walker, HarperCollins, London, 14th edn, 2001

Handlist of Unpublished Finding Aids to the London Collections of the British Library, by R.C. Alston, British Library, London, 1991

Hansard: Parliamentary Debates, 1803 onwards; now published daily during sessions by The Stationery Office (formerly HMSO), London; also on CD-ROM, Chadwyck-Healey, Cambridge (Chadwyck-Healey also publishes various series of Parliamentary Papers from 1715, in microform)

History of the Cinema 1895–1940, 3,574 microfiches plus printed guide and index, Chadwyck-Healey, Cambridge

History Theses, 3 vols, covering the period 1901–90, Institute of Historical Research, London, 1976, 1984, 1994; now annually

Humanities Index, published annually since 1974 by H.W. Wilson, New York; now updated monthly on WilsonWeb and WilsonDisc; also available as *Humanities Full Text*, updated four times a week on WilsonWeb, monthly on WilsonWeb

100 Years 100 Songs, Wise Publications (Omnibus), London, 2000

Index Medicus, published monthly since 1960 by National Library of Medicine, Washington, now in Bethesda, Maryland, USA

Index of English Literary Manuscripts, covering the period 1450–1900, 4 vols to date, Mansell, London, 1980–97 (vol. 4, 1800–1900, ends with Part 3 at 'Patmore'; no further vols scheduled)

Index of Manuscripts in the British Library, 10 vols, Chadwyck-Healey, Cambridge, 1985

Index to Legal Periodicals and Books, published since 1952 by H.W. Wilson, New York, now monthly; online updated weekly on WilsonWeb, monthly on WilsonDisc (retrospective to 1981)

Index to Theses with Abstracts (continuing series *Index to Theses* published since 1950 by Aslib, London), now published by Portland Press Ltd., Colchester, for Aslib, 6 issues per year; also online

Index Translationum, published quarterly 1932–40, and annually since 1949 by UNESCO, Paris; now online at www.unesco.org/culture/trans, updated quarterly

Information Sources in Music, by Lewis Foreman, K.G. Saur, Munich, 2002

Information Sources in the Press and Broadcast Media, eds. Sarah Adair and Selwyn Eagle, K.G. Saur, 2nd edn, 1999

International Bibliography of Bibliographies 1959–1988, ed. State Library of Berlin, K.G. Saur, Munich, 12 vols, 1998

International Bibliography of Printed Music, Music Manuscripts and Recordings, K.G. Saur, Munich, CD-ROM edn, 1999

International Books in Print, K.G. Saur, Munich; not published since 1999

International Dictionary of Film and Filmmakers, ed. Christopher Lyon, 3 vols, Macmillan, Basingstoke, 1987–91

International Index to Music Periodicals, Chadwyck-Healey, Cambridge; Full Text version online

International Journal of the History of Sport, published quarterly by Frank Cass, London; recent issues also online

International Women's Periodicals, Primary Source Microfilm, Reading (150 reels)

International Yearbook of Oral History and Life Stories, Oxford University Press, Oxford, in progress (4 vols to date)

'Introduction to Archive Materials' series of leaflets, available free at the Public Record Office, Kew

ISSN Register (formerly *ISDS Register*), published quarterly on magnetic tape and CD-ROM by the ISSN International Centre, Paris (UK centre: British Library, Boston Spa, Wetherby, West Yorkshire LS23 7BQ)

Keyword Index to Serial Titles (*KIST*), quarterly British Library National Bibliographic Service, Boston Spa, Wetherby (by subscription)

Kobbé's Complete Opera Book, first published 1922; 9th edn, Putnam, London, 1976

Libraries in the United Kingdom and the Republic of Ireland, published annually by the Library Association, now by Facet Publishing, London, 30th edn, 2003

Library and Information Science Abstracts (*LISA*), published monthly, with annual index volume, by Cambridge Scientific Abstracts (CSA), Bethesda, Maryland, USA (UK office, East Grinstead); also as *LISA Plus*, on CD-ROM, updated quarterly, and *LISA Online* (by subscription)

Library of Congress Online Catalog, searchable at www.bl.uk/catalogues/otherlibcats; see also *National Union Catalog*

The Listener, weekly, 1929–91, BBC, London; microform edition, Chadwyck-Healey, Cambridge

Location Register of English Literary Manuscripts and Letters, ed. David Sutton, 4 vols,

British Library, London, 1988–95: *18th and 19th Centuries*, 2 vols, 1995; *20th Century*, 2 vols, 1988

London Catalogue of Books, series of overlapping catalogues covering the years 1700–1855 (first vol., Bent, 1773)

London Directories from the Guildhall Library, 1677–1855, on microfilm, Primary Source Microfilm (The Gale Group), Reading

London Gazette, published since 1665; now daily, Monday to Friday, The Stationery Office (formerly HMSO), London; also sister publications in Belfast and Edinburgh

The Macmillan International Film Encyclopedia, ed. Ephraim Katz, Palgrave Macmillan, Basingstoke, 4th edn, 2001

Manuscript Sources for British History: their Nature, Location and Use, by R.J. Olney, Institute of Historical Research/Royal Commission on Historical Manuscripts, London, 1995

Maps for Historians, by Paul Hindle, Phillimore, Chichester, 1998; reprinted 2002

Maps in the Atlases of the British Library: A Descriptive Catalogue c.850–1800, compiled by R.W. Shirley, British Library, London, 2003

The Media Guide, eds. Steve Peak and Paul Fisher, published annually by Fourth Estate, London (a *Guardian Book*)

Mitchell's Newspaper Press Directory, first published 1846; now *Benn's Media*, q.v.

The Museums and Galleries Yearbook, published annually by the Museums Association, London

National Inventory of Documentary Sources in the United Kingdom and Ireland (*NIDS*), Chadwyck-Healey, Cambridge; also *National Inventory of Documentary Sources in the United States*

National Life Story Collection, in progress at the British Library National Sound Archive, London

National Register of Archives Information Sheets: Sources for 1, *Labour History*; 2, *Colonial History*; 3, *History of Women*; 4, *History of Education*; 5, *Business History*; 6, *Family History*; 7, *History of Film, Theatre and Television*; 8, *History of the Armed Forces*; 9, *Criminal and Legal History*; 10, *Newspaper History*; 11, *Architectural and Garden History*; 12, *Merchant Shipping and Seamen*; 13, *Fine Art and Artists*, available from the Royal Commission on Historical Manuscripts, London

National Union Catalog (US), Library of Congress, Washington: printed vols to 1982; on microfiche from 1983; see also *Library of Congress Online Catalog*

The New Grove Dictionary of Music and Musicians, eds. Stanley Sadie, first published 1980; 2nd edn, ed. Stanley Sadie and John Tyrrell, 29 vols, Macmillan, London, 2001; also online (by subscription)

A New History of Jazz, by Alyn Shipton, Continuum, London, 2002

The New Walford: Guide to Reference Resources, 3 vols and probably companion website, Facet Publishing, London, forthcoming (see below under *Walford's Guide to Reference Material*)

The Newspaper Press in Britain: An Annotated Bibliography, eds David Linton and Ray Boston, Mansell, London, 1987

Nielsen Bookdata, online bibliographic service for the book trade, marketed by VNU Entertainment Media UK, London

Notes & Queries, published since 1849 by Oxford University Press, Oxford, with various index vols and cumulated indexes; now quarterly

Oral History, by Ken Howarth, Sutton Publishing, Thrupp, Glos., 1999

Oral History, journal of the Oral History Society, 1969– (two issues per year)

Oral History: An Annotated Bibliography 1945–1989, compiled by Robert Perks, British Library National Sound Archive, London, 1990

Oral History: Talking about the Past, by Robert Perks, Historical Association, London, 2nd edn, 1995

Oral Traditions and the Verbal Arts: A Guide to Research Practices, by Ruth Finnegan, Routledge, London, 1992

Palmer's Index to The Times, 1790–1941 (out of print); 1790–1905, on CD-ROM and online, Chadwyck-Healey, Cambridge

Pears Cyclopedia, published annually by Penguin Books, Harmondsworth

Periodicals Contents Index, 1770–1995, online from Chadwyck-Healey, Cambridge

Poole's Index to Periodical Literature, 1802–1906, Boston, Mass., reprinted 1938, 1969; *Cumulative Author Index*, Pierian Press, Ann Arbor, Michigan, 1971

The Popular Magazine in Britain and the United States of America 1880–1960, by David Reed, British Library, London, 1997

Popular Song Index, by Patricia P. Havlice, Scarecrow Press, Lanham, Maryland, 1975; supplements, 1978, 1984, 1989

PROCAT [Public Record Office Online Catalogue], searchable at www.pro.gov.uk/catalogues

ProQuest 5000™, Chadwyck-Healey, Cambridge, online (by subscription)

Radio Times, weekly, BBC Worldwide Publishing, London; microform edition, 1923–94, Chadwyck-Healey, Cambridge

Reader's Guide to Periodical Literature, published since 1900 by H.W. Wilson, New York; now monthly, also as *Reader's Guide, Full Text, Mega Edition* updated four times a week on WilsonWeb and monthly on WilsonDisc, and *Select Edition*, updated monthly

Record Repositories in Great Britain, Royal Commission on Historical Manuscripts/PRO Publications, London; regularly revised (latest, 11th edn, 1999); updated online at www.hmc.gov.uk/archon

Reference Sources Handbook, eds. P.W. Lea and A. Day, Library Association, London, 4th edn, 1996 (formerly published under the title *Printed Reference Material and Related Information Sources*)

Research and the Manuscript Tradition, by Frank G. Burke, co-published by Scarecrow Press, Lanham, Maryland, and the Society of American Archivists, 1997

A Rugby Compendium: An Authoritative Guide to the Literature of Rugby Union, compiled by John M. Jenkins, British Library, London, 1998

Serials in the British Library, quarterly, British Library National Bibliographic Service, Boston Spa; *Serials in the British Library 1976–86* (microfiche cumulation), 1988

Sheppard's Book Dealers in Europe, published in alternate years by Richard Joseph Publishers, Farnham

Sheppard's Book Dealers in the British Isles, published annually by Richard Joseph Publishers, Farnham; also on CD-ROM

Skoob Directory of Secondhand Bookshops in the British Isles, Skoob, London, 7th edn, 2000

Social Sciences Index, published since 1974 by H.W. Wilson, New York; updated monthly on WilsonWeb and WilsonDisc; also as *Social Sciences Full Text*, updated 4 times a week on WilsonWeb, monthly on WilsonDisc

Song Catalogue, in *BBC Music Library Catalogue of Holdings*, 4 vols, BBC, London, 1966

Song Index, by M.E. Sears and P. Crawford, H.W. Wilson, New York, 1926; supplement, 1934

Strand Magazine: Index 1891–1950, by Geraldine Beare, Greenwood, Westport, Conn., USA/London, 1982

Subject Guide to Books in Print [US], published annually since 1957 by Bowker, New Providence, N.J., USA; 2002–03 edn, 6 vols

Subject Index to Periodicals, published annually 1915–53, then quarterly with annual cumulations, 1954–61; now the *British Humanities Index*, q.v.

Subjects of Dissertations, Theses and Published Work presented by Successful Candidates at Examinations for Higher Degrees, covering the period 1937–51, University of London Library, London

Surveys of Historical Manuscripts in the United Kingdom: A Select Bibliography, Royal Commission on Historical Manuscripts, London, updated regularly online at www.hmc.gov.uk

300 Years of Fleet Street 1702–2002, by Dennis Griffiths, London Press Club (St Bride's Institute, 14 Bride Lane, Fleet Street, London EC4 8QE), 2002

The Times, London; microfilm edition from 1785, Primary Source Microfilm (The Gale Group), Reading; current subscriptions updated twice-monthly; CD-ROM edn from 1990, Chadwyck-Healey, Cambridge; online at www.thetimes.co.uk

The Times Index, 1785 to present day, currently by subscription, updated monthly, with annual hardback cumulation; 1906–76, on microfilm; on CD-ROM (as part of *British Newspaper Index*) from 1990: all from Primary Source Microfilm (The Gale Group), Reading. Also *Palmer's Index to The Times*, q.v.

The Twentieth-Century Newspaper Press in Britain: An Annotated Bibliography, compiled by David Linton, Mansell, London, 1994

UK and Irish Book Publishers Directory, published annually by the Booksellers Association of the UK and Ireland, London

UKOP, Chadwyck-Healey, Cambridge, CD-ROM and online, updated daily; combines official catalogue of The Stationery Office and *Catalogue of Official Publications Not Published by The Stationery Office*

Ulrich's Periodicals Directory, published annually in 5 vols, by Bowker, New Providence, N.J., US; also on CD-ROM as *Ulrich's on Disc* (annual subscription with quarterly updates), and online as Ulrichsweb.com (by subscription)

Understanding the European Union, by John McCormick, Palgrave Macmillan, Basingstoke, 2nd edn, 2002

UNIBIS Plus, documents and publications of the United Nations Bibliographic Information System, on CD-ROM quarterly (one retrospective disk to 1992), Chadwyck-Healey, Cambridge

The Voice of the Past, by Paul Thompson, Oxford University Press, Oxford, 2nd edn, 1988; reprinted 1989

Walford's Guide to Reference Material, 3 vols: 1, *Science and Technology*, eds. M. Mullay and P. Schlicke, 8th edn, 1999; 2, *Social and Historical Sciences, Philosophy and Religion*, eds. A. Day and M.J. Walsh, 8th edn, 2000; 3, *Generalia, Language and Literature, The Arts*, eds. A. Chalcraft, R. Prytherch and S. Willis, 7th edn, 1998 (*N.B.* This standard work is being thoroughly revised and expanded; from 2004 it will be published as *The New Walford: Guide to Reference Resources*, also in 3 vols, probably with a companion website: vol 1, *Science, Medicine and Technology*, general ed. Ray Lester, is scheduled for 2004. *The Concise Guide to Reference Material*, 2nd edn, 1992, is out of print and no new edition is planned)

Wellesley Index to Victorian Periodicals, 1824–1900, ed. W.E. Houghton, 3 vols, University of Toronto Press/Routledge, London, 1966–79

Whitaker's Almanack, now published annually by A&C Black, London

Whitaker's bibliographic services (chiefly for the book trade and libraries but also available by individual subscription): includes *BookBank, BookBank Global, BookBank OPLibWeb, PubWeb* and *WhitakerWeb*)

Whitaker's Books in Print, published annually (5 vols) by Whitaker, London; on microfiche, updated monthly, also on CD-ROM/DVD and online (by subscription)

Whitaker's Cumulative Book List 1924–83 (re-titled *Whitaker's Book List* in 1984), Whitaker, London; now discontinued

Whitaker's Directory of Publishers (*The Red Book*), published annually by Whitaker, London

Willing's Press Guide (first published in 1871 as *Frederick May's London Press Directory*), now annually, 2 vols, by Waymaker Ltd., Chesham, Bucks; online at www.willingspressguide.com (subscription required – the UK and international volumes may be purchased separately)

Wisden Cricketers' Almanack, published annually since 1864 by John Wisden & Co. Ltd., Alton, Hants

Women's Magazines 1693–1968, by Cynthia L. White, Michael Joseph, London, 1970

Women's Magazines: The First Three Hundred Years, by Brian Braithwaite, Peter Owen, London, 1995

World Bibliographical Series, Clio Press, Oxford, various dates

World Bibliography of Bibliographies, compiled by T. Besterman, 4th edn, 4 vols with index, Societas Bibliographica, Lausanne, 1965, 1966; *Supplement 1964–1974*, ed. Alice Toomey, 2 vols, Bowker, New York, 1977

World Guide to Libraries, K.G. Saur, Munich, 16th edn, 2 vols, 2001; also available as *World Guide to Libraries PLUS*, on CD-ROM, updated annually, and online (by subscription)

World Guide to Special Libraries, K.G. Saur, Munich, 5th edn, 2 vols, 2001

The World of Learning, published annually by Europa Publications, London

Note: Aslib titles are now published by Europa Publications (Taylor & Francis Group), London. Facet Publishing took over Library Association Publishing in April 2002. Chadwyck-Healey and UMI are part of ProQuest Information and Learning Ltd. Research Publications of Reading, later Primary Source Media and now Primary Source Microfilm, are part of Thomson Learning/The Gale Group. Scarecrow Press of Maryland, USA, is now part of Rowman & Littlefield, Oxford. H.W. Wilson titles are distributed in the UK by Thompson Henry Ltd., London Road, Sunningdale, Berks SL5 0EP (tel. 01344 624615; fax 01344 626120; email th@thompsonhenry.co.uk).

Chapter Five

Factual and Historical Research

THE MORE RESEARCH you undertake, the more you learn about sources. If you keep a careful note of every *reliable* source used, either on computer or manually (I find a card index filed under subjects is the best for quick reference), you can build up for yourself a unique and valuable research tool, one that will save you hours of searching whenever a similar problem crops up in your work. It will prove its worth time and time again.

So much is in print these days that there can be scarcely any subject from, say, animated cartoons to Zimbabwe, on which you are not going to find some 'standard' work or encyclopedia; nor any trade, profession, ethnic or religious group for which there is no recognised association, no biographical dictionary or 'Who's Who' – all essential sources for the researcher. And if it is instant up-to-date information you require, you can – provided you have access to the World Wide Web – find a good deal of what you need by simply typing in a keyword and, where appropriate, by clicking on the links provided until you reach your desired subject-matter.

Obviously it is impossible in one short chapter to deal exhaustively with specific sources. Some starting points only, therefore, are suggested here, under the two headings 'Factual' and 'Historical' research, and I combine these with a warning of some of the pitfalls that lie in the path of the unwary.

In all research you have to begin by consulting first one authoritative source, which leads you to the next, and that in turn to another, and so on, until you have satisfied yourself that you have found out all that you need to know. Patience and persistence are the essential qualities. Be aware that a negative result in research may have value.

FACTUAL RESEARCH

The major difficulty here has always been that topical facts and figures are usually out of date by the time they are published. The same applies to all writing on modern society, for nothing stands still in the world, which is developing and changing with every day that passes. To some extent, from the researcher's viewpoint, online cataloguing and access to the Internet has made it easier to get at more up-to-date information than was previously the case. Even so, websites are not always kept as up-to-date as they should be.

For factual information on the UK online, go to the Central Office of Information website www.coi.gov.uk or take out a subscription to *KnowUK* (www.knowuk.co.uk).

A book, once it has gone to the typesetter, may be only lightly corrected at proof stage. That said, if you are expecting some vital new facts or statistics to be released between delivery of your typescript and the day it actually goes to press, you should indicate to your editor at the outset that you may wish to update specific points at the very last moment – either in the body of the book, or (which may be easier) by way of an explanatory footnote. If the editor is willing, then you will have the opportunity of accessing the relevant database or telephoning the source from which your original information came and asking for the most recent facts and figures. All such updatings to your text must be kept to the absolute minimum, however, as anything above an agreed percentage is normally chargeable to the author and will eat into your royalties.

Another problem is that the bases used for the calculation of statistics vary from one subject to another, and from one organisation to another, so that comparison can be, at worst, highly dangerous, and at best, misleading; often, also, you may find it impossible to obtain the precise breakdown you seek. Without expert help and knowledge it is unwise to juggle with statistics: where these do not exactly fit the context, the best solution is to quote them as they are presented and to add a footnote to this effect.

Sources of factual information

The majority of professional researchers and journalists today use computers, have purchased the necessary software, and subscribe to one or more databases relevant to their particular field of writing, which they can access twenty-four hours a day. However, not all writers or researchers are able or wish to work online. In any case, much factual research must still be done from printed sources and by personal contact with experts in the field. Ideally, a combination of both procedures yields the best results.

So far as printed sources are concerned, encyclopedias and yearbooks are an excellent starting point, especially the latter if you subscribe and can access the latest updates online. You can find out what yearbooks exist on a given subject by consulting *Current British Directories* or *Current European Directories*, both of which have detailed subject indexes, or *Ulrich's Periodicals Directory* (which includes the former *Irregular Serials and Annuals*). Other publications most useful to the English writer for quick reference are *Whitaker's Almanack*, *The Statesman's Yearbook*, *Pears Cyclopedia*, *The Annual Register of World Events*, *The Europa World Year Book* and *UK* (formerly *Britain: An Official Handbook*).

The Times newspaper, first published in 1785, is the best source for past and recent events; its *Index* is now published monthly, with annual cumulations. From 1990 there is the *British Newspaper Index* on CD-ROM (see page 63). *Keesing's Record of World Events*, which started in July 1931 as a weekly publication, *Keesing's Contemporary Archives*, is now published eleven times a year (July/August being a double issue); it has an excellent reputation, and most reference libraries subscribe to it (for details look at the website www.keesings.com). You can also rely on its US equivalent, *The Facts on File Weekly World News Digest*.

So far as UK statistics are concerned, the Office for National Statistics (ONS) issues a *Monthly Digest of Statistics* and an *Annual Abstract of Statistics*. There is a great deal more information available, both in printed and in electronic form, and researchers are recommended to contact the National Statistics Information and Library Service, ONS, 1 Drummond Gate, London SW1V 2QQ (tel. 020 7533 5888; email info@statistics.gov.uk; website www.statistics.gov.uk). The historical aspect is well covered by *British Historical Statistics* and by *European Historical Statistics 1750–1975*. The statistical masterfiles of the Congressional Information Service of the United States are held on CD-ROM at the British Library, in the Science reading room (Social Policy Information Service).

On facts in general, the most up-to-date compilation at the time of writing (early 2003) is the new edition of *Chambers Book of Facts* (2002). *The Guinness Book of Records*, first published in 1955 and now re-titled *Guinness World Records*, is a classic, and both *The New Shell Book of Firsts* and the *Penguin Book of Firsts* are crammed with useful information, although not recently brought up-to-date. No one writing about Britain should be without a copy of Bamber Gascoigne's *Encyclopedia of Britain*. A very recent and much acclaimed compendium of general knowledge is *The Daily Telegraph A to Z of* ^{almost} *Everything*.

At the British Library, St Pancras, London, there are three specialist information services which you may use if you have a reader's pass: the Business Information Service (BIS); the Science, Technology and Innovation Information Service; and the Social Policy Information Service (for addresses and telephone numbers, see Appendix I, pages 200–17). Basic enquiries are dealt with free of charge, and a priced, in-depth research service is available on demand. If you want to do your own factual research the British Library *How to Find* and *Key Resource* series of guides, on a wide range of subjects, are on the open shelves and will set you on the right road.

The Information Bureau (51 The Business Centre, 103 Lavender Hill, London SW11 5QL; tel. 020 7924 4414; fax 020 7924 4456; email info@informationbureau.co.uk), formerly the *Daily Telegraph* Information Bureau, offers a general research and information service on a subscription or *ad hoc* basis, using printed and online resources, a vast press cuttings collection, and business and media contacts built up over many years. For non-account subscribers requiring quick checking of dates, facts and figures, or names to contact in associations, there is a minimum charge (valid spring 2003) of £10 + VAT (hourly rate £80 + VAT).

The use of bibliographies, concordances, books of quotations and other basic reference tools has been discussed in the previous chapter. If you are keen on tracking down factual information, you should be able to get at what you need without any problem. Occasionally, however, professional help may be necessary, especially when time is an important factor or where the subject is unfamiliar.

Getting hold of experts

You may sometimes find yourself at a loss as to how to contact experts when there is no one in your immediate circle who can help. Here the best advice to be given is, 'Do not be shy. Go straight to the horse's mouth' – in other words, look up the professional or trade association concerned (or it may be an international company, a bank, or almost any other kind of group), and either write to or telephone the general secretary, press or public relations officer. Remember that all these people have a vested interest in being portrayed correctly, and also that the expert is always flattered to be consulted. If the person you approach is too busy or unable for some other reason to give you what you want, he will usually be able to put you in touch with someone else.

The best way to find out if there is a relevant association is to look in an up-to-date *Ask Hollis* (a directory of UK associations), the *Directory of British Associations* or the equivalent volumes for Europe, the *Directory of European Industrial & Trade Associations* and the *Directory of European Professional & Learned Societies*. Another very useful source is the *Hollis Press & Public Relations Annual*, which lists an enormous number of press contacts (with addresses and telephone numbers) in virtually every field of professional, industrial and commercial life, as well as official and public information sources, PR consultancies and much other invaluable data. The same firm now publishes a similar directory for Europe, *Hollis Europe*. There is also a list of societies and institutions in *Whitaker's Almanack*, but this is not so informative, nor is it as comprehensive as the two publications mentioned above. The researcher concerned with making contacts in the arts or the media will find *The Media Guide* indispensable. Information and press officers in government departments are listed in the *IPO Directory* published by the Central Office of Information. Lastly, do not overlook your local 'yellow pages' directory: there may be some contact on your own doorstep. You can obtain much information on the website www.yell.com.

BT's 'directory enquiries' has recently changed its numbers to 118 500 for UK enquiries and 118 505 for international enquiries. You can make up to ten enquiries per day free online at www.bt.com/directory enquiries.

The *NUJ Online Freelance Directory* is a comprehensive listing of freelance journalists in Britain and Ireland (and some overseas), listed alphabetically, geographically and by subject speciality. It is available at modest cost to non-members and has a useful role to play in the finding of local and specialist contacts.

HISTORICAL RESEARCH

History itself does not change, but the interpretation of history changes constantly. Modern research – most particularly archaeological excavation, backed up by the techniques of carbon-dating and the studies of genetic scientists working on DNA – quite frequently overturns previously held theories, shedding a new light on events and on the lives of ordinary people of past centuries. Old documents and other records turn up in the most unlikely places and necessitate drastic revision of hitherto authoritative works. Thus there will always be a demand for writing that offers a new slant – a reappraisal of events and of people – based on the latest findings. This applies as much to prehistory, and to the history of, say, the 'Dark Ages' as to that of the early 21st century. The writer of history today carries an enormous responsibility to his readers to keep abreast of current research.

When you go to the reference library to look up an historical fact, you will find that the titles are usually grouped in the following manner: history generally, then world history, British history, European history, and (if the collection is large enough) history country by country. In the general section there are all the great standard works published by the Cambridge and Oxford university presses, cheek by jowl with less weightier, more modern volumes. It is advisable to go first to the modern works, to get the benefit of recent research; the 'standard histories' are updated but, being rather learned tomes, not very frequently. Use them for corroborative, in-depth research.

So far as official papers are concerned, in the United Kingdom these are now released for public examination after thirty years. (There are exceptions to this rule in the case of 'sensitive' documents, which may be kept back for up to one hundred years. But this rule is itself occasionally relaxed, as it was early in 2003, when some of the 1936 Abdication papers were made available.)

Every January the Public Record Office braces itself for an onslaught of historians, journalists and researchers who descend sleuth-like upon Kew from all over the world, intent on scrutinising every memo or minute or other scrap of paper emanating from the Cabinet Office, the Foreign and Commonwealth Office and the various ministerial departments. Nearly every year something is pounced upon that makes a headline in the national press. But the bulk of the raw material gathered filters only very gradually into print.

One of the best ways of keeping up-to-date with the latest research is to read the journals and other publications of the major historical societies. If you have time, join one and attend its lectures and conferences. A subscription to the Historical Association's *The Historian* includes membership of a local branch. Go to the Association's website at www.history.org.uk or contact the Secretary at 59a Kennington Park Road, London SE11 4JH (tel. 020 7735 3901; fax 020 7582 4989) and ask for details, including a catalogue of the Association's current publications. You should also look at the *Transactions* and other serial publications of the Royal Historical Society (RHS). The *Writings on British History* series, now renamed the

Annual Bibliography of British and Irish History, is a useful tool, as is the *Studies in History* series. The RHS also publishes a number of handbooks and guides for students and scholars (details on the website www.rhs.ac.uk).

If you are a graduate and undertaking a serious research project you should consider joining the Institute of Historical Research (IHR), which is part of the University of London's School of Advanced Study; or you can become a Friend. The IHR is a great meeting place for historical scholars, and members have the use of a common room and open-access library in Bloomsbury. Among the Institute's many prestigious publications is a quarterly journal, *Historical Research* (formerly the *Bulletin of the Institute of Historical Research*), and more recently an e-journal, *Reviews in History*. (See chapter 4, 'Basic Sources of Information and their Location', page 76, for details of lists of historical theses, and chapter 8, 'Family and Local History', page 159, for the *Victoria County History* series.) There is also *Microforms for Historians: A Finding List of Research Collections in London Academic Libraries*, by D.J. Munro, a most useful tool for researchers.

The IHR maintains a database, *History Online*, which contains over 40,000 records, evaluated links to websites and much other high-quality information relating to historical resources, including details of books and articles published by leading academic history publishers in the UK. You do not have to be a member to browse or search this database on www.ihr.sas.ac.uk/search.

It is impossible in one short chapter to do more than touch on a few of the problems that confront the novice setting out to find historical information. There is one point I should like to stress: in the present climate of obsession with electronic access to information, researchers should never lose sight of the value of the original document. A database is only as good as the information fed into it and is subject to human error of transcription. The original document must always be the primary source.

You should try to purchase as many as you can afford of the standard works on your chosen subject or historical period, both for research purposes and to keep at your elbow as you write. Add to this collection any new books by established historians, or others that have been favourably reviewed.

So far as general titles are concerned, every historical writer, whether of non-fiction or fiction, should in my view possess – and read – Eric Hobsbawm's *The Age of Revolution 1789–1848*, *The Age of Capital 1848–1875*, *The Age of Empire 1875–1914* and *Age of Extremes: The Short Twentieth Century 1914–1991*. Likewise Martin Gilbert's four-volume *History of the Twentieth Century*. Winston S. Churchill's *A History of the English-Speaking Peoples* remains a classic. There are and will be others. One newcomer is *A History of Britain* by Simon Schama, a three-volume work much acclaimed by readers and television viewers alike.

For quick reference on British history I usually turn first to *The Cambridge Historical Encyclopedia of Great Britain and Ireland*. I also consult Charles Arnold-Baker's *The Companion to British History*, a very readable and reliable, if occasionally idiosyncratic, single-volume encyclopedia crammed with information on the history of this country, and also on a wide range of other subjects. Other recommended compilations are *The Oxford Companion to British History*, the two *History Today* publications, *Companion to British History*, and *Who's Who in British History*.

When I need something more specific, I find both the *English Historical Documents* series, covering the period from c. 500 to 1914, and the Macmillan *Historical Facts* series, 1485–1985, very reliable. David and Gareth Butler's *Twentieth Century British Political Facts 1900–2000* is another excellent source.

Some recent social histories of Europe are mentioned in chapter 6, 'Research for Fiction Writers and Dramatists' (pages 100–22). *International Historical Statistics: Europe 1750–2000* and *European Political Facts of the Twentieth Century* are very up-to-date. There are also new editions in the *International Historical Statistics* series for the Americas and for Africa, Asia, Oceania (see the bibliography at the end of this chapter).

It is good news for the researcher seeking quick verification of dates, or a summary of historical events worldwide from earlier times to the present day, that William L. Langer's classic, *The Encyclopedia of World History*, out of print for so many years, has recently been published in a thoroughly revised and updated sixth edition. Not only is this admirable volume of more than 1,000 pages still arranged geographically as well as chronologically, with the usual lists of rulers and wars, maps and genealogical tables, it is now accompanied by a full text CD-ROM for those who prefer to search or browse on screen. A standard work, well worth buying. Otherwise, for quick reference on world history, I can vouch for the *Chambers Dictionary of World History* (though this does not contain the same amount of detail as the Langer).

Space does not permit here the inclusion of sources for the history of individual countries, but some titles are recommended in chapter 10, 'Information from and about Foreign Countries' (pages 170–88) and in Appendix I. Look also at *Walford's Guide to Reference Material*, volume 2, under 'Ancient', 'Medieval' or 'Modern' history and the area of the world (or country), as appropriate.

Conflicting authorities

One of the main problems that you must be prepared to encounter in historical research is that of conflicting authorities. Inevitably at some stage in your work you will come across two, if not three, or more, different dates or interpretations of the same event. How do you know which one to trust?

Wherever possible, you should yourself go back to the original, contemporary source. Where this is not feasible, you have the choice of either weighing up the theories advanced by the various historians and coming down firmly on one side – and sticking to it – or, if you have the space and the inclination, of giving an account of the conflicting views and your reasons for preferring one to all others.

If this interests you, read the intriguing recently published *Truth or Travesty?: Popular Myths, Errors and Controversies in Modern History*, by Ed Rayner and Ron Stapley. [Note that 'modern history' = from the late 18th century onwards.]

Dates

The different reckonings of dates in historical documents often confuse the beginner. Under the Julian calendar, which was in universal use throughout the Middle Ages and in some countries, such as England and Russia, until as late as the 18th and early 20th centuries respectively, the year began on 25 March. The Gregorian calendar, in which 1 January was reckoned as the beginning of each year, was introduced on the Continent in 1582, when ten days were cut out of that year in order to take care of accumulated errors of reckoning. This new calendar was not adopted in England until 1752, although for some years prior to that date a double indication was normally given in official documents (and in some private papers) for dates falling between 1 January and 24 March, as, for example, '24 February 1655/6'. The trap is that during the period 1582–1752 a traveller could leave, say, Italy, on one date and arrive in England several days earlier, because of the discrepancy in the calendar. From the end of the 16th century most English official correspondence with foreign powers carries either both dates, i.e. '12/22 December 1635', or an indication of the reckoning used, i.e. 'O.S.' (Old Style) or 'N.S.' (New Style).

The practice followed by most modern historians is to take the beginning of the historical year as 1 January. All dates between 1 January and 24 March are thus written as, for example, '22 February 1559' rather than '22 February 1558/9', except in quoted matter, where the date should always be copied faithfully as in the original text and an explanatory 'O.S.' or 'N.S.' added in square brackets if necessary. For a full discussion of this whole question, see C.R. Cheney's revised *Handbook of Dates for Students of English History*. This useful book contains, among other information, tables of regnal years, Easter days and calendars for all possible dates of Easter from AD 500 to the year 2100, which will enable you to avoid the most common errors of dating in historical work. Another standard reference work on the subject is the *Handbook of British Chronology. Whitaker's Almanack* contains a 'Calendar for Any Year' from 1770 to 2030. For the 20th and 21st centuries only, you can check dates on the website www.vpcalendar.net.

Dates in private papers sometimes cause the researcher a headache. Letter-writers not infrequently give an incomplete date or omit it altogether; and another trap to watch out for is that at the new year, people through the ages have tended to forget – writing, for example, '5 January 1888' when they meant '5 January 1889'. Where neither contents nor letterheading provide the answer, and the date does not become clear as research progresses, you will have to choose between doing without that particular document and hazarding an intelligent guess – in which case you should make it clear that the original is undated. The Society of Genealogists has published a useful booklet on dating systems of the past, to aid family historians in the interpretation of references: *Dates and calendars for the genealogist*. It will be of use to all who do historical research, as will Lionel Munby's *Dates and Time: A Handbook for Local Historians*. Remember that in the United States it is customary to write the date and month in reverse order to UK practice, i.e. '12/3' for 3 December, whereas we would write '3/12'.

The use of periodicals in historical research

Periodicals of interest to the historical researcher include *Historical Research*, mentioned earlier in this chapter; the Historical Association's quarterly magazine *The Historian*; *History Today*, and the more recent *BBC History Magazine*. *English Historical Review* is published five times a year. Check them all – not forgetting back issues – for articles on your subject. Women's magazines and newspapers are an excellent source for fashion, prices and entertainments at a particular date, while *The Tatler* and *Illustrated London News* contain useful background information on the social scene. Cartoons, from the national press, *Punch* and other sources, may also be of value to the researcher. Advertisements often yield as much information as textual material.

Finally, for all those who use historical documents in their work, there is a splendid guide: *Editing Historical Records* by P.D.A. Harvey, published by the British Library.

The Age of Revolution 1789–1848, *The Age of Capital 1848–1875*, *The Age of Empire 1875–1914*, by Eric Hobsbawm, Cardinal Books, 1988–89; *Age of Extremes: The Short Twentieth Century 1914–1991*, by the same author, Michael Joseph, London, 1994, reprinted 1995; also in paperback editions, Abacus (Time Warner UK)

Annual Abstract of Statistics, Office for National Statistics, published by The Stationery Office (formerly HMSO), London

Annual Bibliography of British and Irish History (previously *Writings on British History*), now published by Oxford University Press for the Royal Historical Society (earlier vols covering years 1946–74 by the Institute of Historical Research)

The Annual Register of World Events, first published 1758; now by Keesings Worldwide, Washington D.C. (UK office: 28a Hills Road, Cambridge CB2 1LA; tel. 01223 508050)

Ask Hollis, published annually by Hollis Publishing, Teddington, Middx

BBC History Magazine, published monthly by BBC Worldwide Publishing, London, 2000–

British Historical Statistics, by B.R. Mitchell, Cambridge University Press, Cambridge, 1988

British Newspaper Index (15 British newspapers including *The Times* from 1990), on CD-ROM, Primary Source Microfilm (The Gale Group), Reading, updated quarterly

The Cambridge Historical Encyclopedia of Great Britain and Ireland, ed. Christopher

Haigh, Cambridge University Press, Cambridge, 1985; paperback edn, 1990
Chambers Book of Facts, Chambers Harrap, Edinburgh, new edn, 2002
Chambers Dictionary of World History, Chambers Harrap, Edinburgh, 2000
The Companion to British History, by Charles Arnold-Baker, Longcross Press, Tunbridge Wells, 1996
Current British Directories, published by CBD Research, Beckenham, 14th edn, 2003
Current European Directories, published by CBD Research, Beckenham, 3rd edn, 1994
The Daily Telegraph A to Z of ^almost *Everything*, ed. Trevor Montague, Little, Brown, London 2001, reprinted 2002; new edn due August 2003
Dates and calendars for the genealogist, by Clifford Webb, Society of Genealogists, London, 1998
Dates and Time: A Handbook for Local Historians, by Lionel Munby, Phillimore, Chichester, 1997
Directory of British Associations, published by CBD Research, Beckenham, 16th edn, 2002; also on CD-ROM
Directory of European Industrial & Trade Associations, published by CBD Research, Beckenham, 6th edn, 1997
Directory of European Professional & Learned Societies, published by CBD Research, Beckenham, 5th edn, 1995
Editing Historical Records, by P.D.A. Harvey, British Library, London, 2000
Encyclopedia of Britain: The A–Z of Britain's Past and Present, by Bamber Gascoigne, rev. edn, Macmillan, London, 1994
The Encyclopedia of World History, ed. William L. Langer, rev. edn ed. Peter N. Stearns, Lutterworth Press, Cambridge, 6th edn, 2002
English Historical Documents, ed. D.C. Douglas, 12 vols, Eyre & Spottiswoode, London, 1953–75
English Historical Review, first published 1886, now by Oxford University Press, five times a year, also online (full text)
The Europa World Year Book, 2 vols, published annually by Europa Publications, London; online as *Europa World* from summer 2003 (by subscription)
European Historical Statistics 1750–1975, ed. B.R. Mitchell, Macmillan, London, 2nd rev. edn, 1981
European Political Facts of the Twentieth Century, eds Chris Cook and John Paxton, Palgrave Macmillan, Basingstoke, 5th edn, 2000
The Facts on File Weekly World News Digest, published by Facts on File, New York
Guinness World Records (formerly *The Guinness Book of Records*), now published by Gullane Publishing, London; latest edn (ed. Claire Folkard) 2002; paperback, Bantam Books, London, 2003
Handbook of British Chronology, Royal Historical Society, London, first published 1939; 3rd edn, eds. E.B. Fryde *et al*, 1986
Handbook of Dates for Students of English History, by C.R. Cheney, 1st edn, 1945; 2nd edn, eds. C.R. Cheney and Michael Jones, Cambridge University Press, 2000

The Historian, quarterly magazine of the Historical Association, London

Historical Facts series, published by Macmillan, London: 6 vols covering the period 1485–1985 (first 2 vols entitled *English Historical Facts*, subsequent vols *British Historical Facts*), 1975–88

Historical Research (formerly the *Bulletin of the Institute of Historical Research*), first published in 1923, now quarterly by Blackwell, Oxford, for the IHR

A History of Britain, by Simon Schama, BBC Worldwide Publications, London, 3 vols, 2002; also on video and DVD

A History of the English-Speaking Peoples, by W.S. Churchill, 4 vols, Cassell, London, first published 1956–58; various reprints; one-volume abridgement, Cassell, London, 1998

History Online, database maintained by the Institute of Historical Research, London, on www.ihr.sas.ac.uk/search

History of the Twentieth Century, by Martin Gilbert, 4 vols, HarperCollins, London, 1997-2001

History Today, published monthly since 1951, London

History Today Companion to British History, eds. Juliet Gardiner and Neil Wenborn, Collins & Brown, London, 1995

History Today Who's Who in British History, ed. Juliet Gardiner, Collins & Brown, London, 2000; paperback, 2002

Hollis Press & Public Relations Annual, published by Hollis Publishing, Teddington, Middx; also *Hollis Europe*, annually

How to Find series, British Library, London

Illustrated London News, weekly from May 1842; now 2 issues per year (summer and Christmas, plus occasional issues on special events), London

International Historical Statistics: Africa, Asia, Oceania 1750–2000, ed. Brian Mitchell, Palgrave Macmillan, Basingstoke, 4th edn, 2003

International Historical Statistics: Americas 1750–2000, ed. Brian Mitchell, Palgrave Macmillan, Basingstoke, 5th edn, 2003

International Historical Statistics Europe 1750–2000, ed. Brian Mitchell, Palgrave Macmillan, Basingstoke, 5th edn, 2003

IPO (Information and Press Officers) Directory, published bi-annually by the Central Office of Information, London

Keesing's Record of World Events (formerly *Keesing's Contemporary Archives*), published since 1931; now 11 issues per year, published by Keesings Worldwide, Washington D.C. (UK office: 28A Hills Road, Cambridge CB2 1LA; tel. 01223 508050; website www.keesings.com). Also available on CD-ROM back to 1960

Key Resource series, British Library, London

The Media Guide, eds. Steve Peak and Paul Fisher, published annually by Fourth Estate, London, (a *Guardian Book*)

Microforms for Historians: A Finding List of Research Collections in London Academic Libraries, by D.J. Munro, Institute of Historical Research, London, 2nd edn, 1994

Monthly Digest of Statistics, Office for National Statistics, The Stationery Office (formerly HMSO), London

The New Shell Book of Firsts, ed. Patrick Robertson, Headline, London, 1995 (formerly entitled *Shell Book of Firsts*, 2nd rev. edn, Michael Joseph, London, 1984)

NUJ Online Freelance Directory, National Union of Journalists, London, updated regularly

The Oxford Companion to British History, ed. John Cannon, Oxford University Press, Oxford, rev. edn, paperback, 2002

Pears Cyclopedia, published annually by Penguin Books, Harmondsworth

Penguin Book of Firsts, ed. Matthew Richardson, Penguin Books, London, 1998

Punch, published weekly 1841–1992, London; relaunched 1996, fortnightly since October 1997 [ceased publication summer 2002]

Reviews in History [e-journal], Institute of Historical Research, London, 1996–

Royal Historical Society Transactions, published annually, now by Cambridge University Press, Cambridge, for the RHS

The Statesman's Yearbook, published annually by Macmillan, London, 140th edn, 2003

Studies in History series, published by Boydell & Brewer, Woodbridge, for the Royal Historical Society, London

The Tatler, first published in 1709, now monthly, London

The Times, London; microfilm edition from 1785, Primary Source Microfilm (The Gale Group), Reading; current subscriptions updated twice-monthly; CD-ROM from 1990, Chadwyck-Healey, Cambridge; online at www.thetimes.co.uk

The Times Index, 1785 to present day, currently by subscription, updated monthly, with annual hardback cumulation; 1906–76, on microfilm; on CD-ROM (as part of *British Newspaper Index*) from 1990: all from Primary Source Microfilm (The Gale Group), Reading. Also *Palmer's Index to The Times*, 1790–1905, on CD-ROM and online, Chadwyck-Healey, Cambridge

Truth or Travesty?: Popular Myths, Errors and Controversies in Modern History, by Ed Rayner and Ron Stapley, Sutton (Haynes Publishing), Thrupp, Stroud, 2002

Twentieth Century British Political Facts 1900–2000, eds. David Butler and Gareth Butler, 8th edn, Palgrave Macmillan, Basingstoke, 2000

UK (formerly *Britain: An Official Handbook*), published annually (January) by The Stationery Office, Norwich

Ulrich's Periodicals Directory, published annually in 5 vols by Bowker, New Providence, N.J., also on CD-ROM as *Ulrich's on Disc* (annual subscription with quarterly updates), and online, updated weekly, at Ulrichsweb.com (also by subscription)

Walford's Guide to Reference Material, vol. 2, *Social and Historical Sciences, Philosophy and Religion*, Library Association, London, 8th edn, 2000 (see chapter 4, page 55 for details of the *New Walford*, due in 2004)

Whitaker's Almanack, published annually by A & C Black, London

Writings on British History, now *Annual Bibliography of British and Irish History*, q.v.

Chapter Six

Research for Fiction Writers and Dramatists

T HE DEPTH OF research to be undertaken by the writer of fiction will depend upon his choice for the story's setting and his own knowledge of that setting, and upon his acquaintance with the kind of people he is writing about. Basically, the research will be concerned with the creation of an authentic background to the plot and with writing dialogue in the correct idiom. As the problems which face the writer of modern fiction and drama differ from those of the writer of historical fiction and drama, they are here examined separately. All that is said about the novel applies equally to the short story and to drama.

THE MODERN NOVEL

Background

There is no substitute for a personal visit to every place in which your story, or scene of a story, is to be set. Only through first-hand experience will you absorb the atmosphere of a place, find out exactly how long it will take your character to get from A to B and what buildings or other landmarks he will pass on the way; by using your eyes and ears and nose, by travelling on the local bus, and by spending a few evenings at the pub, you can learn pretty well everything you need to know about the way the locals live, behave and talk. Make a point of attending at least once, each kind of event that is going to crop up in your story or play – whether it is a boxing match, a race meeting, a sale at Sotheby's, a ballet performance, a court hearing, or anything else.

Inevitably, sometimes, a personal visit is out of the question, and then you have no choice but to rely on secondary sources. If this is the case, equip yourself with a good, large-scale map or two – preferably a street map of each town in which the action of your story is to take place, as well as a map of the whole district. You can obtain much free information of this nature from town halls or tourist offices. If you buy one of the 'interactive' maps in electronic format, you will be able to zoom in on any district you wish and in some cases bring an aerial view up on screen. Travel brochures are always a helpful source, and there are any number of excellent general topographical guides to various regions of the United Kingdom. The *Blue Guides: England* and *London* (separate volumes) are detailed and up-to-date. Arthur Mee's *The King's England* series, originally published in the 1930s, is now available in a facsimile edition. Look also at the publications of the motoring organisations. (How to obtain information on places abroad is dealt with in chapter 10, 'Information from and about Foreign Countries', pages 170–88). The researcher wishing to find out more about the origin and meaning of place-names will find Adrian Room's *Placenames of the World* a useful source. Insofar as English place-names are concerned, both A.D. Mills' *A Dictionary of English Place-Names* and Kenneth Cameron's *English Place-Names* are recommended. For in-depth study consult the volumes (by county) published by the English Place-Name Society.

If you need to describe particular buildings you will find Nikolaus Pevsner's *Buildings of England* series, also one per county, enormously helpful. In addition, all stately homes and castles open to the public produce their own guidebooks, some more comprehensive and informative than others. The AA's *Historic Houses in Britain* has sadly gone out of print, but should be in the libraries. The *Historic Houses & Gardens, Castles & Heritage Sites* publication, and the annual handbooks available to members of English Heritage and the National Trust, all carry brief details of relevant properties. The curators of these historic houses are well informed, but may be too busy to talk to you on days when the public is admitted; a telephone call or preliminary letter beforehand may lead to a special appointment and personally guided tour, with much additional information. Look out for the forthcoming British Records Association publication, *Sources for the History of Houses*.

Other essential reference tools are railway and bus timetables of the area you are describing and, if appropriate, an air timetable: these should save you from making an elementary mistake such as putting a character on a train or plane at the wrong rail or air terminus or misjudging the time taken for a particular journey. A writer setting his tale on board a cruise ship or private yacht will find the *World Cruising Handbook* a mine of information on harbour regulations, ports of call, and much else.

If you are really worried about getting the timing of a journey right, you might consider investing in one of the new pocket-size (battery-operated and relatively inexpensive) digital map distance finders. All you need to do is key in the scale of the map you are using (street map, road map or atlas) plus the estimated travelling speed (on foot, on horseback, by stagecoach, bus, car, taxi, etc.), then trace the desired route on the map. This clever little gadget will then calculate and display both the mileage and the travelling time between start and finish of the journey. Amazing!

Bear in mind that no map or street map can provide essential information such as whether your character would be walking up or down hill, a steep or gentle slope, or if there are steps along the route; nor on the exact surface, i.e. macadamed or cobbled. There is no real substitute for 'on-the-spot' research if this is crucial to the story.

An excellent way to get the 'feel' of a place, when it is not possible for you to visit it, is to take out a subscription to the local newspaper and county magazine; you will find lists of these, under towns, in both *Benn's Media* and *Willing's Press Guide* (see chapter 4, 'Basic Sources of Information', page 61).

People

Often the background to a story or play will concern a particular profession or industry, and here too the best method of research is to mix as much as possible with people in the field. The secretary of the relevant professional or trade association (check names and addresses either in the current *Directory of British Associations*, in the *Hollis Press & Public Relations Annual* or in *Whitaker's Almanack* – see chapter 5, 'Factual and Historical Research', page 91) should be helpful if you do not have any personal contacts, and most large corporations or companies have a press and public relations department or member of staff who will assist you. Do not feel diffident about approaching such people; it is rare for a genuine request for information to be refused point blank, and often a researcher may be invited to visit a factory or training establishment or to attend as an observer one or two meetings of the relevant society – all this is grist to the mill. Nevertheless, it is unfair to impinge too much on someone else's time or expertise – even if this is being paid for by his company – and so a luncheon or dinner invitation is a nice gesture. An incredible amount can be learned from an hour's conversation face to face. Much of what has been said about background research also applies to finding out about people, for there is nothing better than to spend time with whatever age, regional or occupational group you wish to bring into your story. Observe at first-hand how people behave, talk and dress. Every writer should try, therefore, to cultivate a wide circle of friends in all walks of life, and the fiction writer especially should try to get to know a psychologist with whom he can discuss the actions and reactions of his characters, as well as a medical practitioner with whom he can verify medical symptoms and treatments. The crime writer ought to be on friendly terms with at least one member of the police force, active or retired, who is willing to put him right on procedures and jargon. And so on.

Careers pamphlets and training manuals for the relevant trade or profession yield a good deal of information. Biographies, memoirs and diaries of eminent people in that trade or profession should be studied, and also the relevant in-house or trade journals, for these will all provide up-to-date material and jargon, and sometimes also historical detail.

So far as the behaviour of your characters is concerned, personal observation may be supplemented by a simple textbook on psychology or behavioural study. Robert Winston's recent *Human Instinct* is very readable – and revealing. Other recommended titles are Desmond Morris's *Bodytalk: A World Guide to Gestures*, Peter Collett's *Foreign Bodies: A Guide to European Mannerisms* and Roger Axtell's *Gestures:*

The Dos and Taboos of Body Language Around the World. A more academic study is the *Dictionary of Worldwide Gestures*.

Useful sources of information on nicknames (both modern and historical) are the *Handbook of Pseudonyms and Personal Nicknames* compiled by H. Sharp, and *A Dictionary of Pseudonyms and Their Origins, with Stories of Name Changes*, by Adrian Room.

On names in general, there are several first-class sources, the best and most up-to-date of which are *The Oxford Names Companion* and Adrian Room's *Brewer's Dictionary of Names*. The latter title has 8,000 entries and a guide to nearly 100 languages, and covers not only the origins of personal and place names, but brand names, literary characters, rock groups, and almost every other category. For recommendations on literary pseudonyms and names of characters in published fiction, see page 114 of this chapter. Some more academic genealogical studies are mentioned in chapter 8, 'Family and Local History', pages 142–64.

Language

It is highly dangerous for the writer who is unfamiliar with a foreign language, local dialect or occupational slang to dabble in these fields, but if he must do so he should always try to get what he has written verified by an expert. So far as English is concerned, your first step should be to consult the British Library National Sound Archive (96 Euston Road, London NW1 2DB; tel. 020 7412 7440; fax 020 7412 7441; email nsa@bl.uk); an appointment will be arranged for you to listen to relevant recordings. (This can be in London or in Yorkshire, see page 74.) Among printed works, Peter Trudgill's *The Dialects of England* is first class. Most good reference libraries stock the four-volume *Survey of English Dialects* by H. Orton and E. Dieth, and the *English Dialect Dictionary* by J. Wright.

There are a number of so-called 'slang dictionaries', and these have their uses. However, since it is necessary first to know the word or expression whose meaning you wish to look up in them, their value is somewhat limited. Happily there is now *The Thesaurus of Slang*, a splendid compilation containing an alphabetical list of 12,000 standard English words for which you can look up some 150,000 slang terms, common idioms and colloquialisms. The late Eric Partridge's *Slang Today and Yesterday*, with its separate sections dealing with slang spoken in chronological periods and in various occupational groups, is still valid historically. Eric Partridge also compiled *A Dictionary of the Underworld, British and American*, an essential reference book for the crime writer (although this too is arranged as a dictionary), as well as the fascinating *A Dictionary of Catch Phrases* (British and American) from the 16th century to the present day. Fully indexed and cross-referenced, *The Oxford Dictionary of Catchphrases* by Anna Farkas looks at some 800 well-known British and US phrases of the 20th century. Also from OUP is *The Oxford Dictionary of Rhyming Slang*, while a brand-new title from Continuum is Robert Barltrop's *Cockney Dictionary*. There is a 'slang appendix' to *The Official Encyclopedia of Scotland Yard*, which could prove useful to the crime writer.

A comparatively recent compilation by the lexicographer Jonathon Green, *The Cassell Dictionary of Slang*, is set to become a standard work. Among Dr Green's earlier volumes, *Newspeak: A Dictionary of Jargon, Slang Down the Ages* and *The Slang Thesaurus* each still has a different use to the researcher. Other recommended titles include Tony Thorne's *Dictionary of Contemporary Slang* and *The Macmillan Dictionary of American Slang* by R.L. Chapman. The classic Anglo-Indian dictionary, *Hobson-Jobson*, an invaluable source first published in 1886, has recently been reprinted. If none of these help, try the website www.dictionaryofslang.co.uk.

There is an entertaining little paperback on French slang, *Rude French: An Alternative French Phrasebook* by Georges Pillard, which could be useful to the writer introducing Gallic characters into a story – especially as it also offers illustrations and explanations for some well-known French gestures.

Quite often a writer is at a loss to know how one of his characters would address another, perhaps someone in an elevated position. Here either *Debrett's Correct Form*, *Debrett's New Guide to Etiquette and Modern Manners* or *Titles and Forms of Address* will provide the answer, supplying as a bonus a guide to practically every situation likely to arise, socially and professionally, including American usage. These books will also be invaluable for the researcher wishing to know how to write or talk to titled or official persons whom he needs to contact for information.

THE HISTORICAL NOVEL

The writer of an historical novel must be thoroughly familiar with the period in which his story is set, and especially knowledgeable about the manners, customs and daily life of the people concerned. He must also be accurate about major events and prominent people. This will not present too much difficulty so long as he keeps at his elbow as he works a general bibliography and authoritative history of the period, as well as a good biographical dictionary (for suggested titles, see chapter 5, 'Factual and Historical Research', pages 88–99 and chapter 7, 'Biography and Autobiography', (pages 127–29). A trap that inexperienced writers sometimes fall into is that of anachronisms, i.e. the mention of, say, ice cream or zip fasteners at a period before these came on the scene. You can avoid such errors by checking in an encyclopedic dictionary or *The New Shell Book of Firsts*. Or you may be lucky enough to find a library near you which stocks the H.W. Wilson *Famous First Facts, International Edition*; this lists over 5,000 'firsts' from ancient times to the present day and has exceptionally useful subject, name, geographical and chronological indexes.

For reasons of space I have had to be ruthlessly selective in considering which titles to recommend in this chapter, in order to introduce the works of some gifted historians – notably the French writers Fernand Braudel, Georges Duby and Roy Ladurie (all now translated into English) who have added a new dimension to social history, for which we humble researchers, seeking ever more detail on the private lives of people through the ages and throughout the world, must be enormously grateful. Especially recommended are two admirable multi-volume works: *Civilization and Capitalism*, by Fernand Braudel, and *A History of Private Life*, edited by P. Aries and G. Duby: every historical novelist should have copies on his bookshelf. In a different category altogether, but very evocative, is the richly illustrated Time-Life series, *What Life was Like*, which is also international in coverage.

Whether you are setting your novel abroad or at home, it is of the utmost importance to use contemporary sources wherever possible. The *English Historical Documents* series is worth looking at, and also the *They Saw It Happen* and *Human Documents* series; some of these are out of print, but you should find them in most reference libraries.

G.M. Trevelyan's *English Social History* remains one of the best general accounts of life in this country through the ages. I also recommend Asa Briggs' *A Social History of England*. Among numerous social histories relating to particular periods, here are a few, to give readers a taste of what to look out for: E.N. Williams' *Life in Georgian England*; Dorothy Marshall's *English People in the Eighteenth Century*; J.H. Plumb's *Georgian Delights*; Venetia Murray's recent social history of the Regency period, 1788–1820, *An Impolite Society*; John Fisher's *The World of the Forsytes*; A.N. Wilson's *The Victorians*; David Evans' *Victorians Early and Late*, in the *How We Used to Live* series from A & C Black (early Victorian times to the present); Robert Graves' and Alan Hodge's *The Long Week-End* (very good on the years between the two world wars); Piers Brendon's *The Dark Valley: A Panorama of the 1930s*; and Norman Longmate's *How We Lived Then: A History of Everyday Life during the Second World War*. G.D.H. Cole and R. Postgate's *The Common People 1746–1938* has become a standard work; see also *The Common People: A History from the Norman Conquest to the Present*, by J.F.C. Harrison, two studies by E.P. Thompson, *Customs in Common* and *The Making of the English Working Class*, and *The Labourer 1760–1832* by J.L. and Barbara Hammond. J.M. Brereton's *The British Soldier: A Social History* provides a reliable background to army life from the 17th century. *British Trials 1660–1900* contains first-hand accounts of thousands of trials. In lighter vein, but very informative, are C.L. Graves' *Mr Punch's History of Modern England*, covering the years from 1841 to 1914, and Leslie Baily's *BBC Scrapbooks 1896–1939*. Rona Randall's *The Model Wife* is a well-illustrated mine of information about marriage and the role of a wife in the 19th-century household. The lifestyle of the upper classes is well portrayed in Mark Girouard's *Life in the English Country House* and in Phyllida Barstow's *The English Country House Party*, with its 'below stairs' counterpart in *The Country House Servant* by Pamela A. Sambrook. So far as the 20th century is concerned, see R. Graves' and A. Hodge's *The Long Week-End* mentioned above; it is also worth looking at the *Portrait of a Decade* series and at *Yesterday's Britain: The Illustrated Story of How We Lived, Worked and Played*.

Autobiographies and diaries are extremely useful as source material for the historical novelist in that they provide absolutely authentic accounts of day-to-day life and thought of the period, written in the contemporary idiom. *British Autobiographies*, compiled by William Matthews, is an annotated bibliography of material printed or published before 1951. John Burnett has made two useful studies of working-class material: the three-volume *Autobiography of the Working Class*, covering the period 1790–1945; and a paperback, *Useful Toil: Autobiographies of Working People from the 1820s to the 1970s*.

William Matthews' *British Diaries 1442–1942* and John Stuart Batts' *British Manuscript Diaries of the 19th Century* are standard works, both listing the diaries under the year in which they commence, which enables the researcher to ascertain what material exists for a particular period. Matthews also compiled an annotated bibliography of *American Diaries* written prior to 1861 and *American Diaries in Manuscript 1580–1954*. His work has been updated, expanded and continued by another American bibliographer, Patricia Pate Havlice, in an invaluable volume, *And So To Bed: A Bibliography of Diaries published in English*; this contains an index to Matthews' listings and also a general index of authors, editors, titles and subjects. Also worth consulting are *English Family Life 1576–1716: An Anthology of Diaries*, edited by Ralph Houlbrooke, and *Women's Diaries, Journals and Letters: An Annotated Bibliography*, compiled by Cheryl Cline.

Most public libraries maintain a local collection, and you should always ask if there is a book dealing with a particular region, town, industry or local family, in the period about which you are writing. (For further suggestions, see chapter 8, 'Family and Local History', pages 142–64.)

One good method of keeping the story of an historical novel or play in line with world or national events is to refer constantly to a published chronology. The four-volume *Chronology of World History* is expensive, but you can buy the volumes separately. *The People's Chronology*, now out of print but available in libraries, contains much information on human events, inventions, etc. not listed elsewhere, from pre-history to modern times. The Dorling Kindersley *Chronicle of the 20th Century*, with its month-by-month listings, amply illustrated with news photographs, and a good index, is indispensable if you are setting a story in the last hundred years. A more detailed set of chronologies is the ongoing *Day By Day* series, published in the US by Facts on File, 1–2 volumes per decade (so far, the 1940s through to the 1980s).

There is a wide choice of dictionaries of dates from various publishers. In some volumes the major events of each year are listed month by month, while in others also included are annual listings of the developments in the arts, sciences, politics, etc., together with the births and deaths of famous people. For quick reference I recommend the Oxford University Press paperback *A Dictionary of Dates*.

Problems likely to be encountered by the writer of historical fiction and some suggestions as to how they may be solved are discussed below.

Places

Many of the places and buildings you may want to mention in your novel or play still exist today, but have changed out of all recognition in the last few hundred years, and it is not easy to find out exactly how they looked at a particular date. You should always ask at the local library or record office if they have maps of approximately the right date, and where these exist you will find it valuable to keep a photocopy of the map in front of you as you write. There is an historical series of the Ordnance Survey, which may be useful, and you can buy reprints of the first (one inch) edition. A good historical atlas, such as *The Times Atlas of World History*, *The Oxford Atlas of World History*, *The Dorling Kindersley Atlas of World History*, and the *Penguin Atlas of World History*, is essential. Penguin publish an excellent and relatively inexpensive series of historical atlases, with separate volumes for *Ancient*, *Medieval*, *Modern* or *Recent History*, as well as for regions and individual countries. There is a series of *Continental History Atlases* published by Macmillan in the US.

Adrian Room, whose compilations include the *Street Names of England*, has recently produced a new and revised edition of *Place-Name Changes, 1900–1991*. International in coverage, it has an appendix listing the official names of all countries of the world, and also an updated and enlarged bibliography.

Like the writer of modern fiction, the historical novelist should attempt to visit every place or building that comes into his story. If this is quite impossible, the best course is to enquire at your local library or county record office for a reliable parish history and for any books about life in the district during the period in which you are interested. If your story is set in the 18th century or later, there will be a local newspaper which you can study. Where buildings have to be described, Nikolaus Pevsner's *Buildings of England* series, already mentioned, will be most useful. For buildings in London, there is the very detailed *Survey of London*. Other useful sources include Sutton Publishing's *Britain in Old Photographs* series, as well as current guidebooks to the historic castles and stately homes open to the public.

The German publisher Karl Baedeker published his first foreign travel guides in 1829; known worldwide as '*Baedekers*', these are good sources for the historical novelist.

Dates

The problems that arise over dating have been discussed in the previous chapter (see pages 95–6). In historical fiction work the writer will most often need to find out on what day of the week a certain anniversary or religious festival fell. This can be done very easily by first looking up the date of Easter in the chronological table at the back of the *Handbook of Dates for Students of English History* and then by turning to the appropriate calendar section, in which there is a double-page spread for all the years from AD 500 to 2100 in which Easter fell (or is going to fall) on that particular day. In the same *Handbook* you will find a list of saints' days and religious festivals, but if you need more detail on festivals you should consult the *British Calendar Customs* series published by the Folklore Society. *Whitaker's Almanack* contains an 'Any Year' calendar from 1770 to 2030.

Weather

What the weather was like on a certain day, or if a particular winter was severe, or when there was a heatwave and how long it lasted, can be vital to an historical novel. *Whitaker's Almanack* (from 1868) is a good source, and so are local and regional newspapers. *The Times* has employed a regular weather correspondent since the early 1870s, but earlier reports – from 1731 – appeared in *Gentleman's Magazine*, where you will find not only monthly tables giving temperatures and rainfall, but a calendar with brief descriptions against each day, such as 'cloudy morning, but bright later'; 'windy and wet all day'; 'heavy rain in the south, snow in the north'.

Two excellent works which are rare books and to be found nowadays only at the British Library or university libraries are T.H. Baker's *Records of the Seasons, etc.... observed in the British Isles* and E.J. Lowe's *Natural Phenomena and Chronology of the Seasons* (of which Part I only was ever published, containing records from AD 220 to 1753). Among other useful reference books are Ingrid Holford's *The Guinness Book of Weather Facts and Feats*; D. Bowen's *Britain's Weather*, which has an appendix listing notable gales, blizzards, floods and frosts; J.H. Brazell's *London Weather*, with its useful chronology from AD 4 to 1964; and W. Andrews' *Famous Frosts and Frost Fairs in Great Britain*.

The best printed source of information about the weather in different regions of the globe is *The World Weather Guide*. The *World Climate Disc*, on CD-ROM, contains data from 1854 to 1990. For quick reference there is a splendid little book by Maria Harding, *Weather to Travel: The Traveller's Guide to the World's Weather*, which as a bonus suggests appropriate seasonal clothing under each country (useful for the novelist).

In England, the Meteorological Office has published records since the 1860s. Its Library (currently at Bracknell, Berkshire, but moving to Exeter by the end of 2003) houses a collection of meteorological literature dating from the 16th century which is the most comprehensive in the world. Members of the public may use the Library and also the Archive (in the Scott Building nearby, but moving to Exeter in 2004); the records stored here comprise a vast collection of meteorological data and charts from England, Wales and British overseas bases, including many private readings, ships' weather logs, and the archives of the Royal Meteorological Society. (Records from Scotland are stored in Edinburgh, and those from Northern Ireland in Belfast.)

Intending visitors should give prior notice to the Library or Archive Manager. During and after the move to Exeter, which will be effected in stages, the customer centre telephone number will remain 0845 300 0300. There is a website www.metoffice.com with a link to the Library. Meanwhile postal enquiries should continue to be addressed to the National Meteorological Library and Archive, Meteorological Office, London Road, Bracknell, Berks RG12 2SZ (tel. 01344 854841; fax 01344 854840). The Librarian will usually recommend titles or may pass a specific query on to the relevant department; a search fee may be payable if extensive research has to be undertaken by staff. Many of the Library's books may be borrowed (proof of identity required); such loans are best arranged through your local library, but may also be requested by post, in which case there may be a search fee and handling surcharge. (*N.B.* Much of the material in the Archive is classed as public records and may not be loaned.)

Language

Getting the idiom right in historical fiction is often a big worry to the writer. The best advice that can be given is that you should read extensively the best novels and plays of the relevant age; this will give you the 'feel' of the spoken English of the time. Eric Partridge's *Slang Today and Yesterday*, as mentioned earlier in this chapter, has useful sections on the slang spoken at different periods (16th to mid-20th century). *Slang Down the Ages* is arranged by subject, with a word index. Another very informative compilation is *The Chronology of Words and Phrases: A Thousand Years in the History of English*: as a bonus for the historical novelist, entries in this inexpensive paperback are linked to historical events and a host of anecdotes. If you are setting your story in the years 1939–45, you should look at *The Language of World War II*, which covers not only spoken expressions but also the slogans and abbreviations then current, as well as the popular songs of the time.

Cost of living, currencies and wages

How much people earned and what they paid for their food and clothing are queries that frequently crop up in historical writing. J. Burnett's *A History of the Cost of Living* will answer most needs: it has chapters dating from the Middle Ages to the mid-20th century, and also a good bibliography. Unfortunately it has been allowed to go out of print, but most libraries should have it; if you ever spot it on offer secondhand, be sure to snap it up! Lionel Munby's *How Much is that Worth?*, written primarily for family and local historians, is excellent. Another exceptionally informative source is the *What It Cost the Day Before Yesterday Book* by Harold Priestley, which is divided into three periods: 1851–1914, 1915–70 and (to take account of inflation) 1971–78. *Prices and Wages in England from the 12th to the 19th Century* by Lord Beveridge and others is a standard work, and Peter Wilsher's *The Pound in your Pocket 1870–1970* is a readable and well-researched study of the pound and its purchasing power throughout that period.

Newspapers and women's magazines are valuable sources from the early 19th century onwards – Alison Adburgham's *Shops and Shopping* covers the period 1800–1914, whereas a new publication, Bill Lancaster's *The Department Store: A Social History*, deals with the subject from the mid-19th century to the present day, on both sides of the Atlantic.

Currency Conversion Tables: A Hundred Years of Change by R.L. Bidwell is a most useful guide to the fluctuations in rates of exchange of most countries of the world 1870–1970; it also has a table of London gold prices. For money values in earlier times I recommend John McCusker's *Money and Exchange in Europe and America 1600–1775*, Peter Spufford's *Handbook of Medieval Exchange* and Pierre Vilar's *A History of Gold and Money 1450–1920*. For more historical or monetary information, write or telephone to the Bank of England Information Centre, Threadneedle Street, London EC2R 8AH (tel. 020 7601 4715; fax 020 7601 4356; email informationcentre@bankofengland.co.uk).

Fashion, etiquette and food

The best source for the history of costume is the Fashion Research Centre at 4 Circus, Bath, Somerset BA1 2EW (tel. 01225 477752; fax 01225 444793; email costumeenquiries@bathnes.gov.ek). The Centre's extensive library contains books on the history of dress from the medieval period to the present day, as well as a study collection (dress, accessories and textiles) which, by appointment on Thursdays and Fridays only, you can examine at close quarters. (To book a study table, tel. 01225 477752/4.) At the Museum of Costume, in the Assembly Rooms nearby, there are over 30,000 objects including some 200 dressed figures illustrating styles from the late 16th century to modern times. Bibliographies are available free of charge from the Centre (state period and type of costume, i.e. men's dress, underclothes, etc.).

Researchers seriously interested in historical fashion should consider joining the Costume Society of Great Britain. The Society's annual journal, *Costume*, contains articles and book reviews on many aspects of fashion through the ages and is a valuable research tool; it is available to non-members on subscription, and past issues and reprints may be purchased. There is also *Costume: A General Bibliography* [to 1974]. (Note that this bibliography covers articles in *Costume*, not general titles.) Members of the Society have the opportunity to attend lectures and other events throughout the year. Details from the Membership Secretary, 56 Wareham Road, Lytchett Matravers, Poole, Dorset BH16 6DS or on the website www.costumesociety.org.uk.

The classic work on English costume is the series by C.W. and P.E. Cunnington, which consists of *Handbooks* covering the medieval period and the 16th, 17th, 18th, 19th and 20th centuries in separate volumes. For quick reference there is J. Laver's *A Concise History of Costume*. Also useful is the revised edition of A. Racinet's *The Historical Encyclopedia of Costumes*. Alison Lurie's study *The Language of Clothes* is a thoroughly researched and witty comment on dress and manners that will help both the modern and the historical novelist. The *Fashions of a Decade* series, published by Batsford, is useful for the 20th century. On hairdressing there is R. Corson's *Fashions in Hair: The First 5000 Years*, R. Turner Wilcox's *Modes in Hats and Headdress* (from ancient Egyptian to the mid-20th century) and G. de Courtais' *Women's Headdress and Hairstyles in England from AD 600 to the Present Day*.

The best guides to English manners and etiquette are J. Wildeblood and P. Brinson's *The Polite World* (covering the 13th to the 19th centuries) and *A Punch History of Manners 1841–1940*, by A. Adburgham. On eating habits and diet there are Arnold Palmer's *Movable Feasts*, J.C. Drummond and A. Wilbraham's *The*

Englishman's Food: A History of Five Centuries of English Diet, J. Burnett's *Plenty and Want: A Social History of Diet in England from 1815 to the Present Day*, Reay Tannahill's recently revised *Food in History* and Margaret Visser's *The Rituals of Dinner*. Roy Strong's *Feast*, with its apt sub-title *A History of Grand Eating*, is excellent not only on regal and aristocratic banqueting, but also on seating arrangements, table manners, utensils and much else – all succulent fodder for the novelist.

Sport

For historical information on the various sports your characters might take part in, your best sources are probably the relevant club museums (see chapter 4, 'Basic Sources of Information and their Location', page 68). Dennis Brailsford's *British Sport: A Social History* presents a good overview of sport in this country from the Middle Ages to the 1990s. The *International Journal of the History of Sport* is also worth studying; recent issues are online as well as in print.

Transport and travel

Finding out exactly how long a particular journey would have taken at a particular date is not easy. So far as train journeys are concerned, try to find an early *Bradshaw* (first published in 1839) – you may have to settle for the one nearest in date to your story. Stage-coach timetables will be found in the early London directories. OAG Worldwide (formerly ABC International), now part of the Reed Travel Group, have a collection of old rail and air timetables; telephone them on 01582 600111. Alternatively, contact the National Railway Museum Library and Archive, Leeman Road, York YO26 4XJ (tel. 01904 621261; fax 01904 611112; email nrm@nmsi.ac.uk; website www.nrm.org.uk); the Caird Library of the National Maritime Museum, Greenwich, London SE10 9NF (tel. 020 8858 4422; fax 020 8312 6632; website www.nmm.ac.uk); or the Civil Aviation Authority Library and Information Centre, Aviation House, Gatwick Airport South, West Sussex RH6 0YR (tel. 01293 573725; fax 01293 573181; email library-enquiries@srg.caa.co.uk).

There is an important Transport History Collection at Leicester University Library, University Road, Leicester LE1 9QD (tel. 0116 252 2043; email libdesk@lc.ac.uk).

The classic standard work is E.A. Pratt's *History of Inland Transport and Communications*, first published in 1912. Publishers who currently specialise in transport history include Sutton Publishing of Thrupp, near Stroud, Gloucestershire, now part of Haynes Publishing (tel. 01453 731114; fax 01453 731117). Send both for the firm's general catalogue and for their separate listings of 'Road and rail titles' and 'Inland waterway and maritime books'.

CHILDREN'S FICTION

Research done by the children's writer is not much different from that carried out by the writer of stories for adults. Children of all ages being highly critical and quick to spot mistakes, it is very important that background and language are absolutely right.

The correct idiom is vital. It is a good idea, if you are embarking on a modern story, to study a selection of juvenile magazines for a time. You will also want to keep up-to-date with, and read, published children's books. Ask at your local children's library enquiries desk for the *Children's Fiction Index* and *Sequels, Volume II: Children's Books*.

The major collection of children's books in this country is at the National Art Library at the Victoria & Albert Museum, Cromwell Road, London SW7 2RL (tel. 020 7942 2400; website www.nal.vam.ac.uk). (Note that the Children's Literature Collections here now include the Renier Collection of Historic and Contemporary Children's Books spanning five centuries and other book collections formerly held at the Museum of Childhood at Bethnal Green.) You will need a Special Collections reader's ticket for access, for which you must supply two passport-size photographs and the name of a referee.

Children's Literature at Booktrust – formerly called the Young Book Trust – at Book House, 45 East Hill, London SW18 2QZ (tel. 020 8516 2977; fax 020 8516 2978; email info@booktrust.org.uk; website www.booktrust.org.uk) maintains an excellent Children's Reference Library (direct line tel. 020 8516 2985; website www.booktrusted.com). As well as reference titles, this library holds a copy of every children's book published in the past two years. After two years, these books are passed on to the Booktrust Children's Collection at the University of Surrey (Roehampton), Mount Clare, Minstead Gardens, Roehampton, London SW15 4EE (tel. 020 392 3772; email s.mansfield@roehampton.ac.uk or j.mills@roehampton.ac.uk). Access to this collection, which opened in early summer 2003, is strictly by appointment.

For further details see Appendix I, under 'Children (Books and Objects)', pages 221–2.

On sources generally, highly recommended are the *Children's Fiction Sourcebook*, and two works by Tessa Rose Chester, *Children's Books Research: A Practical Guide to Techniques and Sources* and *Sources of Information about Children's Books*. For general reference, in addition to the standard work, *The Oxford Companion to Children's Literature*, you will find Arthur Mortimore's *Index to Characters in Children's Literature* very useful. If you write for young children, you may want to have works such as the *Oxford Companion to Fairy Tales* or the *Oxford Dictionary of Nursery Rhymes* on your reference bookshelf.

So far as school stories are concerned, you cannot do better than delve into Peter Opie's *The Lore and Language of School Children*. Isabel Quigly's *The Heirs of Tom Brown*, with its excellent bibliography, will help with a public-school setting. Another very useful book is *Children's Games in Street and Playground*, by Iona and Peter Opie.

Various slang dictionaries have been mentioned on pages 103–4 and 109. However, it cannot be stressed too strongly that our language is changing all the time – and especially the language of the young – so that there can be no substitute for the writer mixing with, and talking and listening to, the younger generation, in order to get the idiom exactly right.

Background too must be up-to-date: remember single-parent families and the mixed nationalities encountered by children today in playgroup and school!

CRIME FICTION

The best research tool I have come across recently in this field is Douglas Wynn's *The Crime Writer's Handbook*. This slim and inexpensive publication is a goldmine of reference information on methods of murder (including weapons and poisons), methods of detection and forensic science, police procedures and much else. The bibliography will lead you to pretty well every other source you need.

The *Writers' News Book Society* usually has on offer a number of guides specifically for the crime writer.

SCIENCE FICTION

The best source in this country is the Science Fiction Foundation Research Library, at Liverpool University Library, PO Box 123, Liverpool L69 3DA (tel. 0151 794 3142). This collection, which includes the library of the British Science Fiction Association, is the largest in this field outside the United States. Researchers must telephone in advance for an appointment.

A useful reference handbook on published works is *The Ultimate Guide to Science Fiction: An A–Z of Science Fiction Books by Title* by D. Pringle.

FINDING OUT ABOUT PUBLISHED FICTION

In addition to the specific research problems connected with his own work, the fiction writer or playwright frequently wants to know what other novels or plays or short stories have been published with similar themes or backgrounds. He may also wish to check on whether any other writer has used the title which he has in mind. (There is no copyright in titles, but for the exact legal position, see the Society of Authors' *Quick Guide* on the 'Protection of Titles'.)

Most public libraries possess copies of the *Fiction Index*, the *Play Index* and the *Short Story Index*; you should ask for them at the readers' enquiry desk. There are cumulated volumes of the *Fiction Index* for 1945–60 and 1960–69; since 1970 every five years. Titles are listed under some 3,000 subject headings. Another useful tool is the *Reference Guide to Short Fiction*, which covers the 19th and 20th centuries and includes foreign-language writers and translations. There is also the British Library cumulative *Fiction on Fiche*, listing adult and teenage fiction published since 1950;

this has however been discontinued since December 2001. If you want to check up on sequels to published fiction, ask at the library enquiry desk for *Sequels* (*Volume I: Adult Books*; *Volume II: Children's Books*).

The researcher wishing to find out about published historical fiction should consult Daniel S. Burt's *What Historical Novel Do I Read Next?*. This two-volume American compilation covers over 7,000 novels and includes a number of indexes which enable the user to track down historical fiction by author, subject, fictional and historical characters, location and period. It also evaluates the novels for historical accuracy. Persuade your local library to acquire it if they haven't already done so.

Literary pseudonyms may be traced in Frank Atkinson's *Dictionary of Literary Pseudonyms*. There are three useful sources for finding out about characters in published fiction: the *Dictionary of British Literary Characters*, the *Dictionary of Fictional Characters* and the *Dictionary of Real People and Places in Fiction*.

There is now a vast reference source for English and American literature available by subscription from Chadwyck-Healey of Cambridge: *Literature Online*, which contains full texts of poetry, drama and fiction from AD 600 to the present day. There are flexible rates for access (to all, or any single or combination of databases), and it is worth asking whether your library or professional institution subscribes.

Finally, but by no means least, for the advice of a successful novelist (as opposed to that of myself, a humble researcher – albeit one who has delved on behalf of many novelists) read Jean Saunders' *How to Research your Novel*.

American Diaries: An Annotated Bibliography of American Diaries written prior to Year 1861, by William Matthews, University of California Press, Berkeley and Los Angeles, 1945, 1959

American Diaries in Manuscript, 1580–1954, by William Matthews, University of Georgia Press, Athens, 1974

And So To Bed: A Bibliography of Diaries published in English, by Patricia Pate Havlice, Scarecrow Press, Metuchen, 1987

An Athletics Compendium: A Guide to the UK Literature of Track and Field, by Tom McNab, Peter Lovesey and Andrew Huxtable, British Library, London, 2001

Autobiography of the Working Class, by John Burnett, 3 vols, Harvester, Hemel Hempstead, 1984–89

Baedeker travel guides, from 1829

BBC Scrapbooks, by Leslie Baily, 2 vols: 1, *1896–1914*; 2, *1918–1939*, Allen & Unwin, London, 1966–68

Benn's Media, 3 vols, published annually by CMP Information Ltd., Tonbridge

Bodytalk: A World Guide to Gestures, by Desmond Morris, Jonathan Cape, London, 1994

Bradshaw's Monthly Railway Guide, 1839–1961

Brewer's Dictionary of Names, compiled by Adrian Room, Helicon, Oxford, 1995

Britain in Old Photographs series, published by Sutton Publishing (Haynes Publishing), Thrupp, Stroud, Glos.

Britain's Weather, by David Bowen, David & Charles, Newton Abbot, 1969

British Autobiographies: An Annotated Bibliography of British Autobiographies published or written before 1951, by William Matthews, University of California Press, Berkeley and Los Angeles, 1955

British Calendar Customs: England, 3 vols; *Scotland*, 3 vols; *Orkneys and Shetland*, 1 vol, published by the Folklore Society, London, 1936–46

British Diaries 1442–1942: An Annotated Bibliography of British Diaries written between 1442 and 1942, by William Matthews, University of California Press, Berkeley and Los Angeles, 1950

British Manuscript Diaries of the 19th Century: An Annotated Listing, by John Stuart Batts, Centaur Press, Fontwell and London, 1976

The British Soldier: A Social History, by J.M. Brereton, Bodley Head, London, 1986

British Sport: A Social History, by Dennis Brailsford, Lutterworth Press, Cambridge, 1992

British Trials 1660–1900, microfiche series, Chadwyck-Healey, Cambridge

Buildings of England series, originally ed. by Nikolaus Pevsner, 46 vols, 1951 onwards, Penguin Books, Harmondsworth; revised edns, by Bridget Cherry and others, in progress

The Cambridge World History of Food, by Kenneth F. Kiple and Kriemhild Conee Ornelas, Cambridge University Press, Cambridge, 2 vols, 2000

The Cassell Dictionary of Slang, by Jonathon Green, Cassell, London, 1998

Children's Books Research: A Practical Guide to Techniques and Sources, by Tessa Rose Chester, Thimble Press/Westminster College, Oxford, 1989

Children's Fiction Index, published by the Career Development Group of the Library Association, London, 7th edn, eds. Margaret Hobson and Jennifer Madden, 1993

Children's Fiction Sourcebook, compiled by J. Madden and M. Hobson, Scolar Press, London (now Ashgate Publishing, Aldershot), 1995

Children's Games in Street and Playground, by Iona and Peter Opie, Oxford University Press, Oxford, 1969; paperback edn, 1984

Chronicle of the 20th Century, first published by Dorling Kindersley, London, 1988; rev. edn, 1995

The Chronology of Words & Phrases: A Thousand Years in the History of English, by Linda and Roger Flavell, Kyle Cathie, London, 2001

Chronology of World History, 4 vols: 1, *Prehistory–1491AD*; 2, *1492–1775*; 3, *1776–1900*; 4, *1901–present day*, Helicon, Oxford, 1999

Civilization and Capitalism 1400–1800, by Fernand Braudel, 3 vols: 1, *The Structures of Everyday Life*; 2, *The Wheels of Commerce*; 3, *The Perspective of the World*, Collins, London, 1981–85; paperback edns, Orion, London, 2000

The Classic Fairy Tales, by Iona and Peter Opie, Oxford University Press, Oxford, 1974; reprinted 1992

Cockney Dictionary, ed. Robert Barltrop, Continuum, London, 2003

The Common People 1746–1938, by G.D.H. Cole and R. Postgate, Methuen, London, 1938; reprinted 1965

The Common People: A History from the Norman Conquest to the Present, by J.F.C. Harrison, Fontana, London, 1984

A Concise History of Costume, by J. Laver, Thames & Hudson, 1969

Continental History Atlases: vols for *Asia, Europe, North America, South America*, Macmillan, New York, 1998

Costume, illustrated journal of The Costume Society, published annually (available to non-members by subscription from Maney Publishing, Hudson Road, Leeds LS9 7DL)

Costume: A General Bibliography, by P. Anthony and J. Arnold, published by The Costume Society, London, new edn, 1999 (from Maney Publishing, as above)

The Country House Servant, by Pamela A. Sambrook, Sutton Publishing, Thrupp, Stroud, Glos., 2002

The Crime Writer's Handbook, by Douglas Wynn, Allison & Busby, 1997

Currency Conversion Tables: A Hundred Years of Change, by R.L. Bidwell, Rex Collings, London, 1970 (out of print)

Customs in Common, by E.P. Thompson, Merlin, London, 1991

The Dark Valley: A Panorama of the 1930s, by Piers Brendon, Jonathan Cape, London, 2000; paperback, Pimlico, London, 2001

Day by Day series, published by Facts On File, New York, in progress 1983–

Debrett's Correct Form, Headline, London, new edn, 1999; updated paperback edn, 2002

Debrett's New Guide to Etiquette and Modern Manners, by John Morgan, Headline, London, 1996

The Department Store: A Social History, by Bill Lancaster, Leicester University Press (Cassell), London, 1995

The Dialects of England, by Peter Trudgill, Blackwell, Oxford, 1990

Dictionary of British Literary Characters, 18th, 19th and 20th Century Novels, by John R. Greenfield, Facts On File, New York, 3 vols, 1993, 1994

A Dictionary of Catch Phrases British and American, from the Sixteenth Century to the Present Day, by Eric Partridge, ed. Paul Beale, 2nd edn, Routledge, London 1986; paperback edn, 1990

Dictionary of Contemporary Slang, by Tony Thorne, Bloomsbury Reference, London, 1997

A Dictionary of English Place-Names, by A.D. Mills, Oxford University Press, 1991; 2nd edn (paperback), 1998

Dictionary of Fictional Characters, by William Freeman, Everyman Reference series, Dent, London, 3rd edn revised, 1973

Dictionary of Literary Pseudonyms, compiled by Frank Atkinson, Library Association, London, 4th edn, 1987

A Dictionary of Pseudonyms and Their Origins, with Stories of Name Changes, by Adrian Room, McFarland, Jefferson, North Carolina, 3rd edn, 1998

A Dictionary of Dates, ed. C.L. Beeching, Oxford University Press, Oxford, 2nd edn 1997

Dictionary of Real People and Places in Fiction, compiled by M.C. Rintoul, Routledge, London, 1991

A Dictionary of the Underworld, British and American, compiled by Eric Partridge, Routledge, London, 3rd edn revised, 1968

Dictionary of Worldwide Gestures, by Betty J. Bäuml and Franz H. Bäuml, Scarecrow Press, Lanham, Maryland (now part of Rowman & Littlefield Publishing Group, Oxford), 2nd edn, 1997

Directory of British Associations, published by CBD Research, Beckenham, 16th edn, 2002; CD-ROM, 2003

Directory of Publishing (formerly *Cassell Directory of Publishing*), now published annually by Continuum International Publishing Group Ltd., London (29th edn, 2003)

The Dorling Kindersley Atlas of World History, ed. Jeremy Black, Dorling Kindersley, London, 2000

England: Blue Guide, by Ian Ousby, A & C Black, London, 11th edn, 1995

The English Country House Party, by Phyllida Barstow, Sutton Publishing, Thrupp, Glos., 1998

English Dialect Dictionary, compiled by J. Wright, 6 vols, Frowde, London, 1896–1905; new edn, Oxford University Press, Oxford, 1981

English Family Life 1576–1716: An Anthology of Diaries, ed. R. Houlbrooke, Blackwell, Oxford, 1989

English Historical Documents, ed. D.C. Douglas, 12 vols, Eyre & Spottiswoode, London, 1953–75

English People in the Eighteenth Century, by Dorothy Marshall, Longman, London, 1956

English Place-Name Society, volumes by county, in progress since 1923, published by the Society, c/o University of Nottingham

English Place-Names, by Kenneth Cameron, Batsford, London, 1996

English Social History, by G.M. Trevelyan, first published 1944; new edn, Longman, London, 1978; paperback edn, Penguin Books, Harmondsworth, 1986

The Englishman's Food: A History of Five Centuries of English Diet, by J.C. Drummond and A. Wilbraham, Cape, London, 1958; reprinted, Pimlico, London, 1991

Famous First Facts, International Edition, H.W. Wilson, New York, 2000

Famous Frosts and Frost Fairs in Great Britain, by W. Andrews, Redway, London, 1887

Fashions in Hair: The First 5000 Years, by R. Corson, Peter Owen, London, 1965

Fashions of a Decade series (1920s–1990s), published by Batsford, London, 8 vols, 1991–92

Feast: A History of Grand Eating, by Roy Strong, Jonathan Cape, London, 2002

Fiction Index, published by the Association of Assistant Librarians (now the Career Development Group of the Library Association), London, since 1970; cumulated vols covering the period 1945–89, now every 5 years. Latest edns, compiled by Marilyn E. Hicken: *Fiction Index 1995*, published 1997, and *Cumulated Fiction Index 1995–1999*, published 2001

Fiction on Fiche, microfiche, published quarterly by the British Library National Bibliographic Service, Wetherby, Yorks, 1950–2001; now discontinued

Food in History, by Reay Tannahill, Eyre Methuen, London, 1973; updated edn, Headline paperback, 2002

Foreign Bodies: A Guide to European Mannerisms, by Peter Collett, Simon & Schuster, London, 1993

Gentleman's Magazine, 1731–1922; weather reports

Georgian Delights, by J.H. Plumb, Weidenfeld & Nicolson, London, 1980

Gestures: The Dos and Taboos of Body Language Around the World, by Roger E. Axtell, John Wiley, London, 1991

The Guinness Book of Weather Facts and Feats, by Ingrid Holford, Guinness Superlatives, Enfield, 1977

Handbook of Dates for Students of English History, ed. C.R. Cheney, first published 1945; 2nd edn, ed. C.R. Cheney and Michael Jones, Cambridge University Press, Cambridge, 2000

Handbook of English Costume series, by C.W. and P.E. Cunnington, Faber, London, 1952–73

Handbook of Medieval Exchange, by Peter Spufford, Royal Historical Society, London, 1986

Handbook of Pseudonyms and Personal Nicknames, compiled by Harold S. Sharp, 2 vols, Scarecrow Press (formerly of Metuchen, N.J., USA (now part of the Rowman & Littlefield Group, Oxford), 1972; supplements 1975, 1982

The Heirs of Tom Brown, by Isabel Quigly, Chatto & Windus, London, 1982; paperback edn, Oxford University Press, Oxford, 1984

Historic Houses & Gardens, Castles & Heritage Sites, published annually, now by Norman Hudson, Banbury, Oxon.

Historic Houses in Britain, AA Publishing, Basingstoke, 1994; reprinted 1999

The Historical Encyclopedia of Costumes, originally compiled by A. Racinet, rev. edn, Studio Editions, London, 1988

A History of the Cost of Living, by John Burnett, Penguin Books, Harmondsworth, 1969

A History of Gold and Money 1450–1920, by Pierre Vilar, Verso, USA, 1991 (distributed in UK by Marston Book Services, Oxford)

History of Inland Transport and Communication, by E.A. Pratt, 1912; reprinted, David & Charles, Newton Abbot, 1970

A History of Private Life, eds P. Aries and G. Duby, translated from French, 5 vols, Harvard University Press, Cambridge, Mass., 1987–91; also in paperback (distributed in UK by John Wiley & Sons)

Hobson-Jobson: The Anglo-Indian Dictionary, by Henry Yule and A.C. Burnell, 1886; paperback edn, Wordsworth Reference, Ware, Herts, 1996

Hollis Press & Public Relations Annual, published by Hollis Publishing, Teddington, Middx

How Much is that Worth?, by Lionel Munby, Phillimore, Chichester, 2nd edn, 1996

How to Research your Novel, by Jean Saunders, Allison & Busby, London, 1993

How We Lived Then: A History of Everyday Life during the Second World War, by Norman Longmate, Hutchinson, London, 1971; paperback edn, Arrow, London, 1977

How We Used to Live: Victorians Early and Late, by David Evans, A & C Black, London, 1990

Human Documents series, ed. R.E. Pike, Allen & Unwin, London (out of print)

Human Instinct by Robert Winston, Transworld, London, 2002

An Impolite Society: A Social History of the Regency Period 1788–1820, by Venetia Murray, Penguin Books, London, 1998

Index to Characters in Children's Literature, compiled and published by Arthur D. Mortimore, Bristol, 1977

International Journal of the History of Sport, published quarterly by Frank Cass, London; also online from issue 18/1

The King's England series, by Arthur Mee, introductory vol. and 40 vols (county by county), facsimile edition, the King's England Press, Rotherham, South Yorkshire, 1998

The Labourer 1760–1832, by J.L. and Barbara Hammond, 1-vol. paperback edn, Sutton Publishing, Thrupp, Stroud, 1995

The Language of Clothes, by Alison Lurie, Heinemann, London, 1981; paperback edn, Hamlyn, London, 1983

The Language of World War II, compiled by A.M. Taylor, H.W. Wilson, New York, 1948

Life in the English Country House, by Mark Girouard, Yale University Press, New York and London, 1978; paperback edn, Penguin Books, Harmondsworth, 1980

Life in Georgian England, by E.N. Williams, Batsford, London, 1962

Literature Online, by subscription, Chadwyck-Healey, Cambridge; some collections available separately on CD-ROM

London: Blue Guide, by Ylva French, A & C Black, London, 16th edn, 1998

London Weather, by J.H. Brazell, HMSO, London, 1968

The Long Week-End: A Social History of Great Britain 1918–1939, by Robert Graves and Alan Hodge, Hutchinson, London, 1985

The Lore and Language of School Children, by Iona and Peter Opie, Oxford University Press, Oxford, 1959; reprinted 1987

The Macmillan Dictionary of American Slang, compiled by R.L. Chapman, Macmillan, 1995

The Making of the English Working Class, by E.P. Thompson, Gollancz, London, 1980

Mr Punch's History of Modern England, by C.L. Graves, 4 vols, Cassell, London, 1921–22

The Model Wife, by Rona Randall, Herbert Press, London, 1989

Modes in Hats and Headdress, by R. Turner Wilcox, Scribner's, New York, rev. edn, 1959

Money and Exchange in Europe and America 1600–1775, by John McCusker, Macmillan, London, 1978

Movable Feasts: Changes in English Eating-Habits, by Arnold Palmer, Oxford University Press, Oxford, 1984

Natural Phenomena and Chronology of the Seasons, by E.J. Lowe, Part I only, London, 1870

The New Shell Book of Firsts, ed. Patrick Robertson, Headline, London, 1995; previously entitled *The Shell Book of Firsts*

Newspeak: A Dictionary of Jargon, by Jonathon Green, Routledge, London, 1984; paperback edn, 1985

The Official Encyclopedia of Scotland Yard, by Martin Fido and Keith Skinner, Virgin Books, London, 2000

Ordnance Survey: first edition, ed. J.B. Harley, reprinted by David & Charles, Newton Abbot; modern edns, Ordnance Survey, Southampton (also in interactive format on CD-ROM from Dream Direct Ltd., Granville Way, Bicester OX26 4JT (tel. 0870 744 7400)

The Oxford Atlas of World History, ed. Patrick K. O'Brien, Oxford University Press, Oxford, 2002

The Oxford Companion to Children's Literature, by H. Carpenter and M. Prichard, Oxford University Press, Oxford, 1984; paperback edn, 1999

The Oxford Companion to Fairy Tales, ed. Jack Zipes, Oxford University Press, Oxford, 2000

The Oxford Dictionary of Catchphrases, ed. Anna Farkas, Oxford University Press, Oxford, 2002

The Oxford Dictionary of Nursery Rhymes, eds Iona and Peter Opie, Oxford University Press, Oxford, first published 1951; new edn 1997

The Oxford Dictionary of Rhyming Slang, ed. John Ayto, Oxford University Press, Oxford, 2002

The Oxford Names Companion, ed. Patrick Hanks *et al*, Oxford University Press, Oxford, 2002

Penguin Atlas series, various compilers and dates: *Ancient, Medieval, Modern* and *Recent History*; also *Historical Atlases* of individual countries, peoples and regions of the world, Penguin Books, Harmondsworth; regularly revised

Penguin Atlas of World History, 2 vols, Penguin Books, Harmondsworth, 1974; reprinted 1984

The People's Chronology, compiled by James Trager, Heinemann, London, 1980; 3rd rev. edn, Henry Holt, New York, 1992

Place-Name Changes, 1900–1991, ed. Adrian Room, Scarecrow Press (Rowman & Littlefield Publishing Group), Oxford, 2002

Placenames of the World: Origins and Meanings of the Names for Over 5000 Natural Features, Countries, Capitals, Territories, Cities and Historic Sites, by Adrian Room, McFarland, Jefferson, North Carolina, 1997

Play Index, published by H.W. Wilson, New York, since 1949 (10 vols to date, covering 1949–2002)

Plenty and Want: A Social History of Diet in England from 1815 to the Present Day, by John Burnett, Routledge, London, 3rd edn, 1989

The Polite World: A Guide to English Manners and Deportment from the 13th to the 19th Century, rev. edn by J. Wildeblood and P. Brinson, Oxford University Press, Oxford, 1974

Portrait of a Decade series, published by Batsford, London, 9 vols covering the period 1900–1980s

The Pound in Your Pocket 1870–1970, by Peter Wilsher, Cassell, London, 1970

Prices and Wages in England from the 12th to the 19th Century, by Lord Beveridge and others, Frank Cass, London, 1965

'Protection of Titles', Society of Authors *Quick Guide* No. 2, Society of Authors, London

A Punch History of Manners 1841–1940, by Alison Adburgham, Hutchinson, London, 1961

Records of the Seasons and Prices of Agricultural Produce & Phenomena observed in the British Isles, by T.H. Baker, Simpkin Marshall, London, 1883

Reference Guide to Short Fiction, ed. Noelle Watson, St James Press, Detroit, 2nd edn, 1998

The Rituals of Dinner, by Margaret Visser, Penguin Books, Harmondsworth, 1991

Rude French: An Alternative French Phrasebook, by Georges Pilard, Chambers Harrap, Edinburgh, 2002

Sequels: Volume I: Adult Books, compiled by Marilyn E. Hicken, 13th edn scheduled for 2003; *Volume II: Children's Books*, compiled by Margaret Woodcock, 9th edn, 1999; new edn in preparation, Career Development Group of the Library Association, London

Shops and Shopping, by Alison Adburgham, Allen & Unwin, London, 2nd edn, 1981

Short Story Index, published annually with 5-year cumulations by H.W. Wilson, New York; 10 permanent retrospective volumes covering 1900–93; a single volume *Collections Indexed 1900–1978*; now updated quarterly on WilsonWeb and WilsonDisc

Slang Down the Ages, by Jonathon Green, Kyle Cathie, London, 1993; new edn, 2003

The Slang Thesaurus, by Jonathon Green, Penguin Books, Harmondsworth, 1988; rev. edn, 1999

Slang Today and Yesterday, by Eric Partridge, Routledge, London, 4th edn, 1970

A Social History of England, by Asa Briggs, Weidenfeld & Nicolson, London, 1983; paperback, 3rd rev. edn, Penguin Books, Harmondsworth, 1999

Sources for the History of Houses, by Nat Alcock, British Record Association, London, forthcoming (a revision of the 1974 title by John Harvey)

Sources of Information about Children's Books, by Tessa Rose Chester, Thimble Press, Oxford, 1989

Street Names of England, ed. Adrian Room, Paul Watkins, London, 1992

Survey of English Dialects, by H. Orton and E. Dieth, introductory vol. and 4 regional vols, E.J. Arnold, Leeds, 1962–70

Survey of London, 41 vols to date, originally published by the LCC, subsequently by Athlone Press, London, 1900–

The Thesaurus of Slang, compiled by Esther and Albert E. Lewin, Facts on File, New York, rev. 2nd edn, 1997

They Saw It Happen series, published by Blackwell, Oxford; 4 vols covering 55BC–1940 (out of print)

The Times, London; weather reports, from c. 1870

The Times Atlas of World History, HarperCollins, London, 5th edn, 1999; *Concise Times Atlas of World History*, 6th edn, 1997

Titles and Forms of Address: A Guide to Correct Use, A & C Black, London, 20th edn, 1997

The Ultimate Guide to Science Fiction: An A–Z of Science Fiction Books by Title, by D. Pringle, Scolar Press, London (now Ashgate Publishing, Aldershot), 1995

Useful Toil: Autobiographies of Working People from the 1820s to the 1970s, by John Burnett, Penguin Books, Harmondsworth, 1984

The Victorians, by A.N. Wilson, Hutchinson, London, 2002

Weather to Travel: The Traveller's Guide to the World's Weather, by Maria Harding, Tomorrow's Guides Ltd., London, Millennium Edition, 1998

What Historical Novel Do I Read Next?, compiled by Daniel S. Burt, The Gale Group, Detroit, USA, 2 vols, 1997

What It Cost the Day Before Yesterday Book, by H. Priestley, Kenneth Mason, Emsworth, 1979

Whitaker's Almanack, now published annually by A & C Black, London

Willing's Press Guide, 2 vols, now published annually by Waymaker Ltd., Chesham, Bucks; online at www.willingspressguide.com (subscription required)

Women's Diaries, Journals and Letters: An Annotated Bibliography, compiled by Cheryl Cline, Garland, New York and London, 1989

Women's Headdress and Hairstyles in England from AD *600 to the Present Day*, by G. de Courtais, Batsford, London, rev. edn, 1986

World Climate Disc, CD-ROM, Chadwyck-Healey, Cambridge, 1995

World Cruising Handbook, by Jimmy Cornell, A & C Black, London, 3rd edn, 2001

The World of the Forsytes, by John Fisher, Secker & Warburg, London, 1976

The World Weather Guide, by E.A. Pearce and C.G. Smith, Helicon, Oxford, new edn, 1998

Yesterday's Britain: The Illustrated Story of How We Lived, Worked and Played, Reader's Digest Association, London, 1998

Chapter Seven

Biography and Autobiography

BIOGRAPHICAL WRITING MAY consist of a short feature on a celebrity, past or present, to be published perhaps in commemoration of a centenary or an eightieth birthday, or it may be a full-length study. It sometimes happens that a book grows out of the research undertaken for a newspaper or magazine article. Occasionally biographies are written of people who during their lifetime were neither renowned nor eminent, but whose papers (usually diaries or letters) make a unique contribution to the social history of their time. Autobiographies, whether of celebrities or of lesser mortals, are also of value, provided that they are well researched and well written and not mere exercises in self-promotion or name-dropping. Many autobiographies today are written by professional 'ghost' writers. I have nothing to say against this practice here, provided that the 'ghosts' in question write well and – more importantly – do their research thoroughly.

There is a growing trend for biographies to be written while their subjects are still alive, or very soon after their death; this may have something to do with the fear of the modern biographer that once the biographee and his contemporaries have gone, there may be little material to work on, seeing that letter-writing is a dying art and telephoning an increasing convenience. The academic view of such work, however, is that it constitutes a 'study' or 'profile' of the person concerned rather than a true biography, and that while such studies or profiles will undoubtedly be of inestimable value to future biographers, it is generally agreed that a certain number of years should have elapsed before any life can be properly evaluated and seen in perspective to its time.

The autobiography of a well-known personality is often published at the peak of that person's career rather than towards the end of his or her life; subsequent volumes may follow. Marriage to a famous person, or a unique achievement, may also provide the motive. In recent years there has been a spate of childhood memoirs, by no means all written by well-known people, but each with something unique to contribute to the social history of their day.

There is much to be said for starting to write your memoirs early on – or at least assembling the material – while the people you need to mention are alive and events fresh in your mind. You may not know at that stage whether you will achieve the status that merits a published autobiography, but if in the event you do not, then at least you will have written a piece of family history that can be handed down to the grandchildren. And if you deposit a copy with your local record office or at the Society of Genealogists in London, you will have made a worthwhile contribution towards the social history of the period – one for which future researchers and historians will be immensely grateful. Such documentation is going to be decidedly thin on the ground later on in the 21st century!

The writer who embarks on a biographical project normally has some good reason for wanting to do it, such as kinship to the subject, or an intimate working relationship with him or her, and/or the possession of – and access to – original papers. If a number of 'lives' have already been published on the person concerned, he may simply have a burning desire to write from a fresh angle, to 'set the record straight' or to throw new light on some controversial aspects as a result of recent research. It is generally accepted that the famous characters of history will stand new biographies roughly every ten years.

Whatever the motive, it is advisable to try to get the work commissioned and – especially where a full-length book is envisaged – to secure a cash advance, for there will be a considerable amount of research to be undertaken and expenses to be met. In calculating the likely total costs, you should not forget to take into account your own working time. Out-of-pocket expenditure will include travel, meals away from home, postal and telephone charges, photocopying, photographs and stationery, at the very least; there may well be 'extras' such as library search fees, fees payable to a genealogist or research assistant, the cost of professional word-processing and indexing, reproduction fees for illustrations, and so on.

Before a publisher signs a contract, or parts with any money to a writer who is unknown to him, he normally asks to see a synopsis, or maybe even a chapter or two, of the proposed work. The research that has to be done for the purposes of writing this synopsis is roughly the same as that required for a short biographical feature: both must include the salient points of the life and mention the existence of any hitherto unpublished material and/or recent research that provide a new angle. It must be done in sufficient depth so as to convince the potential publisher that the book will be a good investment.

The writer who has reached this stage is bound to be familiar with the outline life of his subject. However, it may not be out of place to record here, as an *aide-mémoire*, the main sources open to biographers and to researchers seeking biographical information for use in other work.

The importance of researching 'in the round' has been stressed earlier in this book. In biographical research this is particularly important: it is essential to uncover the whole person, 'warts and all'. At the research stage, therefore, nothing should be avoided or glossed over or left unexplored. Motives for your subject's actions may be discussed in the final work, and whether you write from a more or a less sympathetic angle is a matter of interpretation rather than one of research: this is a decision each individual writer must make, with the agreement of his publisher, once he has satisfied himself as to the true facts.

PRIVATE PAPERS

One good reason for allowing a certain amount of time to elapse before writing a biography is that there may not be access to private papers for a given number of years after the biographee's death. Although you may have possession of your subject's personal papers and the blessing of the family concerned to make use of them, it is more than likely that much other relevant material exists in the papers of others and that this may be subject to restrictions. Papers deposited in record offices and other archives are normally subject to the thirty-year closure rule or, in special cases, to an even longer period. Permission may be needed from the family or the estate before the documents may be seen. Although the copyright of correspondence belongs to the writer, the actual letters belong to the recipient or to his heirs or executors, or to anyone else who has acquired them; in practice, unless there is some good reason to the contrary, permission is usually forthcoming – but it may be stipulated that the text of the biography must be submitted before going to press. It is important always to make due acknowledgment to the source of such material and to comply with any request for prior submission of the text.

It is true that modern biographies *are* often written without the permission of the subject's family and thus without access to the private papers, but a writer who decides to embark on such a work should be fully aware beforehand of the difficulties that can arise. Quite apart from missing out on material and close family recollections and anecdotes, it may be less easy to obtain other people's help (there is no doubt that when seeking interviews or writing for information, magic phrases such as 'the official biography', 'sanctioned by the family', and so on, do carry weight and often swing the balance in the biographer's favour where someone is hesitant about supplying information). More serious can be the reaction of relatives to an 'unauthorised' biography, with the possibility that if they are seriously displeased they may seek an injunction through the courts.

The location of unpublished source material in general has been discussed in chapter 4, 'Basic Sources of Information and their Location' (see pages 69–76). The biographer needing to find out whether any private papers exist, and, if so, their whereabouts, should first have a look at the National Register of Archives (NRA), maintained by the Royal Commission on Historical Manuscripts (HMC). At the time of writing (early 2003) the Commission (now part of the National Archives) is still at Quality House, Quality Court, Chancery Lane, London WC2A 1HP, but is scheduled to move to the PRO building at Kew towards the end of 2003 (see chapter 4, 'Basic Sources of Information and their Location', page 70). The NRA consists of more than 43,000 unpublished lists and catalogues of major manuscript collections, including those of private individuals; the indexes alone contain some 150,000 references and 300,000 related records. The most useful of these indexes to the biographer is the Personal Index, where you will find details of the nature and location of an individual's papers, including where that person's correspondence is housed in other collections. You can search all the indexes either in person at the HMC or online at their website www.hmc.gov.uk/nra. After the move to Kew, you will need a National Archives reader's pass for access.

The HMC's publications include an ongoing series of *Guide to Sources for British History*, based on private papers and other unpublished information held in the NRA. The twelve volumes published to date include guides to the papers of cabinet ministers, churchmen, colonial governors, diplomats, politicians and scientists (see list in the bibliography to chapter 4, page 81). Another valuable research tool is the Commission's *Surveys of historical manuscripts in the United Kingdom: a select bibliography*, which is maintained online.

The Department of Manuscripts in the British Library and the Public Record Office are both major sources. Many universities also have important holdings. The National Maritime Museum at Greenwich has a comparatively recent manuscript collection of interest to the naval biographer. The Churchill Archives Centre at Churchill College, Cambridge is collecting papers of 20th-century politicians, scientists, and military and naval commanders. To check on other holdings use the 'General Index to Collections' at the back of *British Archives: A Guide to Archive Resources in the United Kingdom*.

The papers of lesser-known persons are more difficult to track down. If you are not in touch with the family or are unable to trace any living relatives, and the local record office has no deposited papers, you may be able to trace executors or other persons likely to be in possession of a deceased person's papers through a will at First Avenue House (see chapter 8, 'Family and Local History', pages 153–4). If you are writing a biography of someone who lived in the last fifty years, even if you do have access to family and private papers, an advertisement in the national or local press may help: many unexpected and valuable 'fish' are netted in this way, in the shape of replies from friends, teachers, colleagues, employees and others who have known, worked with or met the subject at some period of his life, and may produce fascinating and very usable factual or anecdotal material of which you would otherwise be unaware.

It is important to remember that the papers of even the most eminent public personages contain a certain amount of correspondence from people in lesser walks of life, and if you have reason to believe that the subject of your biography had dealings with someone whose papers have been catalogued and/or deposited, do not overlook this source. When researching for biographical information on professional people, it is always worth contacting the librarian or archivist of the relevant society or institution; some of these bodies hold collections of important private papers and most have biographical information that you may not find easily elsewhere, going back to the date of their foundation.

'Private papers' in this context are not limited to correspondence, but may consist of almost any kind of documentary material, such as account books, scrapbooks and photograph albums, visitors' books, personal diaries, and so on.

PRINTED AND OTHER SOURCES

Biographical dictionaries

There are some superb biographical reference tools available to the researcher today, both nationally and internationally.

In this country there is to be a new full edition of the *Dictionary of National Biography* in 2004, a major undertaking for the Oxford University Press, in association with the British Academy. It will be published both in printed and online versions, with illustrations, under the title *Oxford Dictionary of National Biography*. The online version will be updated continuously. The present '*DNB*', as it is known to scholars, librarians and researchers, has been since its inception in 1882 the major source of biographical information on nationals of this country. There are 22 main volumes containing entries in alphabetical sequence for persons who died up to 1900, and a series of supplementary volumes (one per decade originally, then one every five years). A *Missing Persons* volume of entries for some worthy persons 'omitted' from the main *DNB* from its beginning up to 1985 was published in 1993. There is also a very useful *Chronological and Occupational Index to the DNB*.

Few individuals are likely to be able to afford the money or the shelf space for the massively expanded new edition of some 50,000 biographies, but it is good to know that it will be in the libraries for consultation. Whether there will be a *Concise Oxford DNB* or a *Compact* edition (with magnifying glass) as before, remains to be seen. What has been made clear is that the new *DNB* will include entries for those people who were omitted last time round because of scandals in their lives. (If you cannot wait until 2004, I suggest you look at the recently published *Brewer's Rogues, Villains & Eccentrics: An A to Z of Roguish Britons through the Ages*, compiled by William Donaldson.)

Most foreign countries publish their own equivalent to the *DNB*: these are listed under 'Biography' in *Walford's Guide to Reference Material*, vol. 2, under each country.

Probably the most important biographical reference tool currently in progress is the massive World Biographical Information System launched by K.G. Saur Verlag of Munich in 1982. This consists of a series of *Biographical Archives* on microfiche (32 to date), each supplemented by printed index volumes, and also the *World Biographical Index*, a cumulated index of the *Biographical Archives*, available on CD-ROM and online (free) at www.saur.de. Eventually this mammoth project, which has a wide international, regional and occupational coverage and spans many centuries, will cover the entire world. For some countries there is so much source material that there is already more than one series. The German Biographical Archive was the first to be published, in 1982; like the *British Biographical Archive* (*BBA*) and the *British Biographical Index*, it is already in its second series. There are now *Archives* for Africa, America, Australia, China, most European countries and Latin America; also a *Jewish Biographical Archive*. Others in progress and planned include Canada, India, Japan,

Korea, Russia, Turkey, a *Biographical Archive of the Classical World* and an *Arab-Islamic Biographical Archive*. A detailed brochure is available from K.G. Saur Verlag, PO Box 701620, 81316 Munich, Germany.

The Encyclopedia of World Biography, published by The Gale Group of Detroit, USA, is another ongoing major source, comprehensively indexed and cross-referenced. Also from Gale is the regularly updated *Biography and Genealogy Master Index*, which in its microfiche version is known as the '*Bio-Base*'. The information is extracted from hundreds of English-language biographical dictionaries and *Who's Who* compilations. Birth and death dates are stated, together with the source (in abbreviated form), which may be verified in an accompanying booklet. Another major source, albeit with an American bias, is the mammoth *Biography Reference Bank* on the WilsonWeb database (www.hwwilson.com), updated four times a week. From the same publisher are the *Current Biography* printed and online publications (see bibliography at the end of this chapter), as well as the *Wilson Biographies* and *Wilson Biographies Plus Illustrated*, all updated monthly.

With such massive modern tools at the researcher's disposal (see also the sub-heading 'Bibliographies' below), it seems unnecessary to list the many biographical dictionaries on offer. However, every writer needs at least one for quick reference. Outstanding among such compilations is the *Chambers' Biographical Dictionary*. The best quick reference for contemporary British biography is *Who's Who*. There are also ten *Who Was Who* volumes containing entries for those who died during the years 1897–2000, and a *Cumulated Index* volume (1897–2000). *Debrett's People of Today* carries entries for a number of people who have not qualified for inclusion in *Who's Who*.

International reference works of contemporary biography include the *International Who's Who*, the *Dictionary of International Biography* and *Who's Who in International Affairs*. New from Melrose Press is a series of 'Outstanding' short biographies, grouped under field of activity (intellectuals, scholars, scientists, etc.; see the bibliography at end of this chapter). Many foreign countries publish their own *Who's Who* volumes; a selection of these titles is listed under individual countries in chapter 10 (see pages 170–88). The *Almanach de Gotha*, previously an annual German publication long-established as the definitive biographical and genealogical record of European royalty and nobility, reappeared in 1998 under a UK imprint, after an absence of more than half a century. Its two volumes, which now include every living member of every ruling and formerly ruling royal and princely house of Europe and South America, are updated regularly.

There are now biographical dictionaries and *Who's Who* volumes relating to almost every trade or profession from acting to zoology, some of which are published annually and others at irregular intervals. Readers will find some recommended titles listed by subject in Appendix I (see pages 217–38). These should be easily located in the reference library; if not, ask at the enquiry desk for them. *The Oxford Companion* series is another good source of biographical information.

Encyclopedias are invaluable for quick reference, both for contemporary and historical lives; the articles are often followed by a brief bibliography which will lead the researcher on to other sources. The *Who's Who in British History* series covers the British Isles from Roman to Victorian times.

Bibliographies

If you want to find out whether a biography of a particular individual has been published in this country, your best source is the *British National Bibliography* (*BNB*) – look under 'Biographies'. You might also want to check out the national bibliographies of other countries for biographies written in other languages.

In Germany a massive international research tool, the *Index Bio-Bibliographicus Notorum Hominum*, is in progress. Of the 200 volumes planned, 117 have been published to date; it will be some years before it is complete.

Most scholarly non-fiction works contain up-to-date bibliographies, and if you find there is a recently published study of your subject or of any of his close friends or contemporaries, it will pay you to buy rather than to borrow such a book, so that you can keep it beside you as you write and make notes and underlinings in it of special sources, people and places. If you cannot buy the book, then be sure to photocopy the bibliography – this will make an excellent starting point for your research. With luck, it will include references to newspaper and periodical articles. If it does not, then you should make a search in the *British Humanities Index* or, if appropriate, one of the earlier subject indexes to periodicals mentioned in chapter 4, 'Basic Sources of Information and their Location' (see pages 63–4).

Obituaries

Obituaries are an excellent source and often the starting point for biographical research, since the more recent notices usually provide both an outline of a person's life and an evaluation of his career.

To find notices of people who died earlier than the mid-19th century, the six-volume *Musgrave's Obituary* is the first place to look; you should also use the *Indexes to the Biographical and Obituary Notices* in the *Gentleman's Magazine* (the two volumes cover the years 1731–1819) and, if you know the approximate year of death, *The Annual Register of World Events*. For obituaries of prominent persons who have died since the early 1800s, *The Times* is the best source; in recent years as many as 600 obituary notices have been printed annually in that paper. Provided you have an approximate date of death, a search in *The Times Index* should not take long. The three printed volumes, *Obituaries from The Times*, for the years 1951–60, 1961–70 and 1971–75, are out of print but should be in libraries; or ask for the replacement microfilm editions.

Not everyone you may expect to find in *The Times* has achieved an obituary there (much depends on how many other eminent people died the same day), and so the *Daily Telegraph*, the *Guardian* and the relevant local newspapers should be checked.

The local paper of the area in which a person was resident often prints a notice that did not 'make' the nationals or one that goes into greater detail. Professional and trade journals, where appropriate, are especially useful for the evaluation of a person's career.

The Times, the Daily Telegraph and the Guardian do of course carry obituaries of the most prominent people worldwide, but for wider coverage you should look in the national press of the relevant country.

Diaries, letters and memoirs

A great deal of information will be obtained about a person from the published diaries, letters or memoirs of his friends and contemporaries. As research progresses, therefore, it is an excellent plan to keep an ongoing list of all names that crop up and systematically to check these out at the library. Use the indexes to these books to locate the relevant passages. If you think there may be unpublished journals or correspondence, consult the National Register of Archives, as explained earlier in this chapter under the heading 'Private Papers' (see pages 125–6).

School and university records

School and university records provide excellent source-material, both for details of a person's scholastic and academic achievement, and also for information concerning his extra-curricular activities (sports, drama, public-speaking, etc.) and – especially important – the names of contemporaries and friends, schoolmasters and tutors. Should any of these people still be alive, they may have useful contributions to make and can usually be traced through the school or university, or – if they themselves have achieved eminence – in the current Who's Who.

The registers of many universities, schools and colleges in the United Kingdom have been printed. If the particular one you seek is not listed in the library catalogue, get in touch with the college or school secretary. Research of this nature may involve you in a visit to the educational establishment concerned, or you may be put in touch with the secretary of the relevant 'Old Boys' or 'Old Girls' association. Don't overlook the college or school magazines, as these will yield important information on your subject's contemporaries as well as (possibly) on his own classroom or sporting achievements. Addresses, with names of current headmasters and headmistresses, will be found in the Independent Schools Yearbook and the Education Authorities Directory and Annual. Universities and colleges are listed in The World of Learning. The registers of Oxford and Cambridge, Alumni Oxonienses and Alumni Cantabrigienses, and A.B. Emden's Biographical Registers of both these universities to 1500 are of special value to the historian, while the Historical Registers series for Oxford and Cambridge brings the records up to the present day.

Service records

You should encounter no great problem in obtaining details of a person's Service career. Records more than one hundred years old are held at the Public Record Office, where there are also complete runs of the *Army, Navy* and *Air Force Lists*; current volumes of these are usually available in major reference libraries. Guides to the records at the Public Record Office include *Army Records for Family Historians; Records of the Militia and Volunteer Forces 1757–1945; Army Service Records of the First World War; Naval Records for Genealogists; Records of the Royal Marines*; and *Air Force Records for Family Historians*. There is also the admirable, but not now fully up-to-date, *Guide to the Sources of Military History* by R. Higham.

Your first port of call for army records should be the National Army Museum Library, Royal Hospital Road, London SW3 4HT (tel. 020 7730 0717, ext. 2222; fax 020 7823 6573; email info@national-army-museum.ac.uk; website www.national-army-museum.ac.uk). Twentieth-century records only are held at the Liddell Hart Centre for Military Archives, King's College, Strand, London WC2R 2LS (tel. 020 7848 2015; email archives.web@kcl.ac.uk; website www.kcl.ac.uk/lhcma). Regimental histories are another good source and may be traced in the Society for Army Historical Research's *Bibliography of Regimental Histories*. J.M. Brereton's *Guide to the Regiments and Corps of the British Army* includes, along with other information, addresses of regimental headquarters to whom to write for further details. Another highly recommended book, now out of print but available in libraries, is G. Hamilton Edwards' *In Search of Army Ancestry*.

For naval records, as well as the PRO, you should go to the Caird Library at the National Maritime Museum (see Appendix I, under 'Naval', page 230). The Museum has published a useful list, *The Commissioned Sea Officers of the Royal Navy 1660–1815*. Another informative source-book is the PRO's updated *Records of Merchant Shipping and Seamen*.

The first port of call for research into Air Force records should be the Royal Air Force Museum, on the site of the former Hendon airfield (Grahame Park Way, Hendon, London NW9 5LL; tel. 020 8205 2266; fax 020 8200 1751).

Business records

Details of a person's business career can sometimes be obtained from the organisation or company by whom he was employed. Naturally there are restrictions on the amount of information that will be divulged to an outsider, but in special circumstances the researcher may be allowed access to the relevant files. If the person you are interested in was active in business in Britain during the period 1860-1980 you should look him up in the *Dictionary of Business Biography*; unfortunately this publication has not been updated beyond 1980.

There may be a company history, either published or printed for private circulation, which will provide extremely useful background material. You can check this in the *International Directory of Company Histories* or the *International Bibliography of Business History*. Annual returns and other statutory documents, including lists of all directors and company secretaries, of public, private limited and guarantee companies may be inspected (on microfiche) at the Companies House Information Centre (Department of Trade and Industry), 21 Bloomsbury Street, London WC1B 3XD or (original files) at the Companies House, Crown Way, Maindy, Cardiff CF4 3UZ (for all enquiries tel. 0870 333 3636; fax 029 2038 0517; email genenquiries@companieshouse.gov.uk; website www.companieshouse.gov.uk). A modest search fee is payable per file, and there are full photocopying facilities.

The Business Archives Council (BAC), whose objectives include the efficient preservation and use of business records, will advise researchers on the availability and location of archives. Their London office having closed at the end of January 2003, enquiries are now handled by the BAC Hon. Secretary, Fiona Maccoll, Records Manager, Rio Tinto PLC, 6 St James's Square, London SW1Y 4LD (tel. 020 7753 2338; fax 020 7753 2211; email fiona.maccoll@riotinto.com). Note that the BAC continues to publish the occasional survey of historical business records in a variety of fields; ask for a list.

BAC's Scottish counterpart, the Business Archives Council of Scotland, may be contacted at Glasgow University Archive Services (GUAS), 13 Thurso Street, Glasgow GL11 6PE (tel. 0141 330 5515; fax 0141 330 4158; email bacs@archives.gla.ac.uk). Use the enquiry form(s) on the ARCHON directory page for mailing or faxing to the Duty Archivist there.

Company information may also be obtained on the Lloyds-TSB helpline of the British Library Business Information Service (tel. 020 7412 7454/7977; fax 020 7412 7453); brief enquiries are answered free of charge.

Members of Parliament and government officials

Dod's Parliamentary Companion, first published in 1832, is the indispensable British biographical source-book for the modern period. Earlier information will be found in the Institute of Historical Research series (12 volumes published to date), *Office Holders in Modern Britain*. There is one volume per ministry, some of the lists beginning in 1660 and covering the entire period up to 1870; recent additions to the series are volumes on officials of Royal Commissions of Inquiry 1870–1939 and on officers of the Royal Household. Another good source is the four-volume *Members of Parliament*, in which you will find the names of all MPs in England from 1213 and in Scotland and Ireland from 1357 and 1559 respectively; the lists continue up to 1874, for the United Kingdom, and there is an index volume. For further information, or if you fail to find what you are seeking in printed sources, write to the Clerk of the Records at the House of Lords Record Office, House of Lords, London SW1A 0PW; the search room there is open to the public by appointment. For the location of private papers of Members of Parliament and selected public servants, consult the Royal Commission on Historical Manuscripts' *Guides to Sources for British History*, volumes 1 (*Papers of British cabinet ministers 1782–1900*) and 7 (*Papers of British politicians 1782–1900*); also the *Guide to the Papers of British Cabinet Ministers 1900–1951*, published by the Royal Historical Society. The papers of a number of 19th-century British prime ministers, statesmen and politicians are marketed on microfilm by Primary Source Microfilm (The Gale Group/Thomson Learning) of Reading.

Public speeches and broadcasts

Speeches of significance are usually reported in the national press and may be traced in *The Times Index* either under the speaker's name or under the name of the socie-ty or conference addressed. The texts of Members' speeches in Parliament are print-ed in *Hansard: Parliamentary Debates* (separate series for the House of Commons and the House of Lords); transcripts of each day's business are online at noon the next weekday at www.parliament.the-stationery-office.co.uk. Lectures or papers read before learned or professional bodies are normally printed in the transactions or proceedings of such institutions at a later date.

To check on broadcast or televised speeches and interviews, your best plan is first to contact the British Library National Sound Archive, 96 Euston Road, London NW1 2DB (tel. 020 7412 7440; fax 020 7412 7441; email nsa@bl.uk); an appointment will be made for you to listen to or view the relevant transmission, provided it is in their collections. (Note that the NSA includes a collection of Parliamentary sound recordings.)

Once you have ascertained the date, it may be possible to obtain a transcript from the BBC or the independent radio or television company. (The availability of tran-scripts is subject to certain copyright restrictions.) Unfortunately the BBC Written Archives Centre at Caversham Park, Reading, offers access only if you are commis-sioned to write a book or article, or are undertaking accredited academic or com-mercial research (see Appendix I, pages 219–20).

Travel

Obtaining information about a person's travel may be unexpectedly complicated, where no diary or travelogue was kept. Hotel registers and shipping company records are not always retained for more than a few years, although it is always worth asking. (For example, the P & O Group's archives were deposited at the National Maritime Museum in Greenwich in the autumn of 1977.)

British Transport historical records are now at the Public Record Office in Kew, and so are the records of the former Board of Trade (now the Department of Trade and Industry) from c. 1890; the latter contain lists of all arrivals in, and departures from, the United Kingdom, but only a sample (roughly one-tenth) of passengers' lists and ships' logs, so that it is very much a matter of luck whether the information you seek will be obtainable. Factual details such as dates of departure, ports of call, tonnage and which company owns a particular vessel may be quite easily verified in back issues of *Lloyd's Shipping Index* or *Lloyd's Voyage Record*.

The historical archive of the Department for Transport is currently held at the Ashdown House Information Centre at 123 Victoria Street, London SW1E 6DE. All research enquiries should be made in the first instance either in writing or by telephone to the public enquiry unit (tel. 020 7944 3333). For modern transport information you may be directed to one of several site libraries such as that at Great Minster House, 76 Marsham Street SW1P 4DR, a few minutes' walk away.

FURTHER RESEARCH

Having cast your net, and hauled in your initial catch of material, your next task will be to sort the documentation into periods, or other natural chapters, of the life. As you proceed, make a note of any supplementary research to be undertaken. For a short biographical feature or the synopsis of a book, it is fairly safe to rely on the standard or most recent work, plus your own special knowledge; but if you are embarking on a full-length biography you must go through and evaluate for yourself *all* the published material. Make index cards or slips for each book or article read, and keep these in alphabetical sequence; this will take only a few minutes at the time and will be of immense value both for quick reference as you write and at the end of the day, when it comes to compiling the bibliography (see chapter 11, 'Preparation for the Press', page 191).

Some professional help may be required for your chapter on family ancestry (see chapter 9, 'Specialist Research', pages 166–7) and if so, this should be arranged at the earliest possible moment: professional freelance genealogists are usually committed for several months ahead.

At the same time the question of employing outside researchers should also be carefully considered. Where the source material is located at some distance from your home, or if it is essential to go through a run of several years of a particular paper that is available only at the British Library Newspaper Library at Colindale, for instance, it may pay you to offload part of the routine research and leave yourself free to tackle the trickier, more demanding aspects of the work.

Inevitably some travelling will be involved, and it makes sense to plan this so that several sources and/or interviews can be combined on each trip. A visit to the family home, if it still exists, is essential, and on such a visit time must be allowed for conversations with local inhabitants and – particularly important – with anyone close to the family who is still alive, such as a gardener, nanny or cook, where appropriate, or perhaps the vicar or local schoolmaster or publican. It goes without saying that this applies only when you are researching for biographies of people who are either still alive or recently deceased; in the case of subjects who were born, say, earlier than 1900, you have no choice but to rely on documentary sources such as the local newspaper or church magazine, or the records of any local societies with which the family is known to have been connected. The local librarian or secretary of the local historical society will usually be helpful in this respect, and you could strike lucky in that the descendants of an old family retainer may have cherished stories handed down verbally from one generation to the next, along with old photographs or other mementoes, so that any opportunity of visiting such people should always be taken up.

Corroboration of family births, marriages and deaths since 1837 may be obtained at the Family Records Centre, and of divorces, wills and administrations (since 1858) from the Principal Registry of the Family Division now at First Avenue House (for details of these and how to trace earlier records, see chapter 8, 'Family and Local History', pages 142–64). To verify the date of an engagement you may need to search the appropriate pages of *The Times*, *Daily Telegraph* or local newspaper; these papers also carry reports of christenings, weddings, funerals and memorial services in the case of prominent members of society.

If your biographee was involved in any major legal proceedings, you should be able to check this in the *All England Law Reports*, which begin in 1558 and are indexed; or use *The Times Index* and look up the law report in that paper (these have been published since January 1788). Once you have the date of the court proceedings you can, if you require a more popular account or a 'sensational' headline to quote, then go to other newspapers of the same date. Researchers who do not have access to law libraries (normally open only to members of the profession) may like to know that there is a complete set of the *All England Law Reports* on the open shelves at Holborn Public Library, 32–38 Theobalds Road, London WC1X 8PA (tel. 020 7413 6345).

SPECIAL PROBLEMS

The problems most likely to crop up during research for an autobiography or a biography are the following:

Names

In private correspondence and diaries people are often mentioned by nickname or given name only, and their identity may not be clear to you at the outset of research. It is an excellent idea to keep an alphabetical list or card index of everyone who crops up in the course of your work; apart from its value to you personally as a private 'who's who' of identification, it will come in very useful should any editorial note be required (and also later on for the index). Among pitfalls to avoid are the danger of confusing titles (always check on which duke or earl you are referring to at any one time) and the various names by which a woman may be known during her life, due to a series of marriages and/or divorces and the possibility that she may have reverted to her maiden name for professional or other reasons. To add to the confusion, titled persons are sometimes referred to by title and sometimes by surname, which may not be the same.

Dating letters

Letters all too frequently present the biographer with unforeseen problems. Far too many people had (and still have) the habit of dating their correspondence 'Thursday', 'Sunday, 12th' or 'Amsterdam, Monday', or – which is worse from the researcher's point of view – of not dating them at all. You should also be aware that some individuals are prone to stuff free hotel or club stationery into their briefcases and to use it weeks or even months later, so that although such correspondence may be dated, you cannot be absolutely certain that the writer was actually resident at the hotel or club at the time: if there is any doubt at all in your mind on this score, try to verify the date and/or place in another source.

Some expert detective work is often necessary before you can establish the correct chronological sequence of a bundle of correspondence. The most obvious clues are: the address from which the letter is, or is alleged to be, written; the person to whom it is written; the subject-matter. Look also at the handwriting; the ink; the paper: should there be a watermark, this will not give you the precise date of the letter, but it will provide firm evidence that the document cannot have been written earlier than the date of the watermark.

If, on first reading, a letter does not appear to offer any clue of this kind, do not despair. Re-examine it closely for mention of any family, national or world event – perhaps the death of a well-known person, an exhibition or play seen, a new novel read, and so on, the dates of which can then be checked out in the national press, *Whitaker's Almanack* and other sources. Letters that you cannot even guess at dating should be kept apart from the rest; sooner or later, as work progresses, you are more than likely to stumble on some information (nearly always when you are not looking for it) that will enable you to slot such letters into their right sequence. The use of the *Handbook of Dates for Students of English History* or *Whitaker's Almanack* for checking the day of the week of given dates has been explained on pages 95–6.

Handwriting is a great revealer of character, and in recent years many biographers have sought the help of trained graphologists (a trend which spread from France). However, you should not be tempted to try to do it yourself with the aid of any one of a number of books on the subject, entertaining as many of them are (on doodles, for example), as you could go very wrong. It takes years to qualify as a professional graphologist; in the United Kingdom there are approximately only 100 with an internationally recognised diploma. Costs depend on the depth of the analysis required. At the Graphology Bureau Ltd., The Studio, 1B Limpsfield Avenue, London SW19 6DL (tel./fax 020 8780 9530) there is a minimum charge of £150. If you decide to ask for an analysis, you need to send a selection of original – not photocopied or faxed – letters or other documents, preferably of varying dates. Before embarking on this course of action, however, you may like to read the article, 'Graphology and the Biographer', by graphologist Mary Nicholson in the winter 1994 issue of *The Author*.

Verbal information

It is beyond the scope of this chapter to examine in detail all the possibilities open to the biographical researcher. However, if the basic principle is followed of taking each natural phase of the life in turn, verifying dates and events in printed and other records and supplementing the documentary material with the recollections of contemporaries wherever obtainable, you will not go far wrong. A word of warning about the use of verbal information: human nature being what it is, people do frequently tend to try to enhance their own status (either in the researcher's eyes or their own or with a view to their name appearing in print) by exaggerating their intimacy or acquaintance with a well-known person, and memories in general are, sadly, far from infallible. Similarly with autobiography. How many of us can rely on being able to recall with 100 per cent accuracy the exact sequence of events in a particular week or how passionately we felt about something or someone, say, twenty or more years ago? We *think* we remember. But do we – *truthfully*?

Imagining how it was is a poor substitute for the comment recorded at the time. The human memory plays strange tricks. Always therefore make a point of double-checking any story that is told to you or any event you think you remember. If you cannot verify it from a reliable printed source, try to get corroboration from a second person. Confidences must, of course, be respected at all times and care taken to avoid giving offence to relatives or other persons who are still alive. Where private individuals have been especially helpful or informative, it is good manners to let them see the draft text before going to press, and to acknowledge their assistance in the book.

Happily for the responsible writer of biography and autobiography in Britain, the 'infringement of privacy' legislation under discussion a few years ago, and mentioned in two previous editions of this book, appears to have been put on hold for the time being, if not scrapped altogether. The traditional liberty to portray one's subject 'warts and all' remains sacrosanct.

Air Force List, published annually since 1949, formerly by HMSO, now by The Stationery Office, London

Air Force Records for Family Historians, by William Spencer, PRO Publications, London, 2000

All England Law Reports: reprint 1558–1935, 36 vols + index, published 1966–68; since 1936 weekly, with 4 bound vols and cumulative index annually, Butterworth Publishers, London

Almanach de Gotha, published annually in Germany, 1764–1944; since 1998 by Boydell & Brewer, Woodbridge, Suffolk, 2 vols, regularly updated (latest vol I, 2003; vol II, 2001)

Alumni Cantabrigienses: A Biographical List of all known Students, Graduates and Holders of Office to 1900, by J. and J.A. Venn, 10 vols, Cambridge University Press, 1940–54; Kraus reprint, 1974

Alumni Oxonienses: The Members of the University of Oxford 1500–1886, by J. Foster, 8 vols, Parker, Oxford, 1888–92; Kraus reprint, 1968

The Annual Register of World Events, published since 1758; now by Keesings Worldwide, Washington D.C. (UK office: 28a Hills Road, Cambridge CB2 1LA)

Army List, first published 1814, now annually by The Stationery Office (formerly HMSO), London (an earlier series from 1754 may be seen at the PRO, Kew)

Army Records for Family Historians, by Simon Fowler and William Spencer, PRO Publications, London, rev. edn, 1998

Army Service Records of the First World War, by William Spencer, PRO Publications, London, 3rd expanded edn, 2001

Bibliography of Regimental Histories, compiled by A.S. White, Society for Army Historical Research with The Army Museums Ogilby Trust, London, 1965. Now out of print, but the library of the National Army Museum, Royal Hospital Road, London SW3 4HT (tel. 020 7730 0717) maintains a regularly updated interleaved version

Biographical Archive, ongoing international series published on microfiche by Saur, Munich, in progress since 1982; printed index volumes and cumulative *World Biographical Index*, on CD-ROM and online, *q.v.*

Biographical Register of the University of Cambridge to 1500, by A.B. Emden, Cambridge University Press, Cambridge, 1963

Biographical Register of the University of Oxford to 1500, by A.B. Emden, 3 vols, Oxford University Press, Oxford, 1957–59; reissued 1989. *Supplement 1501–1540*, 1974

Biography and Genealogy Master Index, published by Gale Research International (now The Gale Group), Detroit, USA, 2nd edn, 1980– ; on microfiche as *Bio-Base*

Biography Reference Bank, published by H.W. Wilson, New York, online (WilsonWeb) at www.hwwilson.com, updated four times a week*

Brewer's Rogues, Villains & Eccentrics: An A-Z of Roguish Britons through the Ages, compiled by William Donaldson, Cassell, London, 2002

British Archives: A Guide to Archive Resources in the United Kingdom, by Janet Foster and Julia Sheppard, Macmillan, London, 4th edn, 2001

British Biographical Archive (BBA), on microfiche, Saur, Munich, series I, 1984–88; series II, 1991–94

British Biographical Index, Humanities Reference Unit, University of Glasgow, published by Saur, Munich: series I, 4 vols, 1991; series II, 2nd cumulated and enlarged edn, 7 vols, 1998

British Humanities Index (BHI), first published 1915 by the Library Association, London, then by Bowker-Saur, and now by CSA UK, East Grinstead; quarterly, with accumulated annual volume; on CD-ROM as *BHI Plus*, quarterly; updated regularly on www.cas.com

British National Bibliography (BNB), weekly since 1950, with cumulative monthly, annual and some 5-yearly volumes; now published by British Library National Bibliographic Service, Wetherby, weekly in print, monthly on CD-ROM

Chambers' Biographical Dictionary, first published 1897; latest edn, Chambers Harrap, Edinburgh, 2002

The Commissioned Sea Officers of the Royal Navy 1660–1815, National Maritime Museum, London, 1954

Current Biography, published by H.W. Wilson, New York, monthly since 1940; Cumulated Index 1940–2000 volume, 2001; also *Current Biography International Yearbook*, annually; online on WilsonWeb (www.hwwilson.com) as *Current Biography 1940–Present* and *Current Biography Illustrated*, updated monthly*

Debrett's People of Today, published by Debrett's Peerage, London, annually since 1990; available on CD-ROM from 1997, also online at www.debretts.co.uk

Dictionary of Business Biography, ed. David J. Jeremy, 5 vols, Butterworth, London, 1984–86

Dictionary of International Biography, published since 1963; 29th edn, Melrose Press, Cambridge, 2001

Dictionary of National Biography (DNB): to 1900, 22 vols, Oxford University Press, London, 1885–1900; 10 later vols, for the period 1901–90, published 1912–96. *The Concise DNB*, to 1985, 3 vols, 1992. *A Chronological and Occupational Index to the DNB*, 1985. *Missing Persons*, 1993. CD-ROM edition of complete *DNB*, 1996. Will be replaced in 2004 by the *Oxford Dictionary of National Biography, q.v.*

Dod's Parliamentary Companion, published annually since 1832, now by Vacher Dod Publishing Ltd.; updated quarterly as *Vacher's Quarterly*

Education Authorities Directory and Annual, published by the School Government Publishing Company, Redhill

Encyclopedia of World Biography, 2nd edn, 17 vols, The Gale Group, Detroit, 1998; supplementary vols (18–23), 1998–2003; also as CD-ROM and e-book

Gentleman's Magazine: Index to the Biographical and Obituary Notices, 2 vols: *1731–1780*, British Record Society, London, 1891; *1781–1819*, by B. Nangle, Garland Publishing, New York and London, 1980

'Graphology and the Biographer', by Mary Nicholson, *The Author*, Society of Authors, London, winter 1994

Guide to the Papers of British Cabinet Ministers 1900–1951, compiled by C. Hazelhurst and C. Woodland, Royal Historical Society, London, 1974; new edn published by Cambridge University Press for the RHS, 1996

Guide to the Regiments and Corps of the British Army, by J.M. Brereton, Bodley Head, London, 1985

Guide to Sources for British History, Royal Commission on Historical Manuscripts, London, series in progress since 1982, 12 vols to date (see list of titles on page 81)

Guide to the Sources of British Military History, ed. R. Higham, Routledge, London, 1972; reprinted 1989

Handbook of Dates for Students of English History, by C.R. Cheney, first published 1945; 2nd edn, eds. C.R. Cheney and Michael Jones, Cambridge University Press, 2000

Hansard: Parliamentary Debates (House of Commons and House of Lords), 1803

onwards; now published daily during sessions by The Stationery Office (formerly HMSO), London. Chadwyk-Healey, Cambridge, publishes various series of Reports and Parliamentary Papers from 1715 on microfilm, microfiche and CD-ROM

Historical Register series (Universities of Cambridge and Oxford): Cambridge University Press and Oxford University Press respectively

In Search of Army Ancestry, by G. Hamilton-Edwards, Phillimore, Chichester, 1977

Independent Schools Yearbook (*Boys' Schools, Girls' Schools, Co-educational Schools and Preparatory Schools*), published annually by A & C Black, London

Index Bio-Bibliographicus Notorum Hominum, Biblio Verlag, Osnabruck, in progress, 1972– (117 vols to date); also on CD-ROM

International Bibliography of Business History, compiled by S. Goodhall, Routledge, London, 1996

International Directory of Company Histories, St James Press, now part of The Gale Group, Detroit, USA, in progress, 1988– (57 vols to date)

International Who's Who, published annually by Europa Publications, London; now with free online access to purchasers

Jewish Biographical Archive, on microfiche, Saur, Munich, 1994–96, supplement 1998; series II, 2001

Lloyd's Shipping Index, first published as *Lloyds Weekly Index* in 1882, by Lloyd's of London, now weekly by Informa Maritime Transport, London

Lloyd's Voyage Record, published weekly since 1946 by Lloyd's of London, now by Informa Maritime Transport, London

Members of Parliament, 4 vols: I–II, *England 1213–1702*; III, *Great Britain 1705–1796*, *United Kingdom 1801–1874*, *Scotland 1357– 1707*, *Ireland 1559–1800*; IV, *Index*, HMSO, London, 1878–91

Musgrave's Obituary prior to 1800, ed. Sir G.J. Armytage, 6 vols, Harleian Society, London, 1899–1901

Naval Records for Genealogists, by N.A.M. Rodger, PRO Publications, London, 1998

Navy List, published annually since 1814, now by The Stationery Office, London (formerly HMSO); earlier listings at PRO, Kew

Obituaries from The Times, 3 vols covering the period 1951–75, Research Publications International, Reading, 1975–79 (no later vols); microfilm editions, Primary Source Microfilm, Reading

Office Holders in Modern Britain series, Institute of Historical Research, London, 12 vols to date, 1972–

Oxford Companion series (70 titles), Oxford University Press, Oxford, regularly revised; some paperback editions

Oxford Dictionary of National Biography, eds. Colin Matthew and Brian Harrison, Oxford University Press, in association with the British Academy, scheduled for 2004; also online

Papers of British cabinet ministers 1782–1900, Royal Commission on Historical Manuscripts Commission, *Guide to Sources for British History No. 1*, London, 1982

Papers of British politicians 1782–1900, Royal Commission on Historical Manuscripts Commission, *Guide to Sources for British History No. 7*, London, 1989

Records of Merchant Shipping and Seamen, by Kelvin Smith, Christopher T. Watts and Michael J. Watts, PRO Publications, London, 1998; updated edn 2002

Records of the Militia and Volunteer Forces 1757–1945, by William Spencer, PRO Publications, London, 1997

Records of the Royal Marines, by Garth Thomas, PRO Publications, London, 1994

Surveys of historical manuscripts in the United Kingdom: a select bibliography, online at Royal Commission of Historical Manuscripts website www.hmc.gov.uk

The Times Index, 1785 to present day, currently by subscription, updated monthly, with annual hardback cumulation; 1906–76, on microfilm; on CD-ROM (as part of *British Newspaper Index*) from 1990: all from Primary Source Microfilm (The Gale Group), Reading. Also *Palmer's Index to The Times*, 1790–1905, on CD-ROM and online, Chadwyck-Healey, Cambridge

2000 Outstanding Europeans of the 21st Century; 2000 Outstanding Intellectuals of the 21st Century; 2000 Outstanding Scholars of the 21st Century; 2000 Outsanding Scientists of the 21st Century, Melrose Press, Cambridge, 2002

Walford's Guide to Reference Material, vol. 2, Social and Historical Sciences, Philosophy and Religion, Library Association, London, 8th edn, 2000 (see chapter 4, page 86 for details of the *New Walford*, due in 2004)

Whitaker's Almanack, published annually by A & C Black, London

Who Was Who, published by A & C Black, London, 10 vols to date, covering the period 1897–2000; *Cumulated Index 1897–2000*; also available on CD-ROM as *Who's Who 1897–1998*

Who's Who, published annually by A & C Black, London

Who's Who in British History, Shepheard Walwyn, London, 8 vols, hardback and paperback edns; 9th vol. (20th century up to 1945) in preparation

Who's Who in International Affairs, Europa Publications, London, 3rd edn, 2002

Wilson Biographies and *Wilson Biographies Plus Illustrated*, published by H.W. Wilson, New York; updated monthly on Wilson Web (www.hwwilson.com)*

World Biographical Index, Saur, Munich, 10th CD-ROM edn, 2002; also online

The World of Learning, published annually by Europa Publications, London

Note: Space does not permit a full listing of the *Who's Who* volumes for the various professions and foreign countries, of which there are now at least 100 titles published by different firms; researchers should have little difficulty in tracing these in the relevant major library cataloguing systems. Selected titles are listed in chapter 10 (pages 170–88) under country and by subject in Appendix I (pages 217–38).

* H.W. Wilson publications are distributed in the UK by Thompson Henry Ltd., London Road, Sunningdale, Berks SL5 OEP (tel. 01344 624 615; fax 01344 626 120; email thl@thompsonhenry.co.uk).

Chapter Eight

Family and Local History

IN RECENT YEARS people have become increasingly obsessed with tracing their own family ancestry, so much so that genealogy is now rated as the second most popular hobby in the UK – after gardening. (Globally, insofar as the Internet is concerned, there is said to be almost as much interest in genealogy as in pornography.) Millions of people worldwide, it seems, fuelled by the findings of the genetic scientists, are are bent on discovering their roots. Writers, especially those writing their own memoirs, biographies and historical novels, all need to do *some* research in this field; if you are embarking on a book-length family history or a history of your town or village you will have to do more. Students who have worked on a project at school or adult education college often decide to develop it into a more comprehensive study. Some of the problems researchers are likely to encounter have been outlined already in chapters 4 and 6, 'Factual and Historical Research' and 'Biography and Autobiography'.

The first thing to be aware of is that family or local history research can be exceedingly complex and costly, both in terms of working time and of search and certificate fees. If you regard it as a hobby, so that time is not a factor, you need only to be prepared for it to be a lengthy and sometimes frustrating – but, at the end of the day, usually rewarding – occupation. A considerable amount of preliminary study is essential in order to familiarise yourself with the various classes of records available and the kind of information to be derived from them. If you are a writer with a publisher's deadline to meet and you seek only a small detail to incorporate in your book – maybe ancestral research for the first chapter of a biography, or the tracing of a particular will, or a contemporary account of some event in a particular parish featured in an historical novel – I strongly advise you seriously to consider using the services of a professional genealogist or record agent, or a firm such as Debrett's Ancestry Research Ltd. or Burke's Ancestry Research Department (see 'Specialist Research', pages 166–7). Otherwise, the amount of preparatory study will be out of all proportion to the information sought.

Genealogical research has been revolutionised by the new technology. Whereas up to a few years ago the researcher usually had to visit record offices all over the country and spend a great deal of time poring over half-legible handwitten parish registers and other records, or stumping through muddy churchyards in an attempt to decipher the inscriptions on old gravestones, nowadays a lot of the preparatory work can be done at home, working online, or from CD-ROM and microfiche.

There is an ever-growing mountain of dedicated genealogical software on the market to help you to find your way through the labyrinth of databases and records and, most importantly, to make sure you store your retrieved material in the correct way. I do not have space to evaluate the different programs here, and in any case not all of them will suit everyone. Before you start your research, I suggest that you spend a little time studying the genealogical magazines mentioned later in this chapter, or, better still, get professional advice from your local family history society or from a fellow genealogist.

So far as the published guides to online genealogy are concerned, be a little cautious. If you are doing your research in Britain, as I believe the majority of my readers are, it is important to choose a handbook that covers the subject from a British viewpoint. (Quite a few of the widely advertised manuals are published in the United States and are less useful to the novice genealogist over here.) I personally would recommend two first-class, up-to-date titles, both by Peter Christian, who is a much respected lecturer in online genealogy in the UK: *Finding Genealogy on the Internet*, written for the Federation of Family History Societies, and *The Genealogist's Internet*, published by the Public Record Office. There are also two Good Web Guide CD-ROMs, *Genealogy* by Caroline Peacock and *Tracing Your Family History* by Caroline and Jonathan Peacock. One of the best international guides is *Genealogy Online* by Elizabeth Powell Crowe. (For other more general guides to genealogy, see later in this chapter, pages 156–7.)

GETTING STARTED

How to begin the daunting task? Firstly, you should sort and store the papers and photographs you already have in the family. Talk to as many elderly relatives as possible. Then you should consider joining the Society of Genealogists or your local family history society (preferably both): attend their meetings and possibly also take a weekend or longer course of study both in genealogy and in palaeography (the study of old handwriting). It will help if you have some knowledge of Latin. Most adult education centres run courses on local history and genealogy. The opportunities for learning palaeography are rare, although Madingley Hall, just outside Cambridge, usually runs a weekend course for beginners at some stage during the year (details from the Registrar, Madingley Hall, Madingley, Cambridge CB3 8AQ; tel. 01954 280399; website www.cont-ed.cam.ac.uk). In London the Society of Genealogists periodically organises a full-day introductory tutorial. On genealogy itself, if you have the time, there are several courses, including a comprehensive course in Family History Skills, leading to a diploma, that may be followed on a full- or part-time basis, or as a home study course; contact the Registrar, at the Institute of Heraldic and Genealogical Studies, 79–82 Northgate, Canterbury, Kent CT1 1BA (tel. 01227 768664; fax 01227 765617; email ihgs@ihgs.ac.uk; website www.ihgs.ac.uk). The Institute runs a bookshop as well as a library containing many useful indexes and other relevant material.

Members of the Society of Genealogists, 14 Charterhouse Buildings, Goswell Road, London EC1M 7BA (tel. 020 7251 8799; fax 020 7250 1800; website www.sog.org.uk) enjoy free use of the Society's library, with its unique collection of printed, manuscript, microfiche and microfilmed material (including the largest collection of parish register copies in the country), free attendance at tutorials and other events, and the benefit of a reduced rate for research carried out by members of the staff; they also receive a quarterly journal, *Genealogists' Magazine*. The Society's other quarterly periodical, *Computers in Genealogy*, is offered to members at a reduced subscription. A leaflet, 'Using the Library of the Society of Genealogists', is available. The writer who intends to do any extensive genealogical research, and who lives in or with good access to London, will find membership very worthwhile at £43 per year (£40 if you pay by direct debit). Non-members may use the library on payment of a small fee – currently £3.50 for one hour, £9.20 for four hours, and £14.50 for a day, or a day and evening – and may subscribe to both publications.

There are family history societies and local history groups in most counties of the UK. Subscriptions are modest, and members benefit from advice on their researches as well as from the exchange of information with fellow genealogists and historians. An up-to-date list of these societies, giving the secretaries' names and addresses, is available on receipt of a first-class stamped addressed envelope or two international reply coupons from the Administrator, Federation of Family History Societies (FFHS), PO Box 2425, Coventry CV5 6YX (mobile tel. 07041 492032; email info@ffhs.org.uk; website www.ffhs.org.uk).

A subscription to the Guild of One-Name Studies, which is closely associated with the Society of Genealogists and the FFHS, would be worthwhile in the long term, but probably not if you are engaged on a 'one-off' search for the ancestry chapter of one book. Members receive a quarterly journal, *One-Name Studies*, and also a Register listing the names that are currently being researched worldwide, with the name and address of a 'registered member' to contact for information on each name. For a small fee you may register a name, provided it has not already been registered; but in doing so, you give an undertaking to deal with all reply-paid enquiries about that name – so consider carefully before you commit yourself (it could be a drain on your writing time!). The Hon. Secretary of the Guild may be contacted direct at 74 Thornton Place, Horley, Surrey RH6 8RN or c/o Box G, The Society of Genealogists, 14 Charterhouse Buildings, Goswell Road, London EC1M 7BA. The website is www.one-name.org.uk.

The leading publishers of family and local history in this country are Phillimore & Co. Ltd., Shopwyke Manor Barn, Chichester, West Sussex PO20 6BG (tel. 01243 787636; fax 01243 787639; website www.phillimore.co.uk) and Sutton Publishing (now part of Haynes Publishing), Phoenix Mill, Thrupp, Stroud, Gloucestershire GL5

2BU (tel. 01453 731114; fax 01453 731117; email sales@sutton-publishing.co.uk). The Phillimore bookshop, at Shopwyke Manor Barn (address on page 144; email bookshop@phillimore.co.uk) also stocks titles from other publishers and will supply books by post: ask to be put on their catalogue mailing list. The Society of Genealogists' bookshop has recently closed, its publications now being sold direct only to members and the trade (members receive a 20% discount); non-members may order them through the normal bookselling channels, *Family Tree Magazine* (see below), or Amazon. A complete catalogue of FFHS publications is online at www.familyhistorybooks.co.uk. The Society of Genealogists, the FFHS and *Family Tree Magazine* all publish handbooks and leaflets to assist the amateur family and local historian; these are updated regularly.

It is very worthwhile subscribing to one or more of the genealogical magazines. These include *Ancestors*, a relatively new publication from the Public Record Office (six issues a year); *Family History News and Digest*, published twice a year (April and September) by the FFHS; *Family Tree Magazine*; *The Local Historian* (formerly *The Amateur Historian*); and *Practical Family History*. All of them are crammed with useful information. You will also find there the addresses of freelance genealogists, suppliers of software and electronic products, private advertisers selling certificates for which they have no further use and secondhand or re-conditioned equipment such as microfiche readers, and bed-and-breakfast accommodation on offer close to record offices. At *Practical Family History* subscribers have the use of a helpline telephone number for brief enquiries.

A subscription to the annual *Genealogical Research Directory*, published in Sydney, Australia, entitles you to register up to fifteen names in which you are interested; the book is circulated throughout the world and may eventually bring you the bonus of an exchange of information with other subscribers. (See bibliography at the end of this chapter for the address of the UK agent.)

At this stage you are ready to tap the main sources, either by accessing them online or by visiting them personally.

ONLINE SEARCHES

Your best starting point, when working from home, is the *Family Search* database of the Church of Jesus Christ of Latter-Day Saints (known more familiarly as the Mormon Church), of Salt Lake City, Utah in the United States. Through this database (www.familysearch.org) you can access and search the mammoth *International Genealogical Index* (*IGI*), the *Ancestral File*, and the *Family History Library Catalog*.

The *IGI*, which is now updated weekly, has become a major first-port-of-call research tool for genealogists worldwide. Compiled and computerised by the Genealogical Department of the Church, it contains over 200 million records, mostly birth and baptismal (but also some marriage) entries dating from the early 1500s, arranged alphabetically by surname and (so far as the UK is concerned) by county. By keying in a name and a county you can bring up on screen, and print out, a list of all entries under that name. Sadly, it has to be said that the *Index* has never been either comprehensive or 100% accurate: coverage and accuracy vary from county to county. But it is an excellent starting point, provided that you go on to double-check the information in the original sources.

The *Ancestral File*, also maintained by the Mormons of Salt Lake City, consists of family trees donated by researchers and Church members, also containing millions of names.

Searching the *Family History Catalog* under locality and surname will help you to ascertain which records in the UK Library are most likely to be of use to you. This Library, which is open to all, is at the Hyde Park Family History Center of the Church of Jesus Christ of Latter-Day Saints, at 64–68 Exhibition Road, London SW7 2PA (tel. 020 7589 8561). Plenty of computers are available, and there is no need to book in advance. You can print out information at the unbelievably low cost of 5p per page or 50p per floppy disk (or if you take your own disk there is no downloading charge). In addition to the *IGI* and *Ancestral File*, the Library holds some 48,000 films and fiches containing British, Irish and Scottish parish records.

Finally, there are two websites that are worth visiting: www.genuki.org.uk, which is a clear and concise searchable index to the records available for the UK and Ireland; and www.cyndislist.com, a vast American site with some 182,000 links to genealogical sources and 1.5 billion names throughout the world, plus many FAQ and other useful tips for researchers. The FFHS publishes a useful booklet by David Hawgood, *Genuki:UK & Ireland on the Internet*, which explains very clearly how to use the site.

USING COUNTY RECORD OFFICES, ARCHAEOLOGICAL SOCIETIES AND OTHER COLLECTIONS

Your next port of call, when embarking on a family or local history, should be the local record office, where the archivist or an assistant archivist will usually be willing initially to discuss the project with you and to explain what records are available. Some county record offices publish useful pamphlets for students on how to trace the history of a house, a parish or a family, and most have a printed or microfiche guide to their collections, as well as regularly updated lists of parish registers and other documents that have been deposited.

On arrival at the record office or archive centre you will be asked for proof of identity, such as a driving licence or NHS medical card, so that a reader's ticket and/or CARN card may be issued. Some repositories require one or two photographs (check this in advance of your visit). The CARN (County Archive Research Network) card gives the user access to archives in all other participating record offices and archive centres. You will probably be asked to deposit all bags and briefcases and, if you are going to handle original manuscripts, you may be issued with a pair of cotton gloves.

A short list of record offices will be found in Appendix I (pages 203–13). More detailed information is contained in the PRO/HMC booklet *Record Repositories in Great Britain*; this is regularly updated online at ARCHON, on the website of the Royal Commission of Historical Manuscripts (www.hmc.gov.uk). Two excellent printed guides are Jeremy Gibson and Pamela Peskett's *Record Offices: How to Find Them* and *In and Around Record Repositories in Great Britain and Ireland* by Jean Cole and Rosemary Church. The principal public libraries have local history collections, and those of local archaeological societies are usually open to *bona fide* researchers (non-members may be asked to pay a modest search fee). Where information is needed from outside your own district, it is always worth sending a preliminary letter (with self-addressed stamped envelope) to the local archivist or chief reference librarian. Most county archivists used to be happy to answer simple enquiries, such as the verification of not more than one or two entries in a parish register (a baptism, marriage or burial), but nowadays, owing to the severe cutback in local government expenditure, staff no longer undertake searches free of charge. Advice will, however, always be given on the records available for consultation, as well as practical help over any problems encountered in the search room; and most county record offices will, on request, also supply the names and addresses of local freelance record agents. Many record offices and archive centres, and some public libraries, offer a research service on a fee-paying basis, usually at an hourly or half-hourly rate. If you live some distance away this is worth consideration, although you may obtain results faster by employing an agent direct. You should nevertheless always enquire on your first visit whether there is any member of staff who happens to have a special knowledge of, or interest in, your subject. Photocopies, photographs, microfilms and certified copies of most documents are usually obtainable at reasonable cost.

A list of local archaeological societies, with names and addresses of secretaries, will be found in *Whitaker's Almanack*.

THE FAMILY RECORDS CENTRE

Once you have exhausted local sources, you should visit the Family Records Centre (FRC) in London. This is where you will find indexes to births, marriages and deaths, census returns, PCC wills and many other records (see below, under relevant headings).

The Family Records Centre, which opened in July 1997, is administered jointly by the Office for National Statistics (ONS) and the Public Record Office (PRO). At 1 Myddleton Street, London EC1R 1UW, it is within walking distance of several other major sources for family and local history such as the London Metropolitan Archives, the Society of Genealogists, and the Probate Search Rooms at First Avenue House, High Holborn. A useful photocopy map of the area is available from the Centre, showing public transport; there are also instructions on how to get from the FRC to the PRO at Kew. The staff are friendly and helpful; a series of leaflets on how to use the various facilities may be picked up from the New Customers Desk on the first floor, where there is a Research Enquiries Desk. There is also an excellent up-to-date printed handbook, *The Family Records Centre: A User's Guide* by Stella Colwell.

As well as the the records mentioned above, you will also find at the FRC, mostly on microfilm, miscellaneous foreign returns of births, marriages and deaths, death duty registers and Nonconformist registers. Using the computers provided, you can also search there the *Family Search* databases mentioned earlier in this chapter, including the *IGI*. There are photocopying facilities, and a bookshop. It is a popular venue for all family historians and usually quite crowded. For further information telephone the Centre at 020 8392 5300 or visit their website www.familyrecords.gov.uk.

THE NATIONAL ARCHIVES: PUBLIC RECORD OFFICE

Next on your itinerary should be the Public Record Office at Kew (see chapter 4, 'Basic Sources of Information and their Location', pages 71–2). Here again you will find much of the material you need on microfilm, to which you help yourself in the Microfilm Reading Room. Try to get there early in the day to secure a seat: it has become so popular that the genealogists, both professional and amateur, searching there at any one time are said to out-number the historians in the main Reading Room.

The PRO publishes a series of *Pocket Guides to Family History* (twenty-four in all) to help researchers find their way through the labyrinth of records available; you can buy them singly or as a set. Jane Cox's *New to Kew?* and Amanda Bevan's *Tracing Your Ancestors in the Public Record Office* are essential reading.

So much for the general whereabouts of your source material. As to the more specific records, you need to search for the two categories of writing:

FAMILY HISTORY

A family history may have as its starting point a rough tree drawn up by a relative or ancestor, or – if you are lucky – a more professional pedigree; possibly even a collection of papers handed down from one generation to another or recently discovered in an attic of the ancestral home. The first thing to do is to make reasonably sure that a history has not already been written or a tree drawn up. This can be checked in one of several ways: in the catalogue or subject index of one of the copyright libraries; at the library of the Society of Genealogists; at the College of Arms (Queen Victoria Street, London EC4V 4BT; tel. 020 7248 2762; fax 020 7248 6448; email enquiries@college-of-arms.gov.uk; website www.college-of-arms.gov.uk); and at the local record office nearest to the family home. Remember that many family histories are privately printed or may have been deposited at the record office, or donated to the local library, in typescript.

If the family is likely to have been recorded in any of Burke's publications, the place to look is *Burke's Family Index*. This useful volume has references to some 20,000 different family histories.

The next step is to verify, one by one, the dates of all births, marriages and deaths, and – other people's memories being what they are – also to check the names, allowing for variations in spelling. The usual procedure is to work methodically backwards in time, either from yourself or from the person you are writing about, first to the parents, then the grandparents, and so on, generation by generation. As already suggested, if you have a PC, you should make use of some of the specially designed software to help you store and sort the fruits of your research. Alternatively, set up a card index system, with a separate card for each individual, on which you enter each piece of information as it is verified; or there are specially printed genealogical record cards or 'research work-books' on the market (available from the Society of Genealogists, and other genealogical suppliers).

You should draw up your own draft family tree as you proceed; but if the tree is to be published, it is best to have it professionally drawn.

Verifying births, marriages and deaths

Since 1 July 1837 all births, marriages and deaths in England and Wales, together with some overseas (consular) and service returns, births and deaths at sea, etc., have been centrally recorded at the General Register Office (GRO) in London. Formerly at St Catherine's House, these records are now held at the Family Records Centre (see above, pages 147–8, and Appendix I, page 219). In Scotland, where registration began in 1855, the records are housed at the office of the Registrar General, New Register House, Edinburgh EH1 3YT (tel. 0131 334 0380; website www.gro-scotland.gov.uk). In Ireland, the records from 1864 to 1921 are at the office of the Registrar General, Joyce House, 8–11 Lombard Street East, Dublin 2 (tel. 00 3531 6354000; website www.groireland.ie), for the whole of the country and for the Republic since 1922; Northern Ireland records dating from partition are in the care of the Registrar General, Oxford House, 49–55 Chichester Street, Belfast BT1 4HL (tel. 028 9025 2000; website www.groni.gov.uk).

In London searches may be made in person at the Family Records Centre, where there is a computerised link to the indexes at the GRO in Scotland. It should be remembered that access is to the indexes only, not to the actual registers. The index volumes are arranged according to the quarter of the year in which the event (birth, marriage or death) was registered, and alphabetically under surnames. Unless you have an approximate date to go on, you must be prepared for a long haul – and an exhausting one, as pulling out one heavy volume after another is exceedingly tiring. (Eventually all these indexes may be available online, but that is a long way off.) The information given is minimal, so that sometimes you may not be certain that you have found the correct entry; but if you request a copy of the relevant certificate and the parentage and/or spouse does not match with the information you have to give on the application form, a refund will be made. As full certificates currently cost £7 apiece, this is an important consideration. (There is a shorter form of certificate – available for births only – but this is insufficient for genealogical research purposes as it contains only the name, sex, date and place, but *not* the parentage.)*

There is an Adopted Children's Register from 1927 at the FRC, and adopted persons over the age of 18 may apply there for their original birth certificate.

It is always worth getting copies of birth, marriage and death certificates, as the detail given on them – such as the occupation of a child's father, the witnesses to a marriage, the cause of death and the address at which it occurred – will be invaluable and may lead you on to other channels of enquiry. Since 1968 death certificates include the date of birth. For those who live a long way from London (or Edinburgh, Dublin or Belfast), copies of certificates may be obtained by post, in which case a higher fee is charged, currently (from April 2003) £8.50 if you supply the GRO Index reference or £11.50 without a reference; this includes a search carried out by staff over a five-year period. Certificates ordered in person at the FRC are available for collection after four working days, or will be posted first class on the fourth day. Postal applications, with cheque or postal order payable to 'ONS' should be sent to the General Register Office, PO Box 2, Southport, Merseyside PR8 2JD; telephone or fax orders, with payment by debit or credit card, to 0151 471 4800. If the GRO Index reference is quoted, certificates are posted within ten days, those without a reference within twenty-eight days. A priority service is available by post, telephone or fax; certificates will be posted on the day following receipt of application (details of special costs, tel. 0151 471 4816; fax 01704 550013). You can also apply for certificates at the local register office where the event was registered, if you know this.

Parish registers

Ministers in England were first ordered to keep records of all baptisms, marriages and burials in 1538; some registers therefore start in that year, but others were not commenced until a few years later or the earliest volumes have not survived. Not all parish registers have been deposited at the relevant local record office, but current legislation provides that clergy who do not have adequate facilities for preservation and storage must deposit them within a reasonable time.

The best way to find out whether or not a particular parish register has been deposited is to telephone or visit the website of the relevant local record office; with new registers being deposited all the time, the situation is constantly changing. If the record office does not have what you require – and often they will not have registers of recent date – they will give you the name and telephone number of the incumbent in whose possession the relevant registers are, or you can look this up in *Crockford's Clerical Directory*. To obtain access to these current registers, you must write or telephone to make an appointment, as either the minister or his parish clerk must be present at the search. A fee is payable to the incumbent for this service: based either

---

* Copies of birth certificates are currently available on demand, but may in future be subject to some restrictions in order to prevent their fraudulent use as a means of obtaining false passports, driving licences, etc.

on the time spent or on the number of years searched, this is no longer standard, but you can expect to be asked for up to £15 per hour. If you are making a long search, you may be able to negotiate a special rate. To avoid any misunderstanding, it is wise to establish the fee before you make the appointment. (*N.B.* If you cannot get to the vestry yourself and the incumbent agrees to do the search for you, he is entitled to charge a higher fee.)

It is as well to remember that directories such as *Crockford's* go to press months ahead of publication and cannot therefore be totally up-to-date. (The same, alas, applies to this book.) To avoid your letter of enquiry being forwarded on to another parish, should the incumbent listed have moved (which at best will cause delay and may mean that you never receive a reply), it is wise to address it impersonally, i.e. to 'The Incumbent', 'The Rector' or 'Vicar'.

It is important for the novice researcher to remember that parish registers do not record the exact dates of birth or death, but only those of baptism and burial. (A few of the more diligent parish priests also noted the dates of births and deaths, but not many.) In some parishes there are separate registers for baptisms, marriages and burials; in others, the baptisms and burials may be recorded in the same book, starting at different ends, and where the incumbent ran out of space the entries are sometimes continued a few pages later or, worse, may be merged – be careful not to overlook these.

An alternative source, especially when it is difficult to gain access to the registers, are Bishop's Transcripts (copies of parish registers made by each minister and sent annually to the Bishop of his diocese). Unfortunately these are not altogether reliable and indeed are sometimes different, as entries were often copied wrongly, or even omitted. It is essential to make a double-check in the original registers. Many registers have been transcribed and/or printed over the years, and an increasing number are now available for purchase or library study on CD-ROM (for suppliers, see note at end of bibliography, page 164).

There is a *National Burial Index for England and Wales* on CD-ROM, published by the FFHS; it contains over 5.3 million names, dating from 1538 to the modern period.

The National Index of Parish Registers, a vast project started over twenty years ago, is now periodically revising or reprinting some of its earlier volumes. The first three volumes of the *Index* (*I, Sources for Births Marriages and Deaths before 1837*; *II, Sources for Nonconformist Genealogy and Family History*; *III, Sources for Roman Catholic and Jewish Genealogy and Family History*) are especially useful; the remaining volumes are regional, with the two final volumes, *XII, Sources for Scottish Genealogy and Family History*, and *XIII, The Parish Registers of Wales*. The best quick reference tool is *The Phillimore Atlas and Index of Parish Registers*.

Marriage registers and indexes

Marriage registers generally are separate from those of baptisms and burials; some are more informative than others. Supplementary information may be obtained from records of the intention to marry, such as banns, licences, marriage bonds and allegations. Advice on the availability of these will be given by staff on duty in the record office. Many of the Phillimore marriage records and parish registers are marketed on CD-ROM by S & N Genealogy Supplies (see note at end of this chapter, page 164).

Boyd's Marriage Index, compiled by Mr Percival Boyd from parish registers, Bishop's Transcripts and the marriage licences of England, covers most of the English counties in the period 1538–1837. It contains more than 3.5 million names and is housed at the Society of Genealogists in London; a booklet published by the Society and entitled *List of Parishes in Boyd's Marriage Index* gives the dates for each parish included. This is an important source for the researcher who already knows the place or county of the marriage he wishes to trace. However, it is neither complete nor infallible (Mr Boyd died in 1955), and entries should always be verified in the relevant parish register. This is a golden rule in genealogical research when using any printed or transcribed registers or indexes.

Another important marriage index is *Pallot's*, containing some 4.5 million marriages between 1780 and 1837. The original is at the Institute of Heraldic and Genealogical Studies (IHGS) in Canterbury; it is also available on CD-ROM from TWR Computing (see note at end of this chapter, page 164). Enquiries may be sent to the IHGS by post, and searches will be made on a fee-paying basis, currently (early 2003) £15 per half-hour.

You can purchase a catalogue to *Pallot's* (£5) from the Institute, or buy it on CD-ROM. *Boyd's Marriage Index* is available on microfiche.

There are also a number of local marriage indexes compiled both by family history groups and by individuals, and more are in progress. Ask at your local record office, or consult the FFHS booklet, *Marriage and Census Indexes for Family Historians*.

Divorce records

Prior to the mid-19th century a full divorce could be effected only by a private Act of Parliament. Early records of Divorce Bills from 1669 will therefore be found at the House of Lords Record Office, House of Lords, London SW1A 0PW (tel. 020 7219 3074; fax 020 7219 2570; email hlro@parliament.uk; website www.parliament.uk). Since 1859 records have been kept by the Divorce Registry of the Family Division of the High Court, formerly at Somerset House, but now at First Avenue House, 42–49 High Holborn, London WC1V 6NP (tel. 020 7947 7017). Copies of divorce decrees are available (£1 if you can quote the case number; or a ten-year search will be made by staff for £20). These records are useful to the researcher, as they state the date and place of the marriage.

Nonconformist and other records

Nonconformist registers were required by law to be surrendered to the Registrar General in 1840, and these are now at the Family Records Centre. (Some registers were exempt – where they were kept in the same books as other records, such as members' lists, minutes of meetings, etc. – and you may be lucky enough to find them at local record offices.)

The Religious Society of Friends, before surrendering their records, prepared 'Digest Registers' which, together with other valuable Quaker material, may be seen at Friends' House, Euston Road, London NW1 2BJ (tel. 020 7663 1135; website www.quaker.org.uk).

Records of Huguenots in England since the mid-16th century have been published by the Huguenot Society of Great Britain and Ireland, whose library is part of the Special Collections of University College Library, now housed at 140 Hampstead Road, London NW1 2BX (tel. 020 7679 5199; website www.huguenotsociety.org.uk). Note, however, that all written enquiries should go to the Society c/o University College, Gower Street, London WC1E 6BT and that the Library is open, Monday to Wednesday, by appointment.

The archives of the French Protestant Church of London, founded in 1550, may be inspected by appointment with the Honorary Archivist, on Tuesdays and Thursdays, at 8 & 9 Soho Square, London W1V 5DD (tel. 020 7437 5311).

For further information on the existence and whereabouts of Nonconformist registers, see *Sources for Nonconformist Genealogy and Family History* (volume II of the *National Index of Parish Registers*). A useful guidebook for the researcher is Michael Gandy's *Tracing Nonconformist Ancestors*, one of the PRO's *Pocket Guides*.

Researchers seeking material on Roman Catholic or Jewish families should look at volume III of the same series, *Sources for Roman Catholic and Jewish Genealogy and Family History*. You may also like to contact the Jewish Genealogical Society of Great Britain, PO Box 13288, London N3 3WD (email jgsgb@ort.org).

Wills and administrations

Probate records constitute one of the most useful sources of genealogical information. Since 11 January 1858 copies of all wills and administrations and grants of probate in England and Wales have been centralised at the Principal Registry of the Family Division, formerly at Somerset House but now at First Avenue House, 42–49 High Holborn, London WC1V 6NP (tel. (general enquiries) 020 7947 6043; (Probate Search Rooms) 020 7947 7189). Wills and administrations are calendared alphabetically under surnames in the year in which probate was granted (which may be the same as the year of death, but is sometimes later). The calendar volumes are on open shelves, and once you have traced the will or administration you seek, the volume containing it will be produced on payment of a reading fee (currently £15 if you want to see the original, £5 for a copy). Brief notes may be made (in pencil), or alternatively a photocopy ordered, to be sent by post (£5 for one copy, £1 per additional copy, regardless of the length of the will). As with the indexes to births, marriages and deaths, the volumes are pretty massive and heavy to lift; it is envisaged that at some date in the future they may be online. For those unable to visit the search rooms in person there is a probate search service at £5 for a four-year period, plus £3 for each further four-year period; this charge includes a photocopy of the relevant document. (Apply to the Postal Searches and Copies Department, The Probate Registry, Castle Chambers, York YO1 9RG; tel. 01904 666 777; fax 01904 666776.) Researchers may like to know that there is a microfiche set of indexes to wills 1858–1943 at the Family Records Centre.

Prior to 1858 wills and administrations were proved by the courts which had general jurisdiction, of which the most important were the Prerogative Court of Canterbury (PCC) and the Prerogative Court of York (PCY). The PCC wills, formerly at the Public Record Office in Chancery Lane, London (which is now closed), have been transferred to the PRO at Kew, with microfilms (1383–1858) at the Family Records Centre (see above, pages 147–8). PCY wills are held at the Borthwick Institute of Historical Research, University of York, St Anthony's Hall, Peaseholme Green, York YO1 7PW (tel. 01904 642315; website www.york.ac.uk/inst/bihr). A search service is available at £15 per hour (minimum charge £7.50); this includes photocopies of documents. (You can fill in the request form online.) Consult your local record office for details of probate granted by other courts.

As a handbook for the first-time reader of these records I recommend Miriam Scott's *Prerogative Court of Canterbury Wills and Other Probate Records*. The standard work on PCC wills is *An Index to the Wills proved in the Prerogative County of Canterbury 1750–1800* edited by Anthony J. Camp, Director of Research of the Society of Genealogists. Eve McLaughlin's *Wills before 1858* is a useful introduction, and Audrey Collins' *Using Wills after 1858 & First Avenue House* is an up-to-date and invaluable short guide.

Census returns

The 19th-century census returns constitute some of the most valuable sources for the family historian. The complete set is on microfilm at the Family Records Centre, and relevant sections may be read at county record offices. The returns are also gradually being digitised from film and marketed at a reasonable price on CD-ROM and DVD, together with street and name indexes, for London and individual counties. Census returns exist from 1801, but personal names were not recorded until 1841. There is a surname index to the 1881 census on microfiche at the FRC, where the 1891 census (the earliest to contain essential information) is also on microfiche. The Centre also now has on microfilm a complete set of the census returns 1841–91.

As census records are subject to a 101-year rule, the most recent return open to public inspection is currently that of 1901. This is the first census return to have become available online – initially with dire results, when within the first few hours of January 2002 over a million researchers attempted to access the site, causing the entire system to crash. Which serves to emphasise what an exceptionally useful tool the census is to the family historian! (There are plans to put the 1881 and 1891 returns online in due course.) Note that the FRC now has the 1901 census returns on microfiche as well as online.

Searching the index to the online 1901 census is free of charge at www.pro.gov.uk/census; all you need to do is key in the relevant name(s) or place. It costs 75p per page to view a digital image of the original entry; this can then be saved to your own PC or an A3 copy may be ordered, which will be sent by post. To view a transcript of details from the census return costs 50p per individual. Payment is either online by credit card, in advance (minimum charge £5), or by vouchers valid for six months (no minimum charge) which can be purchased in units of £5, £10 and £50 from the Society of Genealogists or the Federation of Family History Societies (Publications), Units 15 and 16, Chesham Business Centre, Oram Street, Bury, Lancashire BL9 6EN (fax 0161 7973846; email orders@ffhs.org.uk; or through their online bookshop at www.familyhistorybooks.co.uk).

Information on the current availability of census returns on CD and DVD may be obtained from S & N Genealogy Supplies (see note at the end of this chapter). At the time of writing, 1891 census sets are on offer for London and a number of other counties, and advance orders are being taken for earlier years (from 1841), as well as for the London 1901 census. (Do not be hoodwinked by a CD-ROM from another source claiming to contain the 1991 census: it consists only of the statistics, *not* the names and addresses and occupations that are of such importance to the researcher; this information will not be released until January 2092.) The relevant census dates are:

6 June 1841
30 March 1851
7 April 1861
2 April 1871
3 April 1881
5 April 1891
31 March 1901

The great value of the census is that you will usually find the whole family (or at least those living under the same roof at the appropriate date) recorded together. The returns of 1851 onwards are the most informative, since they give exact ages and places of birth, and also each person's marital status and relationship to the household, whereas the 1841 census return states only his or her occupation, in what area of the country they were born and, for those over fifteen, ages to the lowest term of five.

It used to be essential to know, if not the exact address at which a family was believed to have been living at the date of the census, at least the parish; but with the

1901 returns now online, and some of the earlier ones digitised and indexed, it has become possible to locate relevant entries simply by keying in a name or place. Should you be unlucky enough to need to search one of the earlier returns not yet on CD-ROM or indexed, you may have to cope with a number of pitfalls: one-half of a street may appear in one enumerator's district and the other half elsewhere; and by no means were all the census enumerators scrupulously accurate. Deciphering the handwriting may be another problem too, especially in the earlier returns, or where the films are faint, but if you are searching at the FRC you will find the staff there very helpful.

Finally, it has to be stressed that delving into census returns nearly always takes longer than one imagines it will, so that the wise researcher allows plenty of time for it.

The best and most up-to-date guides are Susan Lumas' *Making Use of the Census* and Eve McLaughlin's *The 1901 Census and How to Tackle It*. Another excellent handbook is *Census Returns 1841–1891 in Microform: A Directory to Local Holdings in Great Britain, the Channel Islands and the Isle of Man* by Jeremy Gibson and Elizabeth Hampson.

Other records

The above-mentioned are just a few of the sources open to the genealogist/family historian. Searching these should enable you to draw up at least a skeleton family tree as a basis from which to work. The next stage will be to explore the various other classes of records likely to yield further information. Elucidation of the mysteries of Court rolls, Quarter Sessions records, poll books, service records, and so on, is best left to the expert. The genealogists of the future will be able to search present-day electoral registers on CD-ROM.

In the last few years a number of excellent handbooks have been published which will help the researcher. Outstanding among those not already mentioned earlier in this chapter are Mark D. Herber's *Ancestral Trails: The Complete Guide to British Genealogy and Family History*; *Family Names and Family History* and *The Oxford Companion to Local and Family History*, both edited by David Hey; and Stella Colwell's *Family History: A Guide and Troubleshooter*. The classic study remains Sir Anthony Wagner's *English Genealogy*. Other recommended handbooks include *The Family Historian's Enquire Within* by Pauline Saul and F.C. Markwell; and Terrick Fitzhugh's *The Dictionary of Genealogy*. The latter title, although sadly no longer fully up-to-date, contains over a thousand entries: descriptions and locations of records by county, as well as explanations of obsolete terms and translations of those Latin phrases most likely to be encountered in ancestry research. A useful information sheet, *Beginning Family History*, is available from the Royal Commission on Historical Manuscripts. An intriguing little handbook for the modern age is Alan Savin's *DNA for Family Historians*.

Most of the above-mentioned books contain bibliographies which will lead you on to further reading. Write to the Society of Genealogists at 14 Charterhouse Buildings, London EC1M 7BA for their catalogue (arranged under subject), or visit their online bookshop at www.sog.org.uk; also to the Federation of Family History Societies (Publications Department) Ltd., Units 15–16 Chesham Industrial Centre, Oram Street, Bury, Lancashire BL9 6EN (tel. 0161 797 3843; fax 0161 797 3846), whose online bookshop is at www.familyhistorybooks.co.uk. A catalogue of Public Record Office publications is available from PRO Publications Marketing, Kew, Surrey TW9 4DU (tel. 020 8392 5271); details of all titles, including their backlist, will be found on their website www.pro.gov.uk/bookshop.

Use should also be made of the indexes to proceedings of local archaeological societies and to publications of local family history societies (see pages 146–7). Most public libraries and county record offices possess complete sets of those relating to their districts. The standard works and guides mentioned above contain details of the records of special groups such as the Baptists, Huguenots, Methodists and Quakers.

The major printed biographical sources have been discussed in chapter 7, 'Biography and Autobiography' (see pages 123–41), but special mention should be made here of the publications issued by Burke's Peerage Ltd.: the long-awaited new (106th) edition of *Burke's Peerage and Baronetage* was published in 1999; *Burke's Family Index* has already been mentioned. A new compilation, *Burke's Baronage of Scotland*, came out in 2003. Other titles include *Burke's Dormant and Extinct Peerages*, *Burke's Guide to the Royal Family*, *Burke's Irish Family Records*, *Burke's Landed Gentry* and, international in scope, *Ruvigny's Titled Nobility of Europe* (originally published in 1914, reprinted by Burke), *Burke's Presidential Families of the United States of America* and *Burke's Royal Families of the World*. The *Almanach de Gotha*, covering European and South American royalty and their descendants, has recently been reissued after many years out of print.

Debrett's Peerage and Baronetage is revised at five-year intervals. The older, but more comprehensive, *Cockayne's Complete Peerage*, covering extant, extinct and dormant titles from 1265 was reprinted a few years ago; a final volume of addenda and corrigenda was added in 1998, bringing it fully up-to-date. *Cockayne's Complete Baronetage* is also available in a reprint. F.L. Leeson's *Directory of British Peerages*, which covers earliest times to the present day in one continuous alphabetical listing of titles and surnames, is an invaluable finding aid.

A good introduction to heraldic research, written for genealogists and local historians, is Stephen Friar's *Heraldry*. Also recommended is *The Oxford Guide to Heraldry* by Thomas Woodcock and John Martin Robinson. The best place to look up an old coat of arms when you come across one and do not know to which family it belongs is Papworth's *Ordinary of British Armorials*.

LOCAL HISTORY

Local history writing may range from a short feature in the local newspaper or county magazine to a full-length academic study. In all cases painstaking research and a good deal of detective work will be necessary; care must be taken to transcribe original documents accurately and to keep a note of all sources. References should normally be quoted in all but the shortest and most 'popular' articles.

There is a vast store of printed and manuscript material open to the local historian, much of it as yet untapped. Some of these sources have been discussed already under chapter 4, 'Basic Sources of Information and their Location' (see pages 50–87). As with family history, before embarking on a project it is wise to check with the local record office whether the same ground has been covered by someone else; even if nothing has yet been published or deposited, archivists notoriously have their 'ears to the ground' and will usually be aware of any other writers, researchers or students working on parallel lines. A preliminary study of a work of a similar nature, even if it deals with a totally different district, can be of considerable help to a writer wondering how to tackle the particular subject he has in mind.

If you are seeking the location of manorial records, first consult the *Manorial Documents Register* at the Royal Commission on Historical Manuscripts office (currently still at Quality House, Quality Court, Chancery Lane, London WC2A 1HP but moving to the Public Record Office at Kew in the autumn of 2003). Some sections of the *Register* are on the website at www.hmc/gov.uk/mdr, and more will be added in due course. Note that this is a location tool only; the HMC does not hold original manorial documents. Ask for the Commission's information sheet, *The Manorial Documents Register and Manorial Lordships*. An excellent handbook is *Using Manorial Records* by Mary Ellis, published jointly by the Commission and the Public Record Office.

Difficulty may be encountered in reading early documents, and unless you have some knowledge of palaeography and Latin, you may need to use the services of an expert. If however you are serious about learning the necessary skills, and have the time, you might, as suggested earlier in this chapter, consider taking a course on the subject (see pages 143–4). Alternatively, arm yourself with one or two handbooks, such as E.E. Thoyts' excellent *How to Read Old Documents* or *Reading Tudor and Stuart Handwriting* by Steve Hobbs and Lionel Munby. Eve McLaughlin's *Reading Old Handwriting* and *A Secretary Hand ABC Book* are good short guides for beginners. (Most 16th and 17th century records are written in the so-called 'Secretary Hand'; earlier records from the 12th century are written in various 'Court Hands'.)

The Latin of local records differs considerably from school Latin. C.T. Martin's *The Record Interpreter*, with its invaluable list of Latin abbreviations and glossary of Latin words used in English historical manuscripts and records, first published in 1892 and out of print for many years, became available again in a facsimile edition a few years ago. Among other useful reference works are the *Revised Medieval Latin Word-List*, edited by R.E. Latham and *Latin for Local and Family Historians* by Denis

Stuart. Also available is a handy listing in *A Latin Glossary for Family & Local Historians* by Janet Morris.

C.R. Cheney's *Handbook of Dates for Students of English History* and Fryde's *Handbook of British Chronology* are indispensable aids to dating: the former contains not only lists of rulers (with regnal years), popes, archbishops and other officers of state, but also include saints' days and tables that enable you to work out the day of the week of any date from AD 500 to the year 2100. Lionel Munby's *Dates and Time: A Handbook for Local Historians* is another invaluable tool.

As general introductions to the subject, David Dymond's *Researching and Writing History: A Practical Guide for Local Historians*, Robert Dunning's *Local History for Beginners* and John Richardson's *The Local Historian's Encyclopedia* are highly recommended. *The Oxford Companion to Local and Family History* has been mentioned earlier in this chapter. There is also *The Local History Companion* by Stephen Friar and the *Companion to Local History Research* by John Campbell-Kease. Among numerous other titles on the subject are the classics by W.G. Hoskins, *Local History in England* and *Fieldwork in Local History*, and W.E. Tate's *The Parish Chest*. The *Victoria County Histories* (a varying number of volumes per county) are immensely detailed architecturally and topographically. Of more general interest is the revised edition of W.B. Stephens' *Sources for English Local History*. The Historical Association's series, *Short Guides to Records* is always worthwhile. The publications of many local record societies and the Index Library have been produced on microfiche by Chadwyck-Healey (a massive 5,136 microfiches) under the general title of *Publications of the English Record Societies, 1835–1972, and the Index Library*; relevant sections may be available in your local library. Another useful tool is *A Guide to English County Histories*, edited by C.R.J. Currie and C.P. Lewis. The *Darwen County Histories* series begun in 1950 and published by Phillimore of Chichester are regularly revised. From the same publisher are Paul Hindle's *Maps for Historians* (an updated edition of the same author's *Maps for Local History*, published in 1988).

DEPOSITING PAPERS

Every writer of family or local history, whether or not his work achieves publication, should consider depositing a copy of it – together with any original papers that may have come into his possession, and possibly also his research notes – at the appropriate local record office or, in the case of a family history, at the Society of Genealogists in London. By so doing he will be making a valuable contribution to the store of material on English social history and genealogy for the use of future generations of students and researchers.

Almanach de Gotha, Boydell & Brewer, Woodbridge, Suffolk, 2 vols, regularly updated (latest vol. I, 2003; vol. II, 2001)

Ancestors, published by the Public Record Office, London, 6 times a year, since March 2001

Ancestral Trails: The Complete Guide to British Genealogy and Family History, by Mark D. Herber, Sutton Publishing, Thrupp, Stroud, Glos., in association with the Society of Genealogists, 1998; paperback, 2000

Beginning Family History, information sheet available from the Royal Commission on Historical Manuscripts, Quality House, Quality Court, Chancery Lane, London WC2A 1HP

Burke's Baronage of Scotland, Burke's Peerage, London, 2003

Burke's Dormant and Extinct Peerages, Burke's Peerage, London, reprinted 1985

Burke's Family Index, Burke's Peerage, London, 1976

Burke's Guide to the Royal Family, Burke's Peerage, London, 1973

Burke's Irish Family Records, Burke's Peerage, London, 1976; rev. edn, 1986

Burke's Landed Gentry, 3 vols, Burke's Peerage, London, 1965–72; vol. 4, 2001

Burke's Peerage and Baronetage, Burke's Peerage, London, 106th edn, 1999

Burke's Presidential Families of the United States of America, Burke's Peerage, London, 1981

Burke's Royal Families of the World, 2 vols, Burke's Peerage, London, 1977, 1980; vol. 1 reprinted 2003

Census Returns 1841–1891 in Microform: A Directory to Local Holdings in Great Britain, the Channel Islands and the Isle of Man, compiled by Jeremy Gibson and Elizabeth Hampson, FFHS, Bury, Lancs, 6th edn, 1997

[Cockayne's] The Complete Baronetage, reprinted in 6 vols, Alan Sutton, Gloucester, 1982

[Cockayne's] The Complete Peerage of England, Scotland, Ireland, Great Britain and the United Kingdom, Extant, Extinct or Dormant, 13 vols, London, 1910–59; reprinted in 6 vols, Alan Sutton, Gloucester, 1982; vol. XIV: *Addenda and Corrigenda*, ed. Peter Hammond, Sutton Publishing, Thrupp, Stroud, Glos., 1998

Companion to Local History Research, by John Campbell-Kease, A & C Black, London, 1989

Computers in Genealogy, quarterly periodical published by the Society of Genealogists Enterprises Ltd., London, 1982–

Crockford's Clerical Directory, first issued in 1858, now biennially, by Church House Publishing, London

Darwen County Histories series, published by Phillimore, Chichester; regularly revised

Dates and Time: A Handbook for Local Historians, by Lionel Munby, published by Phillimore for the British Association for Local History (BALH), 1997

Debrett's Peerage and Baronetage, published by Debrett's Peerage Ltd. and Macmillan, London, 2000

The Dictionary of Genealogy, by Terrick Fitzhugh, 5th edn, revised by Susan Lumas for the Society of Genealogists, A & C Black, 1998

Directory of British Peerages from earliest times to the present day, ed. F.L. Leeson, Society of Genealogists Enterprises Ltd., London, 1984; rev. edn, 2002

DNA for Family Historians by Alan Savin, FFHS, Birmingham, 2000

English Genealogy, by Anthony Wagner, Phillimore, Chichester, 3rd edn, 1983; reprinted 1990

The Family Historian's Enquire Within, eds. P. Saul and F.C. Markwell, FFHS, Bury, Lancs, 5th edn, 1995, reprinted with amendments 1997; 6th edn in preparation

Family History: A Guide and Troubleshooter, by Stella Colwell, Sutton Publishing, Thrupp, Stroud, Glos., 1999

Family History News and Digest, published twice a year (April and September), by the Federation of Family History Societies (FFHS), Bury, Lancs

Family Names and Family History, ed. David Hey, Hambledon Press (now Hambledon and London), London, 2000

The Family Records Centre: A User's Guide by Stella Colwell, PRO Publications, London, 2002

Family Search, database maintained by the Church of Jesus Christ of Latter-day Saints, Salt Lake City; includes *Ancestral File*, the *International Genealogical Index* and the *Family History Library Catalog*. Searchable online at www.familysearch.org

Family Tree Magazine, monthly since 1984 by ABM Publishing, 61 Great Whyte, Ramsey, Huntingdon, Cambs PE17 1HL

Fieldwork in Local History, by W.G. Hoskins, Faber, London, 1982

Finding Genealogy on the Internet, by Peter Christian, FFHS, Birmingham, 2nd edn, 2002

Genealogical Research Directory, published annually in Sydney, Australia; available from the UK agent, Mrs E. Simpson, 2 Stella Grove, Tollerton, Notts NG12 4EY

The Genealogist's Internet, by Peter Christian, Public Record Office, London, 2001

Genealogists' Magazine, published quarterly by the Society of Genealogists Enterprises Ltd., London

Genealogy by Caroline Peacock, Good Web Guide, London, 2002 [CD-ROM]

Genealogy for Beginners, by A.J. Willis and K. Proudfoot, Phillimore, Chichester, 1997

Genealogy Online, by Elizabeth Powell Crowe, Osborne (McGraw-Hill), New York, 5th edn, 2001

Genuki: UK & Ireland on the Internet, by David Hawgood, FFHS, Bury, Lancs, 2000

A Guide to English County Histories, eds. C.R.J. Currie and C.P. Lewis, Sutton Publishing, Thrupp, Stroud, Glos., 1994; paperback, 1997

Handbook of British Chronology, eds. E.B. Fryde *et al.*, Royal Historical Society, London, 3rd edn, 1986

Handbook of Dates for Students of English History, by C.R. Cheney, first published 1945; 2nd edn, eds. C.R. Cheney and Michael Jones, Cambridge University Press, 2000

Heraldry, by Stephen Friar, Sutton Publishing, Thrupp, Stroud, Glos., 1992; paperback, 1996

How to Read Old Documents, by E.E. Thoyts, Phillimore, Chichester, 1980; reprinted 2001

In and Around Record Repositories in Great Britain and Ireland, by Jean Cole and Rosemary Church, ABM Publishing, Huntingdon, 4th edn, 1998

An Index to the Wills proved in the Prerogative Court of Canterbury 1750–1800, ed. A.J. Camp, 6 vols, Society of Genealogists, London, 1976–93; some vols now out of print but on microfiche

Latin for Local and Family Historians, by Denis Stuart, Phillimore, Chichester, 1995

A Latin Glossary for Family & Local Historians by Janet Morris, FFHS, Bury, Lancs, reprinted 2002

List of Parishes in Boyd's Marriage Index, Phillimore, Chichester, for the Society of Genealogists, London, 6th edn, 1987; reprinted 1994

The Local Historian (formerly *The Amateur Historian*), published quarterly by Phillimore, Chichester, for the British Association for Local History (BALH)

The Local Historian's Encyclopedia, by John Richardson, Phillimore, Chichester, 2nd edn, 1986; reprinted 1993; revised and enlarged edn due 2003

Local History for Beginners, by Robert Dunning, Phillimore, Chichester, 1980

The Local History Companion, by Stephen Friar, Sutton Publishing (now part of Haynes Publishing), Thrupp, Stroud, Glos., 2001

Local History in England, by W.G. Hoskins, Longman, Harlow, 3rd edn, 1984; 4th impression 1990

Making Use of the Census, by Susan Lumas, PRO Publications, London, 4th rev. edn, 2002

The Manorial Documents Register and Manorial Lordships, information sheet available from the Royal Commission on Historical Manuscripts, London

Maps for Historians, by Paul Hindle, Phillimore, Chichester, 1998; reprinted 2002

Marriage and Census Indexes for Family Historians, by Jeremy Gibson and Elizabeth Hampson, FFHS, Birmingham, 8th edn, 2000

National Burial Index for England and Wales, FFHS, Bury, Lancs [CD-ROM]

National Index of Parish Registers, series ed. Cliff Webb, published by Phillimore, Chichester, for the Society of Genealogists, 13 vols, periodically revised and reprinted

New to Kew?, by Jane Cox, PRO Publications, London, 1997

The 1901 Census and How to Tackle It, by Eve McLaughlin, 2002, available from *Family Tree Magazine, q.v.*

One-Name Studies, quarterly journal of the Guild of One-Name Studies, London

Ordinary of British Armorials, by A.W.W. Papworth, 1874; facsimile edn, Tabard Publications, London, 1961

The Oxford Companion to Local and Family History, ed. David Hey, Oxford University Press, Oxford, 1996

The Oxford Guide to Heraldry, by Thomas Woodcock and John Martin Robinson, Oxford University Press, Oxford, 1990

The Parish Chest, by W.E. Tate, Phillimore, Chichester, 3rd rev. edn, 1983; reprinted 1985

The Parish Registers of Wales: vol. XIII of *The National Index of Parish Registers, q.v.*

The Phillimore Atlas and Index of Parish Registers, ed. C.R. Humphery-Smith, Phillimore, Chichester, 2nd edn, 1995

Pocket Guides to Family History series, PRO Publications, London, various dates

Practical Family History, published monthly since summer 1997 by ABM Publishing, Huntingdon, Cambs

Prerogative Court of Canterbury Wills and Other Probate Records, by Miriam Scott, PRO Publications, London, 1997

Publications of the English Record Societies, 1835–1972, and the Index Library, on microfiche, Chadwyck-Healey, Cambridge

Reading Old Handwriting, by Eve McLaughlin, 3rd augmented edn, 1999; available from *Family Tree Magazine, q.v.*

Reading Tudor and Stuart Handwriting, by Steve Hobbs and Lionel Munby, Phillimore, Chichester, 2002

The Record Interpreter, by Charles Trice Martin, originally published 1892; reprinted, Phillimore, Chichester, 2002

Record Offices: How to Find Them, by Jeremy Gibson and Pamela Peskett, FFHS, Bury, Lancs, 9th edn, 2002

Record Repositories in Great Britain, Royal Commission on Historical Manuscripts, PRO Publications, London; revised every few years (latest, 11th edn, 1999); updated online (see page 147)

Researching and Writing History: A Practical Guide for Local Historians, by David Dymond, Phillimore, Chichester, for the British Association for Local History, 1999

Revised Medieval Latin Word-List from British and Irish Sources, ed. R.E. Latham, Oxford University Press, Oxford, 1965

Ruvigny's Titled Nobility of Europe, originally published 1914; reprinted by Burke's Peerage, London, 1980

A Secretary Hand ABC Book by Alf Ison, FFHS (Berkshire Family History Society), 1982

Short Guides to Records series, Historical Association, London, 2 vols (24 guides in each), 1994, 1997

Sources for Births, Marriages and Deaths before 1837: vol. I of *The National Index of Parish Registers, q.v.*

Sources for English Local History, by W.B. Stephens, Phillimore, Chichester, rev. edn, 1994

Sources for Nonconformist Genealogy and Family History: vol. II of *The National Index of Parish Registers, q.v.*

Sources for Roman Catholic and Jewish Genealogy and Family History: vol. III of *The National Index of Parish Registers, q.v.*

Sources for Scottish Genealogy and Family History: vol. XII of *The National Index of Parish Registers, q.v.*

Tracing Your Ancestors in the Public Record Office, by Amanda Bevan, PRO, London, 6th rev. edn, 2002

Tracing Your Family History by Caroline and Jonathan Peacock, Good Web Guide, London, 2002 [CD-ROM]

Using Manorial Records, by Mary Ellis, PRO Publications, London, 1997
'Using the Library of the Society of Genealogists', leaflet published by the Society of
 Genealogists Enterprises Ltd., London
Using Wills after 1858 & First Avenue House, by Audrey Collins, FFHS, Bury, Lancs,
 1998
Victoria History of the Counties of England (*VCH*), over 200 vols published since
 1901; Institute of Historical Research, London (distributed by Oxford University
 Press, Oxford)
Whitaker's Almanack, now published annually by A & C Black, London
Wills before 1858, by Eve McLaughlin, 4th edn, 1992, available from *Family Tree
 Magazine*, q.v.

Note: Publications of the Federation of Family History Societies are obtainable
through local family history societies or from FFHS Publications Ltd., Units 15–16,
Chesham Industrial Estate, Oram Street, Bury, Lancashire BL9 6EN (tel. 0161 797
3843; fax 0161 797 3846; online bookshop www.familyhistorybooks.co.uk; email
sales@ffhs.org.uk). For a list of publications obtainable from *Family Tree Magazine*,
send a stamped addressed envelope to the magazine at 61 Great Whyte, Ramsey,
Huntingdon, Cambs PE17 1HL.

The following are publishers of family history software, CD-ROM/DVDs of parish
records, census returns, street directories and other useful genealogical products:

S & N Genealogy Supplies, West Wing, Manor Farm, Chilmark, Salisbury SP3 5AF
 (tel. 01722 716121; fax 01722 716160; website www.genealogy.demon.co.uk)
Stepping Stones, PO Box 295, York YO31 1YS (tel. 01904 424131; fax 01904 422351;
 secure web page (for orders) www.stepping-stones.co.uk)
TWR Computing, Clapstile Farm, Alpheton, Sudbury, Suffolk C010 9BN (tel. 01284
 828271; email sales@twrcomputing.co.uk; website www.twrcomputing.co.uk)

Chapter Nine

Specialist Research

WHILE IT IS always more rewarding to undertake your own research, there are times when it pays to employ an expert. Books or records to be consulted may be accessible only at some distance; specialist knowledge of a subject may be required, or familiarity with local records which it would take the inexperienced researcher, or one from another district, months, if not years, to acquire – in these circumstances the employment of a qualified researcher or expert will usually save time and money in the long term. If you have press deadlines looming, or other commitments, it may even pay you to offload some of the more routine research as well.

The best advice I can give to anyone looking for a reliable freelance professional researcher is to get a personal recommendation from another writer. Failing that, look in the *Writers' & Artists' Yearbook*, under 'Editorial, Literary and Production Services', and in *The Writer's Handbook*, under 'Miscellany'.

Some of the major libraries and record offices undertake paid research (details on application). The British Library, the Public Record Office and some other libraries and local record offices also maintain lists of researchers/record agents and will pass on names and addresses to enquirers (send a stamped addressed envelope); naturally, they do not accept any responsibility for the work undertaken by these people. Experts willing to do paid research may also sometimes be contacted through the secretaries or librarians of professional or trade societies or institutions; alternatively, an advertisement in a professional or trade journal may yield a suitable result. Some freelancers advertise their services in *The Times*, the *Times Literary Supplement*, *The Author* and similar papers. Teachers and university students often seek research assignments during the long vacation. For details of how to obtain the services of a qualified indexer, see pages 195 and 197.

Contacting a suitable researcher abroad is rather more difficult. You can write to the national library of the country concerned, or to the library or archives centre where you want the research to be done (always enclose a sufficient number of International Reply Coupons for airmail if writing overseas – one is never enough); or you can approach the cultural attaché of the relevant embassy, legation or high commission in London.

The most obvious occasions when a writer may need this kind of help are in the fields of genealogy, when a complicated ancestral search may be necessary for the first chapter of a biography; in local or family history, for which not only a knowledge of the classes of records available is required, but also some skill in reading Latin and in palaeography (transcribing old handwriting); in picture research; and in translation.

GENEALOGY

Experience in palaeography and genealogy is acquired only after considerable study, and there are many traps into which the unwary novice can fall. A working knowledge of Latin is essential for the study of medieval or earlier texts, while later source material demands the ability to read and transcribe both the 'Secretary Hand' (the script in use in England from the mid-16th to the mid-17th centuries) and the later 'Court Hand', each with distinctive forms of capital letters and contractions. Unless you are embarking on your family or local history as a hobby, therefore, and can afford the time to qualify yourself in these subjects, some professional assistance will be desirable.

It is wise to employ someone who lives in the area in which the relevant search is to be made, for he will be familiar both with the local records and with local family names and history, and thus can save the client time and money. He will almost certainly also have a library of indexes to registers and other records on CD-ROM. Most local record offices maintain lists of recommended searchers; alternatively, names and addresses of professional genealogists and record agents who are members of the Association of Genealogists and Researchers in Archives (AGRA) may be obtained from the Joint Secretaries, 29 Badgers Close, Horsham, West Sussex RH12 5RU (enclose £2.50 to cover cost and postage or six International Reply Coupons for overseas). All AGRA members have satisfied their Council as to integrity, qualifications and experience, and they adhere to a strict professional code of practice. There are similar associations in Scotland and Ireland: the Association of Scottish Genealogists and Record Agents (ASGRA), 51/3 Mortonhall Road, Edinburgh EH9 2HN (website www.asgra.co.uk); and the Association of Professional Genealogists in Ireland (APGI), 30 Harlech Crescent, Clonskeagh, Dublin 14 (email apgi@dublin.com). Send a preliminary letter or email to the Hon. Secretary in the first instance.

The College of Arms (Queen Victoria Street, London EC4V 4BT; tel 020 7248 2762; fax 020 7248 6448; email enquiries@college-of-arms.gov.uk; website www.college-of-arms.gov.uk) is open to enquiries of a genealogical and heraldic nature from members of the public (arms and pedigrees of English, Northern Irish and Commonwealth families). For personal visitors only a brief search will be made free of charge to ascertain whether or not a family tree has been drawn up; further research will be conducted on a fee-paying basis.

There are two long-established and highly professional firms in the UK who will conduct comprehensive genealogical research on behalf of clients: Burke's and Debrett's. (Be prepared, however: neither comes cheap!) Burke's Ancestry Research

Department, 209 St John's Hill, London SW11 1TH (tel. 020 7924 5132; fax 020 7924 3369; email burkespeer@aol.com; website www.burkespeer.com), which has the reputation of being very competitive, will give free advice on a genealogical search or provide a detailed feasibility assessment for £48, the cost of which will be deducted if they are commissioned to do further research. Simple research queries (i.e. for specific information) are charged on an hourly basis. At current (2003) rates (£30 an hour) a full family search is likely to cost in the region of £550.

Debrett Ancestry Ltd., which formerly catered only for royalty and the aristocracy, works slightly differently, offering a choice of two research programmes, each tracing the line of one surname: a standard genealogical research programme at £400 plus VAT, and a limited programme at £240 plus VAT. (Two or more programmes, for different names, can be carried out simultaneously.) Contact Debrett Ancestry Ltd., Dept WP, PO Box 379, Winchester, Hants SO23 9YQ (tel. 01962 841 904; email postbox@debrettancestry.co.uk) for a brochure, or visit their website at www.debretancestry.co.uk.

Other firms and individuals offering genealogical research services in various parts of the United Kingdom and abroad advertise in the *Genealogists' Magazine*, the quarterly journal of the Society of Genealogists, and in the various family history magazines mentioned in chapter 8. The Society itself will carry out research, on a fee-paying basis, for members and non-members. Enquiries, accompanied by a stamped addressed envelope, should be addressed to the Director of Research, the Society of Genealogists, 14 Charterhouse Buildings, London EC1M 7BA.

PICTURE RESEARCH

Picture research is immensely complicated and therefore beyond the scope of this book. Sometimes a writer will be expected to provide all the illustrative material for his book or article; in other cases the publisher will employ a professional picture researcher, who may be a member of his staff or a freelancer, to locate and select pictures, commission photographers, and clear the copyright and reproduction fees on a particular project. Whether the author or the publisher foots the bill for the picture researcher is a matter for negotiation. A wise author makes sure that it is stipulated in his contract that it will be the publisher who bears responsibility for print and reproduction fees, since these can be very costly.

Writers wishing to obtain the services of a qualified picture researcher are recommended to contact the Picture Research Association (formerly SPREd – now PRA) at 2 Culver Drive, Oxted, Surrey RH8 9HP (tel. 01883 730123; fax 01883 730144; email chair@picture-research.org.uk; website www.picture-research.org.uk). The Association maintains a Freelance Register (tel. 01727 833676); names and addresses of qualified researchers are supplied free of charge.

An outstanding source for historical pictures, from ancient times to the 20th century, is the Mary Evans Picture Library (59 Tranquil Lane, Blackheath, London SE3 0BS; tel. 020 8318 0034; fax 020 8852 7211; email lib@mepl.co.uk; website www.melp.co.uk). If you are unable to visit the library personally, an 'in-house' team of researchers will help to find suitable illustrations. Ask for a brochure detailing their collections and services.

There have been dramatic changes in picture research in recent years, due largely to the new digital technology, and researchers now need advanced computer and other technological skills. If you are tempted to venture into the field on your own, you should first read the excellent e-book by Julian Jackson, *Picture Research in a Digital Age*, available for purchase online – and instantly downloadable – at www.julianjackson.co.uk, and also on CD-ROM. The same author, who is a consultant to the UK picture research industry, has written an article, 'The picture research revolution' in the current *Writers' & Artists' Yearbook* (*WAYB*), published annually by A & C Black. Both the *WAYB* and *The Writer's Handbook*, published annually by Macmillan, carry lists of picture libraries and agencies in the UK; the *WAYB* also has a useful list by subject area.

Among a variety of practical manuals and useful source-books are the following:

BAPLA Directory, published annually by the British Association of Picture Libraries and Agencies, 18 Vine Hill, London EC1R 5DX (tel. 020 7713 1780; fax 020 7713 1211; email enquiries@bapla.org.uk; website www.bapla.org.uk). Lists all picture libraries and agencies in the UK
The Picture Researcher's Handbook, by Hilary and Mary Evans, 7th edn, Pira, Leatherhead, 2001; updated every few years
Picture Sources UK: A Guide to more than 1200 Public and Private Picture Collections, compiled by R. Eakins, Macdonald, London, 1985 (out of print but available in libraries)
Sources of Illustration 1500–1900, Adams & Dart, London, 1971 (out of print, but still a valuable source, available in libraries)

Note: For recommended titles on cartoons and caricaturists, see Appendix I, page 221.

TRANSLATION

Translation is another field in which professional help may be required from time to time. For basic research purposes a rough translation or précis may be adequate to work on, but any passage to be quoted in print should be prepared by a qualified translator. The best way to find one is to contact the Institute of Translation and Interpreting (ITI), Exchange House, 494 Midsummer Boulevard, Milton Keynes MK9 2EA (tel. 020 7713 7600; fax 020 7713 7650; email info@iti.org.uk; website www.iti.org.uk). The languages and skills of qualified members of the Institute, together with those of some members of the Translators Association of the Society of Authors, are listed in the *ITI Directory*, which is online and on CD-ROM. Alternatively, translation agencies will be found in the yellow pages of most telephone directories, but these normally handle commercial rather than literary texts.

The Translator's Handbook by Rachel Owens (3rd edn, Aslib, London, 1996) is an excellent introduction and source-book for all members of the profession; it will also be of use to writers who need to commission a translator.

RESEARCH FEES

Fees for professional freelance assistance are negotiable and depend on the nature and complexity of the task. Genealogists, record agents and researchers usually work on an hourly basis plus out-of-pocket expenses (travelling, search fees, photocopying, postages, telephone, etc.); short pieces of translation are charged per thousand words. Most freelance workers have a sliding scale of fees; the professional bodies to which the majority of them belong recommend minimum standard rates for the job. If you are asked to pay 'above the odds' it will be either because the assignment is very specialised or complicated, or is needed in a great rush (necessitating weekend and evening work), or because the person engaged has special qualifications. As a guideline the current recommended hourly rates range from £15 to £35 an hour.

It is normal practice for the client commissioning the work to pay a lump sum on account (up to 50 per cent of the total cost estimated) and the balance on completion, but in the case of long-term commissions accounts may be rendered monthly. Estimates will be given on request; but do not expect your researcher to give one with any accuracy – neither he nor you will know at the outset precisely how much time he will spend on the job.

Fees paid to researchers, genealogists, translators and other workers may be set against a writer's income tax.

Chapter Ten

Information from and about Foreign Countries

THE WRITER/RESEARCHER who needs to obtain information about foreign countries or to use published or unpublished material from abroad has relatively few problems these days, thanks to the new technology. Twenty years ago you might have had to budget (or squeeze an advance out of your publisher) for an extended trip in order to look at some vital records lurking the other side of the world. Today you can search vast databases and the catalogues of almost all the great national library and archive collections online, if not from the comfort of your study, then at the local cybercafé or library computer terminal, and either print out or download what you need onto your own PC. An enormous amount of material is available on CD-ROM and in microform, which again you can work on wherever it is you write; and if you so wish you can obtain and/or exchange up-to-date research information with fellow writers worldwide by email without leaving home. What once took weeks, or sometimes months – and a great deal of money – is now more or less instantly accessible at a much more reasonable cost.

It is true that you may still have to travel to get at some of your material. But by doing your initial searching from the home base (which in the first instance usually involves extracting bibliographical information), you will soon discover precisely what exists – and where, if necessary, you must go to examine it. You may find that copies of the books or journals you need are held by some library or archive centre in the UK, or that they are on CD-ROM or have been – or can be – microfilmed. In the case of private papers, however, you will almost always have to go to the source in person, possibly to a university abroad or to visit the family.

When it is a question simply of finding some factual or background information on a foreign country, the best place to start is the reference library. If you are lucky there will be a library not too far away which subscribes to one or more of the global reference databases such as *SYBWorld*, developed by the *Statesman's Yearbook* team at Palgrave Macmillan and updated monthly (for information tel. 020 7843 4612 or visit the website www.sybworld.com). National encyclopedias, bibliographies and current works of reference are normally on open access at the library; many are now online, on CD-ROM and on microfiche. One of the best sources is the *World Bibliographies on CD-ROM* series marketed by K.G. Saur of Munich: containing millions of titles published between the 15th century and the present day, it is fully searchable and each edition (English, French, Italian, Russian, Spanish, etc.) is updated roughly every two years. There are two special large editions covering maps and atlases, and printed music, music manuscripts and recordings, also from the 15th century. Another very useful source is the *World Bibliographical Series* published by Clio Press of Oxford. The use of bibliographies and how to trace books has been outlined in chapter 4.

All the copyright libraries and university libraries in the UK have substantial foreign language holdings, and you should have no difficulty in obtaining most standard works. Use *Walford's Guide to Reference Material* (see chapter 4, page 86) to find them out, looking under each country individually; also the principal encyclopedias, national bibliographies and major works (listed under subject). You can search a number of overseas library catalogues, including the Library of Congress, the National Library of Australia, the National Library of Canada, and several European national libraries on the British Library website at www.bl.uk/catalogues/otherlibcats.

Foreign newspapers and weeklies going back for many years are held at the British Library Newspaper Library in Colindale; there are some gaps during the two world wars. Today they are nearly all purchased on microfilm. You can trace the whereabouts of all foreign periodicals held in British libraries in *Serials in the British Library*. Current publications are listed in *Benn's Media*, *Ulrich's Periodicals Directory* and *Willing's Press Guide* (see chapter 4, pages 61–2).

If you wish to subscribe to a foreign periodical you should contact Nordic Subscription Consultants Ltd., Unit 14, Prees Industrial Estate, Shrewsbury Road, Prees, Whitchurch, Shropshire SY13 1AA (tel. 01948 840321; fax 01948 840063; email subscriptions@nordicsubs.co.uk; website www.nordicsubs.co.uk).

So far as obtaining books published abroad is concerned, Grant & Cutler, 55–57 Great Marlborough Street, London W1V 2AY (tel. 020 7734 2012; fax 020 7734 9272; website www.grantandcutler.com) is the UK's largest foreign language bookseller; the firm holds a large stock of titles from all over the world and will order on any subject.

The number of countries or regions for which there is a *Biographical Archive* (on microfiche, from K.G. Saur, Munich) is growing fast. Many also have a *Biographical Index*, and these are included on the huge Saur database, the *World Biographical Index*, which can be accessed free of charge on www.saur.de or www.saur-wbi.de. In printed form, there are biographical dictionaries and/or *Who's Who* volumes for most countries. For quick factual reference look out for the single-volume encyclopedias such as *Le Petit Larousse* (French), *Der Brockhaus in einem Band* (German) and *Pequeño Larousse Ilustrado* (Spanish), as they contain information not always included in their English equivalents.

For up-to-date general information you should contact the relevant tourist information offices in the UK (listed in the London telephone directory) or the cultural departments or press offices of the embassy or high commission. Many embassies publish short factual booklets about their country which they will send you free of charge. A personal approach is often productive; you will find the addresses, and names of cultural attachés, in the current *London Diplomatic List* (published twice a year by The Stationery Office and usually available at the library enquiry desk). Many of the foreign embassies and high commissions in London are listed in the *Writers' & Artists' Yearbook* section on 'Government offices and public services'. Addresses of embassies and other diplomatic bodies worldwide can be found online at www.embassy.world.com. Europa Publications publishes an *International Relations Research Directory* which contains information on every major research institute concerned with international relations, as well as an alphabetical list of relevant periodicals and journals. Remember that public relations officers of the major international companies are often able to provide useful source material and/or contacts; you will find their names and addresses in the current *Hollis Press & Public Relations Annual* and *Hollis Europe*.

Finally, and by no means least, you will find much first-class information about foreign countries in some of the quality travel guides. The *Blue Guides* published by A & C Black are excellent in this respect; there are volumes for most European countries, some for individual towns and regions, and they are regularly revised. For countries farther afield, look at the *Footprint Handbooks*, now totalling some 80 titles, all regularly updated, containing a wealth of information and very reliable. Ask Footprint Handbooks, 6 Riverside Court, Lower Bristol Road, Bath BA2 3DZ (tel. 01225 469141; email webeditor@footprintbooks.com) for a catalogue, or visit their website and search by title or destination (www.footprintbooks.com). For historical as well as present-day information you will find the celebrated *Baedeker* guidebooks, first published by the German publisher Karl Baedeker in 1829, invaluable.

Foreign libraries in the United Kingdom are listed in the *Aslib Directory of Information Sources in the UK*. The *World of Learning* is international. For information on libraries and the book trade generally, look at the two Bowker annuals, *Literary Market Place*, covering the United States and Canada, and *International Literary Market Place*, for the rest of the world. Other useful tools not already mentioned include the US *Public Affairs Information Service Index (PAIS)*, which is worldwide in coverage, the *Regional Surveys of the World* series and the *Political Chronologies of the World* series, both published by Europa Publications, and the *International Historical Statistics* series published by Macmillan. Do not forget old favourites such as the two-volume *Europa World Year Book* (also online as *Europa World* since summer 2003), the *International Who's Who* and the *Yearbook of International Organizations*. As with every other category of research, you need only one book title, or one contact, to start you off.

Readers who live in or near London may be able to make use of the following:

Bibliothèque de l'Institut Français (French Institute), 17 Queensberry Place, London SW7 2DT (tel. 020 7073 1350; fax 020 7073 1363; email library@ambafrance.org.uk; website www.institut.ambafrance.org.uk). The library is open to the public for reference and information; loans are restricted to members. Tue–Fri, 12.00–19.00; Sat, 12.00–18.00

Commonwealth Resource Centre, Commonwealth Institute, Kensington High Street, London W8 6NQ (tel. 020 7603 4535; fax 020 7603 2807; email crc@commonwealth.org.uk; website www.commonwealth.org.uk). Mon–Sat, 10.00–16.00. *N.B.* The library and archives have recently been transferred to the British Empire and Commonwealth Museum at Bristol (see below, pages 177–8)

German Historical Institute Library, 17 Bloomsbury Square, London WC1A 2LP (tel. 020 7309 2019; fax 020 7404 5573; website www.ghil.co.uk). Open Mon, Thu 10.00–20.00; Tue, Wed, Fri, 10.00–17.00

Goethe-Institut Inter Nationes London (German Cultural Centre) Library and Information Centre, 50 Princes Gate, Exhibition Road, London SW7 2PH (tel. 020 7596 4025; fax 020 7594 0239; email library@london.goethe.org; website www.goethe.de/london). Open to the public, free of charge, for reference and study. Loan service to members only (£20 per year; three- and six-monthly membership, and concessions available). Mon–Thu, 12.00–20.00; Sat, 11.00–17.00

Institute of Commonwealth Studies Library, London University, 27–28 Russell Square, London WC1B 5DS (tel. 020 7862 8844 website www.sas.ac.uk/commonwealthstudies). Open (during term) Mon–Wed, 09.30–19.00; Thu, Fri, 09.30–18.00; (during vacations) Mon–Fri, 09.30–17.30. A fee may be payable

Instituto Cervantes (Cervantes Institute, formerly called the Spanish Institute) Library, 102 Eaton Square, London SW1W 9AN (tel. 020 7201 0757; fax 020 7235 0329; email biblon@cervantes.es; website www.cervantes.es). Mon, 12.30–18.30; Tue–Thu, 09.30–18.30; Fri, 09.30–17.00; Sat, 09.30–13.30

Italian Cultural Institute Library, 39 Belgrave Square, London SW1X 8NX (tel. 020 7396 4425; fax 020 7235 4618). Mon–Fri, 10.00–13.00, 14.00–17.00, for reference only

Oriental and India Office Collections (formerly the India Office Library), now at the British Library, 96 Euston Road, London NW1 2DB (tel. 020 7412 7873; fax 020 7412 7641; email oioc-enquiries@bl.uk; website www.bl.uk). Mon, 10.00–17.00; Tue–Sat, 09.30–17.00. Reader's pass required

Polish Library, 238–246 King Street, London W6 0RF (tel. 020 8741 0474; fax 020 87417724; email bibliotekapolska@posk.library.fsnet.co.uk). Mon, Wed, 10.00–20.00; Fri, 10.00–17.00; Sat, 10.00–13.00; closed Tue and Thu. Reference only (loans to scholars)

School of Oriental and African Studies Library, London University, Thornhaugh Street, Russell Square, London WC1H 0XG (tel. 020 7898 4163; website www.soas.ac.uk). Mon–Thu, 09.00–19.00; Fri, 09.00–17.00; summer vacation, Mon–Fri, 09.00–17.00; closed for one week in June. Reader's ticket required (letter of introduction)

Sir Robert Menzies Centre for Australian Studies, 28 Russell Square, London WC1B 5DS (tel. 020 7862 8854; fax 020 7580 9627; email menzies.centre@kcl.ac.uk; website www.kcl.ac.uk/menzies). Mon–Fri, 10.00–17.30

United States of America Information Service Reference Center, American Embassy, 55/56 Upper Brook Street, London W1A 2LH (tel. 020 7408 8060; website www.usembassy.org.uk). *N.B.* This is not a library open to the public. Telephone enquiry service only, Mon–Fri, 10.00–12.00

SHORT LIST OF FOREIGN SOURCE-MATERIAL (ARRANGED ALPHABETICALLY UNDER AREA OR COUNTRY) *

Africa

Sources of information in the UK:

African Studies Centre Library, University of Cambridge, Free School Lane, Cambridge CB2 3RQ (tel. 01223 334398; fax 01223 334396; website www.african.cam.ac.uk)

The School of Oriental and African Studies, University of London, Thornhaugh Street, Russell Square, London WC1H 0XG (tel. 020 7898 4163; website www.soas.ac.uk)

Recommended titles:

Africa South of the Sahara, published annually by Europa Publications, London

African Biographical Archive, K.G. Saur, Munich, 1994–

The African Book Publishing Record, ed. Hans M. Zell, published quarterly by K.G. Saur, Munich

African Books in Print, ed. Hans M. Zell, K.G. Saur, Munich, 5th edn, 2 vols, 2000

African Historical Dictionaries series, published by Scarecrow Press (Rowman & Littlefield), Oxford

African Studies Abstracts, published quarterly by K.G. Saur, Munich

The Black Handbook: The People, History and Politics of Africa and the African Diaspora, by Evangeline Bute and Harry Harmer, Cassell Academic, London, 1997

East Africa Handbook, Footprint Handbooks, Bath

Government and Politics in Africa, by William Tordoff, Palgrave Macmillan, London, 4th edn, 2002

Guide to Documents and Manuscripts in the British Isles relating to Africa, by J.D. Pearson, 2 vols, Mansell, London, 1993–94

---

* Excluding the general histories and guides already mentioned in the body of this chapter.

Guide to South African Reference Books, by Reuben Musiker and Naomi Musiker, Cassell, London, 6th edn, 1997

International African Bibliography, ed. David Hall, in association with the Centre of African Studies, University of London, K.G. Saur, Munich, online, 4 issues annually (by subscription)

The Middle East and North Africa, published annually by Europa Publications, London

A Political Chronology of Africa, Europa Publications, London, 2001

Reference Guide to Africa: A Bibliography of Sources, eds. Alfred Kagan and Yvette Scheven, Scarecrow Press, Lanham, Maryland, 1999

South Africa Handbook, Footprint Handbooks, Bath

South Africa Yearbook, Pan Macmillan South Africa

Arab States and the Middle East

Sources of information in the UK:

British Library Oriental and India Office Collections, British Library, 96 Euston Road, London NW1 2DB (tel. 020 7412 7873; fax 020 7412 7641; email oioc-enquiries@bl.uk; website www.bl.uk)

Centre for Arab Gulf Studies, Documentation Unit, University of Exeter, Stocker Road, Exeter, Devon EX4 4ND (tel. 01392 264041; fax 01392 264023; website www.iais/info@exeter.ac.uk)

Middle East Centre, St Anthony's College, 68 Woodstock Road, Oxford OX2 6JF (tel. 01865 284764; fax 01865 311475; website www.sant.ox.ac.uk) (collections of papers of individuals involved in the Middle East from 1800 to the present day)

Recommended titles:

Arab-Islamic Biographical Archive, K.G. Saur, Munich, 1995–

A History of the Arab Peoples, by Albert Hourani, Faber, London, 1991; paperback 2002

Index Islamicus 1906–1955, with 5-year supplements to 1985, Mansell, London, 1958–91; published quarterly since 1977; now by Brill Academic, Leiden, The Netherlands, quarterly and in an annual cumulation; also on CD-ROM and online

The Middle East and North Africa, published annually by Europa Publications, London

A Political Chronology of the Middle East, Europa Publications, London, 2001

Who's Who in the Arab World 2003–2004, Publitec Publications/K.G. Saur, Munich, 16th edn, 2002

Asia (see also under The Far East)

Sources of information in the UK:

Asian Studies Centre, St Anthony's College, 68 Woodstock Road, Oxford OX2 6JF (tel./fax 01865 274559; email asian@sant.ox.ac.uk; website www.sant.ox.ac.uk/areastudies/asian)

British Library Oriental and India Office Collections, British Library, 96 Euston Road, London NW1 2DB (tel. 020 7412 7873; fax 020 7412 7641; email oioc-enquiries@bl.uk; website www.bl.uk)

Centre of South Asian Studies, University of Cambridge, Laundress Lane, Cambridge CB2 1SD (tel. 01223 338094; fax 01223 316913; website www.s-asian.cam.ac.uk)

School of Oriental and African Studies Library, University of London, Thornhaugh Street, Russell Square, London WC1H 0XG (tel. 020 7898 4163; website www.soas.ac.uk)

University of Cambridge Faculty of Oriental Studies Library, Sidgwick Avenue, Cambridge CB3 9DA (tel. 01223 335112; fax 01223 335110; www.oriental.cam.ac.uk)

Recommended titles:

Asia: A Selected and Annotated Guide to Reference Works, Mansell, London, 1980

Cumulative Bibliography of Asian Studies 1941–1965, Association for Asian Studies Inc., Boston, Mass; now annually with cumulative volumes

Indian Biographical Archive, K.G. Saur, Munich, 1997–

India Handbook, Footprint Handbooks, Bath

A Political Chronology of Central, South and East Asia, Europa Publications, London, 2001

Proquest Reference Asia, online from Chadwyck-Healey, Cambridge, 2001–

South-East Asia Biographical Archive, K.G. Saur, Munich, 1997–

Who's Who in Asia and the Pacific Nations, Melrose Press, Cambridge, 5th edn, 2002

Australasia

Sources of information in the UK: see under 'Australia' and 'New Zealand'

Recommended titles:

Australasian Biographical Archive, K.G. Saur, Munich, 1990–

The Far East and Australasia, published annually by Europa Publications, London

The Penguin Historical Atlas of the Pacific, by Colin McEvedy, Penguin Press, Harmondsworth, 1998

A Political Chronology of South-East Asia and Oceania, Europa Publications, London, 2001

Who's Who in Asia and the Pacific Nations, Melrose Press, Cambridge, 5th edn, 2002

The Far East

Sources of information in the UK:

British Library Oriental and India Office Collections, British Library, 96 Euston Road, London NW1 2DB (tel. 020 7412 7873; fax 020 7412 7641; email oioc-enquiries@bl.uk; website www.bl.uk)
Great Britain China Centre, 15 Belgrave Square, London SW1X 8PS (tel. 020 7235 6696; fax 020 7245 6885; website www.gbcc.org.uk)
Japan Information and Cultural Centre, Embassy of Japan, 101–104 Piccadilly, London W1V 9FN (tel. 020 7465 6580; fax 020 7491 9347; website www.embajapan.org.uk)
The School of Oriental and African Studies Library, University of London, Thornaugh Street, Russell Square, London WC1H 0XG (tel. 020 7898 4163; website www.soas.ac.uk)
University of Cambridge Faculty of Oriental Studies Library, Sidgwick Avenue, Cambridge CB3 9DA (tel. 01223 335112; fax 01223 335110; website www.oriental.cam.ac.uk)

Recommended titles:

The Cambridge Encyclopedia of China, Cambridge University Press, 2nd edn, 1991
The Cambridge Encyclopedia of Japan, Cambridge University Press, 1993
Chinese Biographical Archive, K.G. Saur, Munich, 2000–
Facts about China, eds. E. Knappman and Xiao-bin Ji, H.W. Wilson, New York, 1999; rev. edn 2002
The Far East and Australasia, published annually by Europa Publications, London
A Guide to Reference Books for Japanese Studies, edited and published by the International House of Japan Library, Tokyo, rev. edn, 1997
Japanese Biographical Archive, K.G. Saur, Munich, 2000–
Korea Annual, published annually by Yonhap News Agency, Seoul
Korean Biographical Archive, K.G. Saur, Munich, 2000–
Republic of China Yearbook, Taipei, 1997
Territories of the People's Republic of China, Europa Publications, London, 2002

The Commonwealth

Sources of information in the UK:

The Bodleian Library of Commonwealth and African Studies at Rhodes House (formerly called Rhodes House Library), South Parks Road, Oxford OX1 3RG (tel. 01865 270909; fax 01865 270912; email rhodes-house.library@bodley.ox.ac.uk; website www.bodley.ox.ac.uk/dept/rhodes)
The British Empire and Commonwealth Museum Library, Clock Tower Yard, Temple

Meads, Bristol BS1 6QH (tel. 0117 925 4980; fax 0117 925 4983; email resources@empiremuseum.co.uk; website www.empiremuseum.co.uk)

Commonwealth Resource Centre, Commonwealth Institute, Kensington High Street, London W8 6NQ (tel. 020 7603 4535; fax 020 7603 2807; email crc@commonwealth.org; website www.commonwealth.org.uk). Mon–Sat, 10.00–16.00. *N.B.* The Library and Archives have recently been transferred to the British Empire and Commonwealth Museum at Bristol (see above)

Commonwealth Secretariat Library, Marlborough House, Pall Mall, London SW1Y 5HX (tel. 020 7747 6164; fax 020 7747 6168; email library@commonwealth.int; website www.thecommonwealth.org)

Foreign & Commonwealth Office Library, King Charles Street, London SW1A 2AH (tel. 020 7270 3925; fax 020 7270 3270; website www.fco.gov.uk)

Institute of Commonwealth Studies, University of London, 27–28 Russell Square, London WC1B 5DS (tel. 020 7862 8844; website www.sas.ac.uk/commonwealth-studies)

Sir Robert Menzies Centre for Australian Studies, 28 Russell Square, London WC1B 5DS (tel. 020 7862 8854; fax 020 7580 9627; email menzies.centre@kcl.ac.uk; website www.kcl.ac.uk/menzies)

Researchers should also contact the various high commissions in London, i.e. Australia House, Canada House, India House, New Zealand House, etc. (addresses and telephone numbers in the *Writers' & Artists' Yearbook*, *Whitaker's Almanack*, *Hollis Press & Public Relations Annual*, and the London telephone directory).

Recommended titles:

General:

Bibliography of Imperial, Colonial, and Commonwealth History since 1600, ed. Andrew Porter, Oxford University Press, Oxford, for the Royal Historical Society, 2002

The Commonwealth Yearbook, published annually by The Stationery Office, Norwich, for the Commonwealth Secretariat

Australia

Australasian Biographical Archive, K.G. Saur, Munich, 1990–

Australian Books in Print, D.W. Thorpe, Melbourne

Australian Dictionary of Biography, Melbourne University Press, in progress

Australian National Bibliography, National Library of Australia, Canberra (previously *Annual Catalogue of Australian Publications*, published 1936–60); weekly since 1972, with monthly and 4-monthly cumulations and annual volumes

Contemporary Australians 1998, D.W. Thorpe, Melbourne, 1997

Monash Biographical Dictionary of 20th Century Australia, D.W. Thorpe, Melbourne, 1994

Official Year Book of the Commonwealth of Australia, published annually by the Government Printing Office, Canberra

Resources for Australian and New Zealand Studies: A Guide to Library Holdings in the United Kingdom, British Library, London and Australian Studies Centre, University of London, 1986

Who's Who in Australia, published triennially since 1906, now by Information Australia, Melbourne

Canada

Canada Yearbook, published annually by Statistics Canada, Ottawa; also on CD-ROM

Canadian Biographical Archive, K.G. Saur, Munich, 2001–

Canadiana, national bibliography published monthly since 1951, with annual cumulations, National Library of Canada, Ottawa; also on CD-ROM

Canadian Encyclopedia, ed. J.H. Marsh, published by Hurtig, Edmonton, Alberta, 2nd edn, 4 vols, 1988

Dictionary of Canadian Biography, University of Toronto Press, in progress

Encyclopedia of Canada's People, ed. Paul Robert Mogocsi, University of Toronto Press, Toronto, 1998

The Oxford Companion to Canadian History, ed. Gerald Hallowell, Oxford University Press, Oxford, forthcoming (2004)

The USA and Canada, published annually by Europa Publications, London

Who's Who in Canada, published annually since 1907, now by Global Press, Toronto

India

Index India, published quarterly by Rajasthan University, Jaipur, since 1967

India: A History, by John Keay, HarperCollins, London, 2000

India: A Reference Manual, published annually since 1953 by the Ministry of Information and Broadcasting, New Delhi

India Handbook 1999, Footprint Handbooks, Bath

India Who's Who, published annually since 1969 by INFA Publications, New Delhi

Indian Biographical Archive, K.G. Saur, Munich, 1997–

Indian National Bibliography, published monthly, with annual cumulations, since 1957 by the Central Reference Library, Calcutta

The Territories and States of India, Europa Publications, London, 2002

New Zealand

Encyclopedia of New Zealand, ed. A.H. McLintock, 3 vols, Owen, Wellington, 1966

New Zealand Books in Print, D.W. Thorpe, Melbourne

New Zealand National Bibliography, monthly since 1967, National Library of New Zealand, Wellington

New Zealand Official Year Book, published annually by the Department of Statistics, Wellington
Resources for Australian and New Zealand Studies, see page 179 under 'Australia'

Regrettably, space does not permit the listing of other Commonwealth countries in this section.

Europe

Given the vast amount of material published each year, readers will understand that it is impossible to do more in the space of this chapter than to list some of the countries of Europe, with the location of their national libraries/archives and a selection of reference works. There are, however, a number of general guides which should first be mentioned. These include:

Biographical Archive of the Benelux Countries, Saur, Munich, 1992–
Dictionary of the European Union, by David Phinnemore and Lee McGowan, Europa Publications, London, 2002
Directory of European Industrial & Trade Associations and *Directory of European Professional & Learned Societies*, CBD Research, Beckenham; updated regularly
European Historical and Political Facts series, published by Macmillan, London
European Historical Dictionaries series, published by Scarecrow Press (Rowman & Littlefield), Oxford
The European Union Encyclopedia and Directory, Europa Publications, London, 4th edn, 2003
The European Union: How Does it Work?, by Elizabeth Bomberg and Alexander Stubb, Oxford University Press, Oxford, 2002
Hollis Europe, published annually by Hollis Publishing, Teddington, Middx
Western Europe, published annually by Europa Publications, London

Note: For purposes of this chapter, 'Europe' refers to Western Europe. The countries of Eastern Europe are included under the heading 'The Russian Federation (formerly the Commonwealth of Independent States) and Eastern Europe'. Readers may like to know of the following regional *Biographical Archives* from K.G. Saur, Munich: the *Arab-Islamic Biographical Archive* (1995–); *Baltic Biographical Archive* (1995–); *Czech and Slovakian Biographical Archive* (1993–); *Scandinavian Biographical Archive* (1989–); *South-East Asian Biographical Archive* (1997–); and *South-East European Biographical Archive* (1998–).

Austria

The Österreichische Nationalbibliothek in Vienna is the national library, and there is also the Staatsarchiv (national archives) in the same city.

Austria, Facts and Figures
Dokumentation und Information in Österreich
Österreich Lexikon
Österreichische Bibliographie
Österreichisches Biographisches Lexikon 1815–1950
Who's Who in Austria

Belgium

The Bibliothèque royale, Albert Ier/Koninklijke Bibliotheek Albert I and the Archives générales du Royaume, both in Brussels, are the major library and archive sources.

Bibliographie de Belge/Belgische bibliografie
Biographical Archive of the Benelux Countries
Documentation sur la Belgique: bibliographie selective et analytique
Inventaire des centres belges de recherche
Who's Who in Belgium and the Grand Duchy of Luxembourg

Denmark – see under 'Scandinavia'.

France

Until recently the Bibliothèque Nationale de France (BNF) was situated in the rue Richelieu in central Paris. There is now a new and elegant building, opened by President Chirac and Madame Mitterand in December 1996, at Quai François Mauriac, between the Pont de Bercy and the Pont de Tolbiac, on the banks of the Seine, in the 13th arrondissement, which houses printed documents, serials, audio-visual and electronic documents. Some specialised collections (manuscripts, maps, drawings and photographs) remain at rue Richelieu. In contrast to its British counterpart, 'Tolbiac' as the new library has become popularly known, is architecturally pleasing both from the outside and inside. Another major difference is that, unlike in our British Library, the major collections of the BNF are accessible by the general public on the *'haut-de-jardin'* level; there is a special research library on the *'rez-de-jardin'* level reserved for researchers. Day or annual passes in the *haut-de-jardin*, and two-day, twelve-day or annual passes in the *rez-de-jardin*, are available at a very reasonable cost (readers seeking access to the *rez-de-jardin* may be subjected to a preliminary interview), and there is every facility you would expect from a purpose-built, up-to-date library. In all the reading rooms assistance is available from staff; there is also an 'Initiation Centre' offering group sessions to readers seeking information on the library and its collections. The full address of the new Bibliothèque Nationale de France is 11 Quai François Mauriac, 75706 Paris Cédex 13 (tel. for information 0033 (1) 53 79 59 59; or online at www.bnf.fr).

Among many other libraries in Paris open to the public is the Bibliothèque Publique d'Information (BPI) at the Centre Georges Pompidou, rue Saint Martin,

Place Georges Pompidou, 75004 Paris (tel. 0033 (1) 44 78 12 33; fax 0033 (1) 44 78 12 15; website www.bpi.fr). Note that the postal address of the BPI is Centre Georges Pompidou, 75197 Paris Cedex 04. If you need to find other libraries in the city, ask at one of the tourist offices or libraries for a most useful free map, *Paris en Bibliothèques*, which lists over a hundred, by name and by subject.

The Archives Nationales are at 60 rue de Francs-Bourgeois, 75003 Paris (tel. the *Centre d'accueil et de recherche des archives nationales* on 0033 (1) 40 27 64 19, or visit their website www.archivesnationales.culture.gouv.fr).

Recommended titles:

Annuaire Statistique de la France, published annually by the I.N.S.E.E., Paris

Le Bottin Administratif (yearbook of government departments and public offices), Bottin, Paris, annually

Dictionnaire de biographie française, Letousey, Paris, in progress, 1929– (approximately one instalment per year)

Electre (Livres Disponibles/French Books in Print), published annually by Editions du Cercle de la Librairie, Paris; also on microfiche, CD-ROM and online (www.electre.com)

French Biographical Archive, K.G. Saur, Munich, 2001–

Grand Larousse Encyclopédique, Larousse, Paris, 10 vols, 1960–64; supplements, 1968, 1975

Life in the French Country House: A Social and Political History, by Mark Girouard, Cassell, London, 2000

Livres Hebdo: Bibliographie de la France, published weekly with monthly and quarterly supplements by Editions Cercle de la Librairie, Paris

Qui est Qui en France/Who's Who in France, published biennially since 1953 by Editions Jacques Lafitte, Paris

The Press Division of the Ambassade de France in London issues from time to time a most informative compact publication, entitled *France: a journalist's guide*, which is invaluable to any writer needing to do research in or about France, and hopefully there may be a new edition soon (it has not been revised since 1999). Contact the Ambassade de France en Grande Bretagne, Service de Presse, 58 Knightsbridge, London SW1X 7JT (tel. 020 7201 1024). There is a great deal of information about France on the Embassy's website www.ambafrance-uk.org. Or try the French equivalent of the UK's yellow pages, on www.pagesjaunes.fr.

Germany

The three major libraries are the Deutsche Bibliothek, in Frankfurt and Leipzig; the Staatsbibliothek Preussischer Kulturbesitz, in Berlin; and the Bayerische Staatsbibliothek, in Munich.

Allgemeine Deutsche Biographie
Brockhaus Enzyklopädie (also on CD-ROM)
Deutsches Biographisches Archiv
Deutsche Biographische Enzyklopädie
Deutsche Nationalbibliographie (since 1991 for the united Germany)
Neue Deutsche Biographie
Wer ist Wer? (also on CD-ROM; includes some Austrian and Swiss entries)
Who's Who in Germany

Greece

The National Library is in Athens.

Greek Bibliography
Greek Biographical Archive
Guide to Greek Libraries and Cultural Organizations
Hellenika Vivla (bibliography)
Modern Greece: A Bibliography
Mega Hellenikon Biographikon Lexikon (biographical dictionary), in progress

Republic of Ireland (Eire)

The National Library of Ireland is at Kildare Street, Dublin 2 (tel. (00-353-1) 6030200; fax (00-353-1) 6766690; email info@nli.ie; website www.nli.ie)
The National Archives are at Bishop Street, Dublin 8 (tel. (00-353-1) 4072300; fax (00-353-1) 4072333; email mail@nationalarchives.ie; website www.nationalarchives.ie)

Directory of Irish Archives
Oxford Companion to Irish History
Royal Historical Society Annual Bibliography of British and Irish History

Italy

The major libraries are the Biblioteca Nazionale Centrale Vittorio Emanuele II in Rome and the Biblioteca Nazionale Centrale in Florence; there are also national libraries in Milan, Naples, Palermo, Turin and Venice.

Bibliografia Nazionale Italiana
Dizionario Biografico degli Italiani
Enciclopedia Italiana di Scienze, Lettre ed Arti
Guida delle Bibliothece Italiane
Historical Dictionary of Modern Italy
Italian Biographical Archive
Italian Books in Print

Lui, Chi, E?
Who's Who in Italy

The Netherlands

The major collection is at the Koninklijke Bibliotheek (Royal Library) in The Hague.

Biographical Archive of the Benelux Countries
Brinkman's Cumulatieve Catalogus van Boeken (Dutch national bibliography)
Digest of the Kingdom of the Netherlands (Government Information Service publication)
Grote Nederlandse Larousse Encyclopedie
Grote Winkler Prins Encyclopedie
Historical Dictionary of The Netherlands
Nieuw Nederlandsch Biografisch Woordenboek
Pythersen's Nederlandse Almanak
Who's Who in the Netherlands
Wie is Dat?

Norway – see under 'Scandinavia'.

Scandinavia

Two biographical dictionaries covering the region are the *Dictionary of Scandinavian Biography* and *Who's Who in Scandinavia*; the *Scandinavian Biographical Archive* (Saur, Munich, 1989–91) contains entries for 155,500 individuals from Denmark, Finland, Iceland, Norway and Sweden.

Denmark

The Kongelige Bibliotek (Royal Library) in Copenhagen is the national library; the archive collection is at the Kobenhavns Stadsarkiv.

Bibliography of Books on Denmark 1900–1965
Dansk Biografisk Leksikon
Dansk Bogfortegnelse (Danish national bibliography)
Denmark: An Official Handbook
Denmark: A Select Bibliography
Historical Dictionary of Denmark
Who's Who in Denmark

Norway

The national library is the Universitetsbiblioteket i Oslo (Royal University Library), and the national archives are at the Riksarkivet, also in Oslo.

Facts about Norway
Guide to Norwegian Statistics
Hvem or Hvem? (Norwegian *Who's Who*)
Norsk Biografisk Leksikon
Norsk Bokfortegnelse (Norwegian national bibliography)
Norway Year Book

Sweden

The Kungliga Biblioteket (Royal Library), the Riksarkivet (National Record Office) and the Statistika Centralbyráns Biblioteket (Library of Statistics) are all in Stockholm.

Facts about Sweden
Svenskt Biografiskt Lexikon
Svensk Bokforteckning (Swedish national bibliography)
Vem är Det? (Swedish *Who's Who*)

Poland

The Biblioteka Narodowa (National Library) and the Instytut Bibliograficzny (Biographical Institute, a division of the National Library) are in Warsaw, as are the Archiwów Panstwowych (Polish State Archives) and the Archiwum Glówne Akt (Central Archives for Historical Documents).

*Books in Polish or relating to Poland**
Polish Biographical Archive

Portugal

The Biblioteca Nacional (National Library) and the Instituto dos Arquivos Nacionals (Institute of National Archives) are in Lisbon.

Historical Dictionary of Portugal
Spanish, Portuguese and Latin American Biographical Archive

Spain

The Biblioteca Nacional is in Madrid, as are the Archivo General de la Administración Civil del Estado (the General Archives of the Civil Administration of the State) and the Archivo Historico Nacional (the National Historical Archives). There is also the Real Biblioteca (Royal Library) at El Escorial, near Madrid. The Archivo de la Corona de Aragon (the Royal Archives of Aragon) are in Barcelona, where there is also the Biblioteca de Catalunya (the Library of Catalonia).

* Available at the Polish Library in London (see page 173).

Bibliografia Española
Enciclopedia Universal Ilustrada Europeo-Americana
Gran Enciclopedia Rialp
Indice Cultural Español (Spanish cultural index)
Quién es quién (Spanish Who's Who)
Spanish, Portuguese and Latin American Biographical Archive
Who's Who in Spain

Sweden – see under 'Scandinavia'.

Switzerland

Thc national library is the Schweizerische Landesbibliothek/ Bibliothèque Nationale Suisse in Berne; the Archives Fédérales (national archives) are in the same city. In Geneva there are the United Nations Library and the International Labour Office Library.

Das Schweizer Buch/Le Livre Suisse (Swiss national bibliography)
Who's Who in Switzerland

Turkey

The Milliî Kütüphane (National Library) is in Ankara. There is also the Beyazit State Library in Istanbul. The Grand National Assembly of Turkey Library and Documentation Center is in Ankara.

Historical Dictionary of Turkey, ed. Metin Heper, Scarecrow Press (Rowman & Littlefield), Oxford, 2nd edn, 2002
Turkey Handbook, Footprint Handbooks, Bath
Turkish Biographical Archive, K.G. Saur, Munich, 1999–
Turkiye Bibliyografyasi (Turkish National Bibliography)

Latin America and the Caribbean

Space does not permit the listing here of major libraries in the various countries and states, but these are in the *World Guide to Libraries*, published by K.G. Saur, Munich, 16th edn, 2001 (also on CD-ROM) and in *The World of Learning*, published annually by Europa Publications, London.

Cambridge Encyclopedia of Latin America and the Caribbean, Cambridge University Press, 2nd edn, 1992
Caribbeana, 1900–1965: A Topical Bibliography, by L. Comitas, University of Washington Press, Seattle and London, 1968
CARICOM Bibliography, Caricom Secretariat, Georgetown, Guyana, 1977

Latin America Bibliography, ed. Juan Manuel Pérez, Scarecrow Press, Lanham, Maryland, 1999
Mexico and Central American Handbook 1999, Footprint Handbooks, Bath
South America, Central America and the Caribbean, published annually by Europa Publications, London
South American Handbook 1999, Footprint Handbooks, Bath
Spanish, Portuguese, and Latin American Biographical Archive, K.G. Saur, Munich, 1986–

The Russian Federation (formerly the Commonwealth of Independent States/Union of Soviet Socialist Republics) and Eastern Europe

The Rossiiskaya Nacionalnaya Biblioteka (National Library of Russia) is in St Petersburg, as are the Central State Historical Archives of the USSR. The State Public Historical Library of Russia and the Central Archives of the USSR are in Moscow.

The Biographical Dictionary of the Former Soviet Union, K.G. Saur, Munich, 2nd edn, 1992
Central and South-Eastern Europe, published annually by Europa Publications, London
Eastern Europe, Russia and Central Asia, published annually by Europa Publications, London
The Great Soviet Encyclopedia (translation of *Bol'shaya Sovetskaya Entsiklopediya*, 3rd edn), 31 vols + 3 index vols, Macmillan, New York/Macmillan, London, 1973–83
Guide to Russian Reference Books, Stanford University, California, in progress, 1962–
Natasha's Dance: A Cultural History of Russia, by Orlando Figes, Penguin Books, Harmondsworth, 2002
Official Publications of the Soviet Union and Eastern Europe 1945–1980: A Select Bibliography, ed. G. Walker, Mansell, London, 1985
Reinterpreting Russia: An Annotated Bibliography of Books on Russia, the Soviet Union and the Russian Federation 1991–1996, by Steve D. Bollard, Scarecrow Press, Lanham, Maryland, 1997
Russia and the Russians, by Geoffrey Hosking, Penguin Books, Harmondsworth, 2002
Russian Bibliography 16th Century to 1999, K.G. Saur, Munich, 2000 [CD-ROM]; also from Saur, *Russian National Bibliography PLUS*, 6th edn. 2001 [CD-ROM]
Russian Biographical Archive, K.G. Saur, Munich, 1997–
The Territories of the Russian Federation, published annually by Europa Publications, London
Who Was Who in the Soviet Union, 2 vols, K.G. Saur, Munich, 1992
Who's Who in Russia Today, K.G. Saur, Munich, 1993

United States of America

The Library of Congress, Washington, D.C. 20540 (tel. (202) 707 5000) is the national library, but it is not the exact equivalent of the British Library in that it does not automatically acquire a copy of every book published in the United States; it does, however, collect and catalogue books published in other countries. The printed volumes of the *National Union Catalog*, which has replaced the old *Library of Congress Catalog*, will be found on open access at the British Library and in major libraries of the UK. The *Pre-1956 Imprints*, an impressive run of 755 volumes, are clear and easy to use; their great value to the researcher is that they provide in one alphabetical sequence, under authors, the holdings of the Library of Congress together with those of the principal libraries of North America. Another bonus is that the *NUC* gives dates of authors (otherwise sometimes difficult to obtain). The Library of Congress Online Catalog can be searched on the British Library website www.bl.uk/catalogues/otherlibcats.

The National Archives and Records Administration is at the National Archives Building, 8th Street at Pennsylvania Avenue NW, Washington, D.C. 20408 (tel. (202) 501 5400; website www.archives.gov). Some archives have been transferred to Maryland (8601 Adelphi Road, College Park, MD 20740-6001). Use the main Washington telephone number in the first instance.

Recommended titles:

American Biographical Archive, K.G. Saur, Munich, 1986–

American National Biography, Oxford University Press Inc., New York, 24 vols. 1999 + 1 supplement to date (2002); also on CD-ROM and online (by subscription)

Books in Print, Books in Print Plus, Books in Print with Book Reviews Plus, Books Out of Print with Book Reviews Plus, Subject Guide to Books in Print, Bowker, New Providence, N.J.; some printed vols, some microfiche, some CD-ROM, some online (by subscription)

The Cassell Dictionary of Modern American History, by Peter Thompson, Cassell, London, 2000

Information Please Almanac, published annually since 1947, now by Houghton Mifflin, Boston, Mass.

National Inventory of Documentary Sources in the United States (*NIDS*), on microfiche in three parts: 1, *Federal Records*; 2, *Manuscript Division, Library of Congress*; 3, *State Archives, State Libraries, Historical Societies, Academic Libraries and Other Repositories*; by subscription, Chadwyck-Healey, Cambridge

Oxford Companion to United States History, Oxford University Press, Oxford, 2001

Statistical Abstract of the United States, published annually since 1879 by the Government Printing Office, Washington, D.C.

The USA and Canada, published annually by Europa Publications, London

Who's Who in America, Who Was Who in America, Who Was Who in American History, Marquis, Chicago, printed vols, fiches, CD-ROM and online. The same publisher issues regional volumes for the East, Midwest, South and Southwest, and West of the United States. There is a printed index vol. entitled *Index to Marquis Who's Who Publications*, and also *The Complete Marquis Who's Who* on CD-ROM, updated every six months

Chapter Eleven

Preparation for the Press

THE RESEARCH IS done, the text drafted and polished to the writer's satisfaction, on screen or in typescript, saved on disk, the length approximately right. (Word-processor owners normally have a built-in word-count facility, but those less fortunate must do it the hard way, taking an average number of words per page and multiplying by the number of pages – remembering to allow for any short pages and inserts – and rounding up the total to the nearest hundred words.)

If the great work is an article, a short story, a novel or a play, all that remains to be done is to produce the fair copy. This you may either type, or have professionally typed; or, using a word processor and printer, the latter preferably of inkjet or laser quality, print out. In all cases it is advisable initially to make three copies, two for the publisher and one for yourself; additional copies when needed, say, for an American or paperback publisher, can be made later. It goes without saying that before despatch to literary agent or publisher you make a final check for spelling mistakes and simple errors.

All typing agencies and most freelance typists today offer a word-processing service, which means that as well as the specified number of typescript copies you will receive one or more floppy disks or, if it is an exceptionally long book, a CD-RW disk. An ever-increasing number of publishers now ask for submission on disk, in which case normally they expect to get at least one copy of the typescript as well (this is known as the 'hard copy').

The non-fiction book requires some extra attention. The prelims must be written, the notes and references section and the bibliography (if any) compiled, and some thought given to the provision of an index, although this will not actually be prepared until later. None of these chores, strictly speaking, comes within the province of 'research', but their importance in giving the finished manuscript a professional look merits their mention here.

The word 'manuscript', abbreviated as MS (MSS in plural), which originally meant a handwritten document, in 20th-century literary jargon has become synonymous with 'typescript', a text that is either typed or prepared on a word processor and printed out. An 'electronic typescript' is a text on disk. As mentioned above, a typed manuscript is now usually referred to as a 'hard copy'.

Writers submitting their work on disk or as email attachments should consult their publishers well ahead of their deadline, in order to ascertain requirements. They may be expected to send their text in an ASCII or RTF format. There are other ways of transferring large quantities of material direct to publishers, i.e. on 'zip' disks, but this need not concern the reader of this handbook. Publishers producing small runs of specialised books sometimes ask for what is called 'camera-ready' copy, which is then photographed and reproduced lithographically. Take professional advice if this is a prerequisite.

There are some excellent works to help the writer with his final preparation. *The New Shorter* or *The Concise Oxford English Dictionary* (*OED*) should be on every writer's bookshelf. Highly recommended is the new *Oxford Style Manual* edited by R.M. Ritter, which deals with virtually every aspect of words in print – abbreviations, capitalization, notes and references, quotations, spelling, and much else. Writers submitting material for online publication and those needing to know how to cite electronic media will find useful information here. There are two early 20th century standard works on English usage: *Fowler's Modern English Usage* and Sir Ernest Gowers' *Plain Words*, both of which have gone into numerous editions over a number of years. *The Macmillan Good English Handbook* is also recommended, and *A Guide to Good English in the 21st Century* by the same author, Godfrey Howard, is fully up-to-date. R.L. Trask's *Mind the Gaffe: The Penguin Guide to Common Errors in English* is authoritative, readable and amusing, dealing with 'blunders' as well as many controversial issues. Another witty book on the subject is Bill Walsh's *Lapsing into a Comma*. If you have any particular problems on language or on the current usage of particular words or phrases, you may find it worthwhile visiting the 'Ask the Experts' section on the www.askoxford.com website.

Punctuation has undergone many changes in the last half-century, which has seen hefty reductions in the use of commas, colons and semi-colons. These should not however be disgarded without careful consideration: the placement of a comma (or the lack of one) can alter a meaning drastically. G.V. Carey's *Mind the Stop*, first published some years ago and now a Penguin Reference paperback, is one of two layman's bibles on punctuation; the other is Eric Partridge's *You Have a Point There*, reprinted in 1999.

Judith Butcher's *Copy-Editing*, although directed more at publishers than writers, contains many valuable hints on the final preparation of text for the printer. *The MHRA Style Book* (now re-titled *Guide*) has long been a standard work, not only for academics and editors, but for all authors writing for publication; its current edition (2002) is online at www.mhra.org.uk. Finally, the relevant *British Standards* are listed at the end of this chapter.

PRELIMS

These are the preliminary pages at the beginning of a book, known in the printing and publishing trade as 'prelims'. Normally they consist of a title page, dedication, list of contents, list of illustrations, acknowledgments, abbreviations, preface or foreword. Not all of these are required for every type of book, and the publisher normally has some say in the matter. It is up to you, the author, to indicate, at this stage, what you intend to provide – for example if you wish to include an 'Author's Note' or not. It does not matter too much if you cannot yet write the text of the prelims – all you need to do is to put a blank sheet in the typescript at the appropriate place or places, stating, for example, 'Acknowledgments' and below this, 'copy to follow'. The important thing is for the production manager and book designer to know that they are coming, so that they can allow for them in their calculations.

NOTES AND REFERENCES

Consistency is the keyword here. If the book has been commissioned, the publisher may have sent you a copy of the 'house style', or will have discusssed with you in advance his preference for the numbering and style of notes and references, such as whether these should appear at the foot of each page, after each chapter, or in a separate section at the end of the book. Failing such instruction, or if you do not yet have a publisher, it is advisable to study some published titles in a similar category of book and follow a similar style. Bear in mind for the future that source references need to include websites, together with the dates accessed. You will find help on this new issue both in *The Oxford Style Manual* and in Jane Dorner's two books, *Creative Web Writing* and *Writing for the Internet*.

BIBLIOGRAPHY

Depending on whether the work is aimed at the popular or the academic market, the bibliography may be as selective or as comprehensive as you deem appropriate. If the latter, it is usual to divide the entries into 'primary' and 'secondary' (or 'printed' and 'manuscript') sources, and to include not only books, but articles in periodicals and learned journals, as well as references to private papers consulted. Provided careful notes have been kept of all material used in the course of research, as suggested in chapter 2, the compilation of a bibliography should be quite straightforward. The normal arrangement of books and articles is in an alphabetical sequence, under the surname of the author. Care should be taken to list the particular editions used and to indicate any subsequent revised editions or reprints of each work, where relevant.

The British Standard *BS 1629: Recommendations for references to published materials*, details an internationally accepted set of rules for the guidance of those compiling bibliographies in books.

PREPARATION OF THE TYPESCRIPT

The cardinal rules for the presentation of material for publication stipulate that the text should be typed on one side of the paper only, in double-spacing, with good margins: 1.5 inches (approximately 4 cm) is the norm, both on left and right, and at top and bottom. It is helpful to the publisher if the same number of lines are typed per page; but try not to carry over onto the next page the last two or three words of a paragraph. Using a word processor you will find that the page-breaks are automatic: when you do your final check-through you should be able to remedy these breaks where necessary: in order to avoid a short line at the top of a page it is best to carry over the last two lines, even though it means that the previous page may be one line short. A4 size paper is now standard. Headings should be consistent throughout, and quoted matter of more than a few lines should be indented, without the use of quotation marks. Except for the first paragraph of a chapter or section, indent five spaces at the beginning of each paragraph, unless the publisher's house style asks for anything different. Start each chapter on a new page.

Apart from the obvious use of italics or underlining as necessary, writers using word processors should resist the temptation to adorn their pages with different fonts and type sizes for headings and sub-headings, etc. This is the publisher's prerogative, and the book designer would far rather have a straightforward typescript to work on. Some publishers insist on a plain text format such as ASCII or RTF, which is fine if you are writing fiction; but in a non-fiction work the use of, say, italics for emphasis and/or foreign words may be essential, and if you are writing in this category you should resist requests for 'plain text'.

First impressions matter. New authors should aim to submit a pristine MS, especially if the work is going to a publisher unsolicited. One of the joys of word processing is that corrections may be made right up to the last minute and the revised texts printed out, without the need for laborious re-typing; beware, however, that major inserts or corrections will alter the pagination.

Established authors often find that their publishers adopt a more relaxed attitude, and that they can get away with a modest number of handwritten additions, deletions or amendments. So long as these are absolutely legible and their place of insertion or deletion clear to the typesetter, it is unnecessary to go to the trouble of re-typing each amended page. Be very careful, however, about numbering pages: an insertion between pages 14 and 15, for example, should be numbered 14a, 14b and so on; but if page 15 is to be deleted altogether, the previous page should be numbered 14/15. (This does not apply to text prepared on a word processor, as pages are automatically re-numbered throughout to take account of all amendments.) Where an insertion does not take up a full page, always rule a line obliquely from left to right through the remaining part of the page to indicate that the text is continuous. When amending typewritten texts, it is better to use white correcting fluid and to type the correction in rather than to risk an erasure and handwritten alteration that may be ambiguous to the copy editor or typesetter. (In the case of 'camera-ready' copy, always typed electronically, with variable spacing and justified lines, each page must of course be perfect, although pure spelling mistakes and punctuation may be corrected – very carefully – again with the aid of correction fluid.)

Those who still use a typewriter should make just one clean copy of their final draft, then photocopy the required number of additional copies. Photocopying has become so inexpensive these days that there is little point in messing about with carbons and flimsy paper, except possibly for correspondence. If you do not have a photocopier at home, take your typescript to a copy shop where you can either have it done for you or, at a reduced cost, use a self-operated machine. You may be able to negotiate a special price for several copies of a long book.

When packing up your typescript for agent or publisher, do remember that staples should never be used. Short texts such as poems, articles or short stories may be fastened with paper clips, but a full-length hard copy should always be delivered as loose sheets, preferably packed into a box. Most copy shops will supply lightweight boxes of A4 size, similar to those in which reams of bond typing paper used to be sold (alas, no longer!).

THE COPY-EDITING PROCESS

Once your book has been accepted by the publisher, and before it goes to the printer, the typescript will be handed over to a copy editor. This copy editor, who may be an 'in-house' member of your publisher's editorial team, but more likely nowadays a freelancer, will go through your text with the eyes of a hawk, ironing out discrepancies, repetitions, and errors of grammar, punctuation and spelling. Be prepared, at this stage, to receive what may appear to be an exasperatingly long list of queries: part of the copy editor's job is to challenge everything that he considers to be less than clear, in need of amplification, or basically incorrect. This is why it is so vital that you should hang on to your research notes; otherwise you could find yourself having to re-do some of that early research.

Some copy editors are more ruthless than others, and authors in general do not take kindly to having their work 'tampered with'. Naturally you should not stand for anyone meddling with your individual style or with the opinions you express, but on most other matters it is wise to bear in mind that, far from 'nit-picking', the copy editor is genuinely trying to improve your book. He may not be knowledgeable about the subject-matter, however, and a good deal of patience, justifying and explanation may be required from you, the expert, as you wade through his queries. At the end of the day it may come as a surprise to you just how many inadvertent slips the copy editor has saved you from making.

That said, standards do vary, which is something that the Society for Editors and Proofreaders (SfEP), founded in 1988, is striving to improve through training and accredited membership. If you are unhappy and wish to check up on your copy editor's qualifications for the job, you could ask the publisher if he is a member of SfEP. You can contact the Society at Riverbank House, 1 Putney Bridge Approach, Fulham,

London SW6 3JD (tel. 020 7736 3278; fax 020 7736 3318; email admin@sfep.org.uk; website www.sfep.org.uk).

Writers should not lose sight of the fact that a first-class copy editor is worth his weight in gold.

PROOF-CORRECTION

As a book writer you will normally be sent one set of page proofs, which you are required to read and correct. At the same time the proofs will be read by the publisher's own proofreader, either in or out of 'house'. If the corrections are heavy, a set of revised proofs will be forthcoming.

It should be borne in mind that while printers' errors are not charged, any changes made by the author at proof stage which amount to more than 10–15 per cent of the cost of composition are payable by him (and will be deducted from royalties). The time to make major last-minute amendments is *before* the copy editor passes the work to the typesetter.

Sometimes, where the work is one of topical interest and some important event has taken place between the date of completion of the manuscript and delivery of proofs, the publisher will find the space to include a brief note to the effect that 'Since this book went to press [such and such] has occurred', but this cannot always be counted on.

A list of signs used in proof correction will be found in Judith Butcher's *Copy Editing*, in the *Writers' & Artists' Yearbook* and in the *British Standard BS 5261C: Marks for copy preparation and proof correction*. The best guide on the market today for spelling, punctuation, division of words, and the use of capital and lower case, is the recently published *Oxford Style Manual* by R.M. Ritter, mentioned earlier in this chapter, which brings together for the first time, two of the most indispensable rule-books for writers ever published: *Hart's Rules for Compositors and Readers* (later revised as *The Oxford Guide to Style*) and *The Oxford Dictionary for Writers and Editors*, which in 1981 had replaced the earlier standard work, the *Authors' and Printers' Directory*. If for any reason you require the services of a qualified proofreader, you should contact the Administration Officer of the Society for Editors and Proofreaders at 1 Riverbank House, Putney Bridge Approach, London SW6 3JD (tel. 020 7736 3278; fax 020 7736 3318; email admin@sfep.org.uk; website www.sfep.org.uk). Some proofreading services are listed in the *Writers' & Artists' Yearbook* under 'Editorial, literary and production services by specialisation'.

THE INDEX

Every non-fiction book merits a good index, and reviewers these days are paying more attention than ever before to the quality of indexing and commenting unfavourably, where appropriate, on the lack of indexes.

Most authors' contracts stipulate that the author shall provide the index, at their expense, but a good agent can sometimes negotiate for the publisher to pay the cost. When, if ever, all publishers accept the Minimum Terms Agreement drawn up by the Society of Authors and the Writers' Guild it should become normal practice for the publisher to contribute 50 per cent of the cost, especially if a professional indexer is to be employed. Some publishers have their own team of freelance indexers on whom they can call; others seek recommendations from the Society of Indexers, which was founded in 1957 to safeguard and improve indexing standards and which maintains a register of indexers suitably qualified in different subjects and types of indexing. To assist authors or publishers seeking an indexer for their work, the Society now issues annually a booklet entitled *Indexers Available*, which is distributed throughout the book trade and may also be searched on their website (www.socind.demon.co.uk); it lists practising members' names, addresses, telephone numbers and their specialist subjects. At the time of writing (spring 2003) the Society's recommended minimum rate for indexing is £16 per hour, or £1.20 per page, for basic skills; specialist work commands more (up to £30 per hour, £5 per page). Rates are revised annually. Note that there is also a useful list of FAQ on indexing on the Society's website.

There has long been controversy as to whether writers should or should not index their own books. Some people feel that an author is the ideal person, but others hold strongly to the view that he may be too close to his own work to be able to produce a truly objective index. Certainly, as a general rule, it will almost always take him longer than the trained professional. The lay person may not realise that there is a great deal more to indexing than extracting the names of people and places and stringing them together in alphabetical order, so that when an author does decide to attempt it, he would be well advised to take the time and trouble to learn the basic rules. Firstly, the indexer must choose – and stick to – the form of alphabetical arrangement most suited to the book: either 'letter-by-letter' or 'word-by-word'. Then – and this is governed largely by space – he should give some thought to the layout and balance of the index and whether the sub-headings and sub-sub-headings (if any) will be indented or run on; both in layout and wording the sub-headings throughout must be consistent. There must be adequate cross-referencing of names and concepts, but not so much as to make the index unnecessarily long; care must be taken to avoid what is known as a 'wild goose chase', i.e. cross-references that never lead to the location of the subject-matter in the text, as in, for example, 'Indexers, Society of, *see* Society of Indexers' and 'Society of Indexers, *see* Indexers, Society of'. The main function of an index is to direct the user quickly to the place or places in the text where he will find precisely the information he seeks.

Indexing is normally undertaken at page proof stage and, for this reason, it nearly always has to be done at speed in order to meet the printers' deadline. Here the computer has really come into its own, and now that there is dedicated software specially designed to meet the professional indexer's needs (see details at end of this chapter), two of what used to be the most tedious and time-consuming stages of the job – the sorting of entries into the required order, and the typing of the edited index copy – are now done electronically and very quickly. Beware, however, of the so-called 'automatic indexing' programs on offer in computer catalogues, as these are inadequate for serious book indexing.

Although most professional indexers now use computers, some manual indexing still goes on, the usual method being to mark on the page proofs (either with high-lighter pen or by underlining) each name or concept to be indexed, and to write these on separate cards or slips which are filed alphabetically in a box as work proceeds; a certain amount of tightening up and editing of entries has to take place when all entries are assembled. It is a good plan for the author who intends to prepare his own index to start building it as he writes, making slips for the main entries and possible sub-headings; these can be edited later and the page numbers added. Page references should always be double-checked at the time of writing – an inaccurate index is worse than no index at all.

In the course of his work the indexer may come across inconsistencies or inaccu-racies that both author and copy editor have missed; these should be telephoned through to the editorial office immediately. An index is normally typed/printed out in double-spacing, with a maximum of 32 characters per line, and submitted on disk and/or hard copy.

The publisher may say that his tight production schedule does not permit him to send the indexer a proof for correction, but this should be insisted on wherever pos-sible. Fortunately nowadays, as indexes are now mostly submitted on disk, misprints of page references are unlikely. But even the best printer's typesetter working on a disk can make a nonsense out of an index by failing to notice that a sub-heading has been incorrectly indented – something that may not be spotted if the index is checked only in the editorial office.

These are but a few of the problems that confront the indexer. Writers interested in acquiring some basic training in indexing, or in taking up indexing professional-ly, should consider taking the 'Training in Indexing' course administered by the Society of Indexers, which can be purchased in either printed or electronic format. Successful completion of this course entitles members of the Society to the status of 'Accredited Indexer' and, ultimately, following assessment of their experience and competence in practical indexing, to that of 'Registered Indexer'. (Details from the Administrator of the Society, see below.) There is a shorter, less expensive course, suitable perhaps for the writer who does not intend to pursue a career in indexing, the Book Indexing Postal Tutorials (BIPT), which offers one-to-one tuition and practical exercises based on short texts. (Details from Ann Hall, The Lodge, Sidmount Avenue, Moffat, Dumfriesshire DG10 9BS; tel. 01683 220 440; email ann@lodge-moffat.co.uk; website www.lodge-moffat.co.uk.) So far as printed text-books are concerned, the three most comprehensive and up-to-date manuals, rec-ommended by and available from the Society of Indexers (at a discount to mem-bers), are Pat F. Booth's *Indexing: the manual of good practice*, Nancy C. Mulvany's *Indexing Books* and Hans Wellisch's *Indexing from A to Z*, the last two published in the USA. The *British Standard BS 1749* and *International Standard BS ISO 999* (details at the end of this chapter) are the authoritative guides to current practice.

R.F. Hunnisett's practical guide to indexing historical texts, *Indexing for Editors*, is published by the British Records Association, 40 Northampton Road, London EC1R 0HB (tel. 020 7833 0428; fax 020 7833 0416). The Society of Indexers publishes a journal twice a year, *The Indexer*, as well as occasional papers dealing with various aspects of the profession, regularly updated.

Names of suitably qualified indexers, general or specialist, may be obtained from the Registrar of the Society of Indexers, Mrs E. Wallis, 25 Leyborne Park, Kew Gardens, Surrey TW9 3HB (tel. 020 8940 4771; mobile tel. 07801 628916). For a copy of *Indexers Available*, or other information, including the Training Course, contact the Administrator, The Society of Indexers, Blades Enterprise Centre, John Street, Sheffield S2 4SU (tel. 0114 292 2350; fax 0114 292 2351; email admin@indexers.org.uk; website www.socind.demon.co.uk).

A LAST WORD OF ADVICE

Once the proofs have been corrected and returned to the publisher, you may safely return all borrowed books and documents to their respective libraries and/or owners. Parcel up and store your original notes and early drafts. *It is important not to throw these away.* When eventually your book is published, there is always the possibility that it may arouse unexpected interest and may even lead to other related commissions; almost certainly you will receive a number of readers' letters either asking you to justify certain statements or to give further information. Some of these enquiries may come from researchers working in the same field. Bearing in mind the enormous help you yourself have derived from the work of others, would it not be churlish and ungenerous to refuse or not to be in a position to pass on the fruits of your own research – especially any information gathered but not used – to other *bona fide* writers?

It should not be forgotten that all writers feed to a lesser or greater extent on the work of other writers. As the Californian playwright Wilson Mizner put it, 'When you steal from one author, it's plagiarism; if you steal from many, it's research.'

Authors' and Printers' Dictionary, compiled by F. Howard Collins, first published 1905, Oxford University Press, Oxford; replaced in 1981 by the *Oxford Dictionary for Writers and Editors*, *q.v.*

British Standards (available from the British Standards Institution, 389 Chiswick High Road, London W4 4AL (customer services tel. 020 8996 9001; fax 020 8996 7001; email info@bsi.org.uk; website www.bsi.org.uk):

BS 1629: 1989	*Recommendations for references to published materials*
BS 1749: 1985	*Recommendations for alphabetical arrangement and the filing order of numbers and symbols*
BS 5261 Part 1: 1975 (1983, 2000)	*Copy preparation and proof correction: recommendations for preparation of typescript copy for printing*

BS 5261 Part 2: 1976 (1995)	*Specifications for typographical requirements, marks for copy preparation and proof correction, proofing procedure*
BS 5261C: 1976	*Marks for copy preparation and proof correction* (extract from BS 5261 Part 2)
BS 5605: 1990	*Recommendations for citing and referencing published material*
BS ISO 999: 1996	*Guidelines for the content, organisation and presentation of indexes* (this has replaced the earlier BS 3700)

Copy-Editing, by Judith Butcher, Cambridge University Press, Cambridge, 3rd edn, 1992; latest reprint, with corrections, 1999

Creative Web Writing, by Jane Dorner, A & C Black, London, 2002

[The New] Fowler's Modern English Usage, ed. R.W. Burchfield, 3rd edn, Oxford University Press, 1996, reprinted 1998

A Guide to Good English in the 21st Century, by Godfrey Howard, Duckworth, London, 2002

Hart's Rules for Compositors and Readers at the University Press Oxford, 1893 (1st published edn, 1904) Oxford University Press; 38 subsequent editions; now incorporated into *The Oxford Style Manual*, q.v.

Indexers Available, annual list of accredited and registered indexers, Society of Indexers, Sheffield

Indexing Books, by Nancy C. Mulvany, University of Chicago Press, Chicago, 1994

Indexing for Editors, by R.F. Hunnisett, first published in 1972; reprinted by British Records Association, London, 1997

Indexing from A to Z, by Hans Wellisch, H.W. Wilson, New York, 2nd edn, 1995

Indexing: the manual of good practice, by Pat F. Booth, Saur, Munich, 2001

Lapsing into a Comma, by Bill Walsh, McGraw-Hill, New York, 2000

The Macmillan Good English Handbook, by Godfrey Howard, Macmillan, London, 1998

The MHRA Style Guide, Modern Humanities Research Association, London, 2002; obtainable from Maney Publishing, Hudson Road, Leeds LS9 7DL (tel. 0113 249 781; fax 0113 248 6983; email orders: maney@maney.co.uk); also online at www.mhra.org.uk

Mind the Gaffe: The Penguin Guide to Common Errors in English, by R.L. Trask, Penguin Group, London, 2001

The Oxford Dictionary for Writers and Editors, Oxford University Press, Oxford, first published 1981; major new edn, 2000; now incorporated into *The Oxford Style Manual*, q.v.

Oxford English Dictionary (*OED*), Oxford University Press, Oxford, 2nd edn, 20 vols, 1989; *The New Shorter OED*, 2 vols, 1993, also available on CD-ROM and online. (The third edition of the *OED* is in preparation and scheduled for 2010.)

The Oxford Guide to Style, (formerly *Hart's Rules, q.v.*), Oxford University Press, Oxford, 2002; now incorporated into *The Oxford Style Manual, q.v.*

The Oxford Style Manual, ed. R.M. Ritter, Oxford University Press, Oxford, 2003

Plain Words, by Sir Ernest Gowers, first published 1948; latest edn, *Complete Plain Words*, Penguin Group, London, 2002

Writers' & Artists' Yearbook, published annually by A & C Black, London; section on 'Editorial, literary and production services'

Writing for the Internet, by Jane Dorner, Oxford University Press, Oxford, 2002

You Have a Point There, by Eric Partridge, Routledge, London, 1978; reprinted 1999

The recommended indexing program is:

MACREX, compiled by Hilary and Drusilla Calvert and available from Macrex Indexing Services, Beech House, Burn Road, Blaydon-on-Tyne, NE21 6JR (tel. 0191 4142595; fax 0191 4141893). At a price of £350 (£290 to members of the Society of Indexers), it is clearly a wise investment for the professional indexer or the non-fiction writer who regularly compiles his own indexes, but less so for the writer with a 'one-off' index to put together. For more information visit the website www.macrex.com

Note: New from the Society of Indexers as this book goes to press is an information leaflet, *Authors and Indexes: DIY or hire a professional*.

Appendix I

Selective List of Major Sources in the United Kingdom

THIS LIST IS limited by space and should be used as a guideline only, in conjunction with the *Aslib Directory of Information Sources in the UK*, the booklet *Record Repositories in Great Britain/ARCHON* and other reference sources mentioned in earlier sections of this book. Unless otherwise stated, the libraries and record offices are open to the public without formality. Addresses, telephone numbers and hours of opening are subject to change with alarming frequency; most libraries and record offices have fax numbers, but some have asked for them not to be listed. Websites and email addresses, where not given here, will be found in the above guides. While every effort has been made to bring information up-to-date at the time of going to press, researchers should check in advance before travelling any distance. All libraries and record offices are closed on the normal public holidays; some close for a week or more during the year for annual stocktaking or during the university summer vacation.

THE COPYRIGHT LIBRARIES

The British Library, 96 Euston Road, London NW1 2DB (general enquiries and advance reservations: tel. 020 7412 7676; fax 020 7412 7609; email reader-services-enquiries@bl.uk and reader-admissions@bl.uk). Reading rooms: Humanities 1 and 2; Rare Books and Music; Oriental and India Office; Maps; Manuscripts; Science, Technology and Business 1, 2 and 3. Admission to reading rooms by reader's pass (apply to Reader's Admissions Office, or tel. 020 7412 7677; fax 020 7412 7794). Mon–Thu, 09.30–18.00; Fri, Sat, 09.30–16.30. For further information and access to online catalogue (BLPC), visit the website www.bl.uk.

Bodleian Library, University of Oxford, Broad Street, Oxford OX1 3BG (tel. (general enquiries) 01865 277000; fax 01865 277182; email enquiries@bodley.ox.ac.uk). Central Bodleian Library (The Old Library, The New Library, and the Radcliffe Camera), plus nine other libraries. Mon–Fri, 09.00–22.00 (term), 09.00–19.00

(vacation), Sat, 09.00–13.00. Admission by reader's ticket (fee may be payable for non-graduates): apply Admissions Office (tel. 01865 277180; fax 01865 277105; email admissions@bodley.ox.ac.uk). General catalogue (OLIS) online at www.lib.ox.ac.uk/olis. Website www.bodley.ox.ac.uk.

[Cambridge] University Library, University of Cambridge, West Road, Cambridge CB3 9DR (tel. 01223 333000; fax 01223 333160; email library@ula.com.ac.uk; website www.lib.cam.ca.uk). Admission by reader's ticket (letter of introduction required; fee payable for non-graduates, £10 for six months). Mon–Fri, 09.00–19.00; Sat, 09.00–17.00. Catalogue (NEWTON) online at www.lib.cam.ca.uk/newton.

National Library of Scotland, George IV Bridge, Edinburgh EH1 1EW (tel. 0131 226 4531; fax 0131 622 4803; email enquiries@nls.uk; website www.nls.uk). Admission by reader's ticket. Mon, Tue, Thu, Fri, 09.30–20.30; Wed, 10.00–20.30; Sat, 09.30–13.00. Website www.nls.uk. Catalogue online at www.bl.uk/catalogues/otherlibcats.

National Library of Wales, Aberystwyth, Ceredigion SY23 3BU (tel. 01970 632800; fax 01970 615709; email holi@llg.org.uk; website www.llgc.org.uk). Admission by reader's ticket. Mon–Fri, 09.30–18.00; Sat, 09.30–17.00. Catalogue online at www.bl.uk/catalogues/otherlibcats.

N.B. Trinity College Library, College Street, Dublin 2, in the Republic of Ireland (tel. 00353 1 6772941; fax 00353 1 9003; email library@tcd.ie) is a copyright library. Mon–Fri, 09.00–22.00; Sat, 09.30–16.00 (vacation, 09.30–13.00). Letter of introduction required. Website www.tcd.ie/library.

PUBLIC RECORD OFFICES

The National Archives: Public Record Office, Ruskin Avenue, Kew, Richmond, Surrey TW9 4DU (tel. 020 8876 3444; fax 020 8878 8905; email enquiry@pro.gov.uk; website www.pro.gov.uk). Admission by reader's ticket. Mon, Wed, Fri, 09.00–17.00; Tue, 10.00–19.00; Thu, 09.30–19.00; Sat, 09.30–17.00. Catalogue (PROCAT) online at www.pro.gov.uk/procat.

National Archives of Ireland (formerly the Public Record Office of Ireland), Bishop Street, Dublin 8, Eire (tel. 00353 1 4072300; fax 00353 1 4072333; email mail@nationalarchives.ie; website www.nationalarchives.ie). Mon–Fri, 10.00–17.00.

The National Archives of Scotland (formerly the Scottish Record Office), Historical Search Room, HM General Register House, Edinburgh EH1 3YY (tel. 0131 535 1334; fax 0131 535 1328; email enquiries@nas.gov.uk; website www.nas.gov.uk). Admission by reader's ticket. Mon–Fri, 09.00–16.45. Refurbishment due for completion 2004. *N.B.* The National Register of Archives Scotland is at West Register House.

Public Record Office of Northern Ireland, 66 Balmoral Avenue, Belfast BT9 6NY (tel. 028 9025 1318; fax 028 9025 5999; email proni@nics.gov.uk; website www.proni.gov.uk). Admission by reader's ticket. Mon–Wed, Fri, 09.15–16.45; Thu, 09.15–20.45 (first Thursday of each month 10.00–20.45). Commercial users (includes journalists and professional genealogists) £4.35 per day, or £100 per year.

GENERAL REGISTER OFFICES

General Register Office (part of the Office for National Statistics): indexes to registers of births, marriages and deaths from 1837, and census returns 1841–91, at the Family Records Centre, 1 Myddelton Street, Islington, London EC1R 1UW (tel. 020 8392 5300; fax 020 8392 5307; email certificate.services@ons.gov.uk; website www.familyrecords.gov.uk). Admission without ticket. Mon, Wed, Fri, 09.00–17.00; Tue, 10.00–19.00; Thu, 09.00–19.00; Sat, 09.30–17.00. Address for postal applications for certificates: General Register Office, PO Box 2, Southport, Merseyside PR8 2JD; or tel. 0151 471 4800 (Mon-Fri, 08.00–20.00, Sat, 09.00–16.00); priority service tel. 0151471 4816/fax 01704 550013.

Principal Registry of the Family Division, First Avenue House, 42–49 High Holborn, London WC1V 6NP (tel. (general enquiries) 020 7947 6043; (Probate Search Rooms) 020 7947 7189; (Divorce registry) 020 7947 7017). Mon–Fri, 10.00–16.30.

General Register Office for Scotland, New Register House, Edinburgh EH1 3YT (tel. 0131 334 0380; fax 0131-314 4400; email records@gro-scotland.gov.uk; website www.gro-scotland.gov.uk). Mon–Fri, 09.30–16.30.

General Register Office (Northern Ireland), Oxford House, 49–55 Chichester Street, Belfast BT1 4HL (tel. 028 90 252000; email (certificates) gro.nisra@dfpni.gov.uk; website www.groni.gov.uk). Mon–Fri, 09.30–16.00. Births and deaths from 1864, marriages from 1845 (some records on microfilm). Assisted searches by staff available (£15 per hour); index searches £6 for up to six hours. *N.B.* The records for the whole of Ireland from 1864 to 1921 are at the office of the Registrar General, Joyce House, 8–11 Lombard Street East, Dublin 2 (tel. 00 353 1 6354000; website www.groireland.ie), which houses the records of the Republic only since 1922.

MANUSCRIPT COLLECTIONS/REGISTERS OF ARCHIVES

British Library, 96 Euston Road, London 2DB: Manuscripts Reading Room (tel. 020 7412 7513; fax 020 7412 7745; email mss@bl.uk) and Oriental and India Collections Reading Room (tel. 020 7412 7873; fax 020 7412 7641). Reader's pass required (apply to Reader Admissions Office, tel. 020 7412 7677; fax 020 7412 7794; email reader-admissions@bl.uk). *N.B.* A higher-level pass is required for access to the Manuscripts Reading Room. Mon, 10.00–17.00; Tue–Sat, 09.30–17.00. Catalogue online at www.molcat.bl.uk.

National Register of Archives (Scotland). This is maintained by the National Archives of Scotland – see above, under 'Public Record Offices'.

Royal Commission on Historical Manuscripts/National Register of Archives, Quality House, Quality Court, Chancery Lane, London WC2A 1HP (tel. 020 7242 1198; fax 020 7831 3550; email nra@hmc.gov.uk; website www.hmc.gov.uk). Mon–Fri, 09.30–17.00. *N.B.* The Commission is now part of The National Archives and will be moving to Kew probably in the late autumn of 2003. A National Archives reader's pass will be required for access there. For up-to-date information visit the website or telephone the Public Record Office on 020 8876 3444.

Many collections of manuscripts are also housed at the various Public Record Offices (see page 201) and at County Record Offices and University Libraries (see below, pages 203–15).

COUNTY RECORD OFFICES/REGIONAL ARCHIVES CENTRES

In this list, opening hours are not given for the individual offices: some are open all day throughout the working week, others close for lunch (or do not produce material during the lunch period); some are open late one evening in the week (but material must be ordered beforehand), others are shut either on Mondays or on Saturdays. It is advisable to check prior to making a visit, as these times are subject to change, and to reserve a seat or, where available, a microfilm reader/computer. Readers' tickets and County Archive Research Network (CARN) cards are normally issued on presentation of proof of identity.

Bedfordshire
Bedfordshire and Luton Archives and Record Service, County Hall, Cauldwell Street, Bedford MK42 9AP (tel. 01234 228833/228777/363222 ext. 2833; fax 01234 228854; email archive@csd.bedfordshire.gov.uk; website www.bedfordshire.gov.uk/archive)

Berkshire
Berkshire Record Office, 9 Coley Avenue, Reading RG1 6AF (tel. 0118 901 5132; fax 0118 901 5131; email ARCH@Reading.gov.uk; website www.berkshirerecordoffice.org.uk)

Buckinghamshire
Centre for Buckinghamshire Studies, County Hall, Aylesbury HP20 1UU (tel. 01296 382587; fax 01296 382771; email archives@buckscc.gov.uk; website www.buckscc.gov.uk/archives)

Cambridgeshire
Cambridge County Record Office, Shire Hall, Castle Hill, Cambridge CB3 0AP (tel. 01223 717281; fax 01223 718823; email county.records.cambridge@cambridgeshire.gov.uk); also at Grammar School Walk, Huntingdon PE18 6LF (tel./fax 01480 375842; email county.records.hunts@cambridgeshire.gov.uk)

Cheshire

Cheshire and Chester Archives and Local Studies, Duke Street, Chester CH1 1RL (tel. 01244 602574; fax 01244 603812; email recordoffice@cheshire.gov.uk; website www.cheshire.gov.uk/recoff)

Cornwall

Cornwall Record Office, Old County Hall, Truro TR1 3AY (tel. 01872 273698/323127; fax 01872 270340; email CRO@cornwall.gov.uk; website www.cornwall.gov.uk/Council-Services)

Royal Institution of Cornwall, Royal Cornwall Museum, River Street, Truro TR1 2SJ (tel. 01872 272205; fax 01872 240514; email RIC@royal-cornwall-museum.freeserve.co.uk)

Cumbria

Cumbria Record Office, Carlisle Headquarters, The Castle, Carlisle CA3 8UR (tel. 01228 607285; fax 01228 607274; email carlisle.record.office@cumbriacc.gov.uk; website www.cumbria.gov.uk/archives); also at County Offices, Kendal LA9 4RQ (tel. 01539 773540; fax 01539 773538; email kendal.record.office@cumbriacc.gov.uk); at 140 Duke Street, Barrow-in-Furness LA14 1XW (tel. 01229 894377; fax 01229 894364; email barrow.record.office@cumbriacc.gov.uk); and at Cumbria Record Office and Local Studies Library, Scotch Street, Whitehaven CA28 7NL (tel. 01946 852920; fax 01946 852919; email whitehaven.record.office@cumbriacc.gov.uk; website (all branches) www.cumbria.gov.uk/archives)

Derbyshire

Derbyshire Local Studies Library, County Hall, Matlock DE4 3AG (tel. 01629 585579; fax 01629 585049; website www.derbyshire.gov.uk)

Derbyshire Record Office, New Street, Matlock DE4 3AG (tel. 01629 585347; fax 01629 57611; email record.office@derbyshire.gov.uk; website www.derbyshire.gov.uk/recordoffice). Postal address: DRO, County Offices, Matlock DE4 3AG

Devon

Devon Record Office, Castle Street, Exeter EX4 3PU (tel. 01392 384253; fax 01392 384256; email devrec@devon.gov.uk; website www.devon.gov.uk/dro)

North Devon Library and Record Office, Tuly Street, Barnstaple EX31 1EL (tel. 01271 388607; fax 01271 388608; email ndevrec@devon.gov.uk; website www.devon.gov.uk/dro/nd)

Plymouth and West Devon Area Record Office, Unit 3, Clare Place, Coxside, Plymouth PL4 0JW (tel. 01752 305940; fax 01752 223939; email pwdro@plymouth.gov.uk; website www.plymouth.gov.uk/star/archives)

Dorset
Dorset Record Office, Bridport Road, Dorchester DT1 1RP (tel. 01305 250550; fax 01305 257184; email archives@dorset-cc.gov.uk; website dorset-cc.gov.uk/archives)

Durham
Durham County Record Office, County Hall, Durham DH1 5UL (tel. 0191 383 3253/3474; fax 0191 383 4500; email recordoffice@durham.gov.uk; website www.durham.gov.uk/recordoffice)

Essex
Essex Record Office, Wharf Road, Chelmsford CM2 6YT (tel. 01245 244644; fax 01245 244655); and at Central Library, Victoria Avenue, Southend-on-Sea SS2 6EX (tel. 01702 464278; fax 01702 464252); Colchester and NE Essex Branch, Stanwell House, Stanwell Street, Colchester CO2 7DL (tel. 01206 572099; fax 01206 574541). All branches email ero.enquiry@essexcc.gov.uk; website www.essexcc.gov.uk/ero

Gloucestershire
Bristol Record Office, 'B' Bond Warehouse, Smeaton Road, Bristol BS1 6XN (tel. 0117 922 4224; fax 0117 922 4236; email bro@bristol-city.gov.uk; website www.bristol-city.gov.uk/recordoffice)
Gloucestershire Record Office, Clarence Row, off Alvin Street, Gloucester GL1 3DW (tel. 01452 425295; fax 01452 426378; email records@gloscc.gov.uk; website www.gloscc.gov.uk/pubserv/gcc/corpserv/archives)

Hampshire
Hampshire Record Office, Sussex Street, Winchester SO23 8TH (tel. 01962 846154; fax 01962 878681; email enquiries.archives@hants.gov.uk; website www.hants.gov.uk/record-office)
Portsmouth Museums and Records Service, Museum Road, Portsmouth PO1 2LJ (tel. 023 9282 7261; fax 023 9287 5276; email info@recordsoffice.portsmouthmuseums.co.uk; website www.portsmouthmuseums.co.uk)
Southampton Archives Office, South Block, Civic Centre, Southampton SO14 7LY (tel. 023 8083 2251/8022 3855 ext. 2251; fax 023 8033 2156; email city.archives@southampton.gov.uk; website www.southampton.gov.uk/education/libraries/arch)

Herefordshire
Hereford Record Office, The Old Barracks, Harold Street, Hereford HR1 2QX (tel. 01432 260750; fax 01432 260066; email shubbard@herefordshire.gov.uk; website www.recordoffice.herefordshire.gov.uk)

Hertfordshire
Hertfordshire Archives and Local Studies, County Hall, Hertford SG13 8DE (tel. 01438 737333; fax 01992 555113; email hertsdirect@hertscc.gov.uk; website www.hertsdirect.org)

Kent
Centre for Kentish Studies, Sessions House, County Hall, Maidstone ME14 1XQ (tel. 01622 694363; fax 01622 694379; email archives@kent.gov.uk; website www.kent.gov.uk/e&l/artslib/archives)
East Kent Archives Centre, Enterprise Zone, Honeywood Road, Whitfield, Dover CT16 3EH (tel. 01304 829306; fax 01304 820783; email EastKentArchives@kent.gov.uk; website www.kent.gov.uk/e&l/artslib/archives). Open Tue, Wed, Thu only.

Lancashire
Lancashire Record Office, Bow Lane, Preston PR1 2RE (tel. 01772 263039; fax 01772 263050; email record.office@ed.lancscc.gov.uk; website www.lancashire.gov.uk/education/dlif/ro)

Leicestershire
The Record Office for Leicestershire, Leicester and Rutland, Long Street, Wigston Magna, Leicester LE18 2AH (tel. 0116 257 1080; fax 0116 257 1120; email record-office@leics.gov.uk; website www.leics.gov.uk)

Lincolnshire
Lincolnshire Archives Office, St Rumbold Street, Lincoln LN4 1NL (tel. 01522 526204; fax 01522 530047; email lincolnshire.archive@lincolnshire.gov.uk; website www.lincolnshire.gov.uk/archives)
North East Lincolnshire Archives, Town Hall, Town Hall Square, Grimsby DN31 1HX (tel. 01472 323585; fax 01472 323582; email JohnWilson@nelincs.gov.uk; website www.nelincs.gov.uk/ic/index)

London
City of Westminster Archives Centre, 10 St Ann's Street, London SW1P 2DE (tel. 020 7641 5180; fax 020 7641 5179; email archives@westminster.gov.uk; website www.westminster.gov.uk/archives/index)
Corporation of London Records Office, PO Box 270, Guildhall, London EC2P 2EJ (tel. 020 7332 1251; fax 020 7710 8682; email clro@corpoflondon.gov.uk; website www.cityoflondon.gov.uk/archives/clro/index)
London Metropolitan Archives, 40 Northampton Road, London EC1R 0HB (tel. 020 7332 3820; fax 020 7833 9136; email ask.lma@corpoflondon.gov.uk; website www.cityoflondon.gov.uk/lma)

Manchester

Greater Manchester County Record Office, 56 Marshall Street, New Cross, Manchester M4 5FU (tel. 0161 832 5284; fax 0161 839 3808; email archives@gmcro.co.uk; website www.gmcro.co.uk)

Merseyside

Merseyside Record Office, Central Library, William Brown Street, Liverpool L3 8EW (tel. 0151 233 5817; fax 0151 233 5886; email recoffice.central.library@liverpool.gov.uk; website www.liverpool.gov.uk)

Wirral Archives, Wirral Museum, Town Hall, Hamilton Street, Birkenhead CH41 5BR (tel. 0151 666 3903; fax 0151 647 3965; email archives@wirral-libraries.net; website www.wirral-libraries.net/archives)

Midlands

Birmingham City Archives, Central Library, Chamberlain Square, Birmingham B3 3HQ (tel. 0121 303 4217; fax 0121 212 9397; email archives@birmingham.gov.uk; website www.birmingham.gov.uk)

Coventry Archives, Mandela House, Bayley Lane, Coventry CV1 5RG (tel. 024 7683 2418; fax 024 7683 2421; email coventryarchives@discover.co.uk; website www.coventry-city.co.uk/archives)

Warwickshire County Record Office, Priory Park, Cape Road, Warwick CV34 4JS (tel. 01926 738959; fax 01926 738969; email recordoffice@warwickshire.gov.uk; website www.warwickshire.gov.uk/countyrecordoffice)

Warwick University Modern Records Centre, University Library, Coventry CV4 7AL (tel. 024 7652 4219; fax 024 7657 2988; email archives@warwick.ac.uk; website www.warwick.ac.uk/services/library/mrc)

Norfolk

Norfolk Record Office, Gildengate House, Anglia Square, Upper Green Lane, Norwich NR3 1AX (tel. 01603 761349; fax 01603 761885; email norfrec.nro@norfolk.gov.uk; website www.archives.norfolk.gov.uk)

Northamptonshire

Northamptonshire Record Office, Wootton Hall Park, Northampton NN4 8BQ (tel. 01604 762129; 01604 767562; email archivist@nro.northamptonshire.gov.uk; website www.nro.northamptonshire.gov.uk)

Northumberland

Northumberland Record Office, Melton Park, North Gosforth, Newcastle-upon-Tyne NE3 5QX (tel. 0191 236 2680; fax 0191 217 0905; website www.swinhope.myby.co.uk/NRO/index)

Nottinghamshire
Nottinghamshire Archives, County House, Castle Meadow Road, Nottingham NG2 1AG (tel. 0115 958 1634; fax 0115 941 3997; email archives@nottswcc.gov.uk; website www.nottscc.gov.uk/libraries/archives/index)

Oxfordshire
Centre for Oxfordshire Studies, Oxford Central Library, Westgate, Oxford OX1 1DJ (tel. 01865 815749; fax 01865 810187; email cos@oxfordshire.gov.uk; website www.oxfordshire.gov.uk/culture)
Oxfordshire Record Office, St Luke's Church, Temple Road, Cowley, Oxford OX4 2EX (tel. 01865 398200; fax 01865 398201; email archives@oxfordshire.gov.uk; website www.oxfordshire.gov.uk)

Shropshire
Shropshire Records and Research Centre, Castle Gates, Shrewsbury SY1 2AQ (tel. 01743 255350; fax 01743 255355; email research@shropshire-cc.gov.uk; website www.shropshire-cc.gov.uk/research.nsf)

Somerset
Bath and North East Somerset Record Office, Guildhall, High Street, Bath BA1 5AW (tel. 01225 477421; fax 01225 477439; email archives@bathnes.gov.uk; website www.batharchives.co.uk)
Somerset Archive and Record Service, Obridge Road, Taunton TA2 7PU (tel. 01823 278805, (appointments) 337600; fax 01823 325402; email Archives@somerset.gov.uk; website www.somerset.gov.uk/archives)

Staffordshire
Staffordshire and Stoke-on-Trent Archive Service: Lichfield Record Office, Lichfield Library, The Friary, Lichfield WS13 6QG (tel. 01543 510720; fax 01543 510715; email lichfield.record.office@staffordshire.gov.uk; website www.staffordshire.gov.uk/archives/lich)
Staffordshire Record Office, County Buildings, Eastgate Street, Stafford ST16 2LZ (tel. 01785 278379; fax 01785 278384; email staffordshire.record.office@stafford-shire.gov.uk; website www.staffordshire.gov.uk/archives)
William Salt Library, County Buildings, Eastgate Street, Stafford ST16 2LZ (tel. 01785 278372; fax 01785 278414; email william.salt.library@staffordshire.gov.uk; website www.staffordshire.gov.uk/archives/salt)

Suffolk
Suffolk Record Office, Bury St Edmunds Branch, Raingate Street, Bury St Edmunds IP33 2AR (tel. 01284 352352; fax 01284 352355; email bury.ro@libher.suffolkcc.gov.uk); also at Gateacre Road, Ipswich IP1 2LQ (tel. 01473 584541; fax 01473 584533; email ipswich.ro@libher.suffolkcc.gov.uk); and at Lowestoft Central Library,

Clapham Road, Lowestoft NR32 1DR (tel. 01502 405357; fax 01502 405350; email lowestoft.ro@libher.suffolkcc.gov.uk). Website www.suffolkcc.gov.uk/sro

Surrey

Surrey History Centre (records of Surrey Record Office and Guildford Muniment Room), 130 Goldsworth Road, Woking GU21 1ND (tel. 01483 594594; fax 01483 594595; email shs@surreycc.gov.uk; website www.surreycc.gov.uk/surreyhistoryservice)

East Sussex

East Sussex Record Office, The Maltings, Castle Precincts, Lewes BN7 1YT (tel. 01273 482349; fax 01273 482341; email archives@eastsussexcc.gov.uk; website www.eastsussexcc.gov.uk/archives)

West Sussex

West Sussex Record Office, Sherburne House, 3 Orchard Street, Chichester (tel. 01243 753600; fax 01243 533959; email records.office@westsussex.gov.uk; website www.westsussex.gov.uk/cs/ro). Postal enquiries to WSRO, County Hall, Chichester, West Sussex PO19 1RN

Teesside

Teesside Archives, Exchange House, 6 Marton Road, Middlesbrough TS1 1DB (tel. 01642 248321; fax 01642 248391; email teesidearchives@middlesborough.gov.uk; website www.middlesborough.gov.uk/it/webdevt/council/LIBSARCH.NSF)

Tyne and Wear

Tyne and Wear Archives Services, Blandford House, West Blandford Square, Newcastle-upon-Tyne NE1 4JA (tel. 0191 232 6789; fax 0191 230 2614; email twas@gateshead.gov.uk; website www.thenortheast.com/archives/index.html)
Local Studies Collection, Gateshead Central Library, Prince Consort Road, Gateshead NE8 4LN (tel. 0191 477 3478; fax 0191 477 7454; email a.lang@libarts.gatesheadmbc.gov.uk; website www.gateshead.gov.uk/ls)

Warwickshire

Warwickshire County Record Office, Priory Park, Cape Road, Warwick CV34 4JS (tel. 01926 412735; fax 01926 412509; email recordoffice@warwickshire.gov.uk; website www.warwickshire.gov.uk/countyrecordoffice)
Warwick University Modern Records Centre, University Library, University of Warwick, Coventry CV4 7AL (tel. 024 7652 4219; fax 024 7657 2988; email archives@warwick.ac.uk; website www.warwick.ac.uk/services/library/mrc)

Isle of Wight

Isle of Wight County Record Office, 26 Hillside, Newport PO30 2EB (tel. 01983 823820; fax 01983 823820; email recordoffice@iow.gov.uk; website www.iwight.com/library/recordoffice)

Wiltshire

Wiltshire and Swindon Record Office, Libraries and Heritage Headquarters, Wiltshire County Council, Bythesea Road, Trowbridge BA14 8BS (tel. 01225 713709; fax 01225 713515; email wsro@wiltshire.gov.uk; website www.wiltshire.gov.uk/heritage/html/wsro)

Worcestershire

Worcestershire Record Office: City Centre Branch, Worcestershire Library and History Centre, Trinity Street, Worcester WR1 2PW (tel. 01905 765922; fax 01905 765925; email WLHC@worcestershire.gov.uk)
County Hall Branch, County Hall, Spetchley Road, Worcester WR5 2NP (tel. 01905 766351; fax 01905 766363; email RecordOffice@worcestershire.gov.uk; website www.worcestershire.gov.uk/records)

East Yorkshire

East Riding of Yorkshire Archive Office, The Chapel, Lord Roberts Road, Beverley, E. Yorks (tel. 01482 885007; fax 01482 885463; email archives.service@eastriding.gov.uk; website www.eastriding.gov.uk/learning). Correspondence address: County Hall, Beverley, E. Yorks HU17
Hull City Archives, 79 Lowgate, Hull HU1 1HN (tel. 01482 615102; fax 01482 613051; email City.Archives@hullcc.gov.uk; website www.hullcc.gov.uk)

North Yorkshire

North Yorkshire County Record Office, Malpas Road, Northallerton DL7 8TB (tel. 01609 777585; fax 01609 777078; email archives@northyorks.gov.uk; website www.northyorks.gov.uk/libraries/archives/default.shtm). Correspondence address: County Hall, Northallerton DL7 8AF
York City Archives Department, Art Gallery Building, Exhibition Square, York YO1 7EW (tel. 01904 551878/9; fax 01904 551877; website www.york.gov.uk/learning/libraries/archives/index.html)

South Yorkshire

Barnsley Archive Service and Local Studies Department, Central Library, Shambles Street, Barnsley S70 2JF (tel. 01226 773950/773938; fax 01226 773955; email Archives@barnsley.co.uk)
Doncaster Archives Department, King Edward Road, Balby, Doncaster DN4 0NA (tel. 01302 859811; email doncaster.archives@doncaster.gov.uk; website www.doncaster.gov.uk)

Doncaster Local Studies Library, Waterdale, Doncaster DN1 3JE (tel. 01302 734307; fax 01302 369749; email Central.LocalHistory@doncaster.gov.uk; website www.doncaster.gov.uk)

Sheffield Archives, 52 Shoreham Street, Sheffield S1 4SP (tel. 0114 273 4756; fax 0114 203 9398; email sheffield.archives@dial.pipex.com)

West Yorkshire

West Yorkshire Archive Service, Wakefield Headquarters, Registry of Deeds, Newstead Road, Wakefield WF1 2DE (tel. 01924 305980; fax 01924 305983; email wakefield@wyjs.org.uk; website www.archives.wyjs.org.uk). Branches at Bradford, Halifax, Huddersfield and Leeds.

Scotland

Aberdeen City Archives, The Town House, Broad Street, Aberdeen AB10 1AQ (tel. 01224 522513; fax 01224 638556; email archives@legal.aberdeen.net.uk; website www.aberdeencity.gov.uk). Branch at Old Aberdeen House.

Angus Archives, Montrose Library, 214 High Street, Montrose DD10 8PH (tel. 01674 671415; fax 01674 671810; email angus.archives@angus.gov.uk; website www.angus.gov.uk/history)

Argyll and Bute Council Archives, Manse Brae, Lochgilphead, Argyll PA31 8QU (tel. 01546 604120; fax 01546 606897)

Ayrshire Archives Centre, Craigie Estate, Ayr KA8 0SS (tel. 01292 287584; fax 01292 284918; email archives@south-ayrshire.gov.uk; website www.ayrshirearchives.org.uk)

Dumfries and Galloway Archives, 33 Burns Street, Dumfries DG1 2PS (tel. 01387 269254; fax 01387 264126; email Lib&I@dumgal.gov.uk; website www.dumgal.gov.uk/lia)

Dundee City Archives, 1 Shore Terrace, Dundee (tel. 01382 434494; fax 01382 434666; email archives@dundeecity.gov.uk; website www.dundeecity.gov.uk/archives). Correspondence address: Department of Support Services, 21 City Square, Dundee DD1 3BY

Edinburgh City Archives, Department of Corporate Services, City of Edinburgh Council, City Chambers, High Street, Edinburgh EH1 1YJ (tel. 0131 529 4616; fax 0131 529 4957; website www.edinburgh.gov.uk)

Falkirk Museums History Research Centre, Callendar House, Callendar Park, Falkirk FK1 1YR (tel. 01324 503779; fax 01324 503711; email carol.snedden@falkirk.gov.uk; website www.falkirkmuseums.demon.uk/museums/ms/hrc.htm)

Glasgow City Archives, The Mitchell Library, 201 North Street, Glasgow G3 7DN (tel. 0141 287 2913; fax 0141 226 8452; email archives@cls.glasgow.co.uk; website www.glasgowlibraries.org)

Highland Council Archive, Inverness Library, Farraline Park, Inverness IV1 1NH (tel. 01463 220330; fax 01463 711128; email archives@highland.gov.uk; website www.highland.gov.uk/cl/publicservices/archivedetails/highlandar)

Midlothian Council Archives, Library Headquarters, 2 Clerk Street, Loanhead,

Midlothian EH20 9DR (tel. 0131 440 2210; fax 0131 440 4635; email local.studies@midlothian.gov.uk)

North Highland Archive, Wick Library, Sinclair Terrace, Wick KW1 5AB (tel. 01955 606432; fax 01955 603000; email phil.astley@highland.gov.uk; website www.highland.gov.uk/cl/publicservices/archivedetails/northarchive.htm)

North Lanarkshire Archives, 10 Kelvin Road, Lenziemill, Cumbernauld G67 2BA (tel. 01236 737114; fax 01236 781762)

South Lanarkshire Archives and Information Management Service, 30 Hawbank Road, College Milton, East Kilbride G74 5EX (tel. 01355 239193; fax 01355 242365)

Orkney Archives, The Orkney Library, Laing Street, Kirkwall KW15 1NW (tel. 01856 873166/875260; fax 01856 875260; email alison@oic4.orkney.gov.uk)

Perth and Kinross Council Archive, A.K. Bell Library, 2–8 York Place, Perth PH2 8EP (tel. 01738 477012; fax 01738 477010; email archives@pkc.gov.uk; website www.scan.org.uk/directory/Perth/perthframeset.html)

Scottish Borders Archive and Local History Centre, Library Headquarters, St Mary's Mill, Selkirk TD7 5EW (tel. 01750 20842; fax 01750 22875; email archives@scotborders.gov.uk)

Shetland Archives, 44 King Harald Street, Lerwick ZE1 0EQ (tel. 01595 696247; fax 01595 696533; email briansmith@sic.shetland.gov.uk; website www.shetland.gov.uk/atoz/ed3.htm)

Stirling Council Archives Services, Unit 6, Burghmuir Industrial Estate, Stirling FK7 7PY (tel. 01786 450745; fax 01786 433005; email archive@stirling.gov.uk)

Wales

Anglesey County Record Office, Shire Hall, Glanhwfa Road, Llangefni LL77 7TW (tel. 01248 752080; email avxed@anglesey.gov.uk; website www.anglesey.gov.uk/english/library/archives/archives.htm)

Carmarthenshire Archive Service, Parc Myrddin, Richmond Terrace, Carmarthen SA31 1DS (tel. 01267 228232; fax 01267 228237; email archives@carmarthenshire.gov.uk; website www.llgc.org.uk/cac/cac0028.htm)

Ceredigion Archives, Swyddfa'r Sir, Marine Terrace, Aberystwyth SY23 2DE (tel. 01970 633697/8; fax 01970 633663; email archives@ceredigion.gov.uk; website www.llgc.org.uk/cac/cac0009.htm)

Denbighshire Record Office, 46 Clwyd Street, Ruthin LL15 1HP (tel. 01824 708250; fax 01824 708258; email archives@denbighshire.gov.uk; website www.denbighshire.gov.uk)

Flintshire Record Office, The Old Rectory, Hawarden, Flintshire CH5 3NR (tel. 01244 532364; fax 01244 538344; email archives@flintshire.gov.uk; website www.llgc.org.uk/cac/cac0032.htm)

Glamorgan Record Office, Glamorgan Building, King Edward VII Avenue, Cathays Park, Cardiff CF10 3NE (tel. 029 2078 0282; fax 029 2078 0284; email glamro@cardiff.ac.uk; website www.glamro.gov.uk)

West Glamorgan Archive Service, County Hall, Oystermouth Road, Swansea SA1 3SN (tel. 01792 636589; fax 01792 637130; email Susan.Beckley@Swansea.Gov.Uk; website www.swansea.gov.uk/archives)

Gwent Record Office, County Hall, Cwmbran NP44 2XH (tel. 01633 644886; fax 01633 648382; email gwent.records@torfaen.gov.uk; website www.llgc.org.uk/cac/cac0004.htm)

Gwynedd Archives:

Caernarfon Record Office, Victoria Dock, Caernarfon (tel. 01286 679095; fax 01286 679637; email archives@gwynedd.gov.uk; website www.gwynedd.gov.uk/archives). Correspondence address: County Offices, Shirehall Street, Caernarfon LL55 1SH

Merionydd Record Office, Cae Penarlag, Dolgellau LL40 2YB (tel. 01341 424444; fax 01341 424505; email archives.dolgellau@gwynedd.gov.uk; website www.gwynedd.gov.uk/archives)

Pembrokeshire Record Office, The Castle, Haverfordwest SA61 2EF (tel. 01437 763707; fax 01437 768539; email Claire.Orr@Pembrokeshire.gov.uk; website www.llgc.org.uk/cac/cac0002.htm)

Powys County Archives Office, County Hall, Llandrindod Wells LD1 5LG (tel. 01597 826088; fax 01597 827162; email archives@powys.gov.uk; website www.archives.powys.gov.uk)

UNIVERSITY LIBRARIES WITH IMPORTANT MANUSCRIPT COLLECTIONS

Students, undergraduates and graduates of other universities are normally admitted without formality; temporary tickets will be issued to other *bona fide* researchers at the Librarian's discretion. (A letter of introduction and/or proof of identity may be required.) At most libraries there are amended opening hours during vacations. Please note that telephone and fax numbers, emails and websites stated here are of the departments of archives, manuscripts and special collections, not of the main libraries. Some collections may be seen only by appointment; in all cases you should write in advance of your visit. For opening times and other information, go to the relevant website. For the libraries of the universities of Cambridge, Oxford and London, where there are in excess of 80 repositories each, only the principal collection is listed here. Again, you should log on to the relevant websites for further information.

England

Birmingham University Information Services, Special Collections Department, Main Library, University of Birmingham, Edgbaston, Birmingham B15 2TT (tel. 0121 414 5838; fax 0121 471 4691; email library@bham.ac.uk; website www.is.bham.ac.uk)

Cambridge University Library, Department of Manuscripts and University Archives, West Road, Cambridge CB3 9DR (tel. 01223 333000; fax 01223 333160; email mss@ula.cam.ac.uk; website www.lib.cam.ac.uk/MSS)

Durham University Library, Archives and Special Collections, Palace Green Section, Palace Green, Durham DH1 3RN (tel. 0191 334 2932; fax 0191 334 2942; email pg.library@durham.ac.uk; website www.dur.ac.uk/library)

Exeter University Library, Stocker Road, Exeter EX4 4PT (tel. 01392 263870; fax 01392 263871; email i.j.f.mortimer@exeter.ac.uk; website www.ex.ac.uk/library/special)

Hull University, Brynmor Jones Library, Cottingham Road, Hull HU6 7RX (tel. 01482 465265; fax 01482 466205; email archives@acs.hull.ac.uk; website www.hull.ac.uk/lib/archives)

Keele University Library, Keele ST5 5BG (tel. 01782 583237; fax 01782 711553; email h.burton@keele.ac.uk; website www.keele.ac.uk/depts/li/specarc)

Leeds University Library, Special Collections, The Brotherton Library, Leeds LS2 9JT (tel. 0113 343 5518; fax 0113 343 5561; email special-collections@library.leeds.ac.uk; website www.leeds.ac.uk/library/spcoll)

Liverpool University: Department of Special Collections and Archives, Sydney Jones Library, University of Liverpool, Chatham Street, Liverpool L7 7AY (tel. 0151 794 2696; fax 0151 794 2681; email mwatry@liv.ac.uk; website www.sca.lib.liv.ac.uk/collections). Correspondence address: Sydney Jones Library, University of Liverpool, PO Box 123, Liverpool L69 3DA

University of London Library, Palaeography Room, Senate House, Malet Street, London WC1E 7HU (tel. 020 7682 8470; fax 020 7682 8480; email historic@ull.ac.uk; website www.ull.ac.uk/ull)

Manchester University: John Rylands Library, 150 Deansgate, Manchester M3 3EH (tel. 0161 834 5343; fax 0161 834 5574; email jr.hodgson@man.ac.uk; website www.rylibweb.man.ac.uk/spcoll)

Newcastle-upon-Tyne University: The Robinson Library, Newcastle-upon-Tyne NE2 4HQ (tel. 0191 222 5146; fax 0191 222 6235; email lib-specenq@nlc.ac.uk; website www.ncl.ac.uk/library/speccoll/spechome.html)

Nottingham University Library, Department of Manuscripts and Special Collections, Hallward Library, University Park, Nottingham NG7 2RD (tel. 0115 951 4565; fax 0115 951 4558; email mss-library@nottingham.ac.uk; website www.mss.library.nottingham.ac.uk)

Oxford University Bodleian Library, Special Collections and Western Manuscripts, Broad Street, Oxford OX1 3BG (tel. 01865 277158; fax 01865 277187; email western.manuscripts@bodley.ac.uk; website www.bodley.ox.ac.uk/dept/scwmss)

Reading University Library, PO Box 223, Whiteknights, Reading RG6 6AE (tel. 0118 931 8776; fax 0118 931 6636; email specialcollections@reading.ac.uk; website www.library.rdg.ac.uk/SerDepts/vl/colls/special/index.html)

Sheffield University Library, Western Bank, Sheffield S10 2TN (tel. 0114 222 7230; fax 0114 222 7290; email l.aspden@sheffield.ac.uk; website www.shef.ac.uk/~lib/special/special.html)

Southampton University Library, Highfield, Southampton SO17 1BJ (tel. 023 8059 2721; fax 023 8059 3007; email archives@soton.ac.uk; website www.archives.lib.soton.ac.uk)

Sussex University Library Special Collections, The Library, University of Sussex Falmer, Brighton BN1 9QL (tel. 01273 606755; fax 01273 678441; email Library.SpecialColl@sussex.ac.uk; website www.sussex.ac.uk/library/speccoll)

Warwick University Modern Records Centre, University Library, Coventry CV4 7AL (tel. 024 7652 4219; fax 024 7657 2988; email archives@warwick.ac.uk; website www.warwick.ac.uk/services/library/mrc)

York University, Borthwick Institute of Historical Research, St Anthony's Hall, Peasholme Green, York YO1 2PW (tel. 01904 642315; fax 01904 633284; website www.york.ac.uk/inst./bihr). *N.B.* Will be closed for a period during summer 2004.

Scotland

Aberdeen University Library, Department of Special Libraries and Archives, DISS, Historic Collections, King's College, Aberdeen AB24 3SW (tel. 01224 272598; fax 01224 273891; email speclib@abdn.ac.uk; website www.abdn.ac.uk/diss/historic/spec/speclib.hti)

Dundee University Archives, Tower Building, Dundee DD1 4HN (tel. 01382 344095; fax 01382 345523; email p.e.whatley@dundee.ac.uk; website www.dundee.ac.uk/Archives)

Edinburgh University Library, Special Collections, George Square, Edinburgh EH8 9LJ (tel. 0131 650 8379; fax 0131 650 6863; email special.collections.library@ed.ac.uk; website www.lib.ed.ac.uk/lib/resources/collections/specdivision)

Glasgow University Library, Special Collections Department, Hillhead Street, Glasgow G12 8QE (tel. 0141 330 6767; fax 0141 330 3793; email special@lib.gla.ac.uk; website www.special.lib.gla.ac.uk)

St Andrews University Library, North Street, St Andrews KY16 9TR (tel. 01334 462324; fax 01334 462282; email nhr@st-and.ac.uk; website www.library.st-and.ac.uk)

Wales

University of Wales Bangor, Department of Manuscripts and Archives, Bangor LL57 2DG (tel. 01248 351151 ext. 2966; fax 01248 382979; email 1ss177@bangor.ac.uk; website www.bangor.ac.uk/is/library/special.html)

CATHEDRAL ARCHIVES AND LIBRARIES

Canterbury Cathedral Archives, The Precincts, Canterbury, Kent CT1 2EH (tel. 01227 865330; fax 01227 865222; email archives@canterbury-cathedral.org; website www.canterbury-cathedral.org/archives). Reader's ticket required (take 2 passport-size photographs and means of identification).

Durham Dean and Chapter Library, The College, Durham DH1 3EH (tel. 0191 386 2489; website www.dur.ac.uk/Library/asc/dioc/dcloi.html). Correspondence address re muniments: Durham University Library, Archives and Special Collections, Palace Green, Durham DH1 3RN

Exeter Cathedral Archives, Old Bishop's Palace, Diocesan House, Palace Gate, Exeter EX1 1HX (tel. 01392 495594; website www.ex.ac.uk/library/cathedral.html)

Salisbury Cathedral Library, 6 The Close, Salisbury SP1 2EF (tel. 01722 555160; website www.salisburycathedral.org.uk/pages/index.html). By appointment (letter of introduction required).

York Minster Archives, Dean's Park, York YO1 2JQ (tel. 01904 611118; fax 01904 611119; email archives@yorkminster; website www.yorkminster.org). By appointment.

Westminster Abbey Muniment Room and Library, East Cloister, Westminster Abbey, London SW1P 3PA (tel. 020 7222 5152 ext. 228; fax 020 7654 4827; email library@westminster-abbey.org; website www.westminster-abbey.org). Letter of introduction required.

Westminster Diocesan Archives (Roman Catholic), 16a Abingdon Road, London W8 6AF (tel. 020 7938 3580), by appointment. Letter of introduction required.

Winchester Cathedral Library, c/o Cathedral Office, 5 The Close, Winchester SO23 9LS (tel. 01962 853137; fax 01962 841519; email John.Hardacre@dial.pipex.com). Letter of introduction required.

OTHER MAJOR REFERENCE LIBRARIES

Belfast Central Library: Belfast, Ulster and Irish Studies Department, Royal Avenue, Belfast BT1 1EA (tel. 028 9050 9150; email buis@libraries.belfast-elb.gov.uk; website www.belb.org.uk/library/irishLocalStudies.htm)

Birmingham and Midland Institute, 9 Margaret Street, Birmingham B3 3BS (tel. 0121 236 3591; fax 0121 212 4577; email admin@bmi.org.uk; website www.bmi.org.uk)

Birmingham Reference Library, Central Library, Chamberlain Square, Birmingham B3 3HQ (tel. 0121 303 4511; fax 0121 303 4458; email central.library@birmingham.gov.uk; website www.birmingham.gov.uk). *N.B.* A major New Library of Birmingham is planned in which the reference library will occupy the three upper floors. For up-to-date information log on to the website as above.

Edinburgh City Libraries, Central Library, George IV Bridge, Edinburgh EH1 1EG (tel. 0131 242 8000; email eclis@edinburgh.gov.uk or central.reference.library @edinburgh.gov.uk; website www.edinburgh.gov.uk/CEC/Recreation/Libraries)

Glasgow City Special Collections, The Mitchell Library, North Street, Glasgow G3 7DN (tel. 0141 287 2937; fax 0141 287 2815; email karl.magee@cls.glasgow.gov.uk; website www.glasgowlibraries.org)

Liverpool Central Library, William Brown Street, Liverpool L3 8EW (tel. 0151 233 5890; fax 0151 207 1342; email clc-central@connect.org.uk)

London: Westminster Reference Library, 35 St Martin's Street, London WC2H 7HP (tel. 020 7641 4636; fax 020 7641 4606; email westreflib@dial.pipex.com; website www.westminster.gov.uk/libraries/westref)

Manchester: Central Library, St Peter's Square, Manchester M2 5PD (tel. 0161 234 1900; email mclib@libraries.manchester.gov.uk; website www.manchester.gov.uk/libraries)

PRIVATE SUBSCRIPTION LIBRARIES

Highgate Literary and Scientific Institution Library, 11 South Grove, Highgate Village, London N6 6BS (tel. 020 8340 3343; fax 020 8340 5632; email admin@hlsi.demon.co.uk). Tue–Fri, 10.00–17.00; Sat, 10.00–16.00. £50 per year (£80 family subscription).

London Library, 14 St James's Square, London SW1Y 4LG (tel. 020 7930 7705; fax 020 7766 4766; email membership@londonlibrary.co.uk; website www.londonli-brary.co.uk). Mon, Fri, Sat, 09.30–17.30; Tue, Wed, Thu, 09.30–19.30. £150 per year (2002).

Space does not permit a complete listing of the twenty-three other surviving private subscription libraries in the provinces, but these will be well known to readers living locally; visit the website at www.independentlibraries.co.uk or consult the yellow pages of the local telephone directories. A descriptive leaflet is available from the Association of Independent Libraries, c/o The Leeds Library, 18 Commercial Street, Leeds LS1 6AL (tel. 0113 245 3071).

SHORT LIST OF SUBJECTS AND SOURCES

Advertising

Advertising Association Information Centre, Abford House, 15 Wilton Road, London SW1V 1NJ (tel. 020 7828 2771; fax 020 7931 0376; email ic@adassoc.org.uk; website www.adassoc.org.uk). Non-members (non-business), Tue–Thu, 14.00–16.00, telephone or visit by appointment only. For opening hours for members/businesses, see website.

History of Advertising Trust, HAT House, 12, The Raveningham Centre, Raveningham, Norwich NR14 6NU (tel. 01508 548623; fax 01508 548478; email archives@hatads.demon.co.uk; website www.hatads.org.uk). Mon–Fri, 09.00–17.00.

Agriculture

Rural History Centre, Reading University, PO Box 229, Whiteknights, Reading RG6 2AG (tel. 0118 378 8660; fax 0118 975 1264; website www.ruralhistory.org). Mon–Thu, 09.30–13.00, 14.00–17.00; Fri, 09.30–13.00, 14.00–16.30, by appointment.

Air Force/Aviation

Royal Aeronautical Society Library, 4 Hamilton Place, London W1V 0BQ (tel. 020 7499 3515; fax 020 7499 6230; email raes@raes.org.uk; website www.aerosociety.com). Mon–Fri, 10.00–17.00.

Royal Air Force Museum Library, Grahame Park Way, Hendon, London NW9 5LL (tel. 020 8205 2266, ext. 274; fax 020 8200 1751; website www.rafmuseum.org.uk). Written enquiries only in first instance.

See also Ministry of Defence Whitehall Library under '*Military*', and under '*World Wars I and II*'.

Architecture

Architectural Association Library, 34–36 Bedford Square, London WC1B 3ES (tel. 020 7887 4036; fax 020 7414 0782; email hsklar@aaschool.ac.uk; website www.aaschool.ac.uk/library). Members only (5-day pass available, £15), Mon–Fri, 10.00–20.00; Sat, 11.00–17.00.

British Architectural Library, Royal Institute of British Architects, 66 Portland Place, London W1N 4AD (tel. 020 7580 5533; fax 020 7631 1802; email bal@inst.riba.org; website www.architecture.com; public information line (50p per minute) 0906 302 0400). Tue, 10.00–20.00; Wed, Thu, Fri, 10.00–17.00; Sat, 10.00–13.30. Free to RIBA members; non-members may purchase day tickets. Priced research service (minimum charge £30).

Art

Art and Design Library, Westminster Reference Library, 2nd floor, 35 St Martin's Street, London WC2H 7HP (tel. 020 7641 4638; fax 020 7641 4604; email westreflib@dial.pipex.com; website www.westminster.gov.uk/libraries/westref). Mon–Fri, 10.00–20.00; Sat, 10.00–17.00.

British Museum, Department of Prints and Drawings, Great Russell Street, London WC1B 3DG (tel. 020 7323 8000; website thebritishmuseum.ac.uk). Proof of identity required. Mon–Fri, 10.00–13.00, 14.15–16.00; Sat, 10.00–13.00.

Courtauld Institute of Art Book Library, Somerset House, Strand, London WC2R 0RN (tel. 020 7848 2777; fax 020 7848 2887; website www.courtauld.ac.uk). Mon–Fri, 09.30–21.00 (term), 10.30–17.00 (vacation); reading room service only, 19.00–21.00. *N.B.* This is a library of last resort, i.e. for material not available elsewhere.

National Art Library, Victoria & Albert Museum Library, Cromwell Road, London SW7 2RL (tel. 020 7942 2000; email enquiries@nal.vam.ac.uk; website www.nal.vam.ac.uk). Tue–Sat, 10.00–17.00. *N.B.* A specially endorsed reader's ticket is required for access to the Special Collections.

National Portrait Gallery Heinz Archive and Library, St Martin's Place, London WC2H 0HE (tel. 020 7306 0055; fax 020 7306 0056; website www.npg.org.uk). Tue–Fri, 10.00–17.00, by appointment only.

Recommended title:
Dictionary of Art, ed. Jane Turner, Macmillan, London, 34 vols, 1996

Banking and Commerce

Bank of England Information Centre, Threadneedle Street, London EC2R 8AH (tel. 020 7601 4715; fax 020 7601 4356; email informationcentre@bankofengland.co.uk; website www.bankofengland.co.uk). Mon–Fri, 09.30–17.30, by prior arrangement only and when information not available elsewhere. *N.B.* The Bank of England and other major banks will grant access to historical records only when applications are supported by a university or other centre of research.

Westminster Reference Library (Business and Official Publications), 35 St Martin's Street, London WC2H 7HP (tel. 020 7641 4634; fax 020 7641 4606; email westreflib@dial.pipex.com; website www.westminster.gov.uk/libraries/westref). Mon–Fri, 10.00–20.00; Sat, 10.00–17.00.

Births, Marriages and Deaths

Family Records Centre, 1 Myddleton Street, Islington, London EC1R 1UW (tel. general enquiries, 020 8392 5300; fax 020 8392 5307; certificates, 0870 243 7788; email certificate.services@ons.gov.uk; website www.familyrecords.gov.uk). See also under '*General Register Offices*' (page 202) and '*Genealogy*'.

Black Culture in Britain

Archives & Museum of Black Heritage, 378 Coldharbour Lane, London SW9 8LF (tel. 020 7926 1060; email info@aambh.org.uk; website www.archivesmuseumblackheritage.org.uk). By appointment, Mon-Fri, 10.00–16.00. Exhibitions (free) open to the public 13.00–16.00.

Broadcasting and Television

BBC Written Archives Centre, Peppard Road, Caversham Park, Reading RG4 8TZ (tel. 0118 948 6281; fax 0118 946 1145; email heritage@bbc.co.uk; website www.bbc.co.uk/thenandnow/wac). Open to *bona fide* researchers for reference only, Wed–Fri, 09.45–17.00, by appointment. Some services are charged.

British Library National Sound Archive, British Library, 96 Euston Road, London NW1 2DB (tel. 020 7412 7440; fax 020 7412 7441; email nsa@bl.uk; website www.bl.uk/nsa). British Library reader's pass required. Mon, Thu, 10.00–18.00; Tue, Wed, 10.00–20.00; Fri, Sat, 10.00–17.00. The Recorded Sound Information Service (tel. 020 7412 7440) is based in the Humanities 2 Reading Room; the Listening & Viewing Service (tel. 020 7412 7418) is in the Rare Books and Music Reading Room; appointments may be made by telephone, fax, email or post. Northern listening service at British Library Document Supply Centre, Boston Spa, Wetherby, West Yorkshire LS23 7BQ (tel. 01937 546070), Mon–Fri, 09.15–16.30, by appointment. Catalogue (CADENSA) online at www.cadensa.bl.uk. *N.B.* The collections include some BBC sound material.

British Universities Film and Video Council (BUFVC), 77 Wells Street, London W1P 3RE (tel. 020 7393 1500; fax 020 7393 1555; email ask@bufvc.ac.uk; website www.bufvc.ac.uk). *Bona fide* researchers may use the library for reference purposes.

Business

British Library Business Information Service, Science 3 Reading Room, British Library, 96 Euston Road, London NW1 2DB. For quick information telephone British Library-Lloyds TSB Business Line (020 7412 7454/020 7412 7977; email business-information@bl.uk), Mon–Fri, 09.00–17.00. Brief enquiries are answered free of charge; in-depth research undertaken at commercial rates. For further information visit website www.bl.uk/bis.

Business Archives Council. Will advise on location of business records. Enquiries to the Hon. Secretary, Fiona Maccoll, Records Manager, Rio Tinto PLC, 6 St James's Square, London SW1Y 4LD (tel. 020 7753 2338; fax 020 7753 2211; email fiona.maccoll@riotinto.com).

Business Archives Council of Scotland, c/o Glasgow University Archive and Business Record Centre, 13 Thurso Street, Glasgow G11 6PE (tel. 0141 330 5515; fax 0141 330 4158; email bacs@archives.gla.ac.uk). Written and telephone enquiries only. Download enquiry form on ARCHON for email/fax enquiries to Duty Archivist.

City Business Library, 1 Brewers' Hall Garden, London EC2V 5BX (tel. 020 7638 8215; fax 020 7332 1847; email cbl@corpoflondon.gov.uk; website www.cityoflondon.gov.uk). Mon–Fri, 09.30–17.30.

Companies Registration Office, Companies House, Crown Way, Maindy Pool, Cardiff CF14 3UZ; London search room at Companies House Information Centre, 21 Bloomsbury Street, London WC1B 3XD. (For all enquiries, tel. 0870 333 3636; email genenquiries@companieshouse.gov.uk; website www.companieshouse.gov.uk). Personal enquiries only at London office, Mon–Fri, 09.00–17.00 (last search 15.00 hours). *N.B.* A small search fee per company is payable. Company files are in Cardiff, microfiche copies in London and at branch offices in Edinburgh, Birmingham, Leeds and Manchester.

Westminster Reference Library, Business & Official Publications section, 35 St Martin's Street, London WC2H 7HP (tel. 020 7641 4634; fax 020 7641 4606; email westreflib@dial.pipex.com; website www.westminster.gov.uk/libraries/westref). Mon–Fri, 10.00–20.00; Sat, 10.00–17.00.

Recommended titles:
Business: A Guide to Searching in Published Sources, by Nigel Spencer, *How to Find* series, British Library, London, 1995
Instant Guide to Company Information Online – Europe, ed. Nigel Spencer, *Key Resource* series, British Library, London, 3rd edn, 1998

Cartoons and Caricature

Cartoon Art Trust Museum, 7–13 Brunswick Centre, Bernard Street, London WC1A 1AF (tel. 020 7278 7172; fax 020 7278 4234; email cartooncentre@freeuk.com; website www.cartoonarttrust.com). Tue–Sat, 10.00-17.00.

The Centre for the Study of Cartoons and Caricature, The Templeman Library, University of Kent at Canterbury, Canterbury, Kent CT2 7NU (tel./fax 01227 823127; website www.library.ukc.ac.uk/cartoons). Mon–Fri, 09.00–17.00.

Punch Cartoon Library, 87–135 Brompton Road, London SW1X 7XL (tel. 020 7225 6710; fax 020 7225 6712; email punch.library@harrods.com; website www.punch.co.uk). Mon–Fri, 10.00–13.00, 14.30–17.30, by appointment only. *N.B. Punch* ceased publication in early summer 2002.

Recommended titles:
Dictionary of British Cartoonists and Caricatures 1730–1980, compiled by Mark Bryant and Simon Heneage, Scolar Press, London, 1994
Dictionary of Twentieth Century British Cartoonists and Caricaturists, compiled by Mark Bryant, Ashgate, Aldershot, 2000

Census Returns

Family Records Centre, 1 Myddelton Street, Islington, London EC1R 1UW (tel. 020 8392 5300; fax 020 8392 5307; email enquiry@pro.gov.uk; website www.familyrecords.gov.uk). Mon, Wed, 09.00–17.00; Tue, 10.00–19.00; Thu 9.00–19.00; Sat 09.30–17.00. Open to the public without ticket. Microform copies of census returns for England and Wales 1841–91. The 1901 census is online at www.pro.gov.uk/census.

Children (Books and Objects)

The Booktrust Childrens Collection, University of Surrey Roehampton, Mount Clare, Minstead Gardens, Roehampton, London SW15 4EE (tel. 020 392 3772; email s.mansfield@roehampton.ac.uk or j.mills@roehampton.ac.uk). Access by appointment only.

Children's Literature at Booktrust (formerly Young Book Trust), Book House, 45 East Hill, London SW18 2QZ (tel. 020 8516 2985; fax 020 8516 2978; website www.booktrusted.com). Children's Reference Library: access for reference only, by appointment, Mon–Fri, 9.00–5.00. Information service and membership by subscription.

Museum of Childhood at Bethnal Green, Cambridge Heath Road, London E2 9PA (tel. 020 8983 5200; fax 020 8983 5225; email bgmc@vam.ac.uk; website www.museumofchildhood.org.uk). Mon–Thu, Sat, Sun, 10.00–17.50; closed on Fridays. Collection of dolls, dolls' houses, toys, etc. (*N.B.* The book collections formerly housed here are now at the National Art Library – see below.)

National Art Library/Children's Literature Collections, Victoria & Albert Museum, Cromwell Road, London SW7 2RL (tel. 020 7942 2400; website www.vam.ac.uk). Tue–Sat, 10.00–17.00. Special Collections reader's ticket required (letter of introduction required).

Costume

Fashion Research Centre, 4 Circus, Bath, Somerset BA1 2EW (tel. 01225 477752/4; fax 01225 444793; email enquiries@bathnes.gov.uk; website www.museumofcostume.co.uk). By appointment: reference library Thu, Fri, 10.30–12.30, 14.00–16.00; study collection Mon, Tue, Wed, 10.30 and 14.30.

London College of Fashion Library, 20 John Prince's Street, Oxford Circus, London W1M 0BJ (tel. 020 7514 7453; website www.linst.ac.uk/library). Open to the public for reference only, by appointment (book well in advance), Mon–Thu, 09.30–20.15; Fri, 10.00–17.15.

Museum of Costume, The Assembly Rooms, Bennett Street, Bath BA1 2QH (tel. 01225 477789; fax 01225 444793; website www.museumofcostume.co.uk). Daily (including Sundays) 10.00–17.00.

European Commission

Commission of the European Communities, Press and Information Office, Jean Monnet House, 8 Storey's Gate, London SW1P 3AT (tel. 020 7973 1992; fax 020 7973 1900/1910). Mon–Fri, 10.00–13.00. Not open to students. Enquiries should be referred through a local public library.

Films and Cinema History

British Film Institute National Library, 21 Stephen Street, London W1P 1PL (tel. 020 7255 1444; fax 020 7436 0165; website www.bfi.org.uk). Mon, Fri, 10.30–17.30; Tue, Thu, 10.30–20.00; Wed, 13.00–20.00. *Note:* The telephone enquiry service is in operation only from 10.00–17.00. Open to non-members for reference only, 5-day and limited day membership available.

British Film Institute National Film and Television Archive, J. Paul Getty Conservation Centre, Kingshill Way, Berkhamsted HP4 3TP (tel.

01442 876 301; fax 01442 289 112; email davidpierce@bfi.org.uk; website www.bfi.org.uk/collections/preservation/index.html). *N.B.* Some film is stored at other sites.

British Universities Film and Video Council (BUFVC), 77 Wells Street, London W1P 3RE (tel. 020 7393 1500; fax 020 7393 1555; email ask@bufvc.ac.uk; website www.bufvc.ac.uk). Houses the British Universities Newsreel Project (database of records of British cinema newsreels 1910–79). By appointment to *bona fide* researchers, or search online.

Folklore

The Folklore Society, c/o The Warburg Institute, Woburn Square, London WC1H 0AB (tel. 020 7862 8564; fax 020 7862 8565).Written and telephone enquiries only.

Vaughan Williams Memorial Library, English Folk Dance and Song Society, Cecil Sharp House, 2 Regent's Park Road, London NW1 7AY (tel. 020 7485 2206 ext. 18/19; fax 020 7284 0523; email library@efdss.org; website www.efdss.org). Tue–Fri, 09.30–17.30; 1st and 3rd Sat in month, 10.00–16.00. Non-members pay daily fee for access (reference only).

Recommended titles:

A Companion to the Folklore, Myths & Customs of Britain, by Marc Alexander, Sutton, Thrupp, Stroud, Glos., 2002

A Dictionary of English Folklore, by Jacqueline Simpson and Steve Roud, Oxford University Press, Oxford, 2000

Larousse Dictionary of World Folklore, Larousse, London, 1995

Food

The Brotherton Library, Department of Special Collections, Leeds University, Leeds LS2 9JT (tel. 0113 233 5518; fax 0113 233 5561; email special-collections@library.leeds.ac.uk; website www.leeds.ac.uk/library/spcoll). Collection of old recipe books.

Recommended titles:

The Cambridge World History of Food, by Kenneth F. Kiple and Kriemhild Conee Ornelas, 2 vols, Cambridge University Press, 2000

Food: A History, by Felipe Fernández-Armesto, Macmillan, London, 2001; paperback, 2002

Food: A Culinary History, eds. Jean-Louis Flandrin and Massimo Montanari, Columbia University Press, 1999

Genealogy and Heraldry

College of Arms, Queen Victoria Street, London EC4 4BT (tel. 020 7248 2762; fax 020 7248 6448; email enquiries@college-of-arms.gov.uk; website www.college-of-arms.gov.uk). Mon–Fri, 10.00–16.00; Sat by appointment. *N.B.* There are no public search rooms. Research is undertaken only by the Heralds and their staff, on a fee-paying basis (brief preliminary search is free).

Family Records Centre, 1 Myddleton Street, Islington, London EC1R 1UW (Census and general enquiries, tel. 020 8392 5300; fax 020 8392 5307; email enquiry@pro.gov.uk; birth, marriage and death certificate enquiries, tel. 0870 243 7788; email certificateservices@ons.gov.uk). Website www.familyrecords.gov.uk. Mon, Wed, Fri, 09.00–17.00; Tue, 10.00–19.00; Thu, 09.00–19.00; Sat, 09.30–17.00.

Huguenot Society of Great Britain and Ireland, 140 Hampstead Road, London NW1 2BX (tel. 020 7679 5199; website www.huguenotsociety.org.uk). Mon–Wed, 10.00–16.00, by appointment.

Hyde Park Family History Center of the Church of Jesus Christ of Latter-Day Saints (of Salt Lake City, Utah, USA), 64–68 Exhibition Road, London SW7 2PA (tel. 020 7589 8561; website www.familysearch.org). Mon, 10.00–17.00; Tue, Thu, 10.00–21.00; Wed, Fri, 10.00–19.00; Sat, 10.00–17.00.

Institute of Heraldic and Genealogical Studies Library, 79–82 Northgate, Canterbury, Kent CT1 1BA (tel. 01227 768664; fax 01227 765617; email ihgs@ihgs.ac.uk; website www.ihgs.ac.uk). Mon, Wed, Fri, 10.00–17.00, by appointment. Library searches undertaken (£15 per half-hour).

The National Archives: Public Record Office, Ruskin Avenue, Kew, Richmond, Surrey TW9 4DU (tel. 020 8876 3444; fax 020 8878 8905; email enquiry@pro.gov.uk; website www.pro.gov.uk). Admission by reader's ticket. Mon, Wed, Fri, 09.00–17.00; Tue, 10.00–19.00; Thu, 09.30–19.00; Sat, 09.30–17.00. (Last document orders on Sat, 14.30 hours.)

Religious Society of Friends Library [Quakers], Friends House, 173–177 Euston Road, London NW1 2BJ (tel. 020 7663 1135; fax 020 7663 1001; website www.quaker.org.uk). Tue–Fri, 10.00–17.00. *Bona fide* researchers providing suitable introductions/letters of recommendation may use the Library on payment of a search fee, or searches will be carried out by staff at a fee.

Society of Genealogists' Library, 14 Charterhouse Buildings, Goswell Road, London EC1M 7BA (tel. 020 7251 8799; fax 020 7250 1800; email info@sog.org.uk; website www.sog.org.uk). Tue, Wed, Fri, Sat, 10.00–18.00; Thu, 10.00–20.00; closed on Mondays. Non-members pay search fees (currently £3.50 for one hour; £9.20 for half-day (4 hours); £14.50 for a day or a day and an evening).

Geography and Maps

British Library Maps Reading Room, British Library, 96 Euston Road, London NW1 2DB (tel. 020 7412 7702; fax 020 7412 7780; email maps@bl.uk; website www.bl.uk/collections/maps). British Library reader's pass required. Mon, 10.00–17.00; Tue–Sat, 09.30–17.00.

Royal Geographical Society/Institute of British Geographers Library, Kensington Gore, London SW7 2AR (tel. 020 7591 3040; fax 020 7591 3001; website www.rgs.org). Library and Map Room currently closed during major refurbishment until end

2003. Archives open to Fellows and members by appointment and written request, Thu, Fri (email archives@rgs.org).

Government and Official Information

British Library Social Policy Information Service, Science 2 North Reading Room, British Library, 96 Euston Road, London NW1 2DB (tel. 020 7412 7536; fax 020 7412 7761). British Library reader's pass required. Mon, 10.00–20.00; Tue–Thu, 09.30–20.00; Fri, Sat, 09.30–17.00.

Central Office of Information, Hercules Road, Westminster Bridge Road, London SE1 7DU (tel. 020 7928 2345). Telephone or written enquiries only.

Foreign & Commonwealth Office Library, King Charles Street, London SW1A 2AH (tel. (enquiries) 020 7270 3925; website www.fco.gov.uk). Open to *bona fide* researchers only, by appointment.

Office for National Statistics Information & Library Service, 1 Drummond Gate, London SW1V 2QQ (tel. 0845 601 3034; 01633 652747; email info@statistics.gov.uk; website www.statistics.gov.uk). Mon–Fri, 9.00–17.00. No appointment necessary.

Oriental and India Office Collections Reading Room, British Library, 96 Euston Road, London NW1 2DB (tel. 020 7412 7873; fax 020 7412 7641; email oioc-enquiries@bl.uk; website www.bl.uk). The former India Office Library. Mon, 10.00–17.00; Tue–Sat, 09.30–17.00.

Public Record Office, Ruskin Avenue, Kew, Richmond, Surrey TW9 4DU (tel. 020 8876 3444; fax 020 8878 8905; email enquiry@pro.gov.uk; website www.pro.gov.uk). Admission by reader's ticket. Mon, Wed, Fri, 09.00–17.00; Tue, 10.00-19.00; Thu, 09.30–19.00; Sat, 09.30-17.00. (Last document orders on Saturdays, 14.30.). *N.B.* The Public Record Office in Chancery Lane is now closed. See also under '*Parliament*'.

Recommended titles:

'*Never Complain, Never Explain*': *Records of the Foreign Office and State Paper Office 1500–c. 1960*, by Louise Atherton, PRO Publications, London, 1994

The Records of the Foreign Office 1782–1968, by Michael Roper, PRO Publications, London, 2002

See also *Calendar of State Papers series* and other publications of the Public Record Office.

International Affairs

Royal Institute of International Affairs Library, Chatham House, 10 St James's Square, London SW1Y 4LE (tel. (enquiries) 020 7957 5723; email libenquiries@riaa.org; website www.riaa.org.uk). Open to non-members by arrangement with the librarian, Mon–Fri, 11.00-17.30. *N.B.* The press cuttings collection for the period 1940–71 has been transferred to the British Newspaper Library, Colindale (indexes at Chatham House).

Ireland

National Library of Ireland, Kildare Street, Dublin 2 (tel. 00 353 1 6030200; fax 00 353 1 6766690; email info@nli.ie or ReadersServices@nli.ie; website www.nli.ie). Mon–Wed, 10.00–21.00; Thu, Fri, 10.00–17.00; Sat, 10.00–13.00 (Manuscripts library closes half an hour earlier.)

Public Record Office of Northern Ireland, 66 Balmoral Avenue, Belfast BT9 6NY (tel. 028 9025 1318; fax 028 9025 5999; email proni@nics.gov.uk; website www.proni.gov.uk). Admission by reader's ticket. Mon–Wed, Fri, 09.15–16.45; Thu, 09.15–20.45 (first Thursday of each month 10.00–20.45). Commercial users (includes journalists and professional genealogists) £4.35 per day, or £100 per year.

For the General Register Office (Northern Ireland) and the Registrar General (Dublin), see above, under 'General Register Offices', page 202.

Recommended titles:

British Sources for Irish History 1485–1641, Irish Manuscripts Commission, Dublin, 1997

Directory of Irish Archives, eds. Seamus Helferty and Raymond Refaussé, Four Courts Press, Dublin, 3rd edn, 1999

Irish History from 1700: A Guide to Sources in the Public Record Office, by Alice Prochaska, British Records Association, London, 1986

The Oxford Companion to Irish History, ed. S.J. Connolly, 2nd edn, Oxford University Press, Oxford, paperback edn, 1999

Law

Use of the law libraries in London is limited to members of the legal profession, but *bona fide* researchers may be able to obtain information by telephone or written enquiry. There are law libraries at a number of universities in the UK. (For these and other law libraries, see the *Aslib Directory of Information Sources in the UK*.)

Gray's Inn Library, 5 South Square, Gray's Inn, London WC1R 5EU (tel. 020 7242 8592; fax 020 7831 8381; email library@graysinn.org.uk; website www.graysinn.org.uk).

Holborn Library (London Borough of Camden public library), 32–38 Theobalds Road, London WC1X 8PA (tel. 020 7924 6345/6; fax 020 7413 6356). Mon, Thu, 10.00–19.00; Tue, Fri, 10.00–18.00; Sat, 10.00–17.00. Closed on Wednesdays.

Inner Temple Library, Inner Temple, London EC4Y 7DA (tel. 020 7797 8217; fax 020 7583 6030; email library@innertemple.org.uk; website www.innertemplelibrary.org.uk).

Institute of Advanced Legal Studies Library, University of London, 17 Russell Square, London WC1B 5DR (tel. 020 7637 1731; fax 020 7436 8824; email ials@sas.ac.uk; website www.ials.sas.ac.uk).

The Law Society Library, 113 Chancery Lane, London WC2A 1PL (tel. 020 7320 5946; fax 020 7831 1687; email lib-enq@lawsociety.org.uk; website www.lawsociety.org.uk). (Holds records of solicitors from 1907; also LEXIS index to newspaper law reports.) Members only.

Lincoln's Inn Library, Lincoln's Inn, Holborn, London WC2A 3TN (tel. 020 7242 4371; fax 020 7404 1864; email library@lincolnsinn.org.uk; website www.lincolnsinn.org.uk).

Middle Temple Library, Middle Temple Lane, London EC4Y 9BT (tel. 020 7427 4830; fax 020 7427 4831; email library@middletemple.org.uk; website www.middletemple.org.uk).

Royal Courts of Justice Library, Strand, London WC2A 2LL (tel. 020 7947 6000)

Recommended titles:
Legal Information – What it is and where to find it, by Peter Clinch, Aslib, London, 2nd rev. edn, 2000

London

Corporation of London Records Office, PO Box 270, Guildhall, London EC2P 2EJ (tel. 020 7332 1251; fax 020 7710 8682; email clro@corpoflondon.gov.uk; website www.cityoflondon.gov.uk/archives/clro). Mon–Fri, 09.30–16.45.

Guildhall Library, Aldermanbury, London EC2P 2EJ (tel. (Printed Books) 020 7332 1868/1870; (Manuscripts) 020 7332 1863; (Print & Map Room) 020 7332 1839); fax 020 7600 3384; website www.corpoflondon.gov.uk). Mon–Sat, 09.30–17.00 (Manuscripts library closes 16.45.)

London Metropolitan Archives Library, 40 Northampton Road, London EC1R 0HB (tel. 020 7332 3822; fax 020 7833 9136; email ask.lma@corpoflondon.gov.uk; website www.cityoflondon.gov.uk). Formerly the Greater London Record Office. Mon, Wed, Fri, 09.30–16.45; Tue, Thu, 09.30–19.30. (Tel. for Saturday opening times.)

Westminster City Archives, 10 St Ann's Street, London SW1P 2XR (tel. 020 7641 5180; fax 020 7641 5179; email archives@westminster.gov.uk; website www.westminster.gov.uk). Mon, Fri, Sat,) 09.30–17.00; Tue, Wed, Thu, 09.30–19.00.

Note: A number of London borough public libraries hold sizeable local history collections (see the current edition of *Record Repositories in Great Britain*, PRO Publications, London, or visit the ARCHON directory at website www.hmc.gov.uk). A British Records Association publication, *Sources for the History of London, 1939–45: A Guide and Bibliography*, by Heather Creaton, London, 1998, is an invaluable reference work for the writer setting a story in wartime London.

Recommended titles:
The Annals of London: A Year-by-Year Record of a Thousand Years of History, by John Richardson, Cassell, London, 2000
London: The Biography, by Peter Ackroyd, Chatto & Windus, London, 2000; paperback, Vintage, London, 2001

The London Encyclopedia, eds. Ben Weinreb and Christopher Hibbert, Macmillan, London, 1983; rev. edn, 1993

Medicine

Marylebone Information Service, Marylebone Public Library, 109–117 Marylebone Road, London NW1 5PS (tel. 020 7641 1039; fax 020 7641 1028; email reflibrarynwi@westminster.gov.uk; website www.westminster.gov.uk/libraries). Mon, Tue, Thu, Fri, 09.30–20.00; Wed, 10.00–20.00; Sat, 09.30–17.00, Sun, 13.30–17.00. Reference and lending facilities (tickets from other public libraries are accepted). *N.B.* There is now a limited collection on medicine/health.

Royal College of Physicians of London Library, 11 St Andrew's Place, London NW1 4LE (tel. 020 7935 1174; fax 020 7487 5218; website www.rcp.london.ac.uk). Mon–Fri, 09.30–17.30. *Bona fide* researchers not members of the profession may use the reference facilities (proof of identity required). Holds *Munk's Roll* (lives of Fellows of the Royal College of Physicians from the 16th century to the present day).

Royal College of Surgeons of England Library, 35–43 Lincoln's Inn Fields, London WC2A 3PN (tel. 020 7869 6555; fax 020 7405 4438; email library@rcseng.ac.uk; website www.rcseng.ac.uk). Letter of introduction required. Mon–Fri, 09.00–18.00.

Royal Society of Medicine Library, 1 Wimpole Street, London W1G 0AE (tel. 020 7290 2940; fax 020 7290 2939; email library@rsm.ac.uk; website www.rsm.ac.uk). Mon–Fri, 09.30–20.30; Sat, 10.00–17.00. Access for reference only, by introduction by Fellow of Society (temporary membership available).

Wellcome Institute for the History & Understanding of Medicine Library, 183 Euston Road, London NW1 2BE (tel. 020 7611 8582; fax 020 7611 8369). Mon, Wed, Fri, 09.45–17.15; Tue, Thu, 09.45–19.30; Sat, 09.45–13.00. By appointment. Reader's ticket required.

For further information see the *Directory of Health Library and Information Services in the United Kingdom and the Republic of Ireland 2002–3*, ed. Julie Ryder, Facet Publishing, London, 11th edn, 2002 (formerly a Library Association title).

Military

Liddell Hart Centre for Military Archives, King's College, Strand, London WC2R 2LS (tel. 020 78482015; email archives.web@kcl.ac.uk; website www.kcl.ac.uk/lhcma). Access by written application (letter of introduction required). *N.B.* 20th-century records only.

Ministry of Defence Whitehall Library, 3–5 Great Scotland Yard, London SW1A 2HW (tel. (general enquiries) 020 7218 4445; fax 020 7218 5413). Telephone or written enquiries only.

The National Archives: Public Record Office, Ruskin Avenue, Kew, Richmond, Surrey TW9 4DU (tel. 020 8876 3444; fax 020 8878 8905; email enquiry@pro.gov.uk; website www.pro.gov.uk). Admission by reader's ticket. Mon, Wed, Fri, Sat,

09.30–17.00; Tue, 10.00–19.00; Thu, 09.30–19.00. (Last document orders on
Saturdays, 14.30 hours.) Closed for stocktaking two weeks usually early
December. *N.B.* The Public Record Office in Chancery Lane is now closed.
National Army Museum, Royal Hospital Road, London SW3 4HT. Library and
Department of Archives, Photographs, Film and Sound (tel. 020 7730 0717 ext.
2222; fax 020 7823 6573; email info@national-army-museum.ac.uk; website
www.national-army-museum-ac.uk). Admission by reader's ticket. Tue–Sat,
10.00–16.30.

Recommended titles:
The Oxford Companion to Military History, ed. Richard Holmes, Oxford University
Press, Oxford, 2001
Records of the War Office and Related Departments, 1660–1964, by Michael Roper,
PRO Publications, London, 1998
See also under '*World Wars I and II*'.

Music
British Library Rare Books and Music Reading Room, British Library, 96 Euston
Road, London NW1 2DB (tel. 020 7412 7772; fax 020 7412 7751; email
music-collections@bl.uk; website www.bl.uk). British Library reader's pass
required. Mon, 10.00–20.00; Tue–Thu, 09.30–20.00; Fri, Sat, 09.30–17.00. Access
to printed and manuscript material and to the Listening and Viewing Service of
the National Sound Archive (see page 231).
Royal College of Music Reference Library, Prince Consort Road, London SW7 2BS
(tel. 020 7591 4325; fax 020 7589 7740; website www.rcm.ac.uk). Admission by
reader's ticket. Mon–Thu, 08.45–19.45; Fri, 08.45–17.30.
Royal Opera House Archive, Royal Opera House, Covent Garden, London WC2E
9DD (tel. 020 7212 9353; fax 020 7212 9489; email archive.enquiries@roh.org.uk;
website www.roh.org.uk). By appointment only (written or email enquiries in
first instance).
Vaughan Williams Memorial Library, English Folk Dance and Song Society, Cecil
Sharp House, 2 Regent's Park Road, London NW1 7AY (tel. 020 7485 2206 ext.
18/19; fax 020 7284 0523; email library@efdss.org; website www.efdss.org).
Tue–Fri, 09.30–17.30; 1st and 3rd Sat in month, 10.00–16.00. Non-members pay
daily fee for access, reference only.
Westminster Music Library, Victoria Library, 160 Buckingham Palace Road, London
SW1W 9UD (tel. 020 7641 4292; fax 020 7641 4281; email
westmuslib@dial.pipex.com; website
www.westminster.gov.uk/libraries/special/music). Mon–Fri, 11.00–19.00; Sat,
10.00–17.00.

Recommended title:
The New Grove Dictionary of Music and Musicians, 2nd edn, eds. Stanley Sadie and John Tyrrell, 29 vols, Macmillan, London, 2001; also online (by subscription)

Natural History

Natural History Museum Library, Cromwell Road, London SW7 5BD (tel. 020 7942 5460; fax 020 7942 5559; email library@nhm.ac.uk; website www.nhm.ac.uk/library). There are five sections: general, botany, earth sciences, entomology, and zoology. Mon–Fri, 10.00–16.30. Proof of identity required for reader's ticket (telephone for appointment). *N.B.* There is a branch at Tring, Herts: see below, under '*Zoology*'.

Royal Botanic Garden Library, 20a Inverleith Row, Edinburgh EH3 5LR (tel. 0131 248 2853; fax 0131 248 2901; email library@rbge.org.uk; website www.rbge.org.uk). By appointment, letter of introduction required.

Royal Botanic Gardens Library and Archives, Kew, Richmond, Surrey TW9 3AE (tel. 020 8332 5414; fax 020 8332 5430). Tue–Thu, 10.00–17.00. By appointment, reader's ticket required.

Naval

Caird Library, National Maritime Museum, Greenwich, London SE10 9NF (tel. 020 8858 4422; email library@nmm.ac.uk; website www.nmm.ac.uk). Mon–Fri, 10.00–16.45; Sat, by appointment. Reader's ticket required. For those unable to visit the Library an independent professional researcher can be provided on a fee-paying basis.

Royal Naval Historical Library, at Ministry of Defence Whitehall Library, see under '*Military*' on page 228.

Newspapers and Periodicals

British Library Newspaper Library, Colindale Avenue, London NW9 5HE (tel. 020 7412 7353; fax 020 7412 7379; email newspaper@bl.uk; website www.bl.uk/collections/newspapers). Admission by British Library reader's pass or Newspaper Library pass. Mon–Sat, 10.00–16.45.

British Library Humanities Reading Rooms, British Library, 96 Euston Road, London NW1 2DB (tel. 020 7412 7676; fax 020 7412 7609; email reader-services-enquiries@bl.uk; website www.bl.uk). Mon, 10.00–20.00; Tue, Wed, Thu, 09.30–20.00; Fri, Sat, 09.30–17.00. Reader's ticket required. Some reference material relating to periodicals is on open access. Journals held at the British Library Document Supply Centre, Boston Spa, Wetherby, West Yorkshire LS23 7BQ may be borrowed on request (through British Library or local public library).

Parliament

House of Lords Record Office, House of Lords, Palace of Westminster, London SW1A 0PW (tel. 020 7219 3074; fax 020 7219 2570; email hllibrary@parliament.uk; website www.parliament.uk). By appointment. Mon–Fri, 09.30–17.00 (Tue to

20.00), when House is sitting. Intending searchers should write to the Clerk of the Records in advance, giving at least one week's notice and details of the nature of their research and/or specific documents they wish to consult. Confirmation of appointment and proof of identity will be checked at Pass Office prior to admission.

Note: The libraries of the House of Commons and House of Lords are for the use of Members only. Outside enquiries may be addressed to the House of Commons Public Information Office, Department of the Library, House of Commons, London SW1A 0AA (tel. 020 7219 4272).
See also under '*Government and Official Information*'.

Politics (20th-century)
British Library of Political and Economic Science, London School of Economics, 25 Southampton Buildings, London WC2A 1PH (tel. 020 7955 7229; fax 020 7955 7454; email library.information.desk@lse.ac.uk; website www.lse.ac.uk). By appointment.

Churchill Archives Centre, Churchill College, Cambridge CB3 0DS (tel. 01223 336087; fax 01223 336135; email archives@chu.cam.ac.uk; website www.chu.cam.ac.uk/archives). Mon–Fri, 09.00–17.00, by appointment with the Archivist (proof of identity required). *N.B.* Certain collections are subject to special conditions of access.

Printing and Publishing
St Bride Printing Library, Bride Lane, London EC4Y 8EE (tel. 020 7353 4660; fax 020 7583 7073; email stbride@corpoflondon.gov.uk; website www.stbride.org). Mon–Fri, 09.30–17.30.

Recorded Sound
British Library National Sound Archive, British Library, 96 Euston Road, London NW1 2DB (tel. 020 7412 7440; fax 020 7412 7441; email nsa@bl.uk; website www.bl.uk/nsa). British Library reader's pass required. Mon, Thu, 10.00–18.00; Tue, Wed, 10.00–0.00; Fri, Sat, 10.00–17.00. The Recorded Sound Information Service (tel. 020 7412 7440) is based in the Humanities 2 Reading Room; the Listening & Viewing Service (tel. 020 7412 7418) is in the Rare Books and Music Reading Room; appointments may be made by telephone, fax, email or post. Northern listening service at British Library Document Supply Centre, Boston Spa, Wetherby, West Yorkshire LS23 7BQ (tel. 01937 546070), Mon–Fri, 09.15–16.30, by appointment. *N.B.* The collections include some BBC sound material.

Religion
Catholic Central Library, Lancing Street, London NW1 1ND (tel. 020 7383 4333; fax

020 7388 6675; email librarian@catholic-library.org.uk; website www.catholic-library.org.uk). Non-members for reference and research only. Mon, Tue, Thu, Fri, 10.30–17.00; Wed, 10.30–19.00.

Church of England Record Centre, 15 Galleywall Road, South Bermondsey, London SE16 3PB (tel. 020 7898 1030; fax 020 7394 7018). Written enquiries preferred. *N.B.* Material for study will be transferred to Lambeth Palace Library, *q.v.*

French Protestant Church of London, 8 & 9 Soho Square, London W1V 5DD (tel. 020 7437 5311). Library open Tue, Thu only, 10.30–13.00 and 14.15–16.45, by appointment with archivist.

Huguenot Society of Great Britain and Ireland, 140 Hampstead Road, London NW1 2BX (tel. 020 7679 5199; website www.huguenotsociety.org.uk). Mon–Wed, 10.00–16.00, by appointment.

Lambeth Palace Library, London SE1 7JU (tel. 020 7928 1400; fax 020 7928 7932; website www.lambethpalacelibrary.org). Mon–Fri, 10.00–17.00. Letter of introduction required.

Methodist Archives and Research Centre, John Rylands University Library, University of Manchester, 150 Deansgate, Manchester M3 3EH (tel. 0161 834 5343; fax 0161 834 5574). Mon–Fri, 10.00–17.15; Sat, 10.00–13.00. *N.B.* The Centre is closing in July 2003 for up to two years, for major refurbishment, but arrangements will be made for those wishing to study material. For up-to-date information visit the website www.rylibweb.man.ac.uk/spcoll.

Parkes Library (Jewish studies), University of Southampton Library, Highfield, Southampton SO17 1BJ (tel. 023 8059 3335; email archives@soton.ac.uk; website www.archives.lib.soton.ac.uk). Mon–Thu, 09.00–17.00; Wed, 10,00–17.00.

Religious Society of Friends Library [Quakers], Friends House, 173–177 Euston Road, London NW1 2BJ (tel. 020 7663 1135; fax 020 7663 1001; website www.quaker.org.uk). Tue–Fri, 10.00–17.00; closed for one week before Spring Bank Holiday and one week at end of November. *Bona fide* researchers providing suitable introductions/letters of recommendation may use the Library on payment of a search fee, or searches will be carried out by staff at a fee.

Dr Williams's Library, 14 Gordon Square, London WC1H 0AG (tel. 020 7387 3727; fax 020 7388 1142; email enquiries@dwlib.co.uk). Mon, 10.00–17.00; Tue, Thu, 10.00–18.30; Wed, Fri, 10.00–17.30. Admission by subscription for borrowers; non-members for reference only (proof of identity required).

See also under '*Cathedral Archives and Libraries*'.

Recommended titles:

Keyguide to Information Sources on World Religions, compiled by Jean Holm, Mansell, London, 1991

Religions of the World, eds. J. Gordon Melton and Martin Baumann, ABC-Clio, Oxford, 4 vols, 2002

The Times World Religions, ed. Martin Palmer, Times Books, London, 2002

Royal Archives

By special permission of the Keeper of the Queen's Archives, Windsor Castle, Berks SL4 1NJ (tel. 01753 868286; fax 01753 831834). Apply in writing.

Science and Technology

British Library Science, Technology and Innovation Information Services (formerly the Science Reference and Information Service/Science, Technology and Business Service), British Library, 96 Euston Road, London NW1 2DB. Five reading rooms: Science 1 South (British and European patents and trademarks); Science 1 North (foreign patents); Science 2 South (Life sciences and technologies, medicine and chemistry); Science 2 North (Official publications and social sciences, engineering,); Science 3 (Business information, physical and earth sciences). Tel. (general enquiries) 020 7412 7494/7496; (patent enquiries) 020 7412 7919; (business enquiries) 020 7412 7454/7977.

Imperial College of Science, Technology and Medicine Libraries, South Kensington, London SW7 2AZ. Central Library (tel. 020 7594 8820; fax 020 7584 3763; email library@ic.ac.uk; website www.lib.ic.ac.uk) and various departmental libraries. Mon–Fri, 09.30–21.00; Sat, 09.30–17.30 (term); Mon–Sat, 09.30–17.30 (vacation).

Royal Society of London Library, 6 Carlton House Terrace, London SW1Y 5AG (tel. 020 7451 2606; fax 020 7930 2170; email library@royalsoc.ac.uk; website www.royalsoc.ac.uk). Mon–Fri, 10.00–17.00. Admission on introduction by a Fellow: *bona fide* researchers by application (proof of identity required).

Science Museum Library, Imperial College Road, off Exhibition Road, London SW7 5NH (tel. 020 7942 4242; fax 020 7942 4243; email smlinfo@nsmi.ac.uk; website www.nmsi.ac.uk/library). Mon–Fri, 09.30–21.00 (closes at 17.30 during vacations); Sat, 09.30–17.30. Access for reference only. Operates jointly with Imperial College Central Library (see above).

See also the Highgate Literary and Scientific Institution Library, listed under '*Private Subscription Libraries*'.

Recommended titles:

Biographical Dictionary of the History of Technology, eds. Lance Day and Ian McNeil, Routledge, London, 1998

How to Find and *Key Resource* series, British Library, London, various dates

The Hutchinson Dictionary of Scientific Biography, eds. Roy Porter and Marilyn Ogilvie, Helicon, Oxford, 2 vols, 2000

ISIS Cumulative Bibliography and the *History of Technology* series, both published by Mansell, London

The New York Public Library Science Desk Reference, Macmillan, New York, 1996

Science: A History 1543–2001, by John Gribbin, Penguin Group, London, 2002

The Timetables of Technology, by Bryan Bunch and Alexander Hellemans, Touchstone (Simon & Schuster), New York, 1993

Science Fiction

Science Fiction Foundation Research Library, Liverpool University Library, PO Box 123, Liverpool L69 3DA (tel. 0151 794 3142). Telephone for appointment.

Recommended title:
Encyclopedia of Science Fiction, compiled by John Clute and Peter Nicholls, Orbit, London, rev. edn, 1993

Scotland

General Register Office for Scotland, New Register House, Edinburgh EH1 3YT (tel. 0131 334 0380; fax 0131 314 4400; email records@gro-scotland.gov.uk; website www.gro-scotland.gov.uk). Mon–Fri, 09.30–16.30.

The National Archives of Scotland (formerly the Scottish Record Office), HM General Register House, Edinburgh EH1 3YY (tel. 0131 535 1314; fax 0131 557 1360; email enquiries@nas.gov.uk). Admission by reader's ticket. Mon–Fri, 09.00–16.45. Website www.nas.gov.uk. *N.B.* The National Register of Archives Scotland is at West Register House.

National Library of Scotland, George IV Bridge, Edinburgh EH1 1EW (tel. 0131 226 4531; fax 0131 622 4803; email enquiries@nls.uk; website www.nls.uk). Admission by reader's ticket. Mon, Tue, Thu, Fri, 09.30–20.30; Wed, 10.00–20.30; Sat, 09.30–13.00.

Recommended title:
The Oxford Companion to Scottish History, ed. Michael Lynch, Oxford University Press, Oxford, 2001

Sport

Association of Sports Historians, 10 Elmete Grange, Menston, Ilkley, Yorks LS29 6LA (written enquiries only). Will undertake in-depth research on fee-paying basis (estimates given, initial deposit required), drawing on their own vast archives, normally available only to members.

Sheffield Public Library Sports Library, Surrey Street, Sheffield S1 1XZ (tel. 0114 273 5929; email sports.library@dial.pipex.com). Mon, Wed, 10.00–13.00 and 14.00–18.00; Tue, Fri, 10.00–13.00 and 14.00–16.30.

Theatre

Raymond Mander and Joe Mitchenson Theatre Collection, Jerwood Library of the Performing Arts, Trinity College of Music, King Charles Court, Old Royal Naval College, London SE10 9JF (tel. 020 83053893; fax 020 8305 3993; email rmangan@tcm.ac.uk; website www.mander-and-michenson.co.uk). Open to *bona fide* researchers by appointment.

National Theatre Archive, Royal National Theatre, South Bank, London SE1 9PX (tel./fax 020 7820 3512; email archive@nationaltheatre.org.uk; website www.nationaltheatre.org.uk). Mon, Wed, Fri, 10.00–17.00.

Society for Theatre Research, c/o Theatre Museum, 1e Tavistock Street, Covent Garden, London WC2E 7PA. Written enquiries only.

Theatre Museum Library and Archive, 1e Tavistock Street, London WC2E 7PR (tel. 020 7943 4700; fax 020 7943 4777; website www.theatremuseum.org). Study Room open Tue–Fri, 10.30–16.30, strictly by appointment, preferably ten days in advance. Entrance to the Study Room is not the Museum entrance, but round the corner in Tavistock Street at basement level, approached by a ramp. The collection includes that of the Enthoven Collection, previously at the Victoria & Albert Museum, and the library of the former British Theatre Association. The Theatre Museum itself is open Tue-Sun, 10.00–18.00.

Recommended titles:
Biographical Dictionary of Actors, Actresses, Musicians, Dancers, Managers and Other Stage Personnel in London 1660–1800, by P.H. Highhill, K.A. Burnim and E.A. Langhans, Southern Illinois University Press, USA, 16 vols, 1973–93
A Directory of Theatre Research, ed. Francesca Franchi, Society for Theatre Research/Library Association, London, 3rd edn, 1998
International Dictionary of Theatre, St James Press, Detroit, 3 vols, 1992–94
The London Stage (day-by-day calendar of plays produced at the major London theatres 1890–1959), Scarecrow Press, Lanham, Maryland (now Roman & Littlefield, Oxford), 1976–93

Transport
Civil Aviation Authority Library and Information Centre, Aviation House, Gatwick Airport South, West Sussex RH6 0YR (tel. 01293 573725; fax 01293 573181; email library-enquiries@srg.caa.co.uk; website www.caa.co.uk). Mon–Fri, 09.30–16.30.

Department for Transport, Library and Information Service, Ashdown House, 123 Victoria Street, London SW1E 6DE (tel. (public enquiry unit) 020 7944 3333). Written and telephone enquiries only.

Leicester University Library, Transport History Collection, University Road, Leicester LE1 9QD (tel. 0116 252 2043; email libdesk@lc.ac.uk). Mon–Fri, 9.00–17.00.

London Transport Museum Library, 39 Wellington Street, Covent Garden, London WC2E 7BB (tel. 020 7379 6344; fax 020 7565 7252; website www.ltmusuem.co.uk). Mon–Fri, 10.00–17.00.

National Motor Museum, Beaulieu, Hants SO42 7ZN (tel. 01590 612345; website www.beaulieu.co.uk)

National Railway Museum Library and Archive, National Railway Museum, Leeman Road, York YO26 4XJ. By appointment (tel. 01904 686235; fax 01904 611112; email nrm@nmsi.ac.uk; website www.nmsi.ac.uk/nrm).

Royal Aeronautical Society Library, 4 Hamilton Place, London W1V 0BQ (tel. 020 7670 4300; fax 020 7499 6230; email raes@raes.org.uk; website www.aerosociety.com). Mon–Fri, 10.00–17.00

Recommended titles:
The Airline Encyclopedia 1900–2000, ed. Myron J. 'Jack' Smith, Jr., Scarecrow Press (Roman & Littlefield), Oxford, 2002
Journal of Transport History, published twice a year by Manchester University Press, Manchester
The Moving Metropolis: London's Transport since 1800, ed. Sheila Taylor, Laurence King, London, 2001
The Oxford Companion to British Railway History, eds. Jack Simmons and Gordon Biddle, Oxford University Press, Oxford, 1997; paperback, 1999
Railway Records: A Guide to Sources, by Cliff Edwards, PRO Publications, London, 2001
Records of Merchant Shipping and Seamen, by Kelvin Smith, Christopher T. Watts and Michael J. Watts, PRO Publications, London, 1998; updated edn, 2002

United Nations

United Nations Library and Information Centre, Millbank Tower (21st floor), 21/24 Millbank, London SW1P 4QH (tel. 020 7630 1981; fax 020 7976 6478; email info@uniclondon.org; website www.unitednations.org.uk). Reference library, Mon-Thu, 09.30–13.00, 14.00–17.00, by appointment. Information Centre, Mon–Fri, 09.30–13.00, 14.00–17.00.

Wales

National Library of Wales, Aberystwyth, Ceredigion SY23 3BU (tel. 01970 632800; fax 01970 615709; email holi@llg.org.uk; website www.llgc.org.uk). Admission by reader's ticket. Mon–Fri, 09.30–18.00; Sat, 09.30–17.00. Online catalogue at www.geacweb.llgc.org.uk:8000.

Weather

National Meteorological Library and Archive. Scheduled to move from its present site in Bracknell, Berkshire, to Exeter, Devon, in 2003–4. The move will take place in several stages. For up-to-date information telephone the Customer Centre on 0845 300 0300 or go to the website www.metoffice.com.

Wills

Borthwick Institute of Historical Research (York University), St Anthony's Hall, Peaseholme Green, York YO1 7PW (tel. 01904 642315; website www.york.ac.uk/inst/bihr). No email enquiries. Mon–Fri, 09.30–16.50, by appointment. (PCY wills.) *N.B.* Will be closed for a period during the summer 2004.
Family Records Centre, 1 Myddleton Street, Islington, London EC1R 1UW (tel. 020 8392 5300; fax 020 8392 5307). Mon, Wed, Fri, 09.00–17.00; Tue, 10.00–19.00; Thu, 09.00–19.00; Sat, 09.30–17.00. (PCC wills 1383–1858, on microfilm).
Principal Registry of the Family Division, First Avenue House, 42–49 High Holborn, London WC1V 6NP (tel. (probate search room) 020 7947 7189). Mon–Fri,

10.00–16.30. (Wills and administrations since 1858.)

Women's Studies

Fawcett Library, see below, The Women's Library Feminist Library Resource and Information Centre, 5–5a Westminster Bridge Road, London SE1 7XW (tel. 020 7928 7789). Tue, 11.00–20.00; Wed, 15.00–20.00; Sat, 14.00–17.00. Free access for reference; books may be borrowed on payment of fee.

The Women's Library, Old Castle Street, London E1 7NT (tel. 020 7320 2222; fax 020 7320 2333; email moreinfo@thewomenslibrary.ac.uk; website www.thewomenslibrary.ac.uk). Opened in 2002 as a cultural and research centre on all aspects of women's history, based on the Fawcett Library collection. Tue–Fri, 09.30–17.00 (Thu to 20.00); Sat, 10.00–16.00.

Recommended titles:

History of Women, Primary Source Microfilm, Reading [collection of 1,248 reels]

Information Sources in Women's Studies and Feminism, ed. Hope Olson, K.G. Saur, Munich, 2002

World Wars I and II

Churchill Archives Centre, Churchill College, Cambridge CB3 0DS (tel. 01223 336087; fax 01223 336135; email archives@chu.cam.ac.uk; website www.chu.cam.ac.uk/archives). Mon–Fri, 09.00–17.00, by appointment with the Archivist. Proof of identity required. (Papers of military and naval commanders, politicians and scientists; certain collections subject to special conditions of access.)

Imperial War Museum Library, Lambeth Road, London SE1 6HZ (tel. 020 7416 5000; fax 020 7416 5374; email books@iwm.org.uk; website www.iwm.org.uk). Mon–Sat, 10.00–17.00, by appointment (at least 24 hours' notice required).

Wiener Library, Institute of Contemporary History, 4 Devonshire Street, London W1N 2BH (tel. 020 7636 7247/8; fax 020 7436 6428; email info@wienerlibrary.co.uk; website www.wienerlibrary.co.uk). Letter of introduction required. Subscription payable for extensive research, but short-term use of reference facilities free. Mon–Fri, 10.00–17.30 *N.B.* The collection of books was mostly transferred to Tel Aviv University in 1980, but the bulk of the material has been retained on microfilm in London.

Recommended titles:

The First World War: An Illustrated History, by John Keegan, Hutchinson, London, 2002

The Oxford Companion to the Second World War, ed. I.C.B. Dear, Oxford University Press, Oxford, 1995

The Second World War: A Guide to Sources, by J.D. Cantwell, PRO Publications, London, 1998

Zoology

Walter Rothschild Zoological Museum, Akeman Street, Tring, Herts HP23 6AP (tel. 020 7942 6171; fax 020 7942 6150; email tring-enquiries@rhm.ac.uk; website www.rhm.ac.uk/museum/tring). Mon–Sat, 10.00–17.00; Sun, 14.00–17.00.

Zoological Society of London Library, Regent's Park, London NW1 4RY (tel. 020 7449 6293; fax 020 7586 5743; website www.zsl.org). Mon–Fri, 09.30–17.30. Access for non-members on payment of fee.

The Writer's Bookshelf

GOOD REFERENCE BOOKS, whether in printed or electronic form, do not come cheap, and no individual writer can afford to compete with a library in keeping his personal collection fully up-to-date. You would be foolish even to try. What you buy, therefore, must be related to your own pocket, the shelf-space you have available, the distance you live away from a well-stocked reference library, and the special nature of your work.

Some basic suggestions for a writer's bookshelf are listed below. It is recommended that a plan for systematic renewal should be worked out, whereby you replace the essential yearbooks annually and other books in rotation. (Do not forget that dictionaries and atlases, as well as reference books, need to be updated from time to time.) Sell those which you discard and put the proceeds towards the purchase of new editions. Excellent reference works may often be picked up in secondhand bookshops, or even in charity shops, for a fraction of their original cost and are a good buy for those not engaged on highly topical work; the information they contain can be supplemented or updated by the occasional visit to the library or, in case of urgent need, by a telephone call to the reference librarian. Now that the Net Book Agreement has gone, there are discount bookshops all over the country where you will find real bargains. It will pay you, too, to keep an eye open for the special promotions on offer from the book clubs.

Oxford University Press has recently marketed a CD-ROM which deserves a place on every writers's shelf: *The Oxford Pop-up English Language Reference Shelf Windows CD-ROM*. This relatively inexpensive disk contains *The New Oxford Dictionary of English*, *The New Oxford Thesaurus*, *The Oxford Dictionary of Quotations* (5th edition) and the *Oxford World Encyclopedia*. It incorporates the latest iFinger 'pop-up' technology: when you move your mouse over a word in the dictionary or thesaurus, the definition or synonym appears in a 'pop-up' window on the document or web page. You can also search the full text of one or all of the four titles at the click of a button.

Paperback reference titles are by no means to be scorned. Naturally they do not stand up to as much handling as hard-covers, but you will be less reluctant to offload them when revised editions become available – and feel less guilty about giving them the full 'working tool' treatment, annotating and marking them as your research progresses. The Oxford Paperback Reference series published by Oxford University Press are excellent value for money.

At the end of a major project you may decide to dispose of a number of books in order to create shelf-space for a new set related to your next work. The secondhand bookseller with whom you are in the habit of dealing should give you a fair price. You might also consider selling online. Do not however be *too* ruthless! (How to locate specialist booksellers will be found on page 51 and details of bookfinding services on pages 58–9.)

SUGGESTED BASIC REFERENCE LIBRARY FOR THE WRITER

The essential items are:

1　A good English dictionary.
　The Oxford English Dictionary (*OED*), 2nd edition, 20 volumes, 1989, and, since March 2000, online by subscription, is clearly ideal, but probably beyond the means of the average writer for home use. There is a second edition of the *Compact OED*, in slipcase with magnifying glass (1991). The *OED* (2nd edn), the *New Shorter OED* (2 vols, 1993) and the *Concise OED* (10th edn, 1999) are also marketed in electronic form (CD-ROM and magnetic tape). A three-volume set, *The Oxford English Dictionary Additions Series*, the first major update of the OED for ten years, was published in the period 1993–97. (*Note*: a third edition of the full *OED* is in preparation and scheduled for publication in 2010; new *Concise* and *Shorter* editions are bound to follow.) Since March 2000 the *OED* has been available online by subscription (this includes the second edition, the *Additions* volumes and quarterly releases of new material), currently £350 per annum.

　　Outstanding among single-volume dictionaries are *The Chambers Dictionary* (latest edn, 2002) and *Chambers 21st Century Dictionary* (rev. edn 2002). For American meanings and spellings you should consider acquiring the *Webster's Third New International Dictionary* (*Unabridged*) (latest edition 2002), available also on CD-ROM. If you are a subscriber to *Encyclopedia Britannica*'s new Premium Service (see below, page 242), you can search the *Merriam-Webster Collegiate Dictionary and Thesaurus* online there.

　　Even though your word processor may have a spellchecker, it is always a good idea to keep a smaller dictionary handy for quick reference, and there are many to choose from. Remember that language is forever changing: ideally you should update your main dictionary every ten years or so, or at least supplement it with a dictionary of current use. *Chambers 21st Century Dictionary*, mentioned above, is compiled from Chambers Wordtrack, a monitoring programme which tracks changes in language use and incorporates authenticated new words regularly. (You can search it online at www.chambers.co.uk.) *Chambers Dictionary of Etymology* is a good reference source for the origin of English words and how their meanings have changed over the years.

2   One or two biographical dictionaries.
An up-to-date *Who's Who*, if you can afford it. A set of *Who Was Who*, together with the index volume, if you do much historical writing. The three-volume *Concise Dictionary of National Biography* is not cheap, but invaluable. (Bear in mind that there is to be a new edition of the full *DNB* in 2004: see chapter 7, page 127.) The best, relatively inexpensive single-volume buy, available both in hardback and paperback, is *Chambers Biographical Dictionary*, latest edn, 2002.

3   A good atlas, plus, if possible, a world gazetteer.
The Times Comprehensive Atlas of the World is currently in its 10th edition (1999) and unrivalled. The smaller *Times of London Concise Atlas of the World* (2001) represents good value, as do any of the atlases from Collins or Philip's, or those from the two big American publishers, Rand McNally and National Geographic. There is an 8th edition (2000) of Philip's *Atlas of the World*, published by Oxford University Press, and a 7th edition (1999) of the National Geographic *Atlas of the World*. A more expensive option is the *Hammond World Atlas: Executive Edition* (3rd edn, 2000). Useful to keep at your elbow is the Rand McNally paperback *Quick Reference World Atlas* (rev. edn 2001).

Webster's New Geographical Dictionary (rev. edn 1997) is an excellent cross between an atlas and a gazetteer. It is unlikely that individual readers will wish to acquire for home use the three-volume *Columbia Gazetteer of the World* (2000), retailing at around £500, but this is the definitive book in the field; you will of course find it in a good map library.

Among the many atlases in electronic format, the *Microsoft Encarta Interactive World Atlas* has been much praised.

For recommendations of atlases of world history, see chapter 6, page 107. N.B. Atlases are revised every few years, and you should buy the latest and the best that you can afford. Take the advice of a firm like Stanford's, 12–14 Long Acre, London WC2E 9LP (tel. 020 7836 1321; fax 020 7836 0189; website www.stanfords.co.uk) before you make any large purchase.

4   A road atlas/gazetteer of the British Isles.
These also go out of date very quickly and should be replaced regularly. The *AA Big Road Atlas Britain* (scale 3 miles to 1 inch) (latest edn 2002) is currently excellent value. An up-to-date copy of *London A–Z* is also a good investment. The *AA Road Book of Britain* is a gazetteer of places, containing much useful historical information.

5   An encyclopedia (or two).
Here the choice depends very much on your needs and your budget. The most recent state-of-the-art encyclopedias online are 'multimedia', presenting information not only as text but with graphics, sound and animation. Supreme among the traditional compilations, the *2002 Encyclopedia Britannica* runs into thirty-two volumes in printed form and is also available at a very reasonable cost in both CD-ROM and DVD editions, updated to 2003. Purchasers receive one month's free online access; thereafter a subscription to EB Online gives you access to a vast database, regularly updated and reviewed by the *Britannica* editorial team, with links to some 130,000 selected sites. If you subscribe to the new Britannica 'Premium Service' online you can access not only the full 32-volume set, but also the *Concise* and *Student* volumes, the *Merriam-Webster Collegiate Dictionary and Thesaurus*, articles from leading magazines and news headlines from the New York Times. (Subscription details and FAQ on www.eb.com or www.britannica.co.uk.) There is also a *Britannica Book of the Year*, published annually, and a *Britannica Concise Encyclopedia*. If that is not enough, new on DVD is the *Britannica 2003 Ultimate Reference Suite*. On CD-ROM is the *Microsoft Encarta Encyclopedia Deluxe 2003* or *Encarta Standard 2003*.

Recommended single-volume encyclopedias include *The Macmillan Encyclopedia*, *The Cambridge Encyclopedia*, the *New Penguin Encyclopedia* and, more recently, *The Chambers Encyclopedia*, in which information is arranged in fourteen thematic sections. It makes sense to buy one of these concise editions and renew them frequently; most are now updated very regularly.* However, if you have the chance to acquire a secondhand set of either the 9th (the so-called 'scholars' edition) or the 11th *Britannica* (with supplements, the most extensive), do not pass it by; these contain much information not included in modern editions. That said, one word of warning: do not be tempted to acquire too many different encyclopedias, or when you come to look things up, you will be driven crazy by conflicting facts!

6   A dictionary of quotations (preferably more than one).
Standard works are *The Oxford Dictionary of Quotations* (5th edn, 1999) and *Bartlett's Familiar Quotations* (10th edn, 2000). (The *Oxford* is included in the OUP *Pop-up English Language Reference Shelf* mentioned earlier in this chapter, and Bartlett's can be accessed online at www.bartleby.com or on www.yahoo.com/reference/bartlett.)

There are any number of paperback editions for quick reference marketed by a variety of publishers. I particularly like the Penguin compilations and find

---

* In 2002 Helicon became part of the electronic publishers RMLearning, and subsequently the Hutchinson reference titles, including the excellent *Hutchinson Almanac* and the *Hutchinson Encyclopedia*, were licensed for an agreed period to HodderHeadline. At the time of writing (early 2003) no information has been forthcoming as to whether or not these titles are to be published again in the foreseeable future.

The Penguin Thesaurus of Quotations, edited by M.J. Cohen (1998, paperback 2000) especially useful in that the quotations are grouped under 800 different themes. Along the same lines, but more substantial, is *The Oxford Dictionary of Thematic Quotations (2000)*. Also from Oxford University Press is a new edition (2002) of *The Oxford Dictionary of Phrase, Saying and Quotation*. The *Cassell Companion to Quotations*, compiled by Nigel Rees (1997), contains explanatory footnotes on the provenance of the quotations included.

In recent years there have been many specialist compilations ranging from biographical to war quotations, even the erotic, the humorous and the insulting – too numerous to list here. Buy a standard work and a few others that best reflect your writing interests.

7 A dictionary of dates and/or chronology of historical events/concise world history.
The Oxford University Press paperback, *A Dictionary of Dates*, edited by C.L. Beeching (2nd edn, 1997) is a good buy, and so is *The Timetables of History: A Horizontal Linkage of People and Events*, compiled by Bernard Grun and Daniel J. Boorstin (Touchstone, New York, 3rd rev. edn, 1991; the 1975 Thames & Hudson, London, edn is out of print). Or you may be able to find a secondhand copy of the classic S.H. Steinberg's *Historical Tables 58 BC–AD 1990* (Macmillan, 12th edn, ed. John Paxton, 1991).

The Encyclopedia of World History, compiled by William L. Langer (rev. edn ed. Peter N. Stearns, Lutterworth Press, Cambridge, 6th edn, 2002) is the long-awaited update of a much-loved standard reference work, arranged both geographically and chronologically (see chapter 5, page 94). *Chambers Dictionary of World History* (latest edn 2000) is an excellent tool for quick reference, with a straightforward A–Z listing, as is *The Chronology of 20th Century World History* by John Paxton (Continuum, 1998). *The Chronology of World History* (4 vols, Helicon, 1999; also on CD-ROM) is expensive and probably best consulted in the library.

8 A thesaurus (or two).
Roget's Thesaurus of English Words and Phrases is the standard work. A special 150th anniversary edition, edited by G. Davidson, was published by Penguin in 2002; also available from the same publisher, in both hardback and paperback, is the revised edition (1998) by E.M. Kirkpatrick. A different style of compilation is *The New Oxford Thesaurus of English*, edited by Patrick Hanks (Oxford University Press, 2000). There is also a new paperback edition of *The Chambers Thesaurus* (2003), which is very straightforward to use.

Except for very quick reference I personally would not recommend any of the so-called 'compact' or 'concise' thesauri available, as they are simply not adequate for the professional writer.

9   A guide to English usage.
Fowler's *A Dictionary of Modern English Usage*, first published in 1926, has long
been the standard, and there have been several revised editions. *The New Fowler's
Modern English Usage*, third edition, revised by R.W. Burchfield, was published
by Oxford University Press, in 1996, and reprinted in 1998. A highly recom-
mended modern work is Godfrey Howard's *A Guide to Good English in the 21st
Century* (Duckworth, 2002); by the same author is a handy reference title, *The
Macmillan Good English Handbook*, 1998, in both hardback and paperback.

10   *Brewer's Dictionary of Phrase and Fable*, originally published in 1870, is now in a
Millennium edition, edited by Adrian Room (Cassell, 1999; paperback 2001). By
the same editor is *Brewer's Dictionary of Modern Phrase and Fable* (Cassell, 2000),
Brewer's Dictionary of Names: People & Places & Things (Helicon, 1995). There is
a *Concise* edition of Brewer's, edited by Betty Kirkpatrick (Cassell, 2001).

11   A current yearbook.
Whitaker's Almanack and *Pears Cyclopedia* are classics. You should however think
carefully before opting for the cheaper concise Whitaker, as some sections are
omitted altogether. (See footnote on page 242 re the *Hutchinson Almanac*.)

12   *Writers' & Artists' Yearbook* (*WAYB*), published annually by A & C Black. Every
writer should possess a current edition. This is one reference book that should
be renewed each year.

13   *The Writer's Handbook*, ed. Barry Turner, published annually by Macmillan.
Another essential annual purchase. It is different in style to the *WAYB* and contains much additional information. If you cannot afford both annually, I suggest
you renew them in alternate years.

14   One or more other directories reflecting your chief interests. For example, the
Directory of Publishing; *Benn's Media*; *Willing's Press Guide*; *The Media Guide* –
all listed in the bibliography at the end of chapter 4. The radio and television
writer will want *Contacts*, an annual publication from Spotlight (7 Leicester
Place, London WC2H 7BP; tel. 020 7437 7631/fax 020 7437 5881; email
info@spotlight.cd.com; website www.spotlightcd.com) which lists all the main
addresses of the radio and television companies, names of heads of department,
agents, producers, etc.

The above titles form a superb nucleus reference library, which can be added to over
the years according to the dictates and fluctuations of bank balance and work
requirements. Some further suggestions (many of which have been mentioned in
various chapters of this book) are:

The Companion to British History, by Charles Arnold-Baker, Longcross Press, Tunbridge Wells, 1996

Debrett's Correct Form, Hodder Headline, London, updated paperback edn, 2002

The Europa World Year Book, published annually by Europa Publications, London

Hollis Press & Public Relations Annual, published annually (September) by Hollis Publishing, Teddington, Middx

The International Who's Who, published annually by Europa Publications, London (with online access)

International Who's Who of Authors' & Writers', formerly published by Melrose Press, now by Europa Publications, London; updated every few years (18th edn, 2003)

Oxford Companion to English Literature, Oxford University Press, 6th edn, ed. by Margaret Drabble, 2000

Record Repositories in Great Britain, Royal Commission on Historical Manuscripts, PRO, London; revised every few years (11th edn, ed. Ian Mortimer, 1999) and updated regularly online (see chapter 4, page 84)

The Statesman's Yearbook, published annually by Macmillan, London

UK (formerly *Britain: An Official Handbook*), compiled by the Office for National Statistics and published annually (January) by The Stationery Office, Norwich

Walford's Concise Guide to Reference Material, compiled by A. Chalcroft *et al.*, Library Association, London, 2nd edn, 1992 (out of print, but still very useful; see chapter 4, page 55 for details of the current 3-volume *Guide* and of the *New Walford* scheduled from 2004 onwards)

Who Was Who, published by A & C Black, London, 10 vols to date, covering the period 1897–2000; also *Cumulated Index 1897–2000*. There is a CD-ROM of *Who's Who 1897–1998*.

Note: Thousands of reference books are now produced in electronic form. While an increasing number of standard works *are* becoming freely available online, it is a fact of modern technological life that if you wish to access some of the specialist or academic data on offer, you (or your library) must be a subscriber. The costs are high and often beyond the reach of the individual. You could spend a small fortune subscribing to even a half-dozen databases. The best plan is to find out which library nearest to you subscribes to the particular database(s) that you need, and weigh up the costs of travelling and convenience against that of a subscription. Unfortunately – or perhaps inevitably – many of the works that are up for grabs free of charge are those that are out of copyright, which is misleading, to say the least. Take, for example, *Roget's Thesaurus*, which can be searched at www.thesaurus.com. This online text turns out to be the 1911 edition, which, to be frank, is not of that much use to the modern writer. (Since I personally find it easier to flip through the pages of the printed book anyway, I have recently acquired the 150th anniversary edition.) On which note, with heartfelt thanks to Dr Peter Mark Roget, who originated the work in 1852, and to all the other compilers of our greatest reference tools, without whose help our research would be a far less enjoyable and rewarding task than it is, I end this seventh edition.

Index

Note: It would be impossible to include in this index every single library, database, book or newspaper title referred to in the text. Entries are therefore restricted to those of major importance and those with special mention in the book. Readers should be able quickly to locate other material by looking up relevant subject entries and by consulting the bibliographies at the end of the various chapters.